Environmental Politics
Domestic and Global Dimensions

Second Edition

Jacqueline Vaughn Switzer
Northern Arizona University

with

Gary Bryner
Brigham Young University

Bedford/St. Martin's   Boston ⚌ New York

For those who stood beside me:

Dr. Claude Curran
Dr. Patrick Gillette
Kevin Keaney, Esq.

Sponsoring editor: Beth A. Gillett
Development editor: Susan Cottenden
Manager, Publishing services: Emily Berleth
Senior editor, Publishing services: Douglas Bell
Project management: York Production Services, Inc.
Senior production supervisor: Dennis Para
Cover design: Evelyn Horovicz
Cover photo: Copyright © 1996/George B. Diebold/The Stock Market

Library of Congress Catalog Card Number: 97-065189

Copyright © 1998 by Bedford/St. Martin's

Manufactured in the United States of America.

3 2 1 0 9
f e d c b

For information write: Bedford/St. Martin's, 75 Arlington Street, Boston, MA 02116 (617-426-7440)

ISBN: 0-312-14988-3 (paperback)
        0-312-16384-3 (hardcover)

Contents

Preface

When the first edition of *Environmental Politics* was written in 1992, issues of environmental protection were increasingly regarded as global rather than purely domestic problems. The reasons for this change of perspective were many: the collapse of the Communist empire and the opening of doors through perestroika and glasnost revealed Eastern Europe's massive environmental degradation;[1] the June 1992 United Nations Earth Summit brought 25,000 observers and delegates from 178 nations to Rio de Janeiro to prioritize and reach agreement on their common problems;[2] and crises, such as the environmental damage resulting from the Persian Gulf War, kept the world's attention focused on the international aspects of preserving and protecting the planet's resources.

As we approach the twenty-first century, an evaluation of both domestic and global environmental policymaking provides a mixed review. There is little doubt that progress has been made in solving some problems, although nongovernmental organizations argue that the pace of implementing laws is agonizingly slow. In the United States, for example, groups such as the American Lung Association have pressured the Environmental Protection Agency to adopt stricter air quality standards as new scientific evidence becomes available concerning the health risks posed by ozone and fine airborne particles. In his 1997 State of the Union Address, President Bill Clinton proposed a new American Heritage Rivers program in an effort to help communities revitalize their waterfronts and clean up pollution, although critics noted that the designation would not impose any new restrictions on river usage and thus the president's action was more symbolic than substantive.

On the international front, indigenous peoples continue to battle for control of their lands and natural resources. In a protest similar to that conducted by groups in Brazil and India, members of the Huxalt people of British Columbia joined with the Forest Action Network and Greenpeace in an attempt to stop a Canadian lumber company from clear-cutting part of the Great Coast Rainforest, one of the world's last great tracts of old-growth temperate rainforest.[3]

Although the 1992 UN conference was ballyhooed as a major step forward in developing a global regime for environmental protection, implementation of the accords reached at the Earth Summit has been made more difficult as political leaders face competing demands for limited financial resources.[4] Although sulfur dioxide emissions in Western Europe have decreased dramatically and reduced the threat posed by acid rain, damage to plant and animal life continues because transboundary agreements are not strict enough to protect fragile ecosystems. Similarly, the 1990 ban on commercial trade in ivory reduced poaching of elephants, but in 1997, several African nations were successful in their efforts to have the ban lifted, potentially increasing poaching elsewhere on the continent and reigniting the issue of endangered species protection.[5] Most observers agree that current patterns of natural resource use are not sustainable, and there is a high likelihood that there will be a global decline in the nature and quality of human life.[6]

The continuing debate over domestic and global environmental protection is framed somewhat differently than it was when *Environmental Politics* was first published, but the purpose of the second edition remains largely the same: to provide a framework for understanding the nature of the environmental problems we face, to review the history and evolution of our efforts to remedy them, and to explore the prospects for effective public policymaking for environmental protection.

This book uses the policy process as a framework for reviewing the broad spectrum of environmental problems facing political leaders today. Although much of the focus is on the development of environmental policy in the United States, there is also considerable attention paid to the globalization of environmental politics. The chapters refer to various environmental regimes—international agreements that may take the form of conventions or protocols—that have been created in an attempt to solve many of the transboundary problems that the book identifies. References are also made to the international body responsible for most regime formation in environmental issues, the United Nations. After the United Nations Conference on the Human Environment, held in Stockholm in June 1972, the UN General Assembly established the UN Environment Programme (UNEP), which has become the lead agency for many of the regimes discussed throughout this book. Other authors have made much more significant contributions to the literature on the role of specific international organizations, regimes, and stakeholders.[7]

Many people interested in the future of our nation and our planet may have only a "headline news" awareness of environmental problems. This book tries to provide a more comprehensive, objective view of issues that have been mired in controversy for decades, avoiding the rhetoric that often distorts the environmental protection debate. In that sense, *Environmental Politics* is designed to serve as a complement to other books that can provide the reader with additional background on the nature of the public policy process, public administration, political history, natural resources, or environmental science.

To put environmental politics in context, it is important to understand how the recognition of environmental conditions as "problems" and attempts to devise solutions make up the policy process. Public policies are those developed by the government, with the policymaking process following a sequential pattern of activity as follows:

1. *Problem identification and agenda formation:* In this stage, policy issues are brought to the attention of public officials in a variety of ways. Some are uncovered by the media; others become prominent through crisis or scientific study. Organized groups may demonstrate or lobby officials to focus attention on the problem or may enlist celebrities to bring it to the government's attention on their behalf.

2. *Policy formulation:* After a problem is identified as worthy of government attention, policymakers must then develop proposed courses of action to solve it. Groups may participate in this stage as well, lobbying officials to choose one alternative or proposal over another.

3. *Policy adoption:* The acceptance of a particular policy is a highly politicized stage that then legitimizes the policy, often involving legislation or rule making. This is usually referred to as the authorization phase of policymaking.

4. *Policy implementation:* To put an agreed-upon policy into effect, this fourth stage involves conflict and struggle as the administrative machinery of government begins to turn. Affected groups must now turn their attention from the legislative arena to the bureaucracy, and, in some cases, the judicial branch to get the policy to work.

5. *Policy evaluation:* An ongoing process, this stage involves various determinations as to whether or not the policy is effective. This appraisal may be based on studies of program operations, systematic evaluation, or personal judgment, but whatever the method, the evaluation may start the policy process all over again.[8]

The elements of this model of policymaking are not separate, distinct events; policymaking is an organic, even messy process of defining and redefining problems, formulating and implementing policies and then reformulating them, and moving off and on the policy agenda. Political scientists have developed a number of models in addition to this process framework to explain political activity. These other models focus on institutional design, the role of elites, the role of organized interests, insights from game theory, the rational calculations of individuals, and the functioning of systems.[9]

No one model can provide a complete assessment of all the factors that affect policymaking, but the process model is a useful paradigm for exploring environmental policy and politics. It focuses attention on the interaction of policymaking institutions such as, in the case of the United States, Congress, the president and the executive branch, and the courts as they compete for influence in formulating and implementing policies. Focusing on process also provides a way to see how nongovernmental actors interact with the formal institutional powers. Ultimately, a process model permits us to understand how policies are made and how they can be made to more effectively address the problems at which they are aimed. Ecological science has made clear the stakes: we are experimenting on a global scale with the natural systems that make life possible. Some mistakes may be irreversible, at least in a human scale of time. There is no greater collective need than to improve our capacity to make good environmental policies.

Environmental Politics begins with an overview of environmental history in Chapter 1 to provide background on the early beginnings of concern about the environment, followed by an explanation of the participants in the environmental debate in Chapter 2. Chapter 3 provides an introduction to the process by which environmental policy is made at the federal, state, and local levels, identifying key agencies and nongovernmental organizations involved in legislation, regime formation, and rule making. Chapters 4 through 8 introduce the essential issues related to the protection of land, waste management, energy, water, air quality, and environmental health. Although many of the problems associated with environmental protection are overlapping and interrelated, these sections bring the reader up to date on the most critical aspects of political decision making in each area. Common to each chapter is a statement of the environmental protection problem, an analysis of the efforts made to solve the problem, an assessment of the most critical issues, and an evaluation of what progress has been made. Chapters 9 through 11 shift in emphasis to those problems with a more global impact, such as transboundary pollution, global climate change, and the human population explosion. Lastly, Chapter 12 reflects on the problems and solutions we now face, and identifies emerging issues as we enter the new millennium.

Any one of these topics merits a complete book-length treatment of its own, and the end of each chapter includes suggestions for further reading. It is hoped that this "taste" of key environmental issues will lead the reader to develop an appetite for more comprehensive studies and research. But taken as a whole, the goal is that all readers—whether students, citizen activists, or government officials—emerge with a better understanding of the totality and scope of environmental politics.

ACKNOWLEDGMENTS

The first edition of *Environmental Politics* was initially written for my own use as an instructor, and the text benefited from the reviews and classroom use by colleagues across the country who shared their reactions on how it might be improved. There are no better critics than students, such as those who enrolled in my own courses, who were unabashed in their commentary. The preparation of the second edition of this book could not have been accomplished without the efforts of Gary Bryner, who agreed to assist in completing this project. He provided a valuable partnership and his own engaging style of writing throughout the text, and I am greatly indebted for his help. We wish also to thank the following individuals who reviewed portions of the manuscript in preparation: Phil Brick, Whitman College; W. Douglas Costain, University of Colorado, Boulder; Robert J. Duffy, Rider University; David H. Folz, University of Tennessee, Knoxville; Carolyn Long, Washington State University, Vancouver; Richard Kranzdorf, California Polytechnic State University; JoAnne Myers, Marist College; Lisa

Nelson, Bowling Green State University; John D. Redifer, Mesa State College; and Richard Young, Seattle University.

Don Reisman and Donna Erickson were responsible for the acquisition of the first-edition manuscript, and without their vision, the book would not have been written. Susan Cottenden and Beth Gillett of St. Martin's Press took on responsibility for the second edition, and I am grateful for their continuing confidence in my work. Lastly, I wish to acknowledge the friends who have given me their support and encouragement while the book was being written, offering me homemade soup, Internet humor of questionable value, quiet afternoon outings along the river, retail therapy, and love.

JACQUELINE VAUGHN SWITZER

NOTES

1. See, for example, Murray Feshbach, *Ecological Disaster: Cleaning Up the Hidden Legacy of the Soviet Regime* (New York: Twentieth Century Fund Press, 1995).

2. See Michael Grubb, et al. *The Earth Summit Agreements: A Guide and Assessment* (London: Earthscan, 1993); Hal Kane and Linda Starke, *Time for Change: A New Approach to Environment and Development* (Washington, D.C.: Island Press, 1992); Peter M. Haas, Marc A. Levy, and Edward A. Parson, "Appraising the Earth Summit," *Environment, 34,* no. 8 (October 1992): 7–11, 26–33; and *The Global Partnership for Environment and Development: A Guide to Agenda 21* (92-1-100481-0) and *Draft Agenda* (91-1-100482-9) (New York: United Nations, 1991).

3. April Bowling, "Canadian Native Peoples Jailed in a Logging Dispute," *World Watch, 9,* no. 6 (November–December 1996): 7.

4. See Hilary F. French, *Partnership for the Planet: An Environmental Agenda for the United Nations* (Washington, D.C.: Worldwatch Institute, 1995).

5. For an analysis of accomplishments and remaining challenges for international environmental governance, see Hilary F. French, *After the Earth Summit: The Future of Environmental Governance* (Washington, D.C.: Worldwatch Institute, 1992).

6. One of the more optimistic views of the possibility of a sustainable future is provided by Donella H. Meadows, Dennis L. Meadows, and Jorgen Randers, *Beyond the Limits: Confronting Global Collapse, Envisioning a Sustainable Future* (Post Mills, VT: Chelsea Green Publishing, 1992). Sustainability as it relates to one of the world's most pressing problems — hunger — is addressed by Lester R. Brown in *Who Will Feed China?* (New York: W.W. Norton, 1995).

7. See, for example, Lamont C. Hempel, *Environmental Governance: The Global Challenge* (Washington, D.C.: Island Press, 1996); Gareth Porter and Janet Welsh Brown, *Global Environmental Politics* 2d ed. (Boulder, CO: Westview Press, 1996); Lawrence E. Susskind, *Environmental Diplomacy: Negotiating More Effective Global Agreements* (New York: Oxford University Press, 1994); Mario F. Bognanno and Kathryn J. Ready, eds., *The North American Free Trade Agreement: Labor, Industry, and Government Perspectives* (Westport, CT: Praeger, 1993); and Peter M. Haas, Robert O. Keohane, and Marc A. Levy, eds., *Institutions for the Earth: Sources of Effective International Environmental Protection* (Cambridge, MA: MIT Press, 1993).

8. Adapted from James E. Anderson, *Public Policymaking: An Introduction,* 2d ed. (Boston, MA: Houghton Mifflin, 1994).

9. For a helpful discussion of models of policymaking, see Thomas R. Dye, *Understanding Public Policy* (Englewood Cliffs, NJ: Prentice Hall, 1992).

About the Authors

Jacqueline Vaughn Switzer teaches in the department of political science at Northern Arizona University, where she specializes in public policy and administration. Professor Switzer holds a Ph.D. in political science from the University of California, Berkeley, where she also attended the graduate school of public policy. She has taught previously at the University of Redlands and Southern Oregon University. Professor Switzer has a broad spectrum of nonacademic experience, including as an aide to a member of the California state legislature, as a program coordinator in the district attorneys' offices in two counties, and as a partner in a political consulting firm. Her environmental background stems from her work with the South Coast Air Quality Management District in southern California and as a policy analyst for Southern California Edison. Professor Switzer's previously published books include the co-authored American government textbook, *The Play of Power,* and *Green Backlash: The History and Politics of Environmental Opposition in the United States.*

Gary Bryner is a professor of political science at Brigham Young University. Since 1992, he has directed the public policy program at BYU, an interdisciplinary BA and MA degree program. He teaches courses in natural resource policy, environmental policy, international development policy, social policy, and policy theory and analysis. His current research interests include reforming environmental law, regulating air pollution, and balancing wilderness preservation and resource development. Professor Bryner has been a Guest Fellow at the Brookings Institution, the National Academy of Public Administration, the Natural Resources Defense Council, and the Natural Resources Law Center at the University of Colorado School of Law. He has a Ph.D. in government from Cornell University and a J.D. from Brigham Young University. He has also served on the Board of Directors of the Utah County Clean Air Coalition and the Rock Canyon Preservation Alliance, as well as the Steering Committee of the National Clean Air Coalition.

CHAPTER 1

A Historical Framework for Environmental Protection

Millions Join Earth Day Observances
  —*New York Times* headline, April 23, 1970

Millions Join Battle for a Beloved Planet
  —*New York Times* headline, April 23, 1990

Most contemporary observers regard Earth Day, 1970, as the peak of the American environmental movement, and the events of April 22 were indeed historic. An estimated twenty million Americans participated: New York Mayor John Lindsay closed Fifth Avenue to traffic during the event, and a massive rally was held in Union Square. Speeches and songs were heard at the Washington Monument, and virtually every college town, from Berkeley to Madison, held teach-ins and demonstrations. Philadelphia held a week-long observance, with symposia by environmental leaders and scientists, including Maine's Senator Edmund Muskie, author Paul Ehrlich, and consumer activist Ralph Nader. The event was highlighted by the appearance of the cast of the Broadway musical *Hair*. In San Francisco, the day was marked by symbolic protests, as a group calling itself Environmental Vigilantes dumped oil into the reflecting pool in front of Standard Oil. In Tacoma, Washington, nearly a hundred high school students rode down the freeway on horseback urging drivers to give up their automobiles.

A review of American history, however, shows that concern about the environment surfaced in the nation's infancy and has been a recurrent theme throughout the past three hundred years. One interesting aspect of that history is that some individuals or events appear to have had a momentary influence on policy development and then virtually disappeared from our historical consciousness. For example, Gifford Pinchot, an advisor to Theodore Roosevelt and leader of the conservation movement during the early twentieth century, had a tremendous impact on policymaking during that period, but his name is unknown to most contemporary members of the environmental movement. There is no Pinchot National Park or building in Washington, nor is the date of his birth celebrated. Like a shooting star, his role was transitory and ephemeral. Similarly, although women's organizations were responsible for bringing urban environmental issues such as solid waste and water quality to the policy agenda, that function ended when it was replaced by the struggle for suffrage.

Equally perplexing are the effects of a number of environmental disasters and crises that made headlines. Some, like the thirty-million-gallon oil spill caused by the sinking of the supertanker *Torrey Canyon* off the coast of England in 1967, have been upstaged by more recent events such as the oil spill resulting from the grounding of the Exxon *Valdez* in Alaska. But the radiation leak at the Soviet Union's Chernobyl plant in April 1986 has become synonymous with concerns about nuclear power and is likely to serve as a catalyst for international protests for years to come.

The development of an environmental policy agenda can be viewed in two ways. First, it is a history of ideas, a philosophical framework about our relationship to nature and the world. This history is punctuated with names ranging from Thomas Malthus and Charles Darwin to Karl Marx and Francis Bacon, along with modern commentary from Barry Commoner, Garrett Hardin, and Paul Ehrlich.[1] Second, it is a factual history, made up of events, individuals, and conditions. This chapter focuses on factual history to identify five distinct periods in the development of policies to protect the environment.

GERMINATION OF AN IDEA: FROM THE COLONIAL PERIOD TO 1900

Even before the states were united there was an awareness of the need to limit the use of the new land's natural resources. As early as 1626, the members of the Plymouth Colony passed ordinances regulating the cutting and sale of timber on colony lands. Other colonial leaders recognized the importance of preserving the region's resources, prohibiting the intentional setting of forest fires, and placing limits on deer hunting. In 1681, William Penn, proprietor of Pennsylvania, decreed that, for every five acres of land cleared, one must be left as virgin forest.[2] In 1691, Massachusetts Bay leaders began to set aside "forest reservations"— large stands of pines valued for their use as ships' masts. Forest preservation became an entrenched principle of colonial land management as early as the seventeenth century.[3]

During the eighteenth century, the nation was consumed with the building of a new government, but individual states made efforts to preserve the resources within their boundaries. Massachusetts in 1710 began to protect coastal waterfowl and in 1718 banned the hunting of deer for four years. Other states, such as Connecticut (1739) and New York (1772), also passed laws to protect game.[4] Political leaders at the beginning of the nineteenth century expressed interest in studying soil erosion; both Washington and Jefferson wrote of their concerns about the lands at their estates. With the opening of the Erie Canal in 1825, bringing pine forests within the reach of eastern markets, states were forced to confront the issue of timber poaching—one of the first environmental crimes.[5]

By midcentury, the public began to be interested in preserving natural resources. George Perkins Marsh's 1864 book, *Man and Nature,* captured attention with its call for protection of songbirds and the use of plantings to prevent soil erosion.[6] In 1866, German scientist and philosopher Ernst Haeckel coined the term *ecology,* and the subject became a thriving research discipline.[7] Still, there was no philosophy of protection that dominated either American or European thought. Studies of the popular literature of the 1870s led some historians to conclude that the environmental movement came alive with the advent of sportsmen's magazines. In October 1871, *The American Sportsman,* a monthly newspaper, marked a watershed in environmental history when it became the first publication to interrelate the subjects of hunting, fishing, natural history, and conservation. Two years later, *Forest and Stream* advocated the protection of watersheds, scientific management of forests, uniform game laws, and abatement of water pollution.[8] Diminishing supplies of fish in the Connecticut River resulted in the development of the fish culture industry and the formation in 1870 of the American Fisheries Society, the first biological society to research a diminishing natural resource. A year later the U.S. Fish Commission was created, the first federal agency responsible for the conservation of a specific natural resource.[9]

Adventure and exploration enhanced the public's interest in the environment throughout the nineteenth century. Lewis and Clark's transcontinental journeys beginning in 1804, and John Wesley Powell's descent down the Colorado River in 1869, increased Americans' awareness of the undiscovered beauty of the frontier.[10]

Tremendous urban population growth between 1870 and the turn of the century led to new environmental problems, including contamination of drinking water sources and garbage and sewage dumping. The problems were most evident in the cities of the Northeast and Midwest, where the population increases were the most rapid. Although New York remained the nation's largest city, nearly tripling its population over the thirty-year period, Chicago had the biggest percentage increase, nearly sixfold. Philadelphia, St. Louis, and Boston nearly doubled the sizes of their populations. Although industrial development did not reach the West Coast's cities as quickly, San Francisco, which served as the major shipping port, doubled its population between 1870 and 1890. The biggest increase was in Los Angeles, which grew to over twenty times its size from 1870 to 1900. American cities became centers of industry, and industry, with its accompanying population growth, meant pollution. By 1880, New York had 287 foundries and machine shops and 125 steam engines, bone mills, refineries, and tanneries. By the turn of the century, Pittsburgh had hundreds of iron and steel plants. Chicago's stockyards railroads, and port traffic filled the city with odors and thick, black smoke.[11]

Pollution problems caused by rapid industrial growth resulted in numerous calls for reform, and women became key leaders in cleaning up the urban environment. Upper-class women with extended periods of leisure time, believing "the housekeeping of a great city is women's work," formed civic organizations dedicated to monitoring pollution and finding solutions to garbage and sanitation problems. The first of these groups, the Ladies' Health Protective Association, was founded in 1884 with the goal of keeping New York's streets free of garbage. The Civic Club of Philadelphia, formed in 1894, began by placing trash receptacles at key intersections. Other groups were organized in Boston (the Women's Municipal League) and St. Louis (Women's Organization for Smoke Abatement).[12]

The nation's environmental awareness was enhanced by the actions of specific individuals. George Catlin first proposed the idea of a national park in 1832.[13] Henry David Thoreau spoke poetically in 1858 of his return to a natural world.[14] Frederick Law Olmstead, the "father of Central Park," was one of the first professional landscape architects in the United States. In 1864, he visited Yosemite and a year later received an appointment as a commissioner to help oversee management of the valley, making what were, at the time, novel suggestions for its preservation.[15] Olmstead's friend George E. Waring built the first separate sewer system in Lenox, Massachusetts, in 1876 and was a pioneer in the study of sanitary engineering. Waring, known as "the apostle of cleanliness," crusaded about the impact of garbage on public health and was responsible for the beginnings of contemporary solid waste science.[16]

The concept of preserving natural areas came from a variety of sources. In 1870, a group of explorers recommended that a portion of the upper Yellowstone River region be set aside to protect its geothermal features, wildlife, forests, and unique scenery. The result, the establishment of Yellowstone National Park in 1872, was the beginning of a pattern of preserving large undisturbed ecosystems. The public endorsed the idea, and Congress responded by creating Sequoia, Kings Canyon, and Yosemite National Parks in 1890, followed by Mount Rainier National Park in 1899. Interest in trees and forests was an important element of preservationism, symbolized by the proclamation of the first Arbor Day on April 10, 1872. The event was the culmination of the work of J. Sterling Morton, editor of Nebraska's first newspaper, and Robert W. Furia, a prominent nursery owner who later became governor. The two men convinced the Nebraska state legislature to commemorate the day with tree plantings to make Nebraska "mentally and morally the best agricultural state in the Union." More than one million trees were planted the first year, and Nebraska became known as the "Tree Planter's State" in 1895. With the Forest Reserve Act of 1891, the U.S. Congress set aside forest lands for preservation for the first time. Several years later President Grover Cleveland ordered lands to be protected because few states were willing to protect their forests from logging.

The founding of the Sierra Club by John Muir in 1892 marked the beginning of interest in a more broadly based environmental organization.[17] Although the early organizations have been called "pitifully weak" in membership and finances, these early groups had a strong sense of determination. Most groups debated the scientific management of resources rather than organizing to protect resources. But the idea of preserving land and natural resources was germinating within American society.[18]

PROGRESSIVE REFORMS AND CONSERVATIONISM: 1900–1945

Despite these whispers of ideas and early efforts, most environmental historians place the beginning of an actual "movement" at the turn of the century, when conservationism became a key element of the Progressive Era. The term *conservation* sprung from efforts by pioneers such as Frederick H. Newell, George Maxwell, and Francis G. Newlands to construct reservoirs to conserve spring flood waters for later use during the dry season. The concept behind conservation was "planned and efficient progress."[19]

In the United States, the infant environmental movement split into two camps: preservationists and conservationists. Under the leadership of Gifford Pinchot, the conservationists, influenced by forest management practices in Europe, believed that sustainable exploitation of resources was possible. The preservationists, led by John Muir, sought to preserve wilderness areas from all but recreational and educational use. Pinchot, a Yale graduate who trained at the French Forest School and later received an appointment as forester on the seven-thousand-acre North Carolina estate of George W. Vanderbilt, became the nation's most publicized environmentalist. In 1898, he became chief of the Division of Forestry (later renamed the U.S. Forest Service) and, as a personal friend of Theodore Roosevelt, had tremendous influence over the development of conservation policy through his connections in Washington, D.C. He convinced Roosevelt of the need to preserve forces and to use scientific forestry techniques to manage them.[20] In contrast, John Muir, who spent much of his life in California's Sierra Nevada, championed the protection of the Yosemite Valley and crusaded against the development of Yosemite's Hetch Hetchy reservoir, which he viewed as misuse of the region's natural resources.[21]

Generally, the conservationists' position won, at least at the national level. Before the turn of the century, there had been little federal consideration for conservation. The zenith can be traced to May 13–15, 1908, when a thousand national leaders met to attend a White House Conference on Resource Management, coordinated by Pinchot. This meeting was one of the first official agenda-setting actions in environmental policymaking.[22] At the end of the conference, the leaders asked the president to create a National Conservation Commission to develop an inventory of all natural resources. Roosevelt did so, appointing Pinchot as its chairman. By mid-1909, forty-one states had created similar organizations.[23] Pinchot organized the Conservation Congresses, which convened to discuss the familiar subjects of forest, soil, and water problems and management and eventually expanded to include issues such as public control of railroads, regulation of speculation and gambling in foodstuffs, coordination of governmental agencies, and creation of better rural schools.[24] The Congresses provided an opportunity for debate among federal, state, and local conservation leaders but were heavily politicized. Bitterness and internal struggles brought an end to the annual events in 1917. Of prime importance to many conservation leaders was the "public land question." The possibilities of unlimited economic growth in the West caused

President Theodore Roosevelt to appoint a Public Lands Commission in 1903. While many hoped the commission would promote orderly growth, there was also concern that the old practice of disposing nonagricultural lands to private owners would give way to public ownership and management.[25] During the presidencies of Theodore Roosevelt, William Howard Taft, and Woodrow Wilson, new national forests were created by Congress, which also passed laws to protect historic sites and migratory birds and enacted the National Park Service in 1916.

The Progressive Era is noted also for the birth of conservation organizations such as the National Audubon Society in 1905, the National Parks Association in 1919, and the Izaak Walton League in 1922. Pinchot organized the National Conservation Association in 1909, with the group's primary interests being limited to water power and mineral leasing, reflecting an extension of Roosevelt's policy. The group disbanded in the 1920s. Progressive Era reforms were focused on *efficiency*, striving to make better use of natural resources. The reformers were not radicals in the traditional political sense, so Progressive conservation posed only a modest threat to the existing distribution of power in the United States.[26]

As the term *conservation* broadened, it gradually lost its initial meaning. Roosevelt began to refer to the conservation of human health, and the National Conservation Congress devoted its entire 1912 session to "the conservation of human life." While conservationists focused attention on the sustainability of natural resource use, progressives in urban areas began to work for new laws and regulations to reduce pollution and protect public health. Cities were the first to regulate air pollution; the first clean air laws were enacted in the late 1800s. Public health advocates and activists such as Alice Hamilton and Jane Addams provided the impetus for state and local regulatory programs to improve water quality, provide for sanitation and waste removal, and reduce workers' exposure to toxic chemicals.[27]

During the 1930s, the environmental movement again became a battle between conservation and preservation. As a result, environmental leaders redoubled their efforts to preserve scenic areas. In 1935, Aldo Leopold founded the Wilderness Society to protect public lands, and the National Wildlife Federation (1936) served as the first of the conservation education organizations, sponsoring National Wildlife Week in schools beginning in 1938. Conservation organizations were closely allied with the four major engineering societies: the American Society of Civil Engineers, the American Society of Mechanical Engineers, the American Institute of Electrical Engineers, and the American Institute of Mining Engineers, all of which spearheaded the drive for efficiency. The Great Depression brought the federal government into new areas of responsibility, including environmental policy. Federal conservation interest intensified with the growth of agencies with specific resource responsibilities, beginning with the Tennessee Valley Authority in 1933, the Soil Conservation Service in 1935, and the Civilian Conservation Corps, which from 1933 to 1942 gave two million unemployed young men productive work.

RECREATION AND THE AGE OF ECOLOGY: POST–WORLD WAR II TO 1969

After World War II, Americans' interest in the environment shifted to a new direction. Concern about the efficient scientific management of resources was replaced with desire to use the land for recreational purposes. Over thirty million Americans toured the national parks in 1950. The parks were, in the words of one observer, "in danger of being loved to death," since roads and services were still at prewar levels.[28] National Park Service Director Conrad Wirth presented Congress with a "wish list" of park needs that came to be known as Mission '66—a ten-year improvement program that would coincide with the fiftieth anniversary of the National Park Service. That plan served as the blueprint for massive growth in both national parks and recreational areas during the next twenty years.[29] Habitat protection became the focus of groups like the Defenders of Wildlife, founded in 1947 to preserve, enhance, and protect the diversity of wildlife and their habitats. In 1951, The Nature Conservancy began to acquire, through either purchase, gift, or exchange, ecologically significant tracts of land, many of which are habitats for endangered species.

The 1960s brought a battle between those who supported industrial growth and those who worried about the effects of pollution caused by growth. It was a decade when an author's prose or a single event could rouse the public's indignation. The 1960s marked the beginning of legislative initiatives that would be fine-tuned over the next thirty years and of tremendous growth in environmental organizations.

Another View, Another Voice

THE GENTLE ANGER OF RACHEL CARSON

If a poll were ever taken of individuals who had made a lasting impact on environmental policy, there is little doubt that the name Rachel Carson would appear near the top of the list. Carson combined an interest in nature and a desire to write into a career that was as influential as it was controversial.

Born in 1907 in Springfield, Pennsylvania, she attended the Pennsylvania College for Women and Johns Hopkins University and did graduate work at the Woods Hole Marine Biological Laboratory in Massachusetts. She joined the zoology staff at the University of Maryland and later served as an aquatic biologist with the Bureau of Fisheries in Washington, D.C. She began writing in 1937 with an essay called "Undersea," which was published in the *Atlantic* and later became her first book, *Under the Sea-Wind: A Naturalist's Picture of Ocean Life,* published in 1941. Other marine-related books followed over the next twenty years, including scientific treatises such as *Food from the Sea: Fish*

(continued)

and Shellfish of New England and similar volumes on fish of the Middle West and middle Atlantic coast. In 1951, she received critical acclaim for *The Sea Around Us,* considered a literary work, which was later made into an Academy Award–winning documentary film.

But it was her 1962 book, *Silent Spring,* that polarized her readers and critics and forever changed the life of the quiet scientist. Her scathing indictment of the chemical and agricultural industries was sufficient to persuade President John F. Kennedy to call for a federal investigation into the use of pesticides. The President's Science Advisory Committee later issued a report agreeing with the basic premise of Carson's book, although she was vilified by the people she exposed. One industry spokesperson referred to her claims as "gross distortions of the actual facts, completely unsupported by scientific, experimental evidence, and general practical experience in the field" and threatened lawsuits against the author. Carson preferred to be thought of as a natural scientist in search of truth. In a CBS broadcast in 1963, she noted, "It is the public that is being asked to assume the risks that the insect controllers calculate. The public must decide whether it wishes to continue on the present road, and it can do so only when in full possession of the facts."

Carson died in 1964, leaving behind not only a literary legacy, but also an awareness of the natural world that did not exist prior to the publication of *Silent Spring.* She has been compared to Charles Darwin and credited with making ecology a household word. Because the public could identify with her writing style more so than with that of other scientists of the period, she reached an audience that might otherwise have never heard of DDT or influenced policymakers who would later enact a series of bills related to toxic chemicals. There is another aspect of Rachel Carson that makes her such a formidable figure in American environmental history. Her dire warnings of what might happen if pesticide use was not controlled served to avert the potential ecological disaster she foretold. None of her major predictions, including an endemic cancer wave and mutations of insects inheriting the earth, have happened. But as one contemporary author notes, Carson's warnings inspired the environmental protection revolution that followed. From the moment her mother introduced her to the natural world, Rachel Carson's one voice would grow into an global movement, which has now become an enduring element of American and international culture.

For Further Reading
Paul Brooks, ed. *House of Life: Rachel Carson at Work.* Boston: Houghton Mifflin, 1972.
Gregg Easterbrook, "Averting A Death Foretold," *Newsweek,* November 28, 1994, 72–73.
Frank Graham, Jr. *Since Silent Spring.* Boston: Houghton Mifflin, 1970.
Gino J. Marco, Robert M. Hollingworth, and William Durham, eds. *Silent Spring Revisited.* Washington, DC: American Chemical Society, 1987.
"Rachel Carson Dies of Cancer; 'Silent Spring' Author Was 56," the *New York Times,* April 15, 1964.

Two authors brought public attention to environmental problems during this decade. Rachel Carson in her book *Silent Spring*[30] and Paul Ehrlich in *The Population Bomb*[31] warned the world of the dangers of pesticides and the population explosion. Several authors served up "doom-and-gloom" predictions of the problems facing the planet, and there was a spirit of pessimism regarding the environmental situation. In January and February 1969, two oil spills five and a half miles off the coast of Santa Barbara, California, hit a public nerve like never before. Only eight days into his administration, President Richard Nixon was faced with an environmental crisis for which he was totally unprepared. The media captured the essence of the spills with images of birds soaked in gooey, black oil and pristine, white beaches soiled with globs of oil that washed up with each tide.[32]

Legislatively, the 1960s heralded a period of intense activity (see Appendix). In a carryover of issues from the postwar period, parks and wilderness remained high on the public's and legislature's agendas. By 1960, the number of national park visitors had grown to seventy-two million, and Congress responded by creating the Land and Water Conservation Fund to add new wilderness areas and national parks. Congress also expanded recreational areas with the passage of the National Wilderness Act in 1964 and the Wild and Scenic Rivers and National Trails Acts in 1968. President Lyndon Johnson, as part of his environmental policy, which he called "the new conservation," sought congressional support for urban parks to bring the land closer to the people.[33] Johnson's wife, Lady Bird, spearheaded the drive to improve the nation's roadways through her highway beautification program and sought and found congressional support for the 1965 passage of the Highway Beautification Act.[34]

Although there were several legislative precursors during the 1940s and 1950s, many of the hallmark pieces of pollution legislation were enacted during the 1960s, with the signing of the first Clean Air Act in 1963 (amended as the Air Quality Act in 1967) and the Water Quality Act in 1965. The Endangered Species Conservation Act (1966) marked a return to federal interest in animal and plant habitat that had begun earlier in the century. The National Environment Policy Act (NEPA), signed by President Nixon in 1970, served as the foundation for policy initiatives that were to follow throughout the next twenty years.

Political leadership on environmental issues during the 1960s focused on several individuals, and environmental organizations began to grow. Senator Edmund Muskie of Maine was among the most visible, but he became the target of considerable criticism, especially when he became a leading contender for the Democratic presidential nomination. A 1969 report by Ralph Nader's consumer organization gave Muskie credit for his early stewardship in the air pollution battle, but accused the senator of losing interest.[35] Other leaders, such as Senator Henry Jackson of Washington (who chaired the Senate Interior and Insular Affairs Committee and was largely responsible for shepherding NEPA through Congress) and Representative John Dingell of Michigan, were primarily involved in the legislative arena. Not only did the number of environmental groups expand during the 1960s, but existing ones experienced tremendous growth. New organizations like the African Wildlife Foundation (1961), the World Wildlife Fund (1961), the Environmental Defense Fund (1967), and the Council on Economic Priorities (1969) broadened the spectrum of group concerns. Meanwhile, the Sierra Club's membership grew tenfold from 1952 to 1969, and the Wilderness Society expanded from twelve thousand members in 1960 to fifty-four thousand in 1970.[36] One of the most compelling themes to emerge from the decade of the 1960s was that the federal government must take a more pervasive role in solving what was beginning to be called "the environmental crisis." The limited partnership between the federal government and the states was insufficient to solve what was already being spoken of in global terms.

EARTH DAYS AND DEREGULATION: 1970–1988

In August 1969, Wisconsin Senator Gaylord Nelson was on his way to Berkeley when he read an article in *Ramparts* magazine about the anti–Vietnam War teach-ins that were sweeping the country. Nelson, who was one of few members of Congress who had shown an interest in environmental issues, thought a similar approach might work to raise public awareness about the environment. In September, he proposed his idea during a speech in Seattle. Later that fall he incorporated a nonprofit, nonpartisan organization, Environmental Teach-In, pledging $15,000 of his own funds to get it started.[37] In December 1969, Nelson asked former Stanford student body president Denis Hayes to serve as national coordinator for what was to become Earth Day on April 22, 1970. Hayes, who postponed plans to enter Harvard Law School, worked with a $190,000 budget, purchasing a full-page ad in the *New York Times* to announce the teach-in. Not everyone was supportive. President Nixon, who had presented a thirty-seven-point environmental message to Congress a few months earlier, refused to issue a proclamation in support of Earth Day. Instead, the White House issued proclamations for National Archery Week and National Boating Week.[38]

Certainly 1970 marked a watershed year for new environmental organizations, with the founding of the Center for Science in the Public Interest, Citizens for a Better Environment, Environmental Action, Friends of the Earth, the League of Conservation Voters, Natural Resources Defense Council, and Save the Bay. Greenpeace and Public Citizen formed the following year. This period marks the beginning of a turnaround in leverage, as business and industry mobilized to slow the pace of environmental legislation (see Chapter 2). Environmental organizations were no longer able to monopolize the policy debate to serve their own interests. The range of environmental issues had become so extensive that organized environmental groups were unable to act effectively in all areas. Even more important, many issues had become matters not for public debate and legislative action but for administrative choice, an area in which politics was dominated by technical issues that placed a premium on the financial resources necessary to command expertise. This gave considerable political advantage to administrators and private corporate institutions that employed far more technical personnel than did environmental organizations.

The American public's attitude about the environment has never been very stable, and the decade of the 1970s is a perfect example. When George Gallup asked respondents in his national survey to identify the most important problem facing the nation in November 1967, the environment did not even make the list, nor did it appear when the question was asked in three surveys in 1968 or one in 1969. The Vietnam War and the economy overshadowed other concerns of Americans during that period. Not until May 1970 (after Earth Day) did the topic appear as an issue, when it ranked second and was mentioned by 53 percent of those responding. By June 1970, the subject dropped off the list, replaced in the number one spot by the campus unrest caused by the Vietnam War. Pollution and ecology returned to the list in March 1971 (ranked sixth with only 7 percent of respondents naming these as the most important problem); by June 1971, the topics ranked tenth. Environmental issues reemerged as a topic of concern in August and October 1972 and in March 1973, when the subject ranked sixth. But in May 1973, although pollution was ranked as the fifth most important problem facing the nation, it began to be overshadowed by another problem—the energy crisis, which ranked thirteenth. In January 1974, Gallup found that the public considered the energy crisis to be its most important problem, named by 46 percent of the public. By July that ranking dropped to number four, mentioned by 4 percent of those surveyed—a figure that stayed relatively constant throughout the rest of the decade.

President Nixon, whose position on environmental protection often reflected public opinion, used the signing of NEPA in 1970 to declare the next ten years as "the environmental decade," instructing his staff to rush through new legislative proposals. With his creation of the Environmental Protection Agency (EPA) by Executive Order in 1970, Nixon moved ahead in the race with Congress to be quicker to take advantage of the public's mood.

In the meantime, Congress was firmly on the environmental protection band-wagon, enacting more than twenty major pieces of legislation, many of which were refinements of earlier bills. Other laws, such as the Marine Mammal Protection Act (1972), the Federal Environmental Pesticides Control Act (1972), the Resource Conservation and Recovery Act (1976), and the Toxic Substances Control Act (1976), brought the federal government into new areas of environmental protection.

As had been the case in the 1960s, unexpected events periodically refocused attention on the environment. The 1973 Arab oil embargo pushed energy to the top of the policy agenda, although a succession of presidents had sought to make the United States "energy-independent." President Jimmy Carter pushed through most of his energy conservation program while turning down the White House thermostat and wearing a sweater indoors. Nuclear power, which was being touted as a cleaner, more reliable alternative to foreign oil, suffered a major setback in 1979 when cooling water at the Three Mile Island nuclear power plant near Harrisburg, Pennsylvania, dipped below safe levels and triggered a meltdown. Although no radioactive fuel escaped and no one was injured, the accident cast a shadow of doubt over the entire nuclear energy program.

During the summer of 1978, media coverage of incidents near the Love Canal in Niagara Falls, New York, reawakened American concerns over toxic waste. The abandoned canal had been used as a dumping ground for waste during the 1940s by the Hooker Chemicals and Plastics Corporation, which filled in the site and sold it to the Niagara Falls Board of Education for $1. A school was built near the site in the midst of a residential area. When local health officials found higher-than-normal rates of birth defects, miscarriages, and other medical problems among Love Canal residents, President Carter ordered the federal government to purchase the 240 homes nearest the site, eventually spending more than $30 million in relocation costs.[40]

Similar incidents occurred in 1979 in Kentucky, where seventeen thousand drums of leaking chemicals were discovered, and in 1983 in Times Beach, Missouri, where high levels of dioxin were thought to have contaminated the entire town. The Hudson River was found to be contaminated by more than a million pounds of polychlorinated biphenyls (PCBs), and wells in the West were filled with cancer-causing carbon tetrachloride trichlorethylene (TCE). The impact of publicity surrounding Love Canal and similar disclosures can be seen in public opinion polls. In July 1978, Resources for the Future (RFF) surveyed Americans' attitudes at a time when the inflation rate topped 10 percent and the tiny snail darter had stopped progress on the Tellico Dam. The RFF survey found environmental public support continued to hold firm with the number of people who felt "we are spending too little on environmental protection" increasing despite widespread economic problems.[41]

Just as the 1969 Santa Barbara oil spill had galvanized public opinion, the December 3, 1984, leak of deadly methyl isocyanate gas at a Union Carbide plant in Bhopal, India, reawakened interest in environmental disasters. The leak, which killed more than two thousand and injured two hundred thousand, was brought closer to home when it was revealed that an identical Union Carbide plant was located in Institute, West Virginia. The public and governmental outcry resulted in a shutdown of the plant for several months for inspections and safety checks. These events also caused a shifting of legislative gears as interest changed to toxic and hazardous waste and the health impacts of pollution. With congressional enactment of the Resource Conservation and Recovery Act and the Toxic Substances Control Act in the 1970s, the foundation was laid for the Comprehensive Environmental Response, Compensation, and Liability Act ("Superfund") in 1980 (reauthorized in 1986) and the Hazardous and Solid Waste Amendments in 1984. Concerns about health found their way into the Safe Drinking Water Act Amendments of 1986 (an expansion of the 1974 law) and the Federal Insecticide, Fungicide, and Rodenticide Act Amendments of 1988.

But the 1980s brought an increase in the pessimistic attitudes Americans had toward the efforts that had been made in the previous decade. A Cambridge Reports survey from 1983 to 1989 found that respondents believed that the overall quality of the environment was worse than it was five years before, with a sharp increase in pessimism beginning in 1987.[42] When the question of "most important problem" was asked again during the 1980s by the Gallup poll, energy often made the list of most important problems, although the environment did not. A separate Gallup survey conducted in September 1989 found that 66 percent of the respondents said they were "extremely concerned" about the pollution of sea life and beaches from the dumping of garbage, medical wastes, and chemicals into the ocean, with the same percentage extremely concerned about the pollution of fresh-water rivers, lakes, and other sources of drinking water. Fifty percent of those surveyed said they were extremely concerned about air pollution, and 41 percent expressed concern over the disposal of household garbage and trash.[43]

The 1980s environmental policy agenda was molded most by the administration of President Ronald Reagan, whose main concern was to reduce the amount of governmental regulation (see Chapter 3). Reagan's budget cuts and personnel decisions and a weakening of the previous decade's legislative efforts had a profound effect on policy for the next ten years. Despite those changes, public concern over environmental degradation has risen substantially in recent years, commanding support from large majorities. What was less clear at the end of the 1980s was the strength of the public's commitment to environmental protection.[44]

GLOBAL AWARENESS AND THE NEW DEMOCRATS: THE 1990s

In 1992, the Gallup International Institute's Health of the Planet Survey showed that concern about the environment is not limited to wealthy industrialized nations of the Northern Hemisphere. Environmental problems were rated as one of the three most serious problems in half of the twenty-two nations surveyed, and only small percentages of people in any nation dismissed environmental issues as not serious. The survey found that air and water pollution are perceived as the most serious environmental problems affecting nations, with the loss of natural resources mentioned most often by residents of other nations.[45]

After declaring himself "the environmental president" during his 1988 campaign, George Bush was faced with not only the Reagan legacy of environmental slash and burn, but with a host of newly discovered environmental problems and crises as well, many with a global focus. Two major pieces of legislation enacted during the Bush administration were the Clean Air Act Amendments of 1990 and the 1992 Energy Policy Act, both of which represented a break in the legislative gridlock that characterized Congress under Republican administrations. Environmental organizations, many of which experienced a decline in membership growth after the initial burst of activity in the early 1970s, received a booster shot with Earth Day 1990. The Gallup organization classified about 20 percent of the American public as hard-core environmentalists—those who call themselves strong environmentalists and feel major disruptions are coming if we do not take drastic environmental actions even at the cost of economic growth.[46]

Perhaps the most important development is the globalization of environmental protection. The 1992 Earth Summit refocused the need for environmental issues to be viewed globally, rather than locally. It also provided dramatic evidence of the need for international cooperation to solve the larger issues of global warming, transboundary pollution, and biodiversity and raised the critical question of whether the industrialized world is willing to pay for environmental protection in developing countries. It also spotlighted the North/South split (the split between nations of the Northern and Southern hemispheres) between industrialized and developing nations—a controversy not likely to be resolved by the end of this decade.

The inauguration of President Bill Clinton and Vice-president Al Gore marked yet another turning point in environmental politics. The vice-president was widely known as an aggressive advocate of environmental regulation and author of a best-selling call to environmental arms, *Earth in the Balance*.[47] Although the environment never surfaced as a key issue in the 1992 presidential campaign, Clinton administration officials immediately called for peaceful coexistence between environmentalists and business as the administration prepared its legislative agenda. Early in 1993, the Clinton administration proposed sweeping changes in public lands policies, including raising grazing fees and imposing hard-rock mining royalties and below-cost timber sales in national forests, as part of a budget bill aimed at reducing the federal deficit. The proposals were immediately attacked by members of Congress from Western states, many of whom were Democrats or represented states where Clinton had won in 1992, and the president quickly retreated and shifted his attention to other policy initiatives.

In October 1993, the administration's initiative to add grazing-fee hikes and new environmental safeguards for grazing lands to the Interior Department appropriations bill failed when the Senate was unsuccessful in ending a filibuster of the bill by Republicans and Western Democrats. The proposals were eventually dropped from the bill, but not until Western Senators blasted the administration as launching a war on the West. However, while the Senate resisted changes, the media gave increasingly favorable attention to Secretary Bruce Babbitt's efforts to get Westerners to pay fair prices for using public lands and to increase environmental protection. Babbitt's agenda of reorienting the Bureau of Reclamation away from dam building and toward water conservation, amending the Endangered Species Act to increase habitat preservation, and updating mining and logging policies raised tremendous opposition among some in the West, while encouraging many others who believed such changes were long overdue. Babbitt argued that public land policy should be guided by the idea of "dominant public use," requiring the preservation of ecosystems, rather than "multiple use," in which logging, mining, and ranching interests dominate. Babbitt argued that dominant public use requires policymakers to look at the needs for biodiversity, watershed protection, and landscape, as well as the opportunities for extractive industries, and to set priorities.[48] However, by the time Congress adjourned in 1994, the only conservationist legislation that was enacted created two new National Parks in California, Death Valley and Joshua Tree, and a third protected area, the Mojave Desert.

In 1994, Republican candidates in a number of western states were successful in running against Babbitt and Clinton's western lands reforms. The Republicans effectively integrated attacks on Democrats for launching a war on the West with antitax, anti-Washington, and antiregulation rhetoric. The election in 1994 of a Republican Congress shifted the attention to the economic costs and regulatory burdens of environmental protection. There was a growing belief that environmental politics had been guided by popular opinion rather than by science. Critics pointed to sweeping governmental regulations enacted during the Reagan and Bush administrations to reduce concentrations of toxic compounds in water, air, and land even when there was little scientific evidence of risk to humans. Congress, responding to highly publicized concerns about the dangers of asbestos, radon, and toxic waste dumps, quickly wrote legislation that has resulted in costing the government and business an estimated $140 billion a year. Even William Reilly, the EPA Administrator under Bush, has said that action in the past was "based on responding to the nightly news. What we have had in the United States is environmental agenda-setting by episodic panic."[49]

When the American economy was relatively healthy, few bothered to question the cost:benefit ratio for such expenditures. But with resources growing more and more scarce, and with the federal government placing a new emphasis on domestic problems like crime, drugs, health care, and the urban infrastructure, this questioning of environmental priorities seems long overdue. The 1994 House Republican "Contract with America," written by Newt Gingrich and other Republican House leaders, outlined a set of national issues for House Republican candidates to run on and played a major role once the Republicans won in shaping the policy agenda. The contract promised to "roll back government regulations and create jobs."[50] Frank Lutz, the Republican pollster who worked with Gingrich in creating the Contract with America, told his clients that "Americans believe Washington has gone too far in regulating and they want to turn the clock and paperwork back." Party strategist William Kristol suggested that Republicans immediately identify regulatory "excesses," and he organized a meeting entitled "What to Kill First: Agencies to Dismantle, Programs to Eliminate, and Regulations to Stop." William Niskanen, head of the Cato Institute, called on Congress to "rein in what I call the 'Nanny State.' Stop telling states where to set speed limits. . . . Stop telling businesses about whether and when employees and customers may smoke."[51] Heritage Foundation analysts published "real life 'horror' stories of individuals who have lost their property or had their business harmed because of overzealous government regulators" and offered the following agenda for reforming regulation: force environmental agencies to base their evaluations of proposed regulations on sound scientific criteria; place a ceiling on the estimated total cost of all regulations promulgated by the agency; force regulators to account for the costs of their proposals, whenever possible; insist that regulators rely on markets rather than red tape; and enact legislation specifying exactly when the federal government must compensate property owners for regulatory takings.[52]

The Contract with America did not mention the environment directly, but included numerous provisions aimed at reducing regulation and promoting economic development rather than preservation. These provisions included requirements that Congress fund the regulatory mandates imposed on states and that agencies perform cost:benefit analyses before issuing regulations, reduce paperwork requirements, compensate landowners for costs resulting from regulation, and formulate a regulatory budget of compliance costs that they impose on business. Republicans in Congress sought to reduce environmental regulation through cutting EPA and Interior Department budgets, attaching riders to appropriations bills that reduced specific protections, and introducing major rewrites of the leading environmental laws.

However, Republican efforts to reduce environmental regulation were short-lived. Environmental groups challenged the new Republican agenda in the spring of 1995. The largest environmental organizations proposed an Environmental Bill of Rights signed by Americans throughout the nation and presented to Congress and the White House.[53] President Clinton began vetoing appropriations bills with provisions aimed at reducing environmental protection and saw his popularity climb. That encouraged more vetoes, and more challenges to the Republican agenda, and by 1996, Republicans had abandoned their attacks on environmental laws and programs. Clinton skillfully positioned himself between the Republican radicals and popular environmental programs during the 1996 presidential campaign, and his reelection was in part the result of his willingness to challenge the congressional Republicans' deregulatory agenda. Bruce Babbitt had become one of the most popular members of the Clinton administration, and he led the criticism of the Republican Congress that contributed so greatly to the president's political rehabilitation in 1996. He was most effective at drawing attention to the Republican Congress's environmental agenda, particularly when he charged that some Republicans were seeking to sell off national parks. Babbitt's shift from public lands issues in the West to national environmental issues defused criticism of him inside the administration and in the environmental community.[54] Congress and the White House came together to pass new pesticide and safe drinking water laws in the summer of 1996 that were widely heralded as examples of the potential of bipartisan environmentalism. But the demands for more environmental protection and less burdensome regulation are not easily satisfied, and much more contentious issues lie ahead as a Democratic White House and a Republican Congress try to work together in 1997 as well as lay the groundwork for fighting each other in the 1998 election.

SUMMARY

Historians and political scientists have identified five distinct periods in the development of American environmentalism, although 1970 is often viewed as the peak of the growth of the environmental movement. With the advent of the first Earth Day celebration, media and public attention focused on the environment. A number of crises, from the 1969 Santa Barbara oil spill to the energy crisis of the 1970s, have brought pressure to bear on policymakers who are charged with protecting the environment; American political history is sprinkled with various legislative successes and failures as a result of those pressures. The debate continues over how best to achieve the goal of a clean, healthy environment, and what are the costs and benefits of alternative ways of reaching that end. If there is a recognizable trend in environmental protection, it may be twofold: a fine-tuning of legislation and a recognition of the globalization of environmental issues.

NOTES

1. For a review of the philosophical underpinnings of the movement, see David Pepper, *The Roots of Modern Environmentalism* (London: Croom Helm, 1984).

2. Roderick Nash, *American Environmentalism,* 3d ed. (New York: McGraw-Hill, 1990), xi. Nash has published numerous works on American environmental history, including *The American Conservation Movement* (St. Charles, MO: Forum, 1974); *Wilderness and the American Mind* (New Haven, CT: Yale University Press, 1982); and *The Rights of Nature: A History of Environmental Ethics* (Madison, WI: University of Wisconsin Press, 1988).

3. The colonial period is also covered in David Cushan Coyle, *Conservation* (New Brunswick, NJ: Rutgers University Press, 1957).

4. Nash, *American Environmentalism,* xi.

5. Coyle, *Conservation,* 8–9, 21.

6. George Perkins Marsh, *Man and Nature; or Physical Geography as Modified by Human Action* (New York: Scribner, 1864). See also, David Lowenthal, *George Perkins Marsh: Versatile Vermonter* (New York: Columbia University Press, 1958).

7. Donald Worster, *American Environmentalism: The Formative Period 1860–1915* (New York: Wiley, 1973), 3.

8. One of the historians who has researched the sportsmen's movement is John E. Reiger, *American Sportsmen and the Origins of Conservation* (Norman, OK: University of Oklahoma Press, 1986).

9. *Ibid.,* 53.

10. The biographical materials on these early pioneers provide an excellent background into the formation of the early conservation movement. See, for example, George T. Morgan, Jr., *William B. Greeley, A Practical Forester* (St. Paul, MN: Forest History Society, 1961), and Wallace Stegner, *Beyond the Hundredth Meridian: John Wesley Powell and the Second Coming of the West* (Boston, MA: Houghton Mifflin, 1954).

11. Another one of the major contributors to the field of American environmental history is Joseph Petulla, *Environmental Protection in the United States* (San Francisco, CA: San Francisco Study Center, 1987), 13–30.

12. Suellen Hoy, "Municipal Housekeeping: The Role of Women in Improving Urban Sanitation Practices," in *Pollution and Reform in American Cities 1870–1930,* ed. Martin Melosi (Austin, TX: University of Texas Press, 1980), 173–198. See also the spring 1984 issue of *Environmental Review* for a summary of the contributions of women in the environmental movement.

13. See Harold McCracken, *George Catlin and the Old Frontier* (New York: Dial, 1959), for a biographical perspective on one of the frontier environmentalists.

14. There are two ways to gauge the impact of Thoreau on the development of the environmental movement, especially his sojourn at Walden Pond. One is to read his own words, such as *The Annotated Walden* (New York: Potter, 1970) and *Consciousness in Concord* (Boston, MA: Hougton Mifflin, 1958). There have been numerous attempts to characterize this complex individual, including these by the following biographers: Milton Meltzer and Walter Harding, *A Thoreau Profile* (New York: Crowell, 1962); Sherman Paul, *The Shores of America: Thoreau's Inward Exploration* (Urbana, IL: University of Illinois Press, 1959); and Robert

Richardson, *Henry Thoreau: A Life of the Mind* (Berkeley, CA: University of California Press, 1986).

15. Olmstead's contributions are many, not only his attempts to develop the urban landscape, but scenic preservation as well. Olmstead's accomplishments are chronicled in several biographies, including Albert Fein, *Frederick Law Olmstead and the American Environmental Tradition* (New York: Braziller, 1972); Charles C. McLaughlin, *The Formative Years* (Baltimore, MD: Johns Hopkins University Press, 1977); Elizabeth Stevenson, *Flo: A Biography of Frederick Law Olmstead* (New York: Macmillan, 1977); and Cynthia Zaitzevesky, *Frederick Law Olmstead and the Boston Park System* (Cambridge, MA: Belknap Press, 1982).

16. The urban sanitation issue became one of the cornerstones of urban environmentalism. See George Rosen, *A History of Public Health* (New York: MD Publications, 1958).

17. There are few comprehensive studies of the early organizations, except for those produced by the groups themselves. See, for example, Michael Cohen, *The History of the Sierra Club 1892–1970* (San Francisco, CA: Sierra Club, 1988).

18. For more information on this early period, see Henry Clepper, *Origins of American Conservation* (New York: Ronald Press, 1966); and Peter Wild, *Pioneer Conservationists of Western America* (Missoula, MT: Mountain Press, 1979).

19. Samuel P. Hays, *Conservation and the Gospel of Efficiency* (Cambridge, MA: Harvard University Press, 1959), 5.

20. Pinchot writes of his efforts in *The Fight for Conservation* (New York: Harcourt Brace, 1910), and *Breaking New Ground* (New York: Harcourt Brace, 1947). Biographers who have identified his critical role in the Progressive movement include Martin Fausold, *Gifford Pinchot, Bull Moose Progressive* (Syracuse, NY: Syracuse University Press, 1961); M. Nelson McGeary, *Gifford Pinchot: Forester-Politician* (Princeton, NJ: Princeton University Press, 1960); and Harold T. Pinkett, *Gifford Pinchot: Private and Public Forester* (Urbana, IL: University of Illinois Press, 1970).

21. In contrast to Pinchot, Muir's views are found in his book, *Our National Parks* (Boston, MA: Houghton Mifflin, 1901), and *The Yosemite* (New York: Century, 1912). One of the most widely researched environmental pioneers, Muir is the subject of dozens of biographers, including Michael P. Cohen, *The Pathless Way: John Muir and the American Wilderness* (Madison, WI: University of Wisconsin Press, 1984); Stephen Fox, *John Muir and His Legacy* (Boston, MA: Little, Brown, 1981); Frederick Turner, *Rediscovering America: John Muir in His Time and Ours* (New York: Viking, 1985); and Linnie M. Wolfe, *Son of the Wilderness: The Life of John Muir* (New York: Knopf, 1945).

22. Nash, *American Environmentalism*, 84.

23. Hays, *Conservation and the Gospel of Efficiency*, 132.

24. The activities of the Conservation Congresses are outlined in Grant McConnell, "The Conservation Movement—Past and Present," *Western Political Quarterly*, 7, no. 3 (September 1954): 463–478.

25. Hays, *Conservation and the Gospel of Efficiency*, 69.

26. Many historians and analysts of the Progressive period have downgraded its importance to contemporary environmentalism. See Geoffrey Wandesforde-Smith, "Moral Outrage and the Progress of Environmental Policy: What Do We Tell the Next Generation about How to Care for the Earth?" in *Environmental Policy in the 1990s*, ed. Norman J. Vig and Michael E. Kraft (Washington, D.C.: Congressional Quarterly Press, 1990), 334–335.

27. For a discussion of the evolution of public health and environmental protection, see Robert Gottlieb, *Forcing the Spring: The Transformation of the American Environmental Movement* (Washington, D.C.: Island Press, 1993).

28. For a summary of the development of the parks and wilderness areas, see Dyan Zaslowsky and the Wilderness Society, *These American Lands* (New York: Henry Holt, 1986).

29. There is a wealth of historical information on the National Park Service and its programs, including William C. Everhart, *The National Park Service* (New York: Praeger, 1972); Ronald A. Foresta, *America's National Parks and Their Keepers* (Washington, D.C.: Resources for the Future, 1984); Alfred Runte, *National Parks: The American Experience* (Lincoln: University of Nebraska Press, 1982); David J. Simon, ed., *Our Common Lands* (Wash-

ington, D.C.: Island Press, 1988); and *Investing in Park Futures: A Blueprint for Tomorrow* (Washington, D.C.: National Parks and Conservation Association, 1988).

30. Rachel Carson, *Silent Spring* (Greenwich, CT: Fawcett, 1962). For biographical material on the woman who is largely credited with reviving the contemporary environmental movement, see Paul Brooks, *The House of Life: Rachel Carson at Work* (Boston, MA: Houghton Mifflin, 1972); Carol Gartner, *Rachel Carson* (New York: Ungar, 1983); H. Patricia Hynes, *The Recurring Silent Spring* (New York: Pergamon Press, 1989); and Philip Sterling, *Sea and Earth: The Life of Rachel Carson* (New York: Crowell, 1970).

31. Paul Ehrlich, *The Population Bomb* (New York: Ballantine, 1968).

32. For an account of this event, see Carol and John Steinhart, *Blowout: A Case Study of the Santa Barbara Oil Spill* (Belmont, CA: Wadsworth, 1972). An extensive bibliography on the spill was compiled by Kay Walstead, *Oil Pollution in the Santa Barbara Channel* (Santa Barbara, CA: University of California, Santa Barbara Library, 1972).

33. Zaslowsky, *These American Lands,* 37.

34. See Lewis L. Gould, *Lady Bird Johnson and the Environment* (Lawrence, KS: University of Kansas Press, 1988).

35. John C. Esposito, *Vanishing Air* (New York: Grossman, 1970), 292.

36. Samuel P. Hays, "From Conservation to Environment," *Environmental Review,* Fall 1982, 37.

37. Jack Lewis, "The Spirit of the First Earth Day," *EPA Journal, 16,* no. 1 (January–February 1990): 9–10.

38. See John C. Whitaker, *Striking a Balance: Environment and Natural Resources Policy in the Nixon-Ford Years* (Washington, D.C.: American Enterprise Institute, 1976), 6.

39. Samuel P. Hays, *Beauty, Health and Permanence: Environmental Politics in the U.S. 1955–1985* (Cambridge: Cambridge University Press, 1987), 61.

40. See Lois Gibbs, *Love Canal* (Albany, NY: State University of New York Press, 1983); and Adeline Gordon Levine, *Love Canal: Science, Politics and People* (Lexington, MA: Heath, 1982).

41. Robert Cameron Mitchell, "The Public Speaks Again: A New Environmental Survey," *Resources, 60* (September–October 1978): 2.

42. David Rapp, "Special Report," *Congressional Quarterly,* January 20, 1990, 138.

43. "Household Waste Threatening Environment; Recycling Helps Ease Disposal Problem," *Gallup Report 280,* January 1990, 30–34.

44. See Riley E. Dunlap, "Public Opinion in the 1980s: Clear Consensus, Ambiguous Commitment," *Environment, 33,* no. 8 (October 1991): 9–15, 32–37.

45. Press release, "Environment Given Priority over Economic Growth in Both Rich and Poor Nations," Washington, D.C., George H. Gallup International Institute, May 4, 1992. See also Riley E. Dunlap, George H. Gallup, Jr., and Alec M. Gallup, *The Health of the Planet Survey* (Washington, D.C.: George H. Gallup International Institute, May 1992).

46. George Gallup, Jr., and Frank Newport, "Americans Strongly in Tune with the Purpose of Earth Day 1990," *The Gallup Poll Monthly,* April 1990, 6.

47. Albert Gore, *Earth in the Balance* (Boston: Houghton Mifflin, 1992).

48. Margaret Kriz, "Quick Draw," *National Journal* (November 13, 1993): 2711–2716, quote on 2713.

49. Keith Schneider, "New View Calls Environmental Policy Misguided," *The New York Times,* March 21, 1993, 1.

50. See Ed Gillespie and Rob Shellhas, eds., *Contract with America* (New York: Times Books, 1994): 125–41. For a discussion of the history and evolution of the Contract with America, see Elizabeth Drew, *Showdown: The Struggle Between the Gingrich Congress and the Clinton White House* (New York: Simon & Schuster, 1996): 28–34.

51. Quoted in Cindy Skryzycki, "Hill Republicans Promise a Regulatory Revolution," *The Washington Post,* January 4, 1995, A1.

52. Craig E. Richardson and Geoff C. Ziebart, *Red Tape in America: Stories from the Front Lines* (Washington, D.C.: Heritage Foundation, 1995): v.

53. B. J. Bergman, "Standing Up for the Planet," *Sierra,* March/April 1995, 79–80.

54. Tom Kenworthy, "In Smooth Water Now," *The Washington Post National Weekly Edition,* December 11–17, 1995.

FOR FURTHER READING

Matthew A. Cahn and Rory O'Brien, eds. *Thinking About the Environment.* New York: M. E. Sharpe, 1996.

Riley E. Dunlap and Angela G. Mertig, eds. *American Environmentalism: The U.S. Environmental Movement 1970–1990.* Washington, D.C.: Taylor and Francis, 1992.

Robert Gottlieb. *Forcing the Spring.* Washington, D.C.: Island Press, 1993.

Samuel P. Hays. *Beauty, Health and Permanence: Environmental Politics in the U.S. 1955–1985.* Cambridge, England: Cambridge University Press, 1987.

Samuel P. Hays. *Conservation and the Gospel of Efficiency.* Cambridge, MA: Harvard University Press, 1959.

Roderick Nash. *American Environmentalism,* 3d ed. New York: McGraw-Hill, 1990.

Kirkpatrick Sale. *The Green Revolution.* New York: Hill and Wang, 1993.

Philip Shabecoff. *A Fierce Green Fire.* New York: Hill and Wang, 1993.

CHAPTER 2

Participants in the
Environmental Debate

"Our goal is to destroy, to eradicate the environmental movement."
—Ron Arnold, author, *The Wise Use Agenda*

"[Wise use] is the dark side of conservation, environmentalism's evil force."
—*National Parks*[1]

There are various approaches to studying the policy process outlined in the Preface, but one theory that appears to be especially applicable to environmental politics is group theory. Adherents to this approach believe that political decisions are the result of the struggles among competing interests who have access to the political process. Key to understanding group theory is the acceptance that some groups will have more access than others, because of superior financial resources, leadership, organization, or public support for their cause.[2]

Although this book does not attempt to delve into the theoretical debate over *how much* influence various groups have in the making of environmental policy, or to apply the pluralist tradition of American politics to other countries to explain their environmental policies, it does describe their *role* in the political debate.[3] This chapter attempts to identify the key groups on both sides of the political debate in the United States as well as to provide an overview of international environmental organizations and green parties. It touches briefly on the groups' strategies, successes, and failures and provides a summary of their participation in the policymaking process.

U.S. ENVIRONMENTAL ORGANIZATIONS

In the one hundred years since the founding of the first American environmental associations, there has been a gradual evolution of the movement. Seven of the ten most powerful groups (known collectively as the "Group of Ten") were founded before 1960. Most have influential local or regional chapters and have broadened their interests from land and wildlife issues to broader "second-generation" issues that are not necessarily site- or species-specific.[4]

These mainstream organizations, identified in Table 2.1, have as a common strategy an emphasis on lobbying, although their specific focus often varies. The Sierra Club, the Wilderness Society, and the National Parks and Conservation Association, for example, have tended to emphasize the preservation of public lands for future generations, while groups such as the National Wildlife Federation and Izaak Walton League, with a large percentage of sports enthusiasts and hunters within their constituency, are more involved with habitat preservation for wildlife. Some groups, such as the American Lung Association, are primarily interested in pollution and its impact on public health. But they sometimes work with nature-oriented groups on issues such as air pollution.

When the Environmental Defense Fund (EDF) was founded in 1967, a new breed of organization joined these mainstream groups. EDF and later the Natural Resources Defense Council made environmental litigation an art form, moving group strategy from the legislative to the judicial arena. These groups have benefited from the citizen suit provisions in virtually every federal environmental statute since the 1970 Clean Air Act. The provisions allow "any person" to sue private parties for noncompliance with the law, and to sue not only for injunctive relief but also for civil penalties. This allows those who sue to recover the cost of attorneys' fees and "mitigation fees" in lieu of, or in addition to, civil fines. The groups often receive from offending companies direct transfer payments, which help fund their operations and projects, making litigation an attractive group strategy (see Chapter 3).[5]

Other mainstream groups, although smaller in size and resources, conduct research or grass-roots campaigns. Two of the most prominent are Environmental Action and the League of Conservation Voters. Founded in 1970, Environmental Action, which merged with the Environmental Task Force in 1988, conducts lobbying, research, education, and organizing efforts. The group developed a

Table 2.1 Ten Largest U.S. Environmental Organizations

Group	Year Founded	1995 Membership
Sierra Club	1892	570,000
National Audubon Society	1905	570,000
National Parks and Conservation Assoc.	1919	450,000
Wilderness Society	1935	310,000
National Wildlife Federation	1936	1.8 million
Nature Conservancy	1951	825,000
World Wildlife Fund	1961	1.2 million
Environmental Defense Fund	1967	300,000
Greenpeace USA	1969	1.6 million
Natural Resources Defense Council	1970	185,000

Source: John Seredich, *Your Resource Guide to Environmental Organizations* (Irvine, CA: Smiling Dolphins Press, 1991), and data from individual organizations.

"Dirty Dozen" campaign to spotlight the environmental records of members of Congress and has actively lobbied against utility companies and for bottle-deposit legislation. Also founded in 1970, the League of Conservation Voters has two goals: to help elect pro-environment candidates and to monitor Congressional performance. It is not the group's members that give it clout, but its annual report, the *National Environmental Scorecard,* which ranks the voting records of each member of Congress on environmental legislation.

Some environmental organizations are characterized by their emphasis on a single issue. These types of groups rarely shift from their area of concern to another issue, although some overlap is developing. Clean Water Action, founded in 1971, conducts research and lobbies on issues related to drinking water and groundwater resources. Recognizing the interrelatedness of pollution, Clean Water Action also became involved in the passage of the 1986 Superfund legislation and the 1990 Clean Air Act Amendments. The Clean Air Network is an umbrella organization that brings together national and grass-roots groups to promote implementation of the Clean Air Act and oppose efforts by industry to weaken its provisions. The Defenders of Wildlife work, as their group's name implies, to protect wildlife habitats through education and advocacy programs. Founded in 1947, the group is now working to strengthen the Endangered Species Act and develop funding for wildlife refuges.

Among the more recently created environmental organizations are those, often with a purely regional base of operation, seeking to preserve individual species. Many of these groups were organized in the 1980s after the initial burst of momentum in the environmental movement had passed. Although these groups limit their activities to individual species, they often form coalitions to preserve natural habitats and wildlife ranges. Their membership is typically smaller (ten thousand to forty thousand) and may include researchers dedicated to scientific study of the species. Typical of such groups are Bat Conservation International, founded in 1982, and the Mountain Lion Preservation Foundation, founded in 1986. Both of these organizations emphasize education as well as research and habitat studies. The Mountain Lion Preservation Foundation, for example, has developed an aggressive media campaign in California to educate the public on the habitat needs of this animal, as well as lobbying for a permanent state ban on the hunting of the mountain lion, also known as the cougar, puma, or panther.

Property-oriented groups, such as The Nature Conservancy and Ducks Unlimited represent examples of two long-standing organizations that focus their efforts on management and preservation. Both groups have invested private funds for purchasing lands that are then reserved for wildlife habitats. One of the older environmental groups, Ducks Unlimited, with chapters throughout the United States, was founded in 1937 by hunters seeking to preserve wetland habitats. The Nature Conservancy, founded in 1951, has privately purchased land for habitat protection throughout the United States as well as global ecological preserves that are home to endangered species.

Another subgroup is comprised of organizations that originated or are based in the United States, have members throughout the world, and have broadened their interests to more global concerns. The largest international environmental organization, Greenpeace, was founded in 1969 as the Don't Make A Wave Committee by a small group of Sierra Club members and peace activists. Greenpeace drew its name from a rented boat used to protest nuclear weapons testing in the Aleutian Islands. Its initial effort was the Save the Whales campaign, later expanded to include other sea animals such as the Steller sea lion and dolphins. Since then, Greenpeace has extended its concerns to issues ranging from the use of chlorine bleach during paper processing to nuclear disarmament and weapons testing to toxic pollution to nuclear power to drift nets to protection of the Antarctic. Greenpeace activities have often bordered on the radical, as was the case in 1989 when a Greenpeace ship protested a Trident missile test and was rammed by a U.S. Navy vessel. The group is known, too, for its ability to use the media to its advantage, as demonstrated when its activists are pictured in small boats placing themselves between whales and whaling ships.[6]

One other type of group participating in the environmental debate is the radical environmentalists, many of whom shun the group label altogether. "A movement, not an organization," is how the members of Earth First! characterize themselves. Radical environmental organizations shun traditional organizational structure and administrative rules, preferring militant action termed "monkeywrenching," "ecotage," and "ecodefense." The group is best known for "spiking," the practice of putting large metal spikes in trees about to be cut by timber workers. The tactic poses a threat to workers when the spikes come into contact with saws either in the forest or at the mill. Other group members have blocked logging roads and threatened to sabotage utility power lines in forested areas. In 1996, the *Earth First Journal* included an announcement from the radical Earth Liberation Front calling for activists to "take action against those who are destroying the Earth" by participating in five "Earth Nights" beginning on Halloween. On October 30, a U.S. Forest Service (USFS) ranger station in Oregon was destroyed in what federal officials termed a suspicious fire, and USFS offices throughout the Northwest tightened security as a precaution against potential violence. The ranger station was located in a region where tensions over federal timber sales had resulted in the arrests of dozens of protestors and where a week earlier vandals had set a truck on fire and painted antilogging slogans on the walls of another USFS station.[7]

Although Earth First! is the most well known of the radical groups, there have been other flare-ups of radical environmental activity throughout the United States, although it is often difficult to trace the violence and militancy to a particular group. During the 1970s, an individual calling himself "The Fox" targeted polluting industries in the Chicago area, and the Billboard Bandits in Michigan and Bolt Weevils in Minnesota also operated sporadically in their regions. Another major radical group, the Sea Shepherd Conservation Society, was founded in 1977 by former Greenpeace Director Paul Watson. The group has called itself "an independent policy body," whose purpose is to protect sea mammals and bird.[8]

Those who have studied radical environmental organizations believe there are several factors that distinguish them from mainstream groups:

1. There is an emphasis on confronting problems through direct action, including breaking the law.
2. The main point of radical protests is the preservation of biological diversity.
3. Most radicals act on their own, without direction from an organizational hierarchy.
4. Most radical environmentalists are destitute by choice.
5. These individuals usually have minimal hope they will be successful at affecting a total policy change.[9]

Radical groups are driven by what has been termed "deep ecology," a form of ecological consciousness founded on the idea that humans are no more important than any other species. Deep ecology has two philosophical underpinnings: self-realization and ecocentrism.[10] Generally, radical groups are shunned by virtually all other environmental organizations, whose members often believe the movement's efforts are hampered by the radical groups' emphasis on violence. But mainstream groups also use the radicals as a foil, realizing the posturing and activities of such groups cause their own agendas to be perceived as much more reasonable and acceptable.

Environmental organizations have periodically attempted to put aside their individual interests and have formed coalitions in an attempt to advance their collective interests. In 1946, the Natural Resources Council of America was formed to bring together conservation organizations to serve as an information-sharing body and sponsor policy briefings and surveys of public opinion on issues such as energy needs and conservation. Coalitions have also been formed to lobby specific pieces of legislation, such as the National Clean Air Coalition, which came together during debate over the 1977 and 1990 Clean Air Act Amendments. Consensus reports are becoming more commonplace, such as the 1985 publication of *An Environmental Agenda for the Future*[11] and the 1989 *Blueprint for the Future,*[12] which was prepared to assist the Bush administration in developing environmental policy. Such reports also give groups the appearance of more clout, since legislators perceive them as presenting a unified front.

The membership of environmental organizations has ebbed and flowed over the past three decades, often in response to the government's environmental initiatives or electoral change. With the flurry of environmental legislation enacted in the late 1960s and early 1970s, the membership of the organizations grew enormously. When energy replaced the environment as a key issue during the Carter administration, the groups' direct mail campaigns generally yielded just enough members to replace those who failed to renew. But two of Reagan's appointees, Secretary of the Interior James Watt and Environmental Protection Agency Administrator Anne Burford, were perceived as a threat to the movement, which resulted in a surge in membership as environmental organizations warned potential members of what might happen if they did not have the funds to closely monitor Reagan administration policies. The Wilderness Society's membership grew by 144 percent between 1980 and 1983, with the Sierra Club increasing by 90 percent and the Defenders of Wildlife and Friends of the Earth by 40 percent each. Another surge took place at the turn of the decade, when the national environmental lobby's U.S. membership exceeded three million and attention was focused on Earth Day 1990. But by the early 1990s, even though the environment appeared to be a core value for most Americans, membership decreased again, with many of the groups reducing staffing, closing field offices, and narrowing their program focus to just a few key issues. Despite the loss of members among the largest organizations, small, grass-roots groups appeared to be gaining in strength, with their concentration on local or regional issues. Still, contribution levels to environmental and wildlife groups showed strong gains at mid-decade, growing to four billion dollars in 1995, an increase of 10 percent over 1994.[13]

There have been two major criticisms relating to the membership of the environmental movement. One complaint is that the movement's size has been grossly exaggerated and actually represents only a small percentage of Americans. A second criticism is that the movement's leadership has failed to include members of ethnic and disadvantaged groups and that environmental groups have failed to address the greater environmental risks affecting minority communities. Such criticisms appear to have been warranted. Surveys have found that environmentalists, when compared to the larger population, are considerably better educated, more likely to have white collar jobs, and more likely to have high incomes.[14] Other critics argue that the environmental movement has been largely based in the West and does not represent the opinions and beliefs of the majority of Americans. They point to the fact that the Sierra Club did not open its first chapter outside California until 1950—over fifty years after its founding.[15] The second criticism—that people of color are noticeably absent from mainstream groups—is part of a perception by minority leaders that environmentalists do not share the same interests as the disadvantaged community. Those complaints were publicized in 1990 when two small but aggressive groups, the Gulf Coast Tenant Leadership Development Project in New Orleans and the Southwest Organizing Project in Albuquerque charged the country's biggest environmental groups with racism.

One survey of African American leaders gave higher priority to issues such as health care, jobs, and education, especially in urban areas.[16] However, African Americans have taken on urban environmental ills through multipurpose organizations rooted in churches and civil rights efforts. Crime, schools, trash collection, lead paint, and incinerators are often all part of the agenda of these groups. Minority group members also participate in local grass-roots organizations such as Mothers of East Los Angeles, Toxic Avengers of Brooklyn, and West Harlem Environmental Action. Minority participation has been tied to the environmental equity movement, which focuses on the disproportionate environmental burden borne by disadvantaged neighborhoods. Environmental equity advocates argue that regulatory agencies are less aggressive and take longer in regulating problems affecting communities of color, that penalties for violations in minority areas are generally smaller than those imposed in white areas, that African Americans and Latinos are much more likely to live in areas with high levels of air pollution than are whites and to have higher levels of lead in their blood, and that governments tend to locate undesirable facilities such as incinerators in those communities because land values are lower and political power is weak.[17]

Like the large mainstream groups, minority organizations are realizing the advantages of coalition-building. Environmental organizations have often emerged from established social action groups that have a broader base of interests. Among Native Americans, for example, many of the grass-roots organizations are an outgrowth of the American Indian Movement and struggles against multinational corporations seeking to site projects on tribal lands. The First National People of Color Environmental Leadership Summit was held in October 1991, bringing delegates from every state and representatives of the mainstream environmental movement as well.[18] In the early 1990s, the Indigenous Environmental Network (IEN) brought together local organizations to defeat a landfill proposal on the Rosebud Reservation in South Dakota. Although there is general support for tribal sovereignty and a desire for environmental protection, some Native American leaders have been criticized for the loss of the jobs that sometimes accompanies environmental activism.[19] Still, civil rights groups nationwide have established programs specifically dealing with issues such as environmental health and the cleanup of toxic waste sites and have forced the EPA and other agencies to look more closely at the ethical issues involved in environmental policymaking.[20]

The environmental justice movement has also forced mainstream groups to reevaluate their own policies and, as political scientist Robert Bullard notes, broadened the very definition of environmentalism. Bullard points out that civil rights organizations such as the National Association for the Advancement of Colored People and the American Civil Liberties Union have begun working side by side with environmental organizations such as the Natural Resources Defense Council. Larger environmental groups, for example, the Sierra Club and The Wilderness Society, have made attempts to diversify their governing boards and staff, with a corresponding "trickling down" to state governments that have begun to enact some form of environmental justice laws.[21]

What is significant about environmental organizations generally is what some observers call a "great schism" between grass-roots activists and the leadership of the large mainstream groups. Part of that perceived split is a result of style. Where the national organizations pay their executive officers high salaries and run massive fund-raising operations, most grass-roots groups are strictly volunteer-based and funded on minimal membership dues. A deeper conflict among the groups may be the substance of their interests. The Association of Sierra Club Members for Environmental Ethics, founded by dissident members in 1991, accused the Sierra Club of compromising its principles in order to get legislation through Congress. The Sierra Club experienced a similar split in 1996 over the issue of whether or not the group should support a ban on all commercial logging, with the issue pitting the club's first executive director, Dave Brower, against former Earth First! founder Dave Foreman. The highly publicized internal controversy resulted in the organization's supporting the logging ban by a two-to-one vote, but it also led to the creation of another spinoff dissident group, John Muir Sierrans, that had supported the logging ban for several years.[22] While such disputes may not be enough to cause a permanent rift among groups, they are symptomatic of the fragmentation in the environmental movement that keeps it from speaking as one voice in the political arena.

ENVIRONMENTAL OPPOSITION IN THE UNITED STATES

The Progressive Era ideals of the conservation movement had almost universal support throughout the early twentieth century, although the early groups were still dominated by business organizations that were much more influential in the political arena. As the goals of the movement began to expand from conservation to environmentalism in the late 1960s and early 1970s, so too did the potential impact on business and industry, which had never really felt threatened before. The development of an organized environmental opposition involved three interests, farmers and ranchers, organized labor, and industry, and has recently coalesced into three grass-roots opposition movements: wise use, property rights, and county supremacy.

The initial concern of farmers and ranchers was the tremendous influx of city dwellers who sought the tranquility of rural life after World War II. "Recreationists," as they were called, brought tourist dollars to rural economies badly in need of them, but they also brought with them litter, congestion, and noise. Urban visitors seldom paid much attention to property lines, and major battles developed over public access along the California coastline and through inland wetlands. Farmers who were used to controlling predators on their private property were suddenly facing raptor protection programs and angry wildlife enthusiasts who sought preservation of wolves and coyotes. Agricultural land use also came under fire, as environmental groups sought to legislate farm practices relating to pesticide use, soils, and irrigation. As development, including oil pipelines and utility transmission lines, began to intrude onto rural areas, farmers felt even more threatened. The two issues that have most galvanized farmers have been proposals to restrict the use of agricultural pesticides and herbicides and agricultural use of water. In the case of pesticide use, rural interests have formed a coalition with chemical companies and their associations, bringing together such disparate groups as the American Farm Bureau Federation and the National Agricultural Chemical Association, along with the National Association of State Departments of Agriculture, the Association of American Plant Food, Pesticide and Feed Control Officers, the National Association of County Agents, and the Christmas Tree Growers Association.[23] But the land-use issue has become even more controversial as a result of the Sagebrush Rebellion and the development of the grass-roots environmental opposition movements discussed later in this chapter.

Organized Labor

There are a number of environmental issues that have had an impact on workers, who have often been forced to take sides in the policy debate. On the one hand, organized labor has traditionally supported attempts to make a safer workplace and working conditions. Most labor unions have also supported programs that involve occupational health issues, such as exposure to airborne particulates and toxic chemicals. The United Steelworkers of America, for example, has long-time supported clean air legislation, an environmental problem caused to some extent by the steel industry.[24] Farm workers in California have been active participants in federal pesticide legislation, and cotton dust exposure led the Amalgamated Clothing and Textile Workers Union to lobby the Occupational Safety and Health Administration to develop rules to protect workers in textile mills.

Labor has often opposed pollution control efforts (and more recently, implementation of the Endangered Species Act) that affect job security. The United Auto Workers have consistently supported environmental regulations except when they affect the auto industry. The fear of loss of jobs because of environmental regulations has permeated many regions of the United States, often when the real reason for job loss is technological change and innovation. Environmentalists working within the energy industry unions have repeatedly argued that energy conservation has no negative impact on jobs and is in fact beneficial to workers.[25]

Industry Interests

Industry interests have traditionally opposed environmental rules for one reason: the cost of complying with regulations threatens a company's ability to make money and there is little incentive for voluntary compliance. Sometimes, their opposition results from disagreement over the goals or means used to protect the environment. Yet, industry leaders recognize that they (and their employees and their families) breathe the same polluted air and face toxic contamination like the rest of America. Industry's role has been described as "marked not by agreement on values but by tactics of containment, by a working philosophy of maximum feasible resistance and minimum feasible retreat."[26]

Businesses were initially slow to recognize the potential impact of the environmental movement on their operations, characterizing the activities of most groups as no more than a fad. But officials within the pulp and paper industry began in the late 1950s to understand how desires for more recreation land would likely mean a call for reduction in logging activities and expansion of wilderness area designations. Eventually, other industry leaders became alarmed at the rapid pace of environmental legislation, which accelerated during the late 1960s and into the 1970s. They countered by forming trade associations and nonprofit research groups or think tanks to further their aims, pouring millions of dollars into education and public relations. The American Forest Institute, for example, was specifically created to justify the need for increased, rather than reduced, timber production. The oil industry has been especially hard hit as the environmental movement gained more clout. Companies have been ordered by the courts to pay for special cleanups or fines and have faced lengthy and costly litigation as a result of compliance suits brought by environmental groups.[27]

Today, industries affected by environmental regulations rely on a threefold approach in their opposition to environmental groups. One, there is a continuation of the public relations campaigns that began in the early 1960s to paint industry with an environmentally green bush. Chevron Oil, for example, ran advertisements in national publications promoting its "People Do" projects to protect the habitat of endangered species to counter the public backlash that results after every oil spill, and Dow Chemical Company's efforts included sponsorship of the 1990 Earth Day activities in the company's hometown of Midland, Michigan.[28]

Two, virtually every sector of the economy relies on a stable of federal and state lobbyists to review legislation that could potentially have an impact on its operations. Southern California Edison, one of the nation's largest publicly owned utilities, hired Leon Billings, an influential former aide to Senator Edmund Muskie, to press its cause in Washington during the debate over the 1990 Clean Air Act Amendments, and has other lobbyists monitoring the state capital in Sacramento. Although federal law prohibits them from contributing directly to candidates, corporations can form political action committees that funnel campaign contributions directly to legislators as a way of enhancing their access to the political system. Companies and trade associations also employ their own scientists, economists, and policy experts to refute the claims made by environmental groups, and usually have more financial resources to devote to this strategy than do grass-roots groups.[29]

Three, once programs reach the implementation stage, most industry interests regroup to press their case through the administrative maze. Since many of the implementation decisions are made by low-level administrators, or in a less public arena than Congress, industry has been much more successful in molding programs at this phase of the policy process. EPA rule development has frequently been hampered by companies who argued that information about products and processes constituted trade secrets or are proprietary. Industry lawyers have also launched a flurry of lawsuits aimed at regulations and enforcement actions.

Perhaps the biggest change in industry's role in opposing environmental legislation is that these efforts have now shifted toward industry's taking an active, rather than a reactive stance, forming coalitions to enhance their overall effectiveness. During debate on the 1990 Clean Air Act Amendments, for example, utility lobbyists brought with them to Washington dozens of amendments designed to reduce the cost of compliance with proposed acid rain legislation. The

Clean Air Working Group, the major industry coalition, actively fought each amendment proposed by environmental groups.[30]

Some industry groups have become more responsive to environmental concerns as negative publicity surrounding their emissions have generated adverse public relations. The chemical industry, which for years was accused of intransigence, decided in the late 1980s to move toward a pollution prevention approach as a way to improve the marketability of its products. They were active in the debate over the 1990 Clean Air Act, and politicians gave the industry's lobbyists credit for drafting its own legislation rather than just opposing what was on the table. Monsanto Company's Charles Malloch told fellow industry representatives that such initiative was imperative at the rule-making phase of the Clean Air Act. "Anyone sitting on their hands waiting for the regs to come out is way behind the eightball."[31] Similarly, the Alliance for Responsible Atmospheric Policy and the Nuclear Energy Institute coordinate the efforts of hundreds of companies, speaking with one voice for their interests and using their financial resources and technical expertise to counter efforts by environmental groups to strengthen existing environmental protection rules.[32]

One reason why industry is taking a more activist role is the tremendous increase in environmental issues finding their way onto the ballot. From the early 1970s to 1986, citizens confirmed eighteen environmental measures placed on the ballot for popular approval. Yet in the single election of November 1988, American voters approved at least seventeen environmentally related propositions, including measures dealing with recycling, water quality, natural resources, and funding for environmental programs.[33] Faced with another round of ballot measures in November 1990, industry coalitions were up against their biggest fight in California with Proposition 128, known as "Big Green." A group of oil and chemical firms spent more than six million dollars to oppose the measure, which would have banned pesticides, prohibited new offshore drilling, stopped the cutting of virgin redwood forests, and mandated major reductions in carbon dioxide emissions from utility plants. The voters defeated the ballot initiative nearly two to one.[34] Both the timber industry and chemical industries decided to fight back by gathering signatures for their own ballot measures—the Global Warming and Clear-Cutting Reduction, Wildlife Protection and Reforestation Act of 1990 and the Consumer Pesticide Enforcement Act, termed by environmentalists as "Big Stump" and "Big Brown," respectively. Such measures are being called "trojan horse initiatives" because they are perceived as disarming the initiative process, one of the most effective tools for environmental protection in California.[35]

Subsequent elections have seen the defeat of recycling and nuclear power measures in Oregon, growth control initiatives in Washington, stream protection laws in Missouri, and environmental bond issues in New York.[36] Despite such defeats, the citizen initiative process is still a key strategy used by environmental groups in states like Oregon. In 1996, for example, environmental organizations submitted comments on four measures, including an expansion of the state's pioneer bottle bill and another measure prohibiting livestock from grazing in riparian areas. But the record is uneven. In 1996, initiatives to protect the Everglades and Maine old-growth forests were defeated because of the well-organized opposition of business groups.

Some industry strategists have attempted to work more closely with environmental groups, leading to charges that some organizations have been captured by big business. Companies like Apple Computer and Hewlett Packard were heavily criticized when they donated equipment for Earth Day 1990, as did Shaklee, the first official sponsor with its $50,000 donation. Businesses have made major financial contributions to previously adversarial organizations or have voluntarily adopted policies to make environmental management an integral part of their operations.[37] While it is unlikely that the two sides' interests will ever coalesce completely, there is a growing sense that business, at least, has more to gain from cooperation than from confrontation. For companies continually under the regulatory hammer, such cooperative efforts may become the rule rather than the exception. Conversely, the Environmental Defense Fund has been forced out of some environmental coalitions because its support for market-based approaches to regulation and negotiations with industries have been seen by some groups as too accommodating to polluters.

Grass-Roots Opposition

In 1988, a different type of environmental opposition surfaced as an outgrowth of a meeting of 250 groups at the Multiple Use Strategy Conference sponsored by the Center for Defense of Free Enterprise. One of the group's leaders, Ron Arnold, applied the phrase "wise use" (originally used by conservationist Gifford Pinchot) in describing twenty-five goals to reform the country's environmental policies, including opening up national parks and wilderness areas to mineral exploration, expanding visitor facilities in the parks, and restricting application of the Endangered Species Act.[38] Now, grass-roots opposition is focused on three movements led by large umbrella organizations: wise use, property rights, and the county supremacy movement. The umbrella groups serve as a clearinghouse for information and share a deep antigovernment sentiment and opposition to efforts by government and environmental groups to further regulate the use of public and private lands and natural resources. Although some of their efforts are supported by private interests, ranging from the Mountain States Legal Foundation to agricultural groups and oil, timber, and mining companies, there is a strong grass-roots component of individuals who perceive the government to be intruding into their lives by telling them what they can do with their private property or how lands and resources within the public domain ought to be used. It is difficult to estimate the membership of these groups, since so many individuals are members simply because they belong to another group that has supported one or more of the umbrella groups' tenets. The four million members of the American Farm Bureau Federation (AFBF), for example, are counted as members of the wise use movement simply because the AFBF has endorsed some wise use policies.

The Sagebrush Rebellion began in the 1970s as an effort by wealthy ranchers and others to gain control of public lands in the West. The movement had proponents in government in the 1980s, particularly Interior Secretary James Watt. The movement was reinvigorated in the early 1990s as the wise use and county supremacy movements garnered attention. Although there are similarities between the wise use movement and the Sagebrush Rebellion of the late 1970s and early 1980s, one difference between the two is that the current efforts are marked by steps to broaden the base of support beyond purely western issues. Like other political movements, the groups employ a wide variety of strategies and tactics to push their agenda forward. For example, the annual September "Fly In For Freedom" lobbying effort in Washington, D.C., sponsored by the Alliance For America brings in representatives from diverse groups who are urged to wear work clothes—with special attention to gloves, boots, hard hats, and bandannas—when they rally. The Blue Ribbon Coalition, which represents motorized recreational interests, tracks legislation and alerts its members to contact their Congressional representatives when a bill affects their members. Some of the more militant opposition groups, like the Sahara Club, boast of vandalizing property or disrupting environmental group activities. In addition to cattle ranchers resisting higher grazing fees, the grass-roots efforts tap into gulf shrimpers opposing the use of turtle-excluding devices, Alaskans seeking to expand oil drilling, and private property owners from eastern states battling the National Park Service over boundary disputes. The three movements are well organized, tapping into an electronic network that keeps even the most isolated adherents in touch with one another.[39] Sporadic violence has occurred, aimed at federal agency facilities and employees.

From a political standpoint, the grass-roots opposition has had moderate success legislatively. During President Clinton's first term, it stalled proposed grazing fee increases and was able to get Congressional approval for a brief moratorium on listings under the Endangered Species Act. Organizations like the Mountain States Legal Foundation and the Individual Rights Foundation have led the legal fight against federal lands. Between 1991 and 1995, fifty-nine western counties passed ordinances that claimed authority to supercede federal environmental and land use laws and regulations, and thirty-four counties in Nevada, California, Idaho, New Mexico, and Oregon had passed ordinances challenging federal control of local lands.[40] The resolutions declared that federal land in the county actually belonged to the state and that the county alone has the authority to manage it. Although the resolutions are not technically law, local officials were enforcing them as though they were. The Justice Department challenged the ordinances as illegal and sought an injunction to ban their enforcement.

The courts have dealt a serious blow to county supremacy groups by striking down ordinances that would have given counties the right to determine how

THE CHRISTIAN ENVIRONMENTALISTS

Environmental activists have almost always been thought of as a part of a liberal social movement, sharing many of the same core values and perspectives as those of the political Left. But during the past few years, a new form of environmentalism has emerged that is closely associated with Christianity, and often its members are part of the more evangelical branches of the faith.

In 1996, the Evangelical Environmental Network announced it was launching a one-million-dollar public education and advertising campaign to support the Endangered Species Act (ESA). What makes this action unusual is that the ESA has traditionally been part of the target deregulation package of the Republican Party. Ron Sider, president of Evangelicals for Social Action, made a special appeal to his fellow Christians and noted, "The religious right are our sisters and brothers. . . . Our plea to them is to go back and reread the scriptures."

The source of Christian environmentalism is a very literal interpretation of the Bible and, in particular, the book of Genesis, in which is described Noah building an ark to save animals from destruction. Christian environmentalists believe that species should be preserved because they are created by God; therefore, species preservation becomes a moral rather than an economic issue. Humanity is given dominion over the world's species, and thus there is a corresponding duty to serve as stewards over animal life. Unlike some animal rights groups that argue that animals should not be eaten or used for exhibition in zoos or circuses, Christian environmentalists use scriptural interpretation to denote the "right use" of animals, including the preservation of species and maintenance of their fruitfulness.

Although the partnership of Christianity and environmentalism is not new, its development into an activist movement is relatively recent. The idea of caring for God's creatures dates back hundreds of years to the writings of St. Cyril of Jerusalem (315–386 C.E.), St. Francis of Assisi (1182–1226 C.E.), and Martin Luther (1483–1546). More recently, religious leaders such as the Reverend Dr. Billy Graham and Pope John Paul II have referenced Christian responsibility for caring for animals.

From a political standpoint, this group of environmental activists began as many grass-roots groups often do, calling awareness to a perceived problem, alerting their members, and then attempting to gain additional public support for their view. In 1995, the Christian Environmental Council of the Evangelical Environmental Network adopted a petition urging Congress to oppose any "action that would weaken, hamper, reduce, or end the protection, recovery and preservation of God's creatures, including their habitats, especially as accomplished under the Endangered Species Act." The group also sought additional funding for endangered species recovery worldwide. The petitions were circulated at various places of worship, and their distribution to Congress was coordinated by The Christian Society of the Green Cross, a nonprofit Pennsylvania-based ministry.

Other forms of Christian environmentalism have begun to emerge, although their overall impact on policy appears to be minimal thus far. Some church groups are attempting to form coalitions with other environmental or social activism organizations to enhance their political efficacy. One group, the National Religious Partnership for the Environment, has coproduced a video, *Endangered Species and the Natural World,* with the Union of Concerned Scientists. Green Cross has sponsored a half-hour Virginia Public Radio program, *Creation Song,* which features interviews with noted Christians on their attitudes about the environment and has developed a book on how congregations can conduct energy consumption audits. Smaller organizations, such as the United Methodist Rural Fellowship, have developed guides on how to make a church "more ecological," and the Evangelical Environmental Network mailed thirty thousand packets nationwide on how to make churches "Noah Congregations" and "Creation Awareness Centers."

In January 1996, leaders of the public awareness campaign met with President Bill Clinton's Secretary of the Interior, Bruce Babbitt, and with House Speaker Newt Gingrich to add their voice to the groups fighting efforts to revise the ESA. Environmental organizations have yet to fully embrace the Christian advocates who share their beliefs about species preservation, but the evangelicals seem committed to the cause with or without the support of the mainstream groups.

For Further Reading
Susan Power Bratton. *Christianity, Wilderness and Wildlife: The Original Desert Solitaire.* Scranton, PA: University of Scranton Press, 1993.
"Christian Writings across the Centuries on Caring for God's Creatures," *Green Cross, 2,* no. 1, Winter 1996, 11–12.
Robert Booth Fowler. *The Greening of Protestant Thought.* Chapel Hill, NC: University of North Carolina Press, 1995.
Mark J. Rozell and Clyde Wilcox, eds. *God at the Grassroots.* Lanham, MD: Rowman and Littlefield, 1995.
Roger Sorrell. *St. Francis of Assisi and Nature: Tradition and Innovation in Christian Attitudes Towards the Environment.* New York: Oxford University Press, 1992.

public lands within their boundaries would be used (see Chapter 4). Most individuals involved in the property rights movement are mired in a legal system that takes years to resolve issues, reducing their ability to accomplish their goals. The grass-roots movements have as much success as they do because they have been led by *policy entrepreneurs,* charismatic individuals who have capitalized on the public's distrust of the government's natural resource policies as well as mistrust of the federal government in general, and turned that distrust into self-perpetuating organizations. Although they have often been at odds with most environmental organizations, some opposition group leaders appear to be seeking common ground and compromise as a more effective way of affecting environmental policy during an era when the vast majority of

Americans still adhere to a protectionist ethic. But the wise use movement's adherents are highly motivated, are well organized through a network of web pages, e-mail, and grass-roots chapters, and continue to press their concerns forcefully.

INTERNATIONAL ENVIRONMENTAL MOVEMENTS, GROUPS, AND PARTIES

Concern about the environment is universal, and although this chapter has thus far focused on the development of the environmental movement and opposition groups in the United States, the environmental debate involves a number of international actors. Some international activism paralleled what was taking place in the United States, beginning with the founding of the Commons, Open Spaces and Footpaths Preservation Society in Britain in 1865. There appears to be a trend in industrial nations that ties the development of environmental awareness to business cycles; in Britain, for example, support for environmental protection has been strongest toward the end of periods of sustained economic expansion. With greater economic prosperity, people shift their interest from immediate material needs to the nonmaterial aspects of their lives. As a result, economic advances in the late 1960s and early 1970s led to a tremendous growth spurt in the membership of existing nature groups and the formation of new groups, paralleling activity in the United States during that same period.[41]

Nongovernmental organizations (NGOs) now play a key role in environmental policymaking in both industrialized and developing countries. The term is used to describe all organizations that are neither governmental nor for-profit, and may include groups ranging from rural people's leagues and tribal unions to private relief associations, irrigation user groups, and local development associations.[42] NGOs can be classified as grass-roots organizations (membership-oriented, often in developing nations), service NGOs (supporting the development of grass-roots groups), or policy-specific (environment, human rights, family planning).[43] One characteristic many of the groups have in common is that they are often parochial—concerned almost exclusively about environmental issues in their region. A typical example is the group Dasohli Gram Swarajya Mandal, which began a logging public awareness campaign in India in 1964 that led to the Chipko Andalan movement. Chipko, which means "to cling to" is literally India's tree huggers, Himalayan Indians who launched protests over logging. Indian environmentalists developed political clout over the issue of proposed dams and hydroelectric projects, but have often limited their activism to specific projects.[44] Not only do these groups help shape policy, but they play a major role in generating demands within individual countries for governments to comply with and implement the global agreements they have signed.

NGOs are growing in both number and influence, particularly in developing nations. Unlike their counterparts in Northern Hemisphere countries, NGOs in the south perform somewhat different functions. They often fill a vacuum left by ineffective or nonexistent government programs or extend the reach of resource-poor national governments. They may also forge links with NGOs whose issues are decidedly nonenvironmental, such as the networking that is beginning to occur with human rights and economic development NGOs. Lastly, NGOs in developing countries may serve as an independent voice for public participation, either in opposition to a government program or by placing pressures on government to create new programs.[45]

Studies of NGOs indicate that they are evolving in three directions: the southern NGOs are seeking greater autonomy from those in the north; NGOs are forming international networks and coalitions to keep abreast of issues; and they are performing new roles in legal defense and policy research. The first trend appears to be the most critical as southern hemisphere NGOs seek to distance themselves from their dependence on their northern partners. Long dependent for financial support on their northern donors, these groups now seek the transfer of the technical expertise they need to gain independence. They hope to set their own environmental protection agendas rather than have the terms of their activities dictated by outside sources whom they perceive to be less familiar with local problems. Technological advances such as facsimile machines and computer-linked networks have allowed groups to coordinate their efforts on a global scale, and they have steadily increased their presence in the diplomatic world as well. NGOs held a parallel conference at both the 1972 and 1992 United Nations environmental meetings, and several organizations were accredited by the UN to participate in the preparatory meetings leading up to the Earth Summit. Although these trends indicate that NGOs are growing in both numbers and importance, their influence on global environmental protection is still limited by a lack of stable funding sources and political sophistication.[46]

Only a handful of organizations, called international NGOs (INGOs), have begun to address the global issues of concern to many of the mainstream organizations in the United States, such as global warming and stratospheric ozone depletion. Friends of the Earth International, for example, has affiliates throughout the world, as does Greenpeace. INGOs often designate specific issues for their political activism and are more structured and financially stable than most NGOs. INGOs are especially important in regions where environmental concern has only recently begun to emerge, as evidenced by the founding of a Russian affiliate of Greenpeace. Without the support of an international organization and its resources, environmental activists in the republics of the former Soviet Union would have little voice for their efforts to draw international attention to decades of environmental degradation.[47]

Cultural differences are the major factor behind the variations in how environmental interests become structured or operate. In democratic nations, the pluralist system legitimizes interest group membership. But acceptable tactics in one nation may be considered unacceptable or even criminal in others. Why, for example, are there few groups demanding better air quality in Mexico, despite the capital city's pollution problems? One study of Mexican political beliefs and values concluded that Mexicans generally do not relate easily to abstract or impersonal organizations but rather to the individual who leads the movement. Mexicans' *personalismo* makes it difficult to start and sustain groups that lack such high-profile figures.[48]

In nondemocratic countries such as the People's Republic of China, the government crackdown on Western influences has made it difficult even for INGOs such as the World Wildlife Fund to have much of an impact, leaving little room for environmental groups, domestic or foreign. International pressure and the government's expanded involvement in international trade and politics have led to substantial advances in China's environmental policies, but they have not come about as a result of organized citizen activism.[49]

The most cohesive and powerful environmental movements are found in western Europe, where public opinion polls have shown that support for the environment is especially strong and continues to grow. Coalition-building is a common strategy, with umbrella groups like the European Environmental Bureau monitoring proposed legislation and lobbying on behalf of more than a hundred organizations within the European Union. Group activism has frequently been focused on the issues of nuclear power and nuclear weapons, leading to massive public protests in 1995 when the French government resumed weapons testing in the South Pacific. The environmental movement in Europe is best characterized as diverse, with each group developing its own structure, strategy, and style.[50]

Green Political Parties

Unlike the environmental movement in the United States, which has failed to capture (or be captured by) one of the two major political parties, green parties have formed in dozens of countries, with the major ones identified in Table 2.2. They vary considerably in strength and impact on their respective political systems, in membership, and in the percentage of the electorate they represent. International green parties are often difficult to track, since they frequently change their names or form new alliances with other groups to bolster their political clout. The term *green party* is sometimes used generically, and many groups represent a broader social movement or consist of activists focused on a single issue. In Hungary, for example, "greens" were called "blues" in reference to the Blue Danube Circle (those opposed to the building of the Nagymaros Dam), and in Poland, the largest environmental organization was not a party, per se, but the Polish Ecology Club.[51]

The first green party was the United Tasmania Group, which contested the local elections in the Tasmanian region of Australia in 1972. Although the party was unsuccessful in the ten elections it contested before its dissolution in 1976, it was instrumental in placing the environment at the top of the Australian political agenda. The major wave of green party activity has been in Europe, primarily because the structure of European political systems allows political parties, even small ones, a role in policymaking.[52] During the 1970s, one of the first green parties to form was in Germany, where a loose coalition of groups, the Bund Burgerinitiativen Umweltschutz (BBU) organized massive demonstrations opposing nuclear energy but exercised little political power. Over the past two decades, the German greens have formed several electoral alliances, becoming what many believe is the most powerful environmental force in Europe. Their increasing role in national politics has come despite the death of one of their most influential leaders, Petra Kelly, in 1992. Although the German green party has been split internally, with some factions seeking to move even closer toward the political center, it has gradually dropped some of the demands made in the party's infancy. In 1996, for example, the party agreed to lift a ten-year boycott of computers, which was exemplary of how out of touch with prevailing social attitudes some of the group's demands had been.[53]

The achievements of the German greens has not been matched elsewhere, however. Initially, green parties' successes seemed to be limited to getting their members elected at the local and regional levels. In countries such as Sweden, where legislative seats are allotted based on a threshold level of representation, green parties have struggled to attract the necessary numbers of voters or often have been shut out of the process entirely. Even in those countries with proportional representation, most green parties have had little support, in large part be-

Table 2.2   Major Green Political Parties

Nation	Political Party	Year Founded
Australia	United Tasmania Group	1972
	Nuclear Disarmament Party	1984
	Rainbow Alliance	1988
Austria	Die Grune Alternative	1982
Belgium	Agalev	1982
	Ecolo	1980
Canada	Green Party of Canada	1984
Denmark	DeGronne	1983
Finland	Vihrea Liitto	1987
France	Les Verts	1982
	Generation Ecologie	1990
Germany	Die Grunen	1980
Ireland	Comhaontas Glas	1981
Italy	Federazione delle Liste Verdi	1986
Luxembourg	Die Greng Alternativ	1983
Mexico	Partido Ecologista de Mexico	1984
Netherlands	De Groenen	1983
New Zealand	Values, Green Party of Aotearoa	1972
Sweden	Miljopartiet de Grona	1981
Switzerland	Le Parti Ecologiste/De Grune Partei	1983
United Kingdom	People/Green Party	1973
United States	Green Party USA	1984

cause they modeled their strategy on the atypical German model.[54] The "fading of the greens," as the phenomenon has been called, is not an indication of the lack of the public's environmental interest or its saliency as a political issue. One observer has argued that in one sense the national green parties simply outlived their usefulness once the major political parties adopted the greens' issues as their own. In addition, many environmental activists, sensing that structural barriers limited their ability to attain status as a potent political entity, shifted their energies toward affecting legislation and policy through the NGOs described earlier.

SUMMARY

The debate over how best to protect the environment has involved a wide spectrum of environmental organizations, from mainstream groups that operate out of Washington, D.C., and utilize traditional interest group strategies such as lobbying, to organizations focused on a single issue to radical groups. Although attempts have been made to form coalitions, the environmental movement remains fragmented. While these groups support an enhanced governmental role in environmental protection, the United States has also experienced waves of environmental opposition, led by industries facing government regulation of their business practices and, more recently, by groups that are part of the wise use, county supremacy, and property rights movements. As a result, industry has more recently taken a proactive approach to legislation, and some efforts at cooperation with environmental organizations are beginning. Internationally, the primary participants in the environmental debate are nongovernmental organizations, international nongovernmental organizations, and green political parties that began to develop in the 1970s, with the strongest political clout represented by the German greens.

NOTES

1. Richard M. Stapleton, "Greed vs. Green," *National Parks, 66,* nos. 11–12 (November–December 1992): 32.

2. For more on group theory, see David Truman, *The Governmental Process* (New York: Knopf, 1951; Earl Latham, *The Group Basis of Politics* (New York: Octagon Books, 1965); and Jeffrey M. Berry, *The Interest Group Society,* 2d ed. (Boston: Little, Brown, 1989).

3. For another view of the role of groups, see Michael S. Greve and Fred L. Smith, Jr. eds., *Environmental Politics: Public Costs, Private Rewards* (New York: Praeger, 1992).

4. Riley E. Dunlap and Angela G. Mertig, "The Evolution of the U.S. Environmental Movement from 1970 to 1990: An Overview," in *American Environmentalism: The U.S. Environmental Movement 1970–1990,* eds. Riley E. Dunlap and Angela G. Mertig (Washington, D.C.: Taylor and Francis, 1992), 14.

5. See Michael S. Greve, "Private Enforcement, Private Rewards: How Environmental Suits Became an Entitlement Program," in *Environmental Politics: Public Costs, Private Rewards,* eds. Michael S. Greve and Fred L. Smith, Jr. (New York: Praeger, 1992), 105–109.

6. See Robert Hunter, *Warriors of the Rainbow: A Chronicle of the Greenpeace Movement* (New York: Holt, Rinehart and Winston, 1979).

7. See Dave Foreman, *Confessions of an Eco-Warrior* (New York: Harmony Books,

1991); and Rik Scarce, *Eco-Warriors: Understanding the Radical Environmental Movement* (Chicago: Noble Press, 1990); and Douglas S. Looney, "Protector or Provocateur?" *Sports Illustrated,* May 27, 1991, 54–57.

8. See Paul Watson, *Sea Shepherd* (New York: Norton, 1982).

9. Scarce, *Eco Warriors,* 4–7.

10. See Bill Devall and George Sessions, *Deep Ecology* (Salt Lake City, UT: Gibbs Smith, 1985).

11. Robert Cahn, ed., *An Environmental Agenda for the Future* (Washington, D.C.: Island Press, 1985).

12. T. Allan Comp, ed., *Blueprint for the Future: A Plan for Federal Action* (Salt Lake City, UT: Howe Brothers, 1989).

13. See Robert Cameron Mitchell, Angela G. Mertig, and Riley E. Dunlap, "Twenty Years of Environmental Mobilization: Trends among National Environmental Organizations," in *American Environmentalism: The U.S. Environmental Movement 1970–1990,* eds. Riley E. Dunlap and Angela G. Mertig (Washington, D.C.: Taylor and Francis, 1992), 15; Robert Cameron Mitchell, "Public Opinion and the Green Lobby: Poised for the 1990s? in *Environmental Policy in the 1990s* (Washington, D.C.: Congressional Quarterly Press, 1990), 90–91; Linda Kanamine and Paul Overberg, "Leaner Times Test Limits of Movement," *USA Today,* October 19, 1994, 1A; and Karen W. Arenson, "Donations to Charities Rose 11% Last Year, Report Says," *New York Times,* May 23, 1996, A–9.

14. Craig R. Humphrey and Frederick H. Buttel, *Environment, Energy and Society* (Belmont, CA: Wadsworth, 1982).

15. Stephen Fox, *The American Conservation Movement* (Madison, WI: University of Wisconsin Press, 1985), 279.

16. See John M. Ostheimer and Leonard G. Ritt, *Environment, Energy, and Black Americans* (Beverly Hills, CA: Sage, 1976). See also Hawley Truax, "Beyond White Environmentalism: Minorities and the Environment," *Environmental Action* 21 (1990): 19–30.

17. Studies identifying evidence of environmental injustice are discussed in Mark Dowie, *Losing Ground: American Environmentalism at the Close of the Twentieth Century* (Cambridge, MA: MIT Press, 1996).

18. See Robert D. Bullard and Beverly H. Wright, "The Quest for Environmental Equity: Mobilizing the African-American Community for Social Change," in *American Environmentalism: The U.S. Environmental Movement 1970–1990,* eds. Riley E. Dunlap and Angela G. Mertig (Washington, D.C.: Taylor and Francis, 1992), 39–49; Marcia Coyle, "When Movements Coalesce," *National Law Journal,* September 21, 1992, S–10; Donald Snow, *Inside the Environmental Movement* (Washington, D.C.: Island Press, 1992); and Laura Pulido, "Restructuring and the Contraction and Expansion of Environmental Rights in the United States," *Environment and Planning, 26* (June 1994): 915–936.

19. Bruce Selcraig, "Common Ground," *Sierra,* May–June 1994, 46–50.

20. See, for example, Robert D. Bullard, *Confronting Environmental Racism: Voices from the Grassroots* (Boston, MA: South End Press, 1993); Robert D. Bullard, "Overcoming Racism in Environmental Decisionmaking," *Environment, 36* (May 1994): 10–20, 39–44; and William C. Scott, "Environmental Justice: A New Era of Community Empowerment, Political Activism, and Civil Rights Litigation," *Environmental Claims Journal, 7,* no. 1 (Autumn 1994): 5–23.

21. Robert D. Bullard, "The Environmental Justice Movement Comes of Age," *Amicus Journal, 16,* no. 1 (Spring 1994): 32–37.

22. See Sharon Begley and Patricia King, "The War among the Greens," *Newsweek,* May 4, 1992, 78.

23. Samuel P. Hays, *Beauty, Health and Permanence: Environmental Politics in the United States 1955–1985* (Cambridge, England: Cambridge University Press, 1987), 295.

24. See United Steelworkers for America. *Poison in Our Air* (Washington, D.C.: United Steelworkers of America, 1969).

25. See Frederick H. Buttel, Charles C. Geisler, and Irving W. Wiswall, eds., *Labor and the Environment* (Westport, CT: Greenwood Press, 1984), 1–2.

26. Hays, *Beauty, Health and Permanence,* 308.

27. Mark Ivey, "The Oil Industry Races to Refine Its Image," *Business Week,* April 23, 1990, 98.

28. See Art Kleiner, "The Three Faces of Dow," *Garbage,* July–August 1991, 52–58.

29. See D. Kirk Davidson, "Straws in the Wind: The Nature of Corporate Commitment to Environmental Issues," in *The Corporation, Ethics and the Environment,* ed. W. Mitchell Hoffman (New York: Quorum Books, 1990); "Where the PAC Money Goes," *Congressional Quarterly Weekly Report,* April 15, 1995, 1058; David Corn, "Shilling in the Senate," *The Nation, 249* (July 17, 1989), 84–87; and Stephen Engelberg, "Business Leaves the Lobby and Sits at Congress's Table," *New York Times,* March 31, 1995, A1.

30. The battle among the groups is outlined in Gary Bryner, *Blue Skies, Green Politics: The Clean Air Act of 1990 and Its Implementation,* 2d ed. (Washington, D.C.: Congressional Quarterly Press, 1995). See also Richard E. Cohen, *Washington at Work: Back Rooms and Clean Air* (New York: Macmillan, 1992); and George Hager, "For Industry and Opponents, a Showdown Is in the Air," *Environment '90* (Washington, D.C.: Congressional Quarterly Press, 1990), 10.

31. Bryan Lee, "Washington Report," *Journal of the Air and Waste Management Association, 41,* no. 8 (August 1991): 1022.

32. For an overview of strategies used by various industries, see George W. Ingle and Beverly Lehrer, "The Chemical Manufacturers Association," *Chemtech, 15* (February 1985), 71–73; Bruce A. Ackerman and William T. Hassler, *Clean Coal, Dirty Air* (New Haven, CT: Yale University Press, 1981); Kim Goldberg, "Logging On," *Columbia Journalism Review, 32* (November–December 1993): 19–20; and Chris Crowley, "With Environmental Opposition to Projects, Fight Fire with Fire," *The Oil and Gas Journal, 90,* no. 31 (August 31, 1992): 30–31.

33. John Mark Johnson, "Citizens Initiate Ballot Measures," *Environment 32,* no. 7 (September 1990): 4–5, 43–45.

34. Several authors have analyzed the initiative, one of the most highly publicized in U.S. electoral history. See Bradley Johnson, "Big Business Attacks Big Green," *Advertising Age, 61* (October 22, 1990): 4; "Black Day for California's 'Big Green,'" *New Scientist,* November 17, 1990, 20; Richard Lacayo, "No Lack of Initiatives," *Time,* September 3, 1990, 52; and Elizabeth Schaefer, "A Daunting Proposition," *Nature, 347* (September 27, 1990): 323.

35. Seth Zukerman, "Flying False Colors," *Sierra, 75,* no. 5 (September–October 1990): 20–24.

36. See Richard Lacayo, "Green Ballots vs. Greenbacks, " *Time,* November 19, 1990, 44.

37. Eve Pell, "Buying In," *Mother Jones,* April–May 1990, 23–27; Jennifer Nash and John Ehrenfeld, "Code Green," *Environment, 38,* no. 1 (January–February 1996): 16–20, 36–45; and George D. Carpenter, "Business Joins Ranks of Environmentalists," *Forum for Applied Research and Public Policy, 9* (Summer 1994): 9.

38. Alan M. Gottlieb, ed., *The Wise Use Agenda* (Bellevue, WA: Free Enterprise Press, 1989).

39. For different views of the grass-roots movements, see Philip D. Brick and R. McGreggor Cawley, eds., *A Wolf in the Garden: The Lands Rights Movement and the New Environmental Debate* (Lanham, MD: Rowman and Littlefield, 1996); David Helvarg, *The War against the Greens: The "Wise Use" Movement, the New Right, and Anti-Environmental Violence* (San Francisco: Sierra Club Books, 1994); John Echeverria and Raymond Booth Eby, eds., *Let the People Judge: Wise Use and the Private Property Rights Movement* (Washington, D.C.: Island Press, 1995); and Ron Arnold, *Ecology Wars: Environmentalism As If People Mattered* (Bellevue, WA: Free Enterprise Press, 1987).

40. Keith Schneider, "A County's Bid for U.S. Land Draws Lawsuit," *The New York Times,* March 9, 1995: A1.

41. David Vogel, "Environmental Policy in Europe and Japan," in *Environmental Policy in the 1990s,* eds. Norman J. Vig and Michael E. Kraft (Washington, D.C.: Congressional Quarterly Press, 1990), 262.

42. See Lester D. Brown, *Understanding World Organizations: Guidelines for Donors* (Washington, D.C.: World Bank, County Economics Department, 1989).

43. Robert Livernash, "The Growing Influence of NGOs in the Developing World," *Environment, 34,* no. 5 (June 1992): 12–20, 41–43.

44. See James Clad, "Greens Find Voice: Environmental Lobby Campaigns Against Dams," *Far Eastern Economic Review,* October 19, 1989, 25; and Douglas Stevens, "The Forest and the Trees," *Commonweal, 115* (October 7, 1988): 526–530.

45. Livernash, "Growing Influence of NGOs," 12–13.

46. See William B. Wood, George B. Demko, and Phyllis Mofson, "Ecopolitics in the Global Greenhouse," *Environment, 31,* no. 7 (September 1989): 12–17, 32–34.

47. See Vladimir Kotov and Elena Nikitina, "Russia in Transition: Obstacles to Environmental Protection," *Environment, 35,* no. 10 (December 1993): 11–20; Alexi Yablokov, "A Perspective from Another Country: The Soviet Task," *EPA Journal, 16,* no. 1 (January–February 1990): 50–52.

48. Cynthia Enloe, *The Politics of Pollution in a Comparative Perspective* (New York: David McKay, 1975), 54.

49. See Lester Ross, "The Next Wave of Environmental Legislation," *China Business Review, 21,* no. 4 (1994), 30–33.

50. See Peter Rawliffe, "Making Inroads: Transport Policy and the British Environmental Movement," *Environment, 37,* no. 3 (April 1995): 16–20, 29–36; Regina S. Axelrod, "Environmental Policy and Management in the European Union," in *Environmental Policy in the 1990s,* 3d ed., eds. Norman J. Vig and Michael E. Kraft (Washington, D.C.: Congressional Quarterly Press, 1997), 299–320; and John McCormick, *British Politics and the Environment* (London: Earthscan, 1991).

51. Anna Bramwell, *The Fading of the Greens: The Decline of Environmental Politics in the West,* (New Haven, CT: Yale University Press, 1994).

52. See Dick Richardson and Chris Rootes, eds., *The Green Challenge: The Development of Green Parties in Europe* (London: Routledge, 1995); and Sara Parkin, *Green Parties: An International Guide* (London: Heretic Books, 1989), 80.

53. See Allison Abbott, "Prospects of Power Prompt Rethink for German Greens," *Nature, 380* (April 11, 1996): 470; John Templeman, "The Green Who Would Be Germany's Kingmaker," *Business Week,* September 18, 1995, 70; E. Gene Frankland, "Parliamentary Politics and the Development of the Green Party in West Germany," *The Review of Politics, 51,* no. 3 (Summer 1989): 386–412; and Thomas Poguntke, "Unconventional Participation in Party Politics: The Experience of the German Greens," *Political Studies, 40,* no. 2 (June 1992): 239–254.

54. See Martin Rhoades, "The Italian Greens: Struggling for Survival," *Environmental Politics, 4* (Summer 1995): 305–312; Camilla Berens, "Greens Grasp for Alliance with Direct Action Groups," *New Statesman and Society, 8* (October 20, 1995): 9; and Martin Bennulf, "The 1994 Election in Sweden: Green or Gray?" *Environmental Politics, 4* (Spring 1995): 114–119.

FOR FURTHER READING

Anna Bramwell. *The Fading of the Greens: The Decline of Environmental Politics in the West.* New Haven, CT: Yale University Press, 1994.

Bunyan Bryant, ed. *Environmental Justice: Issues, Policies, and Solutions.* Washington, D.C.: Island Press, 1995.

Mark Dowie. *Losing Ground: American Environmentalism at the Close of the Twentieth Century.* Cambridge, MA: MIT Press, 1995.

Paul R. Ehrlich and Anne H. Ehrlich. *Betrayal of Science and Reason: How Anti-Environmental Rhetoric Threatens Our Future.* Washington, D.C.: Island Press, 1996.

Charles T. Rubin, *The Green Crusade: Rethinking the Roots of Radical Environmentalism.* New York: Free Press, 1994.

Donald Snow, ed. *Inside the Environmental Movement: Meeting the Leadership Challenge.* Washington, D.C.: Conservation Fund, 1992.

Laura Westra and Peter S. Wenz, eds. *Faces of Environmental Racism: Confronting Issues of Global Justice.* Lanham, MD: Rowman and Littlefield, 1995.

CHAPTER 3

The Political Process

> "We have had it up to here with the federal government. The people born
> and raised down here feel they know how to handle this land better than people
> in Washington or in the Wasatch Front."
> —Colin Winchester, Kane County, Utah, attorney[1]

In late 1996, President Bill Clinton faced reelection knowing that his record on the environment did not match the promises he delivered on the campaign trail in 1992. With his selection of Al Gore as vice president, Clinton had won the support of environmental groups who believed the two democrats would bring an end to the budget cutting and gridlock that had typified the previous Republican administrations. Choosing to place other issues such as health care and welfare reform ahead of the environment during his first term in office, Clinton lost even more of his ability as president to move forward with an environmental agenda of his own when the Republicans gained control of Congress in 1995. Environmental leaders were angry and many admitted publicly that they were disappointed with Clinton's choice of priorities and the lack of attention being paid to issues and legislation that they considered to be integral to a comprehensive environmental policy.

With that scenario in mind, Clinton decided to use one of the few elements of presidential power still under his control—the executive order. On September 18, 1996, he designated 1.7 million acres of land in southeastern Utah as the Grand Staircase-Escalante National Monument, bypassing Congress entirely. In a ceremony at Grand Canyon national Park—which President Theodore Roosevelt had protected under a similar executive order in 1908—Clinton tried to woo back his environmental supporters by creating the largest national monument in the lower forty-eight states. Invoking the 1906 Antiquities Act, under which objects of "historic or scientific interest" can be set aside by executive order without congressional approval, the president said the designation would protect the landscape's scenic beauty and rich resources for future generations, and avoided mention of the political controversy and protests that accompanied the announcement. In Kanab, Utah, residents released dozens of black balloons and waved signs reading, "Shame on you, Clinton." In Escalante, Utah, Clinton and Secretary of the Interior Bruce Babbit were hanged in effigy. The area is one of the least-visited wild areas in the Southwest and has been called "a fierce and dangerous place . . . wilderness right down to its burning core," by the Utah Wilderness Coalition, a group that had pushed for wilderness designation for the land to prevent it from being mined for coal, oil, and natural gas. For years, Congress had grappled with how much of the region should be protected, with environmental groups such as the Southern Utah Wilderness Alliance lobbying to have as much as 5.7 million acres protected. Utah's congressional delegation hoped to leave open for development much of the area Clinton chose to designate in the executive order, including the six-hundred-thousand-acre Kaiparowitz Plateau, where a Dutch company has mineral rights. Utah Senator Orrin Hatch, one of the sponsors of legislation that would have allowed the area to be developed, called the president's monument declaration a "war on the West," and the state's governor, Mike Leavitt, criticized the action because he had not been advised of the president's intentions.[2]

The use of the executive order is just one of the ways in which a president can use the political process to circumvent Congress. This chapter identifies the institutions and actors (more commonly referred to as "official policymakers") who possess the legal authority to engage in the formation of environmental policy. Some, such as members of Congress or state legislators, have primary policymaking authority that stems from a constitutional source. Others, such as agency administrators, are termed supplementary policymakers because they gain their authority to act from others or from legislation.[3]

This institutional overview begins with an analysis of the two agencies with the principal responsibilities for stewardship of the environment in the United States, the Department of the Interior and the Environmental Protection Agency, and the role of the presidential leadership. The chapter discusses the role of Congress and key legislative committees and the function of the courts in reviewing and enforcing environmental policy. (Agencies with more narrow environmental jurisdiction, such as the U.S. Forest Service, Bureau of Land Management, and National Park Service, are discussed more fully in subsequent chapters relating to their functions.) The chapter concludes with a brief overview of the role of state and local governments and the fragmentation of environmental policy.

THE EXECUTIVE BRANCH AGENCIES

Despite the prolonged public interest in conservation and environmental protection outlined in Chapter 1, the federal government's involvement is actually relatively recent. During the first hundred years after the nation's founding, both the president and Congress were much more deeply involved with foreign affairs, paying little attention to internal domestic problems until the growth of the country literally demanded it. The creation of a federal environmental policy was sporadic and unfocused, with responsibility for the environment scattered among a host of agencies.[4] Today, the Department of the Interior, established by Congressional legislation in 1849, and the Environmental Protection Agency, created by executive order in 1970, have jurisdiction over the implementation of most of the nation's environmental policies.

Under its first secretary, Thomas Ewing, the Department of the Interior was given domestic housekeeping responsibilities different from today's cabinet-level department. Initially, the Department controlled the General Land office, Office of Indian Affairs, Pension Office, and Patent Office, as well as supervised the Commissioner of Public Buildings, Board of Inspectors, the Warden of the District of Columbia Penitentiary, the census, mines, and accounts of marshals of the U.S. courts. Gradually, a shift occurred as the agency's responsibilities were transferred to other agencies within the executive branch. Eventually, the need to manage newly discovered public resources, especially land and mineral rights, led to the development of several agencies that later came under the Department of the Interior's umbrella, as seen in Table 3.1. The Secretary of the Interior is nominated by the president and confirmed by the Senate, as are the agency directors.

Table 3.1 Agencies of the U.S. Department of the Interior

Agency	*Established*
Bureau of Indian Affairs	1824*
Bureau of Land Management	1946†
Bureau of Mines	1910
Bureau of Reclamation	1902
Minerals Management Service	1982
National Park Service	1916
Office of Surface Mining Reclamation and Enforcement	1977
U.S. Geological Survey	1879
U.S. Fish and Wildlife Service	1940‡

*Originally in War Department; transferred to Interior in 1849.
†Combined the responsibilities of the General Land Office, created in 1812, and the Grazing Service, established in 1934.
‡Combined responsibilities of the Bureau of Fisheries, established in 1871, and the Bureau of Biological Survey, created in 1885.

The Environmental Protection Agency (EPA), in contrast, is an independent agency in the executive branch, headed by an administrator, a deputy, and nine assistant administrators, all nominated by the president and confirmed by the Senate. The EPA has responsibility for administering a broad spectrum of environmental laws. In one sense, it is a regulatory agency, issuing permits, setting and monitoring standards, and enforcing federal laws, but it also gives grants to states to build waste water treatment and other facilities.

The president also receives policy advice on environmental matters from the

Council on Environmental Quality (CEQ), created as part of the 1970 National Environmental Policy Act. Its members recommend policy to the president and to some degree evaluate environmental protection programs within the executive branch and environmental impact statements prepared by federal agencies. The CEQ does not have any regulatory authority, its recommendations are purely advisory. The CEQ's staff and budget were reduced under both Reagan and Bush, and the agency's primary task became the preparation of an annual report on the environment. Although the EPA and Interior Department are responsible for most policy implementation, they share jurisdiction with a number of other federal agencies, as seen in Table 3.2.

Table 3.2   Other Federal Agencies and Commissions with Environmental Policy Jurisdiction

Department	Agency/Commission
Agriculture	Agriculture Stabilization and Conservation Service
	Soil Conservation Service
Commerce	National Bureau of Standards
	National Oceanic and Atmospheric Administration
Defense	Army Corps of Engineers
Energy	Federal Energy Regulatory Commission
	Office of Conservation and Renewable Energy
Health and Human Services	Food and Drug Administration
	National Institute for Occupational Safety and Health
Labor	Mine Safety and Health Administration
Transportation	Federal Aviation Administration
	Federal Highway Administration
	Materials Transportation Bureau
	National Transportation Safety Board
	U.S. Coast Guard

Commissions/Regulatory Agencies

Consumer Product Safety Commission
Federal Maritime Commission
Federal Trade Commission

Sometimes, an agency may have powers and an interest level comparable to that of the Department of the Interior or EPA, as is the case with the Nuclear Regulatory Commission, which authorizes the construction of nuclear power plants and supervises their operation. Other agencies, such as the Federal Aviation Administration, may not have environmental concerns as their primary mission but may be affected by regulations or legislation implemented by other agencies. Thus, the Federal Aviation Administration (FAA) was consulted in 1990 when air-quality officials within the EPA began to consider legislation that would govern the amount of particulates released in aircraft exhaust emissions.

The process of implementing environmental policy is complicated by interest groups, which are playing an increasingly significant role at this stage of policy development. Industry, especially, has made great strides in crafting policies that parallel their needs. Industry groups have often appeared to "give up" their interests at the policy adoption or legislative stage, only to come back stronger than ever during the implementation phase. Generally, this strategy has been successful in influencing environmental legislation. During the policy formulation and adoption phase, which is highly visible and public, industry, ever mindful of its public image, has often accepted or provided only token resistance to proposed legislation that would negatively affect it. Instead, industry has done its best to circumvent costly or logistically difficult environmental regulations when they reach the implementation stage—the responsibility of bureaucratic organizations and agencies such as the EPA.

One way in which environmental groups have been kept out of the implementation process is through industry efforts to remove rule making from the public domain. The kinds of complex, time-consuming procedures that are typical of the rule-making process provide a shield to regulated industries against government intervention and a legitimate basis for resisting demands for information that might be obtained by competitors. The rule-making process involved with the implementation of the seven-hundred-page 1990 Clean Air Amendments is exemplary of this problem. The EPA was required to complete 150 regulatory activities, including one hundred rule makings, during the first two years after passage of the amendments—an unheard of time frame. Surprising nearly everyone, the agency issued most of the regulations on time. To put the process in perspective, consider that in the past the EPA has issued seven or eight major regulations *per year* on all phases of environmental law—from pesticides to solid waste to air and water pollution. Although the issue of nitrogen oxide emissions (one of two acid rain–causing chemicals) took only two pages of the act itself, the regulations crafted by the EPA are expected to take up two hundred or more pages.

Participation by interest groups is made even more difficult by the short comment periods (usually thirty or sixty days) necessitated by the scheduling. From the perspective of those interested in influencing the rule, the tight deadlines mean that the agency has likely already made up its mind and that comments will not bring about many changes in direction.[5] Implementation is also hampered by the complexity of the rule-making process itself. Although the Resource Conservation and Recovery Act (RCRA) was enacted in 1976, it took the EPA four years to implement the first rules under the act. In the meantime, state governments held their own agonizingly slow rule makings or waited until federal funds were made available, giving industry more time to muster its defenses.[6]

The responsibility for implementing policy has often been left to agencies and commissions ill-equipped for the task. In 1979, for example, when RCRA rule making was finally underway, the process was considered so technical and complex that both the EPA and the environmental community suffered from a lack of expertise. Most of the comments that were received on the individual rules were from companies subject to them.[7] During the implementation of the 1990 Clean Air Act, the EPA was forced to hire outside consultants, many of them drawn from industry, to draft preliminary rules, especially those dealing with air-borne toxins, on which the EPA's expertise is notoriously lacking.

Finally, policy implementation is an incremental process. It is made in a series of small steps, each one dependent on the previous one. The process is time-consuming and seldom results in any major legislative or policy advances. The history of water-quality legislation, for example, is one of fine-tuning rather than abrupt or dramatic change. Congress has been unwilling to orchestrate a complete revamping of the legislation initially passed in 1965, and as a result, agencies such as the EPA have followed suit. There have been no major advances in water-quality issues, and none are expected until the legislation is reauthorized.

PRESIDENTIAL LEADERSHIP

Historically, the president has had a limited role in environmental politics, with much of the power delegated to the executive branch agencies. Not until Richard Nixon's tenure began in 1969 did the environment become a presidential priority, and even then, Nixon was reluctant to act. After years of study and staff negotiations, Nixon agreed to a federal reorganization plan calling for an independent pollution control agency, which later became the EPA.

The agency opened its doors under the stewardship of William Ruckelshaus, a graduate of Harvard Law School and former Indiana assistant attorney general. Although he had virtually no background in environmental issues, Ruckelshaus had the support of Nixon's attorney general, John Mitchell, and was confirmed after only two days of hearings. On the day of his selection as administrator, Ruckelshaus was briefed by Nixon, who gave him the impression that he considered the environmental problem "faddish."[8] Ruckelshaus came to the EPA with three priorities: to create a well-defined enforcement image for the agency, to carry out the provisions of the newly amended Clean Air Act, and to gain control over the costs of regulatory decision making.[9] In setting up the agency, Ruckelshaus decided each regional organization within the EPA should mirror the full agency's structure, with staff capabilities in every program area and delegation of responsibility to regional offices, creating an organizational structure that gave the agency a rare capability to make decisions, move programs ahead, and motivate people to produce high volumes of work.[10] Inside the EPA, morale was high, in large part resulting from the accessibility of Ruckelshaus to his staff. Outside, he became a forceful spokesperson for the public interest and was well respected by both sides in the environmental debate. Early on, Ruckelshaus concentrated on air and water pollution, assigning three-quarters of his staff to that task. As a result, there was an improvement in noncompliance with air-quality standards in most cities, and the agency effected a change from aesthetic concerns about the recreational uses of water to health concerns.[11]

Nixon's efforts to give credibility to the Department of the Interior were not nearly as successful. It appears that the creation of the EPA relegated the Department of the Interior to backseat status as far as environmental issues were concerned. A succession of secretaries came and went (see Table 3.3) while the EPA administrators garnered publicity and notoriety. Despite these efforts, there is some doubt as to how much Nixon really cared about the environment as an issue. Some staff members believed the Nixon reorganization experts were neither proponents nor opponents of environmental reform; their specialty was management and organization. They focused on the environment because that was the area in which political pressures were creating a demand for action.

Table 3.3 Environmental Agency Leadership, 1970–1997

President	Secretary of the Interior	EPA Administrator
Nixon	Rogers Morton (1971–74)	William Ruckelshaus (1970–73)
Ford	Rogers Morton (1974–75)	Russell Train (1973–77)
	Stanley Hathaway (1975)	
	Thomas Kleppe (1975–77)	
Carter	Cecil Andrus (1977–1981)	Douglas Costle (1977–1981)
Reagan	James Watt (1981–83)	Anne (Gorsuch) Burford (1981–83)
	William Clark (1983–85)	William Ruckelshaus (1983–85)
	Donald Hodel (1985–89)	Lee Thomas (1985–89)
Bush	Manuel Lujan (1989–92)	William Reilly (1989–92)
Clinton	Bruce Babbitt (1993–)	Carol Browner (1993–)

Typical is the case of Walter Hickel, whom Nixon chose in late 1968 as the new Interior Secretary, setting off a storm of protest. Hickel, who had grown up in Kansas and lived on a tenant farm during the Depression, was a Golden Gloves boxer who loved to fight. As Governor of Alaska, he was accused of being a pawn of the U.S. Chamber of Commerce and of the oil industry. After four days of defensive hearings, his nomination was confirmed. Hickel's bold style was his undoing; he offended the president in a rambling letter about Nixon's policies (eventually leaked to the press) after the Kent State shootings. The gaffe came at a time when the president's staff was considering the reorganization proposal that would have elevated Hickel to head the new Department of Natural Resources. He was fired Thanksgiving Day, 1970.[12]

To Nixon's credit, it should be noted that it was under his administration that the United States first began to take a more global approach to environmental protection. Ruckelshaus was successful in convincing Nixon of the important role the United States could play at the United Nations Conference on the Human Environment in June 1972 in Stockholm. Although the United States was not totally in agreement with the priorities of the United Nations Environment Programme, which grew out of the Stockholm conference, Nixon persuaded Congress to pay the largest share (36 percent) of the new secretariat's budget.[13]

When Gerald Ford took over as president upon Nixon's resignation, he made few changes in the way environmental policy was being conducted. Russell Train remained head of the EPA under Ford and served in that position until Ford was defeated by Jimmy Carter in 1976. Carter kept most of Nixon's other environmental appointees, including Interior Secretary Rogers Morton. For the most part, the crush of environmental programs that marked the Nixon years slowed considerably under Ford for three reasons. One, the energy shortage created by the 1973 Arab oil embargo pushed pollution off the legislative agenda for several years (see Chapter 6). A second factor was a growing concern that the cost to industry to comply with EPA standards was slowing the economy at a time when expansion was needed. Lastly, the environmental momentum of the early 1970s faded by 1976, and Ford did little to refuel it. Congressional initiatives expanded the EPA's authorities with the Safe Drinking Water Act of 1974, the Toxic Substances Control Act of 1976, and the Resource Conservation and Recovery Act of 1976 (legislation discussed in later chapters), but Ford's unsuccessful presidential campaign made him an observer, rather than a participant, in the policymaking process. The environmental slate for Gerald Ford is a clean, albeit empty, one.

In 1976, groups such as the League of Conservation Voters gave presidential candidate Jimmy Carter high grades for his environmental record as governor of Georgia, although his campaign focused more on other issues, such as human rights and the economy. President Carter openly courted environmental groups during his single-term administration, and he counted on their support to carry him through to reelection in 1980, when he lost to Ronald Reagan. He received high marks from environmental groups who believed he would emphasize environmental issues in his administration, but he initially offended one of the environmental movement's heroes, Maine Senator Edmund Muskie. Carter began by choosing Douglas Costle to head the EPA over the objections of Muskie. Costle, a Seattle native, attended Harvard and the University of Chicago Law School and had worked at the Office of Management and Budget under Nixon. His main environmental credential was a stint as Commissioner for Environmental Affairs in Connecticut, but he had a strong financial management background from working at the Congressional Budget Office.

Under Costle, the EPA became the first federal agency to adopt Carter's plan of zero-based budgeting. Costle's main aim in taking over the agency was "to convince the public that EPA was first and foremost a public health agency, not a guardian of birds and bunnies."[14] Taking Costle's lead, Congress responded by passing the Superfund authorization in late 1980, establishing a $1.6 billion emergency fund to clean up toxic contaminants spilled or dumped into the environment. The result was a major shift in the agency's regulatory focus from conventional pollutants to toxics. This allowed the agency room to grow and justification for a 25 percent budget increase at a time when the president was preaching strict austerity.

Carter had a number of environmental achievements during his term, including passage of the landmark Alaska Land Bill in 1980, which brought millions of acres of pristine wilderness under federal protection. As part of his attempt to gain group support, Carter convinced Congress to consider a windfall profits tax on oil to fund solar research and pushed stronger energy conservation measures.[15] But the inability of Congress to develop a comprehensive energy policy under his administration has led most observers to conclude that Carter was not an especially effective leader in environmental policy or in protecting the environment.

The eight years of Ronald Reagan's administration mark a stormy chapter in environmental politics. Critics believe that he almost single-handedly destroyed the progress that had been made in the area of pollution control. Supporters point to his legislative achievements and say the picture was not so bleak after all, but critics argue that those successes came as a result of Congressional initiative, not from Reagan. During his stints as governor of California and then as president, Reagan was heavily influenced by probusiness interests like Colorado brewer Joseph Coors, who urged him to take a more conservative approach to environmental regulation. Coors and his allies were represented in Reagan's inner circle by Nevada Senator Paul Laxalt, and they focused their attention on the appointment of a conservative Secretary of the Interior who would show prudent respect for development interests, especially in the West.[16]

Their candidate was James Watt, a Wyoming native who had served as a legislative aide to Senator Milward Simpson. He had served as a member of the Nixon transition team in 1968 to help Walter Hickel through his confirmation hearings as Secretary of the Interior and was then appointed deputy secretary for water and power. In 1977, he founded the Mountain States Legal Foundation, a conservative anti-environmental regulation law firm, and was later connected to the leadership of the Sagebrush Rebellion (see Chapter 4). Although some of Reagan's advisors preferred Clifford P. Hansen, former Governor and Senator from Wyoming, for the Department of the Interior slot, Watt's rhetorical style and ability to bring in dollars as a conservative fundraiser for Reagan gave him a decided edge. He was a spokesperson for the New Right, among those who believed Reagan was drifting too close to the political center.[17]

Watt divided people into two categories—liberals and Americans—and called the Audubon Society "a chanting mob."[18] He perceived environmentalists as "dangerous and subversive, suggesting they sought to weaken America and to undermine freedom. He called them extremists and likened them to Nazis."[19] More telling, however, was the comparison of Watt to his predecessor, Cecil Andrus, who had said, "I am part of the environmental movement and I intend to make the Interior Department responsive to the movement's needs."[20] Watt discovered he had great independence in molding the agency to conform to his policy interests. Among his first directives, he ordered a moratorium on any further National Park acquisitions and announced his intention to open up federal lands to mining and logging. He proposed to permit leasing of 1.3 million acres off the

California coast for offshore oil and gas exploration and auctioned off 1.1 billion tons of coal in the Powder River Basin of Montana and Wyoming, actions that infuriated environmentalists. By summer 1981, Watt had made enough enemies that the Sierra Club, National Wildlife Federation, and Audubon Society gathered more than one million signatures seeking Watt's ouster. Together, ten organizations urged President Reagan to fire Watt in a stinging indictment that purported to show how he had subverted environmental policy.

His supporters, however, point out that under Watt the federal government spent more than one billion dollars to restore and improve the existing national parks, and 1.8 million acres were added to the nation's wilderness system. Watt's vision was to develop America's energy resources and to remove what many perceived as excessive regulation of business, efforts at which he was successful.[21] But by late 1982, Watt was under heavy criticism for his actions, although he was blunt enough to say out loud what many in the Reagan administration were thinking. Reagan called Watt's record "darn good"[22] but urged him to reconcile with environmental groups, to whom he had stopped speaking just six weeks into his job. They continued to criticize him for refusing to touch more than one billion dollars in the Land and Water Conservation Fund, which had been set aside for national park acquisition, and for spending only about half of the amount of funds for land acquisition appropriated by Congress.[23]

Watt's bluntness turned out to haunt him after he banned the Beach Boys from performing on the Capital Mall, embarrassing the President and the First Lady (a great admirer of the group), who rescheduled the concert. Then, in a speech before Chamber of Commerce lobbyists, Watt recalled that an Interior Department coal advisory panel was comprised of "a black, a woman, two Jews and a cripple," a remark widely criticized in the press, eventually making Watt a major liability to Reagan, who then asked for his resignation. Shortly thereafter, to head the Department of the Interior Reagan appointed William Clark, a man whose term was as undistinguished as Watt's had been tumultuous. Clark served less than a year and a half and was replaced by Donald Hodel, another moderate.

Reagan's appointment of Anne (Gorsuch) Burford as Administrator of the Environmental Protection Agency proved to be even more of an embarrassment than Watt. Burford, a former member of the Colorado legislature, became one of the youngest of Reagan's appointees despite her lack of administrative experience. She began her term as administrator by reorganizing the agency, abolishing divisions only to reestablish them later. The EPA's highly politicized staff members demoralized careerists, and the agency was constantly under siege both from environmental groups (who believed Burford's appointment signaled Reagan's support for industry interests) and from members of Congress. More telling, perhaps, was the loss of a fifth of the EPA's personnel and the major cuts in the agency's budget that began in 1980.[24]

Under Burford, the Office of Enforcement was dismantled, and personnel within the agency found their positions downgraded. Environmental professionals were often passed over for promotion by political appointees, and neither of the two original associate administrators served more than one hundred days.[25] The Reagan administration became embroiled in further controversy when several top EPA administrators, including the agency's general counsel, were investigated or accused of conflict of interest, perjury, giving sweetheart deals to polluters who had influential political ties, and other misdeeds. By the end of his third year in office, more than twenty senior EPA employees had been removed from office and several key agency officials had resigned under pressure.[26]

The biggest fall was Burford's. In fall 1982, John Dingell, chairman of the House Committee on Energy and Commerce, initiated an investigation of alleged abuses in Superfund enforcement and sought EPA documents as part of the case. Dingell subpoenaed Burford to appear to provide the committee with the documents, but on the basis of Justice Department advice, she declined to do so, citing the doctrine of executive privilege. In December 1982, the House voted to declare her in contempt of Congress. Eventually a compromise was struck that allowed the committee to examine nearly all the documents they sought, and the contempt citation was dropped.

The contempt charge was coupled with charges of EPA mismanagement of cleanup operations after discovery of the toxic chemical dioxin in roadways at Times Beach, Missouri. The project had been handled by EPA Assistant Administrator for Hazardous Waste, Rita Lavelle, who was eventually fired by Reagan. Lavelle was the only EPA official to face criminal charges, and she was convicted of perjury and obstructing a congressional investigation. She was sentenced to six months in prison and fined $10,000. The incident cast further doubt on Burford's ability to manage the agency, and she resigned March 9, 1983. At a press conference two days later, Reagan said he believed that it was he, not Burford, who was the real target of Congress's action. He said that he never would have asked for her resignation.[27] Congress did not let up even after Burford resigned. At the end of August 1984, a House Energy and Commerce Oversight Committee concluded that from 1981 to 1983, "top level officials of the EPA violated their public trust by disregarding the public health and environment, manipulating the Superfund program for political purposes, engaging in unethical conduct, and participating in other abuses."[28]

To return the agency to some semblance of credibility, Reagan called upon the EPA's first administrator, William Ruckelshaus, who returned to coordinate salvage operations. Ruckelshaus restored morale to the middle-level EPA staff, reversed the adversarial posture of EPA toward Congress and the media, and brought in new and experienced administrators to replace political appointees.[29] During his second stint as administrator, Ruckelshaus revised the standards for the lead content in gasoline and declared an emergency ban on ethylene dibromide (EDB), a pesticide widely used in grain and food production. Ruckelshaus served until after Reagan's reelection, when the President appointed his third EPA administrator, Lee Thomas.

Thomas, a South Carolina native, became the first nonlawyer to head the agency. He had previously worked in the Federal Emergency Management Administration and headed the Times Beach Task Force that led to Rita Lavelle's firing. When Lavelle left, Thomas took over her position as coordinator of hazardous waste, Superfund, and RCRA programs. Seen as a career EPA employee, he redefined the agency's mission. On the one hand, he focused attention on localized concerns such as medical waste and the garbage crisis that was threatening urban areas. At the same time, he brought attention to global concerns like the weakening of the ozone layer and chlorofluorocarbons (CFCs). Thomas made sure that the EPA became an active participant in international forums and returned the environment to the policy agenda.[30] Another major achievement was the full restoration of the EPA's reputation for strong enforcement, especially after the agency reached a 1985 agreement with Westinghouse Corporation to spend $100 million to clean up toxic waste at its Indiana facilities. This was followed in 1986 by an agreement with Aerojet General to clean up a toxic dump near Sacramento (estimated to cost the company $82 million) and in 1988 by a $1 billion cleanup agreement with Shell Oil and the U.S. Army at the Rocky Mountain arsenal near Denver.

Many environmentalists believed George Bush's campaign promise to be "the environmental president" when he appointed William Reilly to head the EPA in 1989. Reilly, who had previously served as head of the U.S. branch of the World Wildlife Fund, was the first environmental professional to serve as administrator. He had also established a reputation as a moderate while serving with the Washington, D.C.–based Conservation Foundation. The Sierra Club took a wait-and-see attitude, declaring that Reilly was "clearly tagged to be the administration's good guy in a very tough job."[31] Reilly's agenda was different from those of the Reagan appointees. In several early speeches and articles, he reiterated the need for pollution prevention as "a fundamental part of all our activities, all our initiatives, and all our economic growth," making it the theme of EPA's Earth Day celebrations in April 1990.[32] He also pointed to science and risk assessment "to help the Agency put together a much more coherent agenda than has characterized the past 20 years."[33] Reilly and Bush were jointly praised for having broken the legislative gridlock that characterized clean air legislation since the amendments had last been revised in 1977 (see Chapter 9).

Some observers believe, however, that Reilly's efforts were often derailed by members of the White House staff, especially by then Chief of Staff John Sununu, who ridiculed EPA pronouncements on global warming and wetlands preservation, and by budget director Richard Darman, who once called Reilly "a global rock star."[34] Sununu was criticized by environmentalists, who believe he blocked serious international negotiations on global warming. Reilly was caught up in White House politics again in June 1992 when a memo to President Bush on negotiations at the Earth Summit were leaked to the press; some insiders believe that Vice President Dan Quayle's office was responsible.

Bush's other appointees were given mixed reviews, from Michael Deland, head of the Department of Environmental Quality (DEQ) and an ardent environmentalist, to James Watkins, Bush's Secretary of Energy, who won praise for his commitment to alternative energy and energy conservation policy, although critics of the administration felt that his views had not been translated into substantive policy change. The appointment of Manuel Lujan, Jr., a former Congressional representative from New Mexico, as Secretary of the Interior, was criticized by environmental groups that believed he favored the logging and mining interests of the West. Lujan's critics became even more alarmed when Lujan agreed in October 1991 to convene the so-called Endangered Species "God Squad" to review the denial of timber permits on Bureau of Land Management property because they threatened the habitat of the Northern spotted owl, a species that had been declared threatened the previous year. But the Secretary's supporters argued that he was taking a more reasonable approach to the Endangered Species Act and simply invoking a mechanism provided for under law. Equally controversial was the President's wetlands policy. By redefining what constitutes a wetland, the Administration had exempted thousands of acres of land from federal protection—a move that pleased the business community and angered environmentalists who took the matter to court.

Did Bush live up to his claims as "the environmental president"? In his 1991 message on environmental quality, Bush pointed to adoption of an international agreement on CFCs, enactment of the Oil Pollution Act of 1990, enactment of an environmentally progressive farm bill, and his commitment to environmental stewardship. He noted that in 1990, the EPA's enforcement staff had a record of felony indictments that was 33 percent higher than that of 1989. His America the Beautiful tree-planting initiative hoped to add one billion new trees annually over the next ten years.[35] In December 1990, he established the President's Commission on Environmental Quality to build public/private partnerships to achieve concrete results in the area of pollution prevention, conservation, education, and international cooperation. Critics counter that under Vice President Dan Quayle, the Council on Competitiveness thwarted Congressional intent by preventing agencies from issuing regulations required by environmental laws. House Subcommittee on Health and the Environment Chairman Henry Waxman accused the Council of "helping polluters block EPA's efforts" through its regulatory review process.[36] Proving that almost everything he does offends someone, Bush was criticized by both environmentalists and conservatives.

Voters had a clear choice on environmental issues in the 1992 presidential election. While Bush proposed giving greater consideration to protecting jobs in enforcing the Endangered Species Act, Bill Clinton ran on an environmentalist's dream platform. One of the key provisions of the Clinton campaign was a promise to limit U.S. carbon dioxide emissions to 1990 levels by the year 2000 to halt global warming—an issue for which Bush was soundly criticized for not supporting at the Earth Summit. Clinton also pledged to create recycling and energy conservation incentives, to set national water pollution runoff standards, and to support a forty-miles-per-gallon fuel standard. In direct contrast to Bush, Clinton promised to restore to the United Nations Population Fund monies that had previously been cut off (see Chapter 11) and to oppose drilling in the Arctic National Wildlife Refuge. These viewpoints, along with his appointments to executive branch agencies, gave environmentalists room for hope and a sense of renewed executive branch leadership.

Clinton faced a unique situation during his first term. During his first two years as president, he worked with a Democratic Congress, while the sea change Congressional elections of 1994 made a historic transfer of power of both houses to the Republicans, effectively bottling up the few legislative initiatives the administration tried to make. Even during the first two years, Clinton's environmental successes were minimal. Clinton's White House staff initially set the tone by eliminating the Council on Competitiveness, which both Bush and Reagan had used to sidestep EPA regulations, and by proposing to replace the CEQ with a new White House environmental policy office. The CEQ was a statutory agency of Congress, not subject to presidential fiat and, therefore, could not be abolished. But it was merged in 1994 with the new Office of Environmental Policy, headed by Gore protégé Kathleen McGinty. The president also appointed a Council on Sustainable Development, made up of business leaders, representatives from environmental groups, and government officials, which issued a 1996 report calling for a change from conflict to collaboration to maximize environmental protection. Less than a month into his administration, Clinton also endorsed a Senate bill to create the Department of the Environment, elevating the EPA to cabinet-level status. Similar legislation had been introduced each session since 1989, but never gained sufficient support, especially when the Republicans took control of Congress. His Office of Environmental Justice, established in 1994 by Executive Order, was the first effort by any administration to deal with what appears to be a pattern of inequities in environmental protection in minority and rural communities.

Clinton's first term was marked by the signing of only two environmental measures of any significance—the 1994 California Desert Protection Act and bipartisan-supported revisions in safe drinking water amendments in 1996. In both cases, the groundwork for passage had been laid by Congress, and both measures reflect legislative momentum rather than presidential leadership. The majority of the nation's most important domestic environmental problems— grazing fees on public lands, designations of wetlands, storage of hazardous and nuclear waste, reauthorization of Superfund legislation—remained trapped in the legislative gridlock of a divided government. Environmentalists criticized the administration for switching sides and accepting a logging compromise in 1995 that opened old-growth forests to salvage timber cuts and compromising with automakers on implementation of the 1990 Clean Air Act Amendments. Industry groups were just as upset with the White House. There were some small preservationist victories, such as the reintroduction of wolves into Yellowstone National Park and continuation of protection of the Arctic National Wildlife Refuge and the Tongass National Forest in Alaska. The 1997 Interior Department appropriations bill avoided the controversies that plagued the 1996 bill and actually increased overall spending for the department because of emergency funds for fighting Western fires.[37] However, the first Clinton term was hard on the EPA, resulting in staff cutbacks for research by one-third and a shift toward external rather than in-house research. One report on the agency found that the agency's ability to produce sound environmental studies had been diminished and that the "quality of science produced in EPA has plummeted into a state of crisis."[38]

In the area of global environmental politics, Clinton had promised to accelerate and expand U.S. involvement in international preservation efforts, expecting support from Gore and a new legion of activist Democratic members to implement a wide-ranging but unfocused plan. The president failed to establish a timetable to meet proposals to reduce emissions of greenhouse gases, but Clinton can be credited with his prompt signing of the biodiversity treaty that had been adopted at the Earth Summit in 1992. (The Senate, however, had not, as of January 1997, ratified the treaty.) Clinton followed up by establishing a National Biological Service to survey American species—a program that immediately became the target of Republican budget slashers. Clinton also followed up on a campaign promise to restore support for international family planning programs and the Global Environmental Facility, a fund to help developing countries meet their global environmental obligations under international treaties, but these programs also were slashed by the new Republican majority in Congress. Clinton promised early in his first term that the United States would take the lead in addressing global climate change, and he proposed an energy tax in 1993 as part of his deficit reduction plan, but he abandoned both of those efforts in the face of strong opposition from the Republican-controlled Congress. These policy failures undermined the United States' leadership in global environmental diplomacy that seemed so certain when the Clinton-Gore ticket was first elected. By 1996, the administration had given modest support to legally binding limits on greenhouse gases, limits to be set sometime after the year 2005, and had failed to rally support to ratify the biodiversity convention.[39]

Clinton's first term will be remembered as one in which the president was successful in blocking Republicans who sought a major regulatory overhaul for laws covering issues such as wetlands, mining reform, and the Endangered Species Act and who tried to use the budget process to reduce environmental regulations and agency activities. But environmental policy did not become a priority of the administration until blocking congressional environmental protection rollbacks became politically potent. Despite his efforts to reinvent government and make regulation more efficient, Clinton met with resistance virtually every time he sought collaborative agreements on environmental problems. He had largely abandoned global environmental concerns in his reelection campaign while his promises to protect the environment, education, and health care from Republicans became core issues.

CONGRESSIONAL POLICYMAKING

The most striking thing about environmental policymaking in Congress is its fragmentation. The authorizing committees have primary responsibility for writing environmental laws. In the House, the Resources Committee is the primary focus of bills dealing with public lands and natural resources. The Commerce Committee has broad jurisdiction over energy, environmental regulation, and health. The Transportation and Infrastructure Committee has responsibility for water projects. Several other committees regularly get involved in environmental issues: Agriculture, Government Reform and Oversight, International Relations, Science, and Small Business. Then there are committees that have a say in how much money is raised from special environmental taxes (the Ways and Means Committee), how much is spent on environmental programs in general (the Budget Committee), and how funds are distributed to specific agencies and programs (the Appropriations Committee). Each committee is further divided into subcommittees that create additional overlaps. The Senate is almost as fragmented for environmental policy, with a similar set of budget-related committees (the tax committee is Finance rather than Ways and Means). The Energy and Natural Resources and the Environment and Public Works committees are the major players, but the Agriculture, Commerce, Foreign Relations, Governmental Affairs, and Small Business committees are also regular participants in major environmental initiatives.

The House and Senate leaders also play primary roles in environmental policy, as they set the agenda for their chambers and determine what issues will be given priority. The House leaders have taken a particular interest in environmental regulation, vowing to reduce its cost and intrusiveness. The House Government Reform and Oversight and Senate Governmental Affairs, as well as the other committees, have given particular scrutiny in oversight hearings and investigations to the Interior Department and the EPA. The chairs of committees play enormously important roles in deciding what bills are moved through the process and what committee resources are aimed at what issues.

Although Congress has primary responsibility for policy formulation and adoption, the nature of the institution has hampered that role.[40] Congress's current inability to develop an overall national environmental policy has been termed "environmental gridlock"[41] referring to the contrast between the institution's rapid pace and initiative during the 1960s and 1970s in comparison with the body's current inability to move forward with a legislative agenda. There are a number of reasons to explain current Congressional inaction:

1. The fragmentation of the committee system decentralizes both power and the decision-making process. Environmental issues do not "belong" to any one committee within Congress. Eleven of the Senate's standing committees and fourteen of those in the House claim some environmental jurisdiction. Depending on the title of a particular piece of legislation and the subject matter, there is a great deal of latitude in deciding which committee(s) should have jurisdiction. For ex-

ample, a bill dealing with global warming could be heard by the Senate's Agriculture, Appropriations, Commerce, Science and Transportation, Energy and Natural Resources, or Environment and Public Works committee, since each claims some degree of jurisdiction over that subject. Similarly, in the House, the same bill might be heard by either the Agriculture, Appropriations, Foreign Affairs, or Committee on Technology and Competitiveness committee. When environmental issues are "hot," a certain rivalry exists that causes competition among committees as to which one will have the greatest chance of influencing the bill's content.

2. The pressures of an increasing number of "green" groups and industry interests have made it more difficult to build Congressional consensus. The same committee fragmentation that is a characteristic of the modern Congress also gives interest groups more access to the legislative process. If a group feels one committee is less accommodating to their interests, they may seek a more favorable venue before another committee or subcommittee. At any one point in the legislative process, there may be dozens of groups vying for members' attention, and environmental groups have lost the power advantage they once enjoyed at the problem-identification stage of the policy process.

3. Members of Congress often lack the time and expertise needed to produce sophisticated legislation. One of the more recent criticisms of Congress is that it is "an assembly of scientific amateurs enacting programs of great technical complexity to ameliorate scientifically complicated environmental ills most legislators but dimly understand."[42] Nowhere is this incapacitation better viewed than in the Congressional hearings on the 1990 Clean Air Act Amendments. Many of the more technical aspects of the legislation, such as those applicable only to utility oil-fired boilers, were so obtuse that several members left it up to their staff to dicker with industry lobbyists over the feasibility of proposed controls. Similarly, when debate on highly sophisticated bills dealing with stratospheric ozone depletion becomes a battle of one expert's research against another, many members of Congress are at a loss about whom to believe. The result is often legislation that is watered down or intentionally vague. The hectic pace of lawmaking also has an impact on Congressional policymaking. Staff members taking notes on the 1990 Clean Air Act Amendments hurriedly jotted down proposed amendments, the authors of which were often unsure of exactly where they would fit in the mammoth bill. Lobbyists, watching the markup process, found that their notes from committee sessions often differed from those of staff, and it was not unusual to see the two groups huddling over pages of red-lined, handwritten legislation.

4. Localized reelection concerns override a "national" view of environmental policymaking. It is difficult for a member of Congress from northern California to convince a colleague from an urban district in New York of the relative importance of a bill barring timber exports to Japan. As reelection pressures mount (especially in the House, where the fever strikes every two years), bargaining becomes an essential style of policymaking. Members with little personal interest in an issue could often care less about the legislative outcome, and only by bargaining for something of value to their own district do they have a reason to become

involved. Votes on pork barrel projects such as dams and parklands, for example, are often based on the "you-scratch-my-back-I'll-scratch-yours" principle, with no thought given to consistency or even to the regional impact of the decision. Local concerns determine which grants get funded and which do not, and legislators in positions of seniority, especially members of the powerful Appropriations Committees, are particularly adept at bringing projects and facilities "back home."

5. The election of a Republican Congress in 1994 and 1996 seriously challenged the existing structure of environmental law, and political ineptitude dashed any chance of improving environmental law. Republican leaders sought to rewrite the major laws, reduce the resources of the EPA and other agencies, and reshape the regulatory process so that agencies would be much less likely to intrude on industrial and commercial activities, but the extreme, antiregulatory agenda was blocked by moderates within the Republican Party who joined with Democrats and, eventually, by White House vetoes. The Republican antiregulation rhetoric was strikingly harsh. House Majority Leader Dick Armey could not think of an environmental regulation he favored. House Majority Whip Tom De-Lay referred to the EPA as the "Gestapo" and kept a book in his office listing how much the 400 largest political action committees (PACs) gave to Republicans and Democrats during the past two years.[43] The access given in return to lobbyists was remarkable, even by Washington standards. Lobbyists were invited to write bills and sit with committee members in hearings.[44] Journalists described lobbyists ensconced in rooms next to the House Chamber, tapping out on their laptops, talking points for Republican members to use in floor debates.[45] Senator Slade Gorton, a Washington Republican, was singled out for having lobbyists draft a public lands bill and then having to ask the lobbyists to explain the provisions in the bill he was sponsoring: an aide wrote to him that the "coalitions delivered your ESA bill to me on Friday. . . . I know that you are anxious to get the bill introduced, however, it is important that we have a better than adequate understanding of the bill prior to introduction."[46]

The failure of the Republican regulatory relief effort was ultimately its failure to take into account widespread public support for environmental, health, and safety regulation. This strong underlying support caused a split among Republicans and gave the Clinton administration the incentive to block congressional efforts to cut regulation. Public support for environmental protection has been constant in the face of congressional flip-flops. Demands for government services and support for virtually all existing national government programs remain high even among people who express dissatisfaction with government in general. A 1995 survey by GOP pollster Linda DiVall found strong support for federal environmental law even among respondents who believe there is too much government regulation in general.[47] Among the results of her study were the following:

- Nearly six in ten respondents believe there is too much government regulation; 58 percent believe government is doing too many things better left to businesses and individuals, while 35 percent believe government should do more.

- Twenty-one percent of respondents believe there is too much environmental regulation, while 36 percent believe there is not enough, and 31 percent say the current level of regulation is about right.
- Only 35 percent of respondents would vote to reelect a member of Congress who supported cutting the EPA's budget by one-third; 46 percent said they would vote against a candidate taking such a strong position.
- Of the environmental laws discussed, the Clean Water Act has the strongest support; 46 percent of respondents believe no modifications should be made, while 42 percent would accept some changes that would give local environmental quality experts more control.

DiVall warned Republicans that "attacking the EPA is a non-starter." Not even a majority of Republicans "trust the GOP most on environmental matters." She found strong support for a campaign emphasizing "the quest for a reasonable balance between the environment and the economy."[48] But the ability to strike that balance has eluded Congress in recent years. The weakening of the Republican leadership as a result of the ethics problems of Speaker Newt Gingrich and the way they were mishandled in late 1996 and early 1997 may provide new opportunities for moderate members from both parties to fashion compromise legislation to address the numerous shortcomings of environmental policy.

Environmental policy, until the 1980s, was often viewed as a bipartisan issue. Both political parties had platforms that promised to clean up pollution and preserve natural resources. Many Republicans have played leading roles in fashioning environmental policy. But environmental regulation has increasingly become a wedge issue in American politics. Both parties promise strong support for the environment, but they offer extremely different policies to accomplish that goal. Democrats have become the strongest supporters of environmental groups, and Republicans have responded to their business constituencies with promises in their platforms to reduce the costs and burdens of regulations.

COURTS AND ENVIRONMENTAL POLITICS

The courts have two primary functions in the making of environmental policy: to exercise their authority for judicial review and to interpret statutes through cases brought to them. In doing so, they use the constitution to determine the legality of actions of the executive and legislative branches and define the meaning of laws that are often open to differing interpretations. Often courts have the authority to determine who has access to the judicial process and may play an activist role in policymaking through their decisions.

Before the passage of the major environmental laws of the 1970s, most courts' involvement in environmental issues was limited to the adjudication of disputes between polluting industries and citizens affected by pollution under the common law of nuisance. The result in most cases was a cease-and-desist order and perhaps a fine. The new generation of environmental laws opened up a variety of opportunities for private parties, usually environmental groups, to use the courts to compel agencies to take actions mandated by statutes or to sue polluters when government officials failed to enforce the law. Administrative requirements for environmental assessments of projects funded or carried out by federal agencies under the National Environmental Policy Act (NEPA) spawned hundreds of lawsuits challenging agency actions. Studies of NEPA litigation show that the willingness of the courts to review agency decisions, especially in the early 1970s, resulted from a number of factors, including public support for the environment, a tendency toward strict enforcement of statutory procedural requirements, and most importantly, timing. NEPA was enacted at a time when the courts were generally tightening their review of agency decision making and increasingly taking a "hard look" at agency actions.[49]

Several important environmental decisions came about during this period of judicial activism. Interpreting Congressional intent in the opening words of the 1970 Clean Air Act, the U.S. Supreme Court upheld a district court order that instructed the EPA to prevent the "significant deterioration" of air quality in regions that had already met federal standards.[50] A 1973 decision by the District of Columbia Circuit Court forced the EPA to prepare plans to reduce ozone and carbon monoxide (key components of smog) for cities using transportation control measures.[51] The legal concept of "standing"—the right of an individual or group to bring an issue before a court—was greatly expanded as well. The constitutional basis for standing is found in Article III, which gives courts the authority to decide "cases and controversies," and has been historically interpreted to mean that an individual had the right to bring a suit only when there was a clear showing that the person had been harmed, in terms of either personal injury or loss of property. Thus, most suits against polluting industries could be brought only by citizens actually affected by the pollution. Environmental groups found it difficult to qualify as litigants in most suits because environmental harm was not considered by most courts to be personal in nature, so litigation was infrequent.[52] Gradually, however, the courts began to allow members of environmental groups to sue on behalf of the public interest, increasing the number of lawsuits against industries, and later against agencies, that failed to comply with environmental laws and regulations.[53]

There is much evidence to conclude that the courts are now becoming the arena of choice for resolving all types of environmental disputes. Lawsuits have been filed challenging 80 percent of the EPA's major rule makings.[54] On the one hand, environmental groups have been particularly successful in using the courts to compel enforcement of environmental regulations. A suit by the Coalition for Clean Air against the South Coast Air Quality Management District, the agency responsible for controlling stationary sources of air pollution in the Los Angeles Basin, compelled the agency to move forward on preparing a State Implementation Plan (SIP) to meet federal air-quality standards. Coalition members criticized the agency for stalling on the preparation of the EPA-mandated plan, and only legal action got the plan moving forward.

On the other hand, it is usually to industry's advantage to litigate environmental regulations because the process has the net effect of stalling the implementation of new rules. Industry can demur during the policy formation and adoption stage, thereby avoiding the bad press that comes from intrusive lobbying, in hopes of moving the courts closer to their position.[55] Judicial challenges to agency actions have come to dominate the process of issuing regulations. Thousands of jobs for lawyers have been created. Virtually every major agency decision will be highly scrutinized. Regulatory officials must anticipate a lawsuit anytime they take an action of any consequence. It is difficult to assess the benefits that have come from more careful agency action with the disadvantages of a regulatory process that is slow, expensive, and cumbersome.

STATE AND LOCAL POLICYMAKING

Most analysts give the federal government low marks to date, and as one observer notes, fragmentation has been the prevailing pattern in the formation and implementation of federal environmental policy. Efforts to integrate the federal role in environmental management have been sporadic and have had minimal impact.[56] State and local attempts to deal with environmental problems have been similarly fragmented. Although most states developed resource management agencies by 1950 (especially to deal with forests or mines), there was little interest in environmental protection. In the early 1950s, local health departments were given authority over air quality as scientists began monitoring the negative health effects of air pollution. In contrast, jurisdiction over water pollution was taken away from health officials and made a separate agency in most cities.[57]

State agencies expanded in response to federal mandates in the late 1960s and early 1970s, initially creating environmental agencies on a single-media basis, such as state air-quality boards or water commissions. The federal statutes relied on state agencies for implementation, providing funds for planning, monitoring, management, and technical studies.[58]

Gradually, two patterns of state initiative emerged. Some states, such as New York and Washington, created "superagencies" or "little EPAs" for purposes of administrative efficiency. In some cases, this was done for political acceptability, rather than to integrate an entire program of environmental management.[59] Minnesota, for example, created its Pollution Control Agency in 1967 and shifted responsibility for water-pollution control to it and out of the state health department and gave it air and solid waste authority as well. Most of these consolidated programs have a part-time citizen board, which is often subject to attack because members lack sufficient technical expertise. A second pattern was to create a totally new environmental agency focusing on pollution control. Illinois, for example, created a powerful, full-time, five-member Pollution Control Board with a full research staff, the Institute for Environmental Quality.[60]

As the technical competence of state government grew, so too did an "environmental presence," which business and industry interests found unacceptable. They turned to the federal government for regulatory relief and federal preemption of state authority.[61] The New Federalism, which actually began with the State and Local Fiscal Assistance Act of 1972, is exemplified by the Reagan administration's philosophy of "getting government off the backs of the people."[62] Reagan's belief in a reduction in the scope of federal activity, privatization, and the devolution of policy and fiscal responsibility to the states resulted in the an EPA unwilling to serve as policy initiator or Congressional advocate. To fill that void, state officials began to band together to lobby collectively. In the area of air quality, for example, eight states formed Northeast States for Coordinated Air Use Management (NESCAUM) to actively lobby for reauthorization of the Clean Air Act in 1987 when the EPA was no longer its Congressional policy advocate. The group prepared legislative proposals, technical support, and documentation for its position, termed "a complete role reversal, with states serving as policy initiators."[53]

However, in general, states have not been willing to take a position of leadership. A study of the implementation of the 1986 Superfund amendments found that few states had complied with a requirement that governors designate a state official to serve as a trustee for the state's natural resources. The trustee has the authority to bring natural resource damage claims in federal court. By April 1988, eighteen months after enactment of the Superfund provisions, only one-third of the states had designated a trustee, and by April 1989, only thirty-nine states had complied. The survey found that several states were in complete ignorance of the requirement, while others had complied even before the implementing regulations were drafted.[64]

Policy analyst James Lester has sought to explain why there is such a variation in the way in which states respond to environmental problems. One reason is the "severity argument"—that those states with the most concentrated population growth and urbanization (and therefore the most severe pollution problems) take the most active the role in dealing with them. A second reason, the "wealth argument" states that there is a direct relationship between the state's resource base and its commitment to environmental protection. Third, the "partisanship argument" is that states with a Democratic-leaning legislature are more likely to work toward environmental protection than those that are Republican-controlled. Lastly there is the "organizational capacity argument," which states that administrative and organizational reforms are the best predictors of environmental policy outputs, so that professional legislatures are more likely to enact environmental legislation than those that are part-time, unprofessional ones.[65] Since most federal statutes require state implementation, local governments have played relatively subordinate roles to that of the state. The exceptions have been in the states where the environmental movement has been strong and has pressured local officials to enact environmental regulations more stringent than those of the federal or state government, as is the case in several Western states.

Many states and communities have made tremendous progress in developing their capacity to pursue environmental protection goals. States have experimented with innovative ways of integrating pollution-control programs to streamline and integrate different regulatory programs and ensuring that emissions are actually reduced rather than simply transformed from one form to another.[66] San Diego's City Council devised in 1997 a plan to protect hundreds of thousands of acres of land in Southern California. This plan won the support of developers and environmentalists and was heralded by many as a model for national efforts to protect biodiversity.[67] However, there have been problems as well. EPA officials have regularly complained that some states have not effectively enforced environmental laws. The EPA announced in February 1997 a plan to give states more freedom to develop innovative regulatory programs, but then withdrew the plan a few weeks later when critics charged that the proposal would permit states to circumvent federal laws and regulations by claiming that they were simply experimenting with new approaches.[68]

Several studies have found that there is a much stronger level of environmental interest in the West in comparison with other regions.[69] That interest is found in both public opinion polls and legislative voting records, as well as in measures of the use of wilderness areas and in legislation. To some extent, statewide groups such as the Colorado Environmental Council and regional branches of national organizations such as the Sierra Club and Audubon Society have found a sympathetic audience at the state level. Pioneering legislation such as Oregon's bottle bill and California's recycling programs is generally a result of an effective environmental lobby. Since political values are often based on a specific place where citizens live, work, and play, it is not surprising that local governments are beginning to play a larger role in policy formation. Local initiatives may be the result of a smoke plume from a local factory, or of an attempt to make a town more aesthetically pleasing to residents or tourists. But local officials must also balance those concerns with the historic tradition and prevailing mood of business toward development and growth, combined with a steadily decreasing revenue base, which precludes many otherwise desirable environmental projects from being funded.[70]

The one issue the Clinton administration and the Republican Congress did agree on in 1995 was the need for the federal government to be more sensitive to the financial burdens it imposes on states when it enacts environmental and other laws. In March 1995, Congress passed and President Clinton signed the Unfunded Mandates Reform Act, which made it more difficult for the federal government to impose regulatory responsibilities on state and local governments without appropriating money for them. Bills that include unfunded mandates on states and localities are subject to special procedural provisions that permit members of Congress to block passage of the bills until specific votes are taken.[71] Passage of the bill signaled a new willingness of Congress and the White House to begin to rethink the relationship between the federal and state governments in the formulation and implementation of environmental policy.

SUMMARY

Even though Congress holds the constitutional responsibility for enacting legislation to protect the environment, the Department of the Interior and the Environmental Protection Agency are the two lead agencies in the development of environmental policy. Their ability to protect the environment is affected, to a large extent, by the resources given to them. The level of presidential support has been among the most important factors that determine how effective environmental agencies will be. This phenomenon was especially apparent during the eight years of the Reagan administration, when the EPA's budget was slashed and the agency underwent traumatic reorganization and personnel changes. The next eight years under Presidents Bush and Clinton were only marginally better in terms of providing the agency with the resources necessary to accomplish the tasks given it. The protection of the environment has been a priority when it has been a focus of the president and his staff and has slipped when other interests have come first. Many observers believe that the judicial arena is taking on new importance in the settling of environmental disputes, especially by environmental organizations and individuals frustrated by the slow pace of administrative rule making.

NOTES

1. Quoted in James Brook, "A Monumental Debate: Resources or Reserves?" *The Oregonian,* October 13, 1996, A22.

2. See Alison Mitchell, "President Designates a Monument across Utah," *New York Times,* September 17, 1996, A15; and Matthew Brown, "A Wilderness to Really Be Alone," *The Oregonian,* September 22, 1996, A22; "A New and Needed Monument," *New York Times,* September 18, 1996, A22.

3. James E. Anderson, *Public Policy Making: An Introduction* (Boston: Houghton Mifflin, 1990), 51.

4. For the historical background of the nation's earliest attempts at environmental protection, see U.S. Department of the Interior, *Creation of the Department of the Interior* (Washington, D.C.: U.S. Department of the Interior, 1976); and Donald C. Swain, "Conservation in the 1920s," in *American Environmentalism,* 3d ed., ed. Roderick Nash (New York: McGraw-Hill, 1990), 117–125.

5. Henry V. Nickel, "Now, the Rush to Regulate," *The Environmental Forum, 8,* no. 1 (January–February 1991): 19.

6. See Joseph Petulla, *Environmental Protection in the United States* (San Francisco, CA: San Francisco Study Center, 1987), 98–99.

7. Marc K. Landy, Marc J. Roberts, and Stephen R. Thomas, *The EPA: Asking the Wrong Questions* (New York: Oxford University Press, 1990), 117.

8. Alfred A. Marcus, *Promise and Performance: Choosing and Implementing an Environmental Policy* (Westport, CT: Greenwood Press, 1980), 87.

9. Ibid. 85.

10. John Quarles, *Cleaning Up America: An Insider's View of the EPA* (Boston: Houghton Mifflin, 1976), 34.

11. Steven A. Cohen, "EPA: A Qualified Success," in Sheldon Kamieniecki, et al. *Controversies in Environmental Policy* (Albany, NY: State University of New York Press, 1986).

12. Quarles, 17–19.

13. John McCormick, *Reclaiming Paradise: The Global Environmental Movement* (Bloomington, IN: Indiana University Press, 1989), 110.

14. Landy et al., 41.

15. See C. Brant Short, *Ronald Reagan and the Public Lands* (College Station, TX: Texas A&M University Press, 1989), 47.

16. Lou Cannon, *President Reagan: The Role of a Lifetime* (New York: Simon & Schuster, 1991), 530–531. Cannon has spent much of his life as a Reagan biographer, chronicling both of Reagan's terms as governor and as president.

17. Short, 57.

18. Cannon, 531.

19. Jonathan Lash, Katherine Gillman, and David Sheridan, *A Season of Spoils: The Reagan Administration's Attack on the Environment* (New York: Pantheon Books, 1984), 231.

20. Ron Arnold, *At the Eye of the Storm: James Watt and the Environmentalists* (Chicago: Regency Gateway, 1982), 94.

21. Arnold, 93.

22. Cannon, 532.

23. Lash, 287–297.

24. Needless to say, Burford's account of the personnel loss and her subsequent fall from grace is somewhat different. She attributes the changes to natural attrition within the agency. See Anne Burford with John Greenya, *Are You Tough Enough?* (New York: McGraw-Hill, 1986).

25. See Richard E. Cohen, "The Gorsuch Affair," *National Journal*, January 8, 1983, 80.

26. Haynes Johnson, *Sleepwalking Through History: America in the Reagan Years* (New York: W. W. Norton, 1991), 170.

27. *Public Papers of the President of the United States: Ronald Reagan, 1983* (Washington, D.C.: Government Printing Office, 1984), 388–389.

28. Johnson, 171.

29. Landy, 251–252.

30. Landy, 256.

31. Tom Turner, "Changing the Guards," *Mother Earth News,* May–June, 1989, 56.

32. William K. Reilly, "Pollution Prevention: An Environmental Goal for the '90s," *EPA Journal, 16,* no. 1 (January–February 1990): 5.

33. "A Vision for EPA's Future," *EPA Journal, 16,* no. 6 (September–October 1990): 5.

34. "William Reilly's Green Precision Weapons," *The Economist,* March 30, 1991, 28.

35. Executive Office of the President. Council on Environmental Quality. *The 21st Annual Report of the Council on Environmental Quality* (Washington, D.C.: Government Printing Office, 1991).

36. "Quailing over Clean Air," *Environment, 33,* no. 6 (July–August 1991): 24.

37. Allan Freedman, "After Interior's Smooth Ride, Some Issues Left Behind," *Congressional Quarterly Weekly Report,* October 5, 1996: 2858.

38. Gary Lee, "Agency Takes a Hit from One of its Own," *Washington Post,* June 27, 1996: A27.

39. Robert L. Paarlberg, "A Domestic Dispute: Clinton, Congress, and Environmental Policy," *Environment* (October 1996): 16–28.

40. For a general discussion of Congress and environmental policymaking, see Richard A. Cooley and Geoffrey Wandesforde-Smith, *Congress and the Environment* (Seattle, WA: University of Washington Press, 1970). A less contemporary but still accurate view is provided by Henry M. Jackson, "Environmental Policy and the Congress," *Public Administration Review, 28,* no. 4 (July–August 1968): 303–305.

41. Michael E. Kraft, "Environmental Gridlock: Searching for Consensus in Congress," in *Environmental Policy in the 1990s,* eds. Norman J. Vig and Michael E. Kraft (Washington, D.C.: Congressional Quarterly Press, 1990), 103–124.

42. Walter A. Rosenbaum, *Environmental Politics and Policy,* 2d ed. (Washington, D.C.: Congressional Quarterly Press, 1991), 83.

43. Nancy Gibbs and Karen Tumulty, "Master of the House," *Time,* December 25, 1995/January 1, 1996, 68.

44. Associated Press, "A Lobbyists' Perk Will Die," *The New York Times,* May 25, 1995, A13.

45. David Maraniss and Michael Weisskopf, "Cashing In: The GOP revolutionaries have

a sure-fire way of telling friend from foe," *The Washington Post National Weekly Edition,* December 4–10, 1995: 6–7.

46. League of Conservation Voters, "The Anti-Environment Revolution: Let the Lobbyists Write the Laws" (n.d.).

47. Linda DiVall, American Viewpoint, Inc., memorandum to the Superfund Reform Coalition, December 12, 1995.

48. Gary Lee, "GOP Is Warned of Backlash on Environment," *Washington Post,* January 24, 1996, A6; Linda DiVall, American Viewpoint, Inc., memorandum to the Superfund Reform Coalition, December 12, 1995.

49. Frederick R. Anderson, *NEPA in the Courts* (Baltimore, MD: Johns Hopkins University Press, 1973), 17.

50. *Sierra Club v. Ruckelshaus,* 344 F.Supp. 2253 (1972).

51. *Natural Resources Defense Council v. EPA,* 475 F.2d 968 (1973). For a thorough analysis of the courts' review of the Clean Air Act, see R. Shep Melnick, *Regulation and the Courts: The Case of the Clean Air Act* (Washington, D.C.: The Brookings Institution, 1983).

52. Werner F. Grunbaum, *Judicial Policy Making: The Supreme Court and Environmental Quality* (Morristown, NJ: General Learning Press, 1976), 4.

53. The case that generally is regarded as opening the door to environmental group litigation is *Scenic Hudson Preservation Conference v. Federal Power Commission,* 453 F.2d 463 (2nd Cir., 1971). The local conservation group challenged the application of New York Edison Company to build a power plant on Storm King Mountain in the Hudson River Valley and was granted standing by the Second Circuit Court under the Federal Power Act, which directs the Federal Power Commission to consider the impact of proposed projects.

54. Marianne Lavelle, "Talking about Air," *The National Law Journal,* June 10, 1991, 30.

55. See Lettie M. Wenner, *The Environmental Decade in Court* (Bloomington, IN: Indiana University Press, 1982).

56. Barry G. Rabe, *Fragmentation and Integration in State Environmental Management* (Washington, D.C.: The Conservation Foundation, 1986), 17.

57. J. Clarence Davies, *The Politics of Pollution* (New York: Pegasus, 1970), 128.

58. See Samuel P. Hays, *Beauty, Health and Permanence: Environmental Politics in the United States 1955–1985* (Cambridge, England: Cambridge University Press, 1987), 441.

59. Rabe, 31.

60. See Elizabeth Haskell, "State Governments Tackle Pollution," in *Managing the Environment.* United States Environmental Protection Agency. Document EPA/600/5-73-010. (Washington, D.C.: U.S. Environmental Protection Agency, 1973), 135, 138.

61. Hays, 443.

62. For an explanation of the emerging trends of state innovation, see James P. Lester, "A New Federalism?" *Environmental Policy in the 1990s,* eds. Norman J. Vig and Michael E. Kraft (Washington, D.C.: Congressional Quarterly Press, 1990), 59–79.

63. Edward Laverty, "Legacy of the 1980s in State Environmental Administration," in *Regulatory Federalism, Natural Resources, and Environmental Management,* ed. Michael S. Hamilton (Washington, D.C.: American Society for Public Administration, 1990), 68–70.

64. Susan J. Buck and Edward M. Hathaway," Designating State Natural Resource Trustees under the Superfund Amendments," in *Regulatory Federalism, Natural Resources, and Environmental Management,* ed. Michael S. Hamilton (Washington, D.C.: American Society for Public Administration, 1990), 83–94.

65. Lester, 70–71.

66. See Barry G. Rabe, "Integrated Environmental Permitting: Experience and Innovation at the State Level," *State and Local Government Review, 27,* no. 3 (1995); and Rabe, "Power to the States: The Promise and Pitfalls of Decentralization," *Environmental Policy in the 1990s,* 3d ed., eds. Norman J. Vig and Michael E. Kraft (Washington, D.C.: Congressional Quarterly Press, 1997): 31–52.

67. William K. Stevens, "Conservation Plan for Southern California Could Be Model for Nation," *The New York Times,* February 16, 1997, A12.

68. John H. Cushman, Jr., "EPA Withdraws Plan Giving States More Say in Enforcement," *The New York Times,* March 2, 1997, A13.

69. See, for example, Samuel P. Hays, "The New Environmental West," *Journal of Policy History, 3,* no. 3 (1991): 223–248; and The Continental Group, *Toward Responsible Growth: Economic and Environmental Concern in the Balance* (Stamford, CT: The Continental Group, 1982).

70. To understand how states organize their programs, see Deborah Hitchcock Jessup, *Guide to State Environmental Programs* (Washington, D.C.: Bureau of National Affairs, 1990).

71. Public Law No. 104-4; see U.S. Senate, Committee on Governmental Affairs, *Unfunded Mandate Reform Act of 1995,* Senate Report 104-1 (January 11, 1995).

FOR FURTHER READING

Anne Burford with John Greenya. *Are You Tough Enough?* New York: McGraw-Hill, 1986.

Daniel J. Fiorino. *Making Environmental Policy.* Berkeley, CA: University of California Press, 1995.

Peter M. Haas, Robert O. Keohane, and Marc A. Levy. *Institutions for the Earth: Sources of Effective International Environmental Protection.* Cambridge, MA: MIT Press, 1993.

Thomas More Hoban and Richard Oliver Brooks. *Green Justice: The Environment and the Courts.* Boulder, CO: Westview Press, 1996.

Kenneth M. Holland, F. L. Morton, and Brian Galligan, eds. *Federalism and the Environment.* Westport, CT: Greenwood Press, 1996.

Cornelius Neil Kerwin. *Rulemaking: How Government Agencies Write Law and Make Policy.* Washington, D.C.: Congressional Quarterly Press, 1994.

Marc K. Landy, Marc J. Roberts, and Stephen R. Thomas. *The EPA: Asking the Wrong Questions from Nixon to Clinton.* Expanded ed. New York: Oxford University Press, 1990.

Jonathan Lash, Katherine Gillman, and David Sheridan. *A Season of Spoils: The Reagan Administration's Attack on the Environment.* New York: Pantheon Books, 1984.

Alfred A. Marcus. *Promise and Performance: Choosing and Implementing an Environmental Policy.* Westport, CT: Greenwood Press, 1980.

Mark Neuzil and William Kovarik. *Mass Media and Environmental Conflict.* Thousand Oaks, CA: Sage, 1996.

Barry G. Rabe. *Fragmentation and Integration in State Environmental Management.* Washington, D.C.: The Conservation Foundation, 1986.

John C. Whitaker. *Striking a Balance: Environment and Natural Resources Policy in the Nixon-Ford Years.* Washington, D.C.: American Enterprise Institute, 1976.

CHAPTER 4

Stewardship or Exploitation?
Public and Private Lands

Legislators and overzealous regulators, fueled by the apocalypse rhetoric and junk science of the radical environmental movement, are waging the greatest war on private property rights in the history of this Nation.
—Peggy Reigle, founder, Fairness to Land Owners Committee[1]

When the United States was in its infancy, "public lands" referred to the entire area west of the thirteen original colonies. The government, however, was not interested in being in the land business and began selling millions of acres to private owners as quickly as possible. The disposal process started with the Ordinance of 1785, which allowed the sale of parcels of land to the highest bidder at a minimum price of one dollar per acre, with a 640-acre minimum. The disposal process did not end until 1934, when President Franklin Roosevelt signed the Taylor Grazing Act, which ended private settlement and established grazing districts on the remaining federal lands. By then more than one billion acres of public land had been brought under private ownership, with 170 million acres remaining under public domain.

The federal government slowed its marketing approach to public land in 1872 when it established Yellowstone National Park. This shift in both attitude and policy—from selling land to preserving it—was mainly the result of the Progressive Era and the pleas of Thoreau and Emerson for government intervention to protect natural areas. Under growing pressure from the conservation movement, Congress began to tighten up the government's somewhat cavalier attitude toward land in the public domain. With passage of the 1891 Forest Reserve Act (repealed in 1907) the federal government began to set aside forest land to protect future timber supplies. Subsequent legislation in 1906 gave the president authority to withdraw federal lands from settlement and development if they had national or historic interest, and the 1920 Mineral Leasing Act authorized leases, rather than outright sales, of public lands for extraction of oil, gas, coal, and other minerals.

Congress has designated five major uses for public lands under its control: wilderness (lands set aside as undeveloped areas), national forests (areas reserved to ensure a continuous supply of timber, not exclusive of other uses), national parks (which are open to the public for recreational use and closed, for the most part, to resource development), national wildlife refuges (which provide a permanent habitat for migratory birds and animals); and rangelands (open for livestock grazing on a permit basis).

Today, the following agencies hold responsibility for managing over 650 million acres of public lands: the Bureau of Land Management (270 million acres), the U.S. Forest Service (191 million acres), the U.S. Fish and Wildlife Service (92 million acres), the National Park Service (87 million acres), the Department of Defense (25 million acres) and all other federal agencies (8 million acres). Each agency has its own clientele, some of which overlap, and its own agenda in how it implements federal law. The conflicts created by shared jurisdiction are epitomized by the term *multiple use,* which refers to those federal lands that have been designated for a variety of purposes, ranging from grazing to recreation. By its very name, multiple-use designation means that groups compete for the permitted right to use the land. A second component of the multiple-use policy is sustained yield, which means that no more forage or timber may be harvested than can be produced.

Several legislative efforts demonstrate the government's continued commitment to the multiple-use concept. Congress enacted the Multiple Use Sustained Yield Act of 1960, and four years later, the Classification and Multiple Use Act. These two pieces of legislation recognized that land held within the public domain might be used for activities other than logging and grazing, although the laws were minimally successful in changing patterns of use that had existed for decades. When the Federal Land Policy and Management Act was enacted in 1976, it reiterated the government's position on multiple use. The legislation required full public participation in land management decisions and specified that all public lands under federal management were to continue under federal ownership unless their sale was in the national interest. Critics of multiple use, however, call the policy a charade, arguing that it is a smokescreen used by the federal government to justify the exploitation of public lands and resources by favored commodity interests.[2]

This chapter outlines the challenges now facing the federal government as it seeks to manage its public lands. There are several continuing debates that will be explored, including the perspectives of the stakeholders involved with each issue. The chapter continues with an overview of contemporary land-use issues and how environmental politics affects management decisions dealing with both public and private lands.

GRAZING RIGHTS AND WRONGS

In 1934, the Taylor Grazing Act established a federal Division of Grazing to work with the General Land Office to establish grazing districts, set fees, and grant permits for use. The two agencies later merged to become the Bureau of Land Management (BLM). Fees are calculated on the basis of an Animal Unit Month (AUM)—the amount of forage required to feed a cow and her calf, a horse, or five goats or sheep for a month. Access to federal lands is fixed to base property ownership, so that those who own the greatest amount of property get priority for federal grazing privileges.[3] Grazing is also permitted on many national wildlife refuges and within some national parks. When the Taylor Act went into effect in 1936, the fee was five cents per AUM, although the U.S. Forest Service and BLM have often differed in the rates they charged. Congress passed legislation in 1978 to require a uniform grazing fee, which reached a high of $2.36 per AUM in 1980. Shortly thereafter, the Public Rangelands Improvement Act required fees to be set by a formula that took into account production costs and beef prices.[4]

Environmental organizations want the federal government to bring the charges more in line with what it costs to graze animals on the private market, rather than subsidizing ranchers. Ranchers rely on the subsidies as a way of providing their industry with a stable source of forage for their livestock. They also believe that public subsidies keep the cost of meat at a reasonable level for consumers and help to sustain the economic base for the rural West. So far, efforts to raise grazing fees (with increases pegged at anywhere from $2.56 to $8.70 per AUM) have been unsuccessful.[5]

In addition to the financial subsidies provided by the federal grazing program, critics point to the ecological damage caused by livestock. Overgrazing is claimed to have led to erosion and stream sedimentation in riparian habitats and to have devastated populations of game birds, song birds, and fish. In one study, the General Accounting Office (GAO) found that more U.S. plant species are wiped out or endangered by livestock grazing than by any other single factor. Livestock are also major consumers of one of the West's most precious resources—water—which is needed to irrigate hay and other crops. Grazing also forces out populations of wildlife that cannot compete for forage and water.[6]

Besides fee increases, several solutions have been proposed to deal with the grazing issue. Some environmental groups have lobbied for a complete prohibition against grazing on federal lands. Others believe that agencies like the BLM simply need more funds to repair overgrazing damage and to monitor land use. A third option, proposed by the Sierra Club, would be to allow grazing on those lands that have not been abused, but to ban the practice on those that are already in unsatisfactory condition. That option is viewed as an acknowledgment that conservationists' achievements are not keeping up with chronic abuse of public lands.[7]

The powerful livestock lobby has dominated the grazing issue.[8] One 1988 GAO report found that "the BLM is not managing the permittees, rather, permittees are managing the BLM."[9] Occasionally, environmental groups have been successful in forcing the federal government to analyze the impact of grazing, as was the case in 1974 when the Natural Resources Defense Council won a landmark suit that forced the BLM to develop 144 environmental impact statements on grazing. But in response, ranchers fought back in a Rocky Mountain West movement during the late 1970s, which environmentalists called "The Great Terrain Robbery," better known as "The Sagebrush Rebellion."

During the late 1970s, several western groups were formed by conservatives and ranchers dissatisfied with the policies of the Bureau of Land Management. The movement had three objectives: to convince state legislators to pass resolutions demanding that Bureau of Land Management and Forest Service lands be transferred from the federal government to individual states, to create a financial war chest for legal challenges in the federal courts, and to develop a broad public education campaign to get western voters to support the movement. The rebellion was portrayed as a "states' rights" issue, although it became obvious that what the organizers really wanted was to eliminate the federal government from having any say in how ranchers used the land. The Sagebrush Rebellion was the first organized and politically viable challenge to the environmental movement since the early 1950s. One observer, however, believes that, although there was a rebellion for a time, only one side showed up to fight.[10]

The movement was successful in gaining favorable legislation in Arizona, New Mexico, Utah, and Wyoming, but by 1982 it had fizzled as a significant factor in western politics, especially in urban areas. Efforts to join the rebellion failed in Idaho, Montana, Oregon, South Dakota, and Washington and were ended by gubernatorial veto in California and Colorado. Supporters believed that the election of Ronald Reagan in 1980, and his subsequent appointment of James Watt as secretary of the interior, would enhance their efforts, and there was certainly a more conservative approach to land policy taken during his administration. In 1982, Watt ordered his staff to investigate the disposal of federal lands, and Congress introduced bills to sell public lands as a way of reducing the federal deficit.

By late 1982, the Sagebrush Rebellion came under siege from those who believed the states were ill equipped to manage public lands properly. Government officials such as former Interior Secretary Cecil Andrus and Arizona governor Bruce Babbitt, members of the hunting and fishing lobby, and organized environmental organizations such as the Sierra Club and Audubon Society all criticized the movement as insensitive to the preservation of public lands. Under an umbrella group called Save Our Public Lands, the preservation lobbyists targeted Watt until he became a major liability to Reagan and was forced to resign in late 1983. Eventually, legal funds dried up, congressional legislation withered, and Reagan backed away from the cause.

The movement was reinvigorated in the early 1990s as the wise use and county supremacy movements garnered attention. Organizations such as the Mountain States Legal Foundation and the Individual Rights Foundation have led the legal fight against federal lands. Counties passed ordinances challenging federal control of local lands, and state legislators proposed bills calling for state ownership of federal lands.[11] The Western states rebellion reached Washington, D.C., in 1995 when the Republicans became a majority in Congress. The Republican agenda of a smaller federal government fit well with calls for devolution of power to local government and transfer of federal lands to states. The Clin-

THE "REAL" ENVIRONMENTALISTS?

To Clark Collins, Executive Director of the Blue Ribbon Coalition (BRC), the goals of off-highway vehicle (OHV) users, or "motorheads" as they are sometimes derisively called, have been misrepresented by many of their critics. "Anti-recreation access organizations appear to be deliberately misstating our position on Wilderness access for their own political purposes," he says. To Collins and those who comprise the OHV lobby (such as snowmobile clubs, motorcycle owners, trail associations, and mountain and dirt bike enthusiasts) efforts to blur the lines between wilderness (what BRC leaders refer to as "backcountry" areas) and Wilderness (formally federally designated areas) make it difficult for mechanized users to gain access to public lands for recreational purposes.

The BRC's motto, "Preserving our natural resources FOR the public instead of FROM the public," is indicative of the nationwide group's perspective on not only recreational access but also the ways in which natural resources are managed. Like other interest groups, the BRC urges its members to organize letter-writing campaigns and to testify at hearings in opposition to proposals that would have a negative impact on balanced recreation and resource use.

Collins, a former electrician who is a native of Boise, Idaho, became an OHV activist in the 1970s after serving as an officer in several motorcycle organizations. In 1987, he helped form the Idaho Public Land Users Association, and later that same year, the BRC. The organization led the legislative battle for the 1991 passage of the Symms Recreational Trails Fund Act, which sets aside a percentage of the federal tax on gasoline for use in developing recreational trails and facilities. The bill had been opposed by the nation's largest environmental organizations, and it marked a watershed victory for the BRC and its half million members.

Environmental organizations (called Green Advocacy Groups, or GAG by Collins) criticize off-road-vehicle enthusiasts out of concern that fragile ecosystems are being destroyed by users who are unaware of the damage they or their vehicles cause to plants, soil, and trails. Some environmental leaders believe that federal agencies are too lax in enforcing trail closures and have accused officials of allowing companies such as Kawasaki and Yamaha to influence land use policy.

Collins and others, in turn, refer to themselves as the "real environmentalists" and emphasize that the organization's members are family-oriented, self-policing, and participate in numerous volunteer efforts to build and restore trails and recreational sites. They believe that their interests represent a valuable contribution to the American economy, citing studies indicating that personal watercraft sales are the fastest growing segment of the motorized consumer products business and a California survey that showed that OHV

(continued)

recreation annually generates $3 billion in economic activity for the state of California. BRC literature claims that "environmental extremists" are threatening "our sport, our recreation, our jobs and homes. They work to lock up public land—land that belongs to everyone. They assault our rights and liberties."

Many of the advocates for off-highway recreation believe that there is a widening gap separating them from the members of mainstream environmental groups. Some observers believe that the growing distrust on both sides stems from a perceived class difference, with motorized recreationists portrayed as blue collar workers aligned with the Republican Party, and environmental group members more closely associated with Democrats and viewed as elitists who are unwilling to share public lands. Between are federal agencies such as the Bureau of Land Management and the U.S. Forest Service, which have been only moderately successful in bringing the two sides to the negotiating table.

In recent years, OHV users have joined with other segments of the wise use movement to lobby on issues ranging from energy resources and forest reform to opposing the reintroduction of grizzly bears in Idaho. The symbiotic relationship among diverse interests has given the BRC an opportunity to speak with a louder, if not altogether more politically effective, voice.

For Further Reading
John Echeverria and Raymond Booth Eby, eds. *Let the People Judge: Wise Use and the Private Property Rights Movement.* Washington, D.C.: Island Press, 1995.
David Helvarg. *The War against the Greens: The "Wise Use" Movement, the New Right, and Anti-Environmental Violence.* San Francisco, Sierra Club Books, 1994.
Elizabeth Manning. "Motorheads: The New, Noisy, Organized Force in the West." *High Country News, 28,* no. 23 (December 9, 1996): 1, 10–13.
William Perry Pendley. *It Takes a Hero: The Grassroots Struggle against Environmental Oppression.* Bellevue, WA: Free Enterprise Press, 1994.
Todd Wilkinson. "Snowed Under." *National Parks, 69,* no. 1–2 (January–February 1995), 32.
Ted Williams. "Greenscam." *Harrowsmith Country Life* (May–June 1992), 31–37.

ton administration's public land policies became a high priority of the new leaders of Congress. When President Clinton named Bruce Babbitt as interior secretary, the former governor found himself in a position to reform public lands policy, particularly grazing policy. In 1990, 1991, and 1992, the House passed grazing fee increases (as high as $8.70 per AUM) but the bills died in the Senate or were stripped from the bills in the conference committees.[12]

The Clinton administration then entered the grazing lands reform debate through the budget process, proposing to raise the grazing fee from $1.92 to $5.00 per AUM as part of its fiscal stimulation package. Western Senators quickly opposed the administration's initiative and the president just as quickly retreated, dropping his demands for public land reform and reduction of subsidies. The failure of congressional reform prompted a series of twenty meetings throughout the West convened by Secretary Babbitt and others, which culminated in a March 1994 Department of the Interior proposal to raise the grazing fee, broaden public participation in rangeland management, and require environmental improvements on rangelands. The proposal, called Rangeland Reform '94, went into effect in August 1995. Rangeland Reform '94 created Resource Advisory Councils (RACs)—comprised of ranchers, conservationists, and other stakeholders to help create grazing policy—authorized permit holders to not use land for up to ten years for conservation purposes and to graze fewer animals than permitted without losing leases, allowed federal officials to consider a permittee's past performance when determining future permits, required grazing land improvements to be owned by the federal government, raised fees to approximately $3.68 per AUM and subsequent fees to be negotiated, and required changes in grazing practices to ensure recovery and protection of endangered species and protect rangelands.

As Rangeland Reform '94 was evolving through the administrative process, opponents in Congress tried to enact legislation to overturn it. In May 1995, Senator Pete Domenici (R-New Mexico) and Representative Wes Cooley (R-Oregon) introduced their Public Grazing Act of 1995.[13] The Senate version was reported out of the Energy and Natural Resources Committee in June. Negotiations continued, and a substitute bill, the Public Rangelands Management Act, was reported by the committee in November and passed by the Senate in March 1996.[14] The Senate bill would have placed BLM and Forest Service grazing lands under one law, removed the National Grasslands from the National Forest System, lengthened grazing permits from ten to twelve years, limited the application of National Environmental Policy Act (NEPA) reviews to land use plans and not grazing permits, given ranchers more control over management of the lands that they use and more influence in agency decision making, created local advisory councils of ranchers and other interests (but not the "interested public"), and increased fees by 30 percent. The House Resources Committee approved a similar bill in April 1996, but opposition from Democrats and moderate Republicans kept it from reaching the House floor. In June 1996, House Parks Subcommittee Chair Jim Hansen (R-Utah) attached the grazing bill to the omnibus parks bill that had been passed by the Senate in May. Babbitt threatened that the president would veto the entire parks bill if the grazing provisions were attached, and House leaders stripped them before the parks bill was brought for a final, successful vote.

Wise use advocates had achieved few of their policy goals by the beginning of Clinton's second term. But they had successfully placed their concerns on the policy agenda, and federal agencies, environmentalists, and members of Congress were all scrambling to anticipate their attacks on public lands policy and their defense of the traditional West.

"THE BEST IDEA AMERICA EVER HAD":
THE NATIONAL PARKS

When President Woodrow Wilson signed the National Park Service Act in 1916, he brought thirty-six national parks under a single federal agency in what was termed by former British ambassador to the United States James Bryce as "the best idea America ever had." The concept of a national park has now been copied by more than 120 other nations worldwide. Since it was created, the U.S. system has been enlarged to nearly 400 sites on 87 million acres,[15] and with such growth has come a wealth of management and policy problems. On the occasion of the National Park Service's (NPS) seventy-fifth anniversary in 1991, the question of the role of the national park system in protecting the public lands once again gained a place on the policy agenda.

The debate on the future of the NPS focuses on four primary issues, best outlined in a three-year study by the National Parks and Conservation Association (NPCA), an independent organization whose purpose is to support the national parks. The study outlines the group's concerns on how best to operate the system into the next century.[16] First, despite the rapid growth of the number of sites within the system, there is concern over attempts to include virtually every site within the nation's borders that needs protection as a national park. Some authorities believe that not every monument, site, or region needs federal protection, but would be better served by state or local government, or even by private groups. Some efforts have been made to establish joint responsibility, such as the Lyndon B. Johnson National Historical Park in Texas, and groups such as the Nature Conservancy have privately purchased lands not yet protected by other jurisdictions. Congress has largely resisted demands to include sites as national parks that do not have sufficient national value to merit such a designation. But a number of groups have identified some parks that should be given other designations. Members of Congress introduced in 1995 the National Park System Reform Act, designed to establish new criteria for the designation of parks, and ordered NPS to reassess the existing system. The proposal was widely attacked by those who feared a major cutback in protection of the nation's priceless national heritage.[17]

The NPCA noted that continued expansion of the park system is necessary to keep pace with the influx of visitors, which is expected to rise from an estimated 270 million in 1995 to 500 million by 2010. The group recommended the NPS begin acquiring the two million acres of private land located within the parks (with an estimated value of $2 billion), and enhance its mapping capability to make whatever boundary adjustments are necessary to include sensitive or valuable sites currently outside park borders. Concerns have also been raised about the encroachment of commercial development along park boundaries and into wildlife habitats. Boundaries for the parks have typically been segments of latitude and longitude, thereby threatening fragile ecosystems by bisecting them. Other concerns are more aesthetic and visual. For example, a cable television tower tops Red Hill, a ridge overlooking Antietam National Battlefield in Maryland, and new homes and a shopping mall are planned for Grove Farm, where President Abraham Lincoln and General George McClellan met following the Antietam battle. When historians and conservationists fought proposed development on a part of Virginia's Manassas battlefield in 1988, they relied on computer simulations to convince members of Congress to purchase adjacent property, evidence that, as population grows, the battle to preserve scenic and historic sites heats up.[18] Controversies like these are proof that the "battle over the battlefield" is ongoing.

Based on a 1972 NPS study recommending the addition of a minimum of 196 areas, the NPCA identified forty-six natural areas, forty sites of historical significance, and ecological reserves and marine and estuarine ecosystems that should be added to the system. Congress has created several new parks. In 1994, Congress passed the California Desert Protection Act, creating more than 7.5 million acres of federally protected areas in the California desert. This was the largest land withdrawal since the Alaska National Interest Lands Conservation Act of 1980 (ANILCA) and the largest wilderness law in any of the lower forty-eight states. The act included the creation of three national parks, totaling nearly four million acres: Joshua Tree, Death Valley, and East Mojave. The first two parks had been managed as wilderness areas by the NPS for more than a decade.[19] In the final days of the 104th Congress, in September 1996, members passed a 700-page omnibus parks bill that they had been considering for months, which included federal funds to help purchase the Sterling Forest on the border of New Jersey and New York, creation of a trust to preserve the Presidio in San Francisco, creation of a tallgrass prairie reserve in Kansas, a swap of lands in Utah for a ski resort, and dozens of other projects affecting forty-one states.[20]

Critics of expanding the park system question whether growth is warranted when many existing parks are in need of infrastructure improvement and more maintenance and are suffering from personnel shortages. The NPCA estimates that the parks are already suffering from a $4 billion backlog in maintenance needs. Each summer there are widely publicized accounts of the problems of park overcrowding and needed repairs and upkeep. Parks such as Padre Island in Texas cannot afford to hire lifeguards to patrol beaches. Some thirty-two of the thirty-six buildings at Ellis Island, New York, are in need of repair. Temporary concrete barriers have been erected in Glacier National Park where the road's stone restraining wall has crumbled. Campgrounds, trails, roads, sewer lines, and other park facilities are swamped with growing numbers of users.[21]

Second, the parks are walking what has been called "a tightrope between preservation and enjoyment."[22] Studies have already shown that many of the parks, such as Yosemite, have exceeded their carrying capacity for automobiles. Conflicts have arisen among users seeking to restrict mountain bikes or horses and pack animals on park trails. The Grand Canyon, Zion, and Yosemite National Parks have developed plans to eliminate automobiles from the most crowded areas of the parks, replacing them with mass transportation systems. The Grand Canyon's general management plan concluded that "the most pressing issue in the park today is the impact created by the annual crush of nearly five million visitors and their private cars on the few developed areas along the canyon rims."[23] The NPCA has urged Congress to develop an independent research arm and a consistent, long-term visitor management policy, including designations of some uses as inappropriate in a park setting. Those concerns were underscored by another study released in August 1992 by the prestigious National Research Council. The group's report, which was requested by National Park Service Director James Ridenour, noted that NPS officials are called upon to make far-reaching choices between preserving natural treasures and providing service to mounting numbers of campers and sightseers without having an adequate science capability for those decisions. An August 1995 report of the U.S. General Accounting Office focused on twelve of the nation's most popular parks and found them locked in a cycle of increased visits and decaying infrastructure.[24]

Third, the activities of concessionaires and those with leases inside the parks have been the target of considerable legislative and public criticism. In 1965, Congress enacted the Concessions Policy Act, which was designed to limit concessions to those "necessary and appropriate" to the parks' purposes. The vagueness of the legislation has brought beauty parlors, banks, and video arcades to the parks along with more compatible enterprises like lodging and restaurants. The concessions operations, which range from family-run companies to large corporations, pay the U.S. Treasury a franchise fee, although officials argue the fees are too low and result in a virtual giveaway at public expense.[25]

Another controversy involves mining within the national parks. Most Americans are unaware that there are several thousand mining claims and six million acres of mineral rights within NPS boundaries, and that a section of the agency, the Mining and Minerals Branch, oversees mineral development within the parks. Some mineral rights were established before the areas became national parks, while others stem from the 1872 General Mining Law, which granted almost limitless rights to extract ore from public lands. An individual who discovers mineral ore may stake a claim on federal land and pay a $2.50-per-acre fee to establish a patent, which transfers ownership from public to private hands—a provision that has been called "the law with no brain."[26] The landowner also receives the right to develop the property, even for nonmining purposes. New mining claims were terminated with passage of the Mining in the Parks Act in 1976, but abandoned mines and shafts still pose a formidable health and safety hazard. A 1989 NPS study found mining debris including barrels of fuel, solvents, and dynamite at Wrangell–St. Elias National Park, and dangerous radiation leaks just off the footpath off the West Rim Drive in Grand Canyon National Park. Groups like the Western States Public Lands Coalition believe the right to mine should transcend all public lands, including national parks, but environmental organizations feel the original intent of the law is now obsolete.[27]

Fourth, a study commissioned to examine the NPS on its seventy-fifth anniversary concluded that the agency is so weakened by internal problems and is so overwhelmed by outside pressures that it is on the verge of being unable to perform its job. A fourteen-member committee of park service officials, conservationists, and academics produced the report, known as the "Vail Agenda," in 1992. The document is highly critical of the way the agency treats its employees and portrays an agency hobbled by budgetary problems and poor pay, morale, and training. It cites examples where the NPS is not living up to its mandate of educating the public and interpreting its sites and recommends that the NPS be more aggressive in defending its properties against threats from activities outside park boundaries, especially in the Rocky Mountain West.[28]

Several groups believe that the National Park Service should be removed from the Department of the Interior and made an independent agency. Critics point to staffing problems, interference by the department in congressional hearings, staff shortages (NPCA recommends the immediate hiring of twelve hundred new rangers), and a lack of recruitment and training programs. Others point to the NPS's handling of the 1988 summer fire in Yellowstone National Park and the extensive forest fires in 1996 that consumed more than 5.7 million acres by the end of the summer as examples of mismanagement and confusion over how the parks should be run. The first in 1996 were a result of decades of fire-suppression efforts and timber harvesting policy, as dead and dying trees accumulated in forests over a hot, dry summer. The timber industry has urged the Forest Service to increase logging as a way to reduce the risks of fires; environmentalists counter with fears that this will be an excuse to go after old-growth trees. Most foresters agree that some fires are necessary for the overall health of the forests, but the relentless push of construction into forest areas makes it politically impossible to let fires burn.[29] There is no doubt that the management record of the NPS has been tumultuous—three of its directors were fired in five years—but the problems of the national parks go far beyond directors and staff. The unanswered question, as former NPS director George B. Hartzog, Jr., puts it, is: Whose parks are these, and for what purposes?[30]

TRENDS IN LAND USE AND MANAGEMENT

Given these examples of current land use controversies, what does this tell us about trends in how America's land use policies have developed?

First, attitudes about the management of public lands have evolved slowly in the United States, from a policy of divestiture and conservation to one of preservation. Those attitudes reflect the changing consciousness about the environment, which has had its peaks and valleys throughout U.S. history. When citizens are concerned about land use, they demand to be involved and participate fully. When they are apathetic, decisions get made without them.

Second, land use policies are tempered by politics. Frustrated by their attempts to influence presidential policymaking, environmental groups have often turned to Congress or the president in hopes of exploiting regional and partisan rivalries. Many of the legislative mandates given to the agencies responsible for land management are vague and often contradictory, and Congress has seldom seemed eager to be more explicit in its direction. This is partly the result of congressional sidestepping of many of the more controversial conflicts in resource use. Should deserts be opened up to all-terrain vehicles, or left in a pristine condition where no one can enjoy them? Should the national parks be made more accessible so that they can accommodate more visitors, or should traffic be limited to not destroy their scenic beauty through overuse? Should private property owners be told by governmental regulatory agencies how their land can be used? The answers to those questions depend largely on which member of Congress, in what region of the country, is answering them.

Third, the future of public lands appears to have a price tag attached. Although there is a general sense that Americans want to preserve wilderness areas, scenic wonders, and some historic sites, they become less willing to do so when the decisions directly affect their pocketbooks. They may be willing to pay slightly higher fees to use state or national parks, but they rebel when the choice is between preservation of a single species and putting food on their family's table. As a result, land use policies are more likely to take into account the economic rather than scientific impact of decisions.

Fourth, decisions about land use policies are often made in the cloistered setting of administrative hearing rooms, hearings poorly attended by those affected by the decision-making process and only marginally publicized. The language of resource management is esoteric, and the science often unsubstantiated. Thus, the debate over the future of public lands has historically been dominated by resource users, such as timber and mining companies. More recently, however, environmental groups have "learned the language" of land and forest management, often hiring former industry experts. Still, most Americans know little about what is happening to the millions of acres still under federal control, and only well-organized groups that closely monitor regulatory actions (most of them based in the West) are in a position to speak for the public interest.[31]

Lastly, there is evidence of a growing rebellion against government intrusion, especially among small property owners who are fighting land-use restrictions, and by members of the wise use movement discussed previously. Sometimes the protesters can convince officials to soften their rules. Elmyra Taylor's modern home in Hanover, Virginia, was lumped into a historic district in 1988 without her consent, limiting her ability to make any changes without approval from a local architectural board. In response, she and her neighbors decorated their homes with Christmas lights and pink flamingos. The board of supervisors later eased its restrictions.[32]

PRIVATE PROPERTY AND PUBLIC LANDS

One of the most controversial land use issues of the decade—regulatory takings—has galvanized private property owners through the United States who feel the government has unfairly appropriated their land without paying them for its value. The basis for their position is the Fifth Amendment to the Constitution, which states that private property may not be taken for public use without just compensation, and a 1922 United States Supreme Court case that affirmed the concept of a regulatory taking.[33] For years the courts have attempted to interpret the meaning of the amendment, especially in cases where privately owned land was needed for public use, such as the construction of a new freeway. Local governments routinely have condemned houses in the freeway path, paying the owners damages, usually the fair market value of the home.

In 1985, University of Chicago law professor Richard Epstein published a controversial book that placed the concept of takings in a regulatory context.[34] Epstein argued that all forms of government regulations are subject to scrutiny under the takings clause, leading private property rights advocates to demand that the government pay them for the loss of the right to use their land, regardless of the reason. They were joined in their efforts by conservative organizations like the Cato Institute and the Federalist Society, who used the takings and property rights issue to bolster their attempt to reduce government intervention. Since Epstein's book was published, the concept of takings has been applied to a broad range of environmental legislation, from wilderness and wetlands designations to the protection of endangered species.

Under the Endangered Species Act, for example, the federal government has the power to prevent landowners from altering their property in any way if it threatens a species or its habitat. From a legal perspective, the reasoning is that the protection of a species (the common good or public interest) must be weighed against the interest of an individual property owner. Proponents of property rights counter that view by arguing that the government should be prevented from imposing on individual landowners the cost of providing public goods. They cite regulations, such as those that restrict development that would adversely affect wetlands, as examples where individuals are unfairly being asked to give up the use of their land without compensation for their loss. Other cases have involved the expansion of national park boundaries and wilderness designations or instances where a private property owner's land is appropriated for a wildlife refuge or recreational area. In order to press their demands upon the political system, individuals with property grievances have joined grassroots organizations like the American Land Rights Association, Defenders of Property Rights, and Stewards of the Range. The groups have sought to gain media attention for their cause, and have sought remedies in both the judicial and legislative arenas.[35]

The Supreme Court has not provided clear guidelines for determining when a taking has occurred and when compensation is due. There is little question that, when the government actually takes possession of land, fair compensation must be awarded the previous owner; the problem comes when government regulation places some limit on how property owners can use their land. The decisions of the Court send mixed signals concerning the difference between a compensable taking and a regulation that must be complied with by property owners. In some cases, if the government requires a physical intrusion, the Court has required compensation. The Court assesses the economic impact of a regulation in determining whether it crosses the line to become a taking. But the justices have been unable to decide on enduring principles. They have devised some criteria for assessing government actions, but the weight given each factor varies from case to case. Many decisions appear to be the result of a judgment about whether the Court concludes that a regulation serves an important public purpose and is valid or whether it is unjustifiably meddling in the affairs of landowners and is a taking.[36] Property rights activists have also pursued their cause in the U.S. Court of Federal Claims, which hears claims against the U.S. Treasury involving $10,000 or more. In two 1990 cases heard in this venue, the court seemed to indicate its willingness to expand compensation to property owners when all, or virtually all, viable economic use of the land is removed through federal regulation, such as that of the Clean Water Act permit requirements.[37]

In the legislative arena, activists have sought to gain protection for private property in both state legislatures and in Congress. One type of proposal, called "look before you leap," requires governments to assess the takings implications of laws, regulations, and other governmental actions. The bills seek to deter governments from taking actions that would require compensation to property owners, thus saving the government money. However, since there is no widely accepted definition of what constitutes a taking, the standards to be used are unsettled. A second type of legislative proposal (introduced in both state legislatures and as a part of the Republican Contract With America) would trigger compensation when a property's value is diminished by a specific percentage as a result of government regulation. Supporters have also sought a "takings impact analysis" similar to that called for under the National Environmental Policy Act. The concept was advanced in an executive order during the administration of President Ronald Reagan, and calls for an evaluation of whether or not a government regulation would deprive a property owner of the use of the land. But the proposals have been criticized by environmental groups who warned that such legislation would slow down the wheels of government regulation and would bankrupt the government.[38]

When takings proposals have been placed before the voters in state referendums, they have largely failed. The opposition to such measures is mainly a result of their projected costs and the likelihood that they will result in higher taxes. Opponents fear that takings regulations will become a "nightmare of dueling appraisers and dueling lawyers" who will argue over every analysis and every assessment, becoming an expensive new entitlement program that would have a chilling effect on environmental regulation.[39]

Environmental organizations have somewhat belatedly realized the potential impact of the property rights movement as it relates to public land use. Their lethargy may have been because much of the debate was being carried out in the courts, where the judicial wheels move slowly and the justices seldom make sweeping new judicial interpretations. But highly publicized cases, a flurry of state initiatives, and the changeover to a Republican-controlled Congress have mobilized environmental groups to monitor state and federal legislation more closely. So far, they appear to have been successful in confining property rights issues to the judicial arena where policymaking is more likely to be incremental and limited.

SUMMARY

The stewardship of America's public lands is exemplary of major policy shifts in the federal government's attitudes toward environmental protection. Initially, the government sought to dispose of millions of acres by selling them to homesteaders, a process that began in 1785. This policy not only encouraged expansion into the western frontier but also brought hard currency into the growing nation's coffers. During the Progressive Era and the blossoming of the conservation movement, the policy changed as attempts were made to preserve natural areas, especially during the development of the national park system. Today, the public lands debate flourishes on several fronts. For example, angry environmentalists believing western lands are being exploited by ranchers who graze their cattle on subsidized federal land and ranchers reacted during the late 1970s in the Sagebrush Rebellion. Another battle pits timber companies and their workers against those who believe agencies such as the U.S. Forest Service are no longer protecting either trees or the public interests. The National Park Service has come under fire by organizations who believe the program has expanded unnecessarily, and by those who feel the parks' infrastructure and staffing levels are deteriorating because of overuse and budget cuts. Among the most controversial of the public lands debate is the issue of property rights. Landowners are pressuring policymakers to enact legislation that would provide compensation when government regulations reduce property values through takings or other actions.

NOTES

1. Quoted in William Perry Pendley, *It Takes a Hero: The Grassroots Struggle against Environmental Oppression* (Bellevue, WA: Free Enterprise Press, 1994):87.
2. Denzel and Nancy Ferguson, *Sacred Cows at the Public Trough* (Bend, OR: Maverick Publications, 1983), 171–172.
3. George Wuerthner, "How the West Was Eaten," *Wilderness, 54,* no. 192 (Spring 1991): 28–37.
4. See Wesley Calef, *Private Grazing and Public Lands* (Chicago: University of Chicago Press, 1960); Phillip O. Foss, *Politics and Grass* (Seattle: University of Washington Press, 1960); and Gary D. Libecap, *Locking Up the Range* (Cambridge, MA: Ballinger, 1981).
5. See Phillip A. Davis, "Grazing Fee Increase OK'd by Interior Subcommittee," *Congressional Quarterly Weekly Report,* June 8, 1991, 1497.
6. George Wuerthner, "The Price is Wrong," *Sierra, 75,* no. 5 (September–October 1990): 38–43.
7. Rose Strickland, "Taking the Bull by the Horns," *Sierra, 75,* no. 5 (September–October 1990): 46–48.
8. See William Voigt, *Public Grazing Lands* (New Brunswick, NJ: Rutgers University Press, 1976).
9. Wuerthner, "How the West Was Eaten," 36.
10. William L. Graf, *Wilderness Preservation and the Sagebrush Rebellions* (Savage, MD: Rowman and Littlefield, 1990), 229.
11. Paul Rauber, "National Yard Sale," *Sierra* (September/October 1995): 28–33.

12. 104th Congress, H.R. 643.

13. 104th Congress, S 852, H.R. 1713.

14. 104th Congress, S. 1459.

15. For a map and listing of the NPS sites, see Paul Pritchard, "The Best Idea America Ever Had," *National Geographic, 80*, no. 2, (August 1991): 36–59.

16. National Parks and Conservation Association, *Investing in Park Futures, The National Park System Plan: A Blueprint for Tomorrow* (Washington, D.C.: 1988). The nine-volume study includes an executive summary of the organization's recommendations.

17. Robin W. Winks, "Debating Significance," *National Parks, 69*, no. 34 (March–April 1995): 24–25.

18. Randolph Harrison, "Protecting U.S. National Parks," *Environment, 32*, no. 1 (January–February 1990): 18–19.

19. The California Desert Protection Act, P.L. 103–433.

20. John H. Cushman, Jr., "Senate Approves Parks Bill after Deal on Alaskan Forest," *The New York Times,* October 3, 1996, A1.

21. Allan Freedman, "Long-Term Solutions Elusive for Stressed Park System," *Congressional Quarterly Weekly Report* (August 24, 1996): 2386–2389.

22. *Investing in Park Futures,* 11.

23. Tom Kenworthy, "Shhhhh! Park Ahead," *Washington Post National Weekly Edition* (August 19–25, 1996): 31.

24. The report is summarized in Freedman, "Long-Term Solutions Elusive for Stressed Park System," 2386–2387.

25. Dale Bumpers, "Profit from the Parks," *National Parks, 65,* nos. 3–4 (March–April 1991): 16–17.

26. Todd Wilkinson, "Undermining the Parks," *National Parks, 65,* nos. 1–2 (January–February 1991): 28–31.

27. Ibid., 31.

28. Tom Kenworthy, "It's No Day at the Beach for the National Park Service," *Washington Post National Weekly Edition,* April 13–19, 1992, 34.

29. Tom Kenworthy, "Burn Now or Burn Later," *Washington Post National Weekly Edition* (September 9–15, 1996): 31.

30. George P. Hartzog, Jr., *Battling for the National Parks* (Mt. Kisco, NY: Moyer Bell Limited, 1988). Hartzog served as director of the National Park Service from 1963 to 1972.

31. See Walter Rosenbaum, *Environmental Politics and Policy* (Washington, D.C.: Congressional Quarterly, 1991), 279–98.

32. Lisa J. Moore, "When Landowners Clash with the Law," *U.S. News & World Report,* April 6, 1992, 80–81.

33. *Pennsylvania Coal Co. V. Mahon,* 260 U.S. 393 (1922).

34. Richard Epstein, *Takings: Private Property and the Power of Eminent Domain* (Cambridge, MA: Harvard University Press, 1985).

35. For a discussion of the strategies used by property rights groups, see, Bruce Yandle, ed. *Land Rights: The 1990s' Property Rights Rebellion* (Lanham, MD: Rowman and Littlefield, 1995); John D. Echeverria and Raymond Booth Eby, eds., *Let the People Judge: Wise Use and the Private Property Rights Movement* (Washington, D.C.: Island Press, 1995); David Helvarg, *The War Against the Greens: The "Wise-Use Movement, the New Right, and Anti-Environmental Violence* (San Francisco: Sierra Club Books, 1994), and Jacqueline Vaughn Switzer, *Green Backlash: The History and Politics of Environmental Opposition in the U.S.* (Boulder, CO: Lynne Rienner, 1997).

36. The Court's actions are discussed by Roger W. Findley and Daniel A. Farber, *Environmental Law* (St. Paul, MN: West Publishing, 1992), 279–292.

37. See Karol J. Ceplo, "Land-Rights Conflicts in the Regulation of Wetlands," in Yandle, ed., *Land Rights,* 106.

38. See Patricia Byrnes, "Are We Being Taken By Takings?" *Wilderness, 58*, no. 208 (Spring 1995): 4–5; and Neal R. Peirce, "Takings—The Comings and Goings," *National Journal, 28* (January 6, 1996): 37.

39.   See Barbara Moulton, "Takings Legislation: Protection of Property Rights or Threat to the Public Interest?" *Environment, 37,* no. 2 (March 1995): 44–45.

FOR FURTHER READING

Philip D. Brick and R. McGreggor Cawley, eds. *A Wolf in the Garden: The Land Rights Movement and the New Environmental Debate.* Lanham, MD: Rowman and Littlefield, 1996.

Lynton Keith Caldwell and Kristin Schrader-Frechette. *Policy for Land: Law and Ethics.* Lanham, MD: Rowman and Littlefield, 1993.

Charles Davis, ed. *Western Public Lands and Environmental Politics.* Boulder, CO: Westview Press, 1996.

Henry L. Diamond and Patrick F. Noonan. *Land Use in America.* Cambridge, MA: Lincoln Institute of Land Management, 1996.

Robert H. Nelson. *Public Lands and Private Rights: The Failure of Scientific Management.* Lanham, MD: Rowman and Littlefield, 1995.

Frederick Wagner, et al., eds. *Wildlife Policies in the U.S. National Parks.* Washington, D.C.: Island Press, 1995.

Bruce Yandle. *Land Rights: The 1990s Property Rights Rebellion.* Lanham, MD: Rowman and Littlefield, 1995.

Dyan Zaslowsky and T. H. Watkins. *These American Lands: Parks, Wilderness, and the Public Lands.* rev. ed. Washington, D.C.: Island Press, 1994.

CHAPTER 5

Dilemmas of Waste and Cleanup: Super Mess and Superfund

We will not budge on the principle that big polluting companies should pay for cleanups.
—Carol Browner, EPA Administrator under President Bill Clinton[1]

In 1996, residents of Strasburg, Pennsylvania, learned firsthand how difficult it would be to get the federal government to pay attention to a problem that had been facing their community for years. Local officials were informed that a scheduled $10 million cleanup of a toxic waste dump in their area would be postponed because of a shortage of federal funds. The twenty-two-acre site, located in a wooded area thirty miles west of Philadelphia, had long been a popular area for dumping garbage and industrial waste. In the mid-1980s, state officials found toxic chemicals at the site and closed it down, with nearby residents concerned that rainwater might carry harmful chemicals into local wells and water supplies. The runoff from the area flows into rivers popular with local trout fishers and is a source of drinking water for communities downstream. The landfill is sometimes used as a playground by children and as hunting grounds by local residents who ignore the sturdy metal fencing surrounding it. In 1989, the dump was placed on a list of sites requiring cleanup under federal law, and after six years of study, the Environmental Protection Agency (EPA) decided that the landfill needed a new liner to keep chemicals from seeping through a cap and landscaping. But the citizens of Strasburg and the residents near fifty-four other sites scheduled for cleanup would have to wait for the government to find sufficient funds to begin work on the site under a federal program commonly known as Superfund.[2]

Over the past decade, the job of cleaning up humanity's mess, whether it be household garbage or radioactive material produced from nuclear power plants, has become a more visible and acute problem on the environmental policy agenda. In years past, the issue has literally and figuratively been buried at the bottom of the pile of environmental problems facing policymakers. Historically, we have simply covered up the refuse of life with dirt or dumped it where it was out of sight (and out of mind). Now, old habits are coming back to haunt us as we (1) produce more waste than ever before and (2) run out of places to put it.

This chapter explores the management of waste and the strategies that are being developed to try to deal with this ongoing and highly politicized problem. The discussion begins by identifying the various types of waste produced and what attempts have been made to deal with it. The main focus of the chapter is an analysis of the regulatory framework of waste management and the role of different levels of government that are grappling with a growing problem that has fewer resources for its solution. The chapter concludes with an overview of how the dilemmas experienced by the United States are being mirrored on a global scale, with the creation of international regimes to control the hazardous waste trade, and the difficulties of dealing with the contamination that has been discovered in Eastern Europe and the former Soviet Union.

THE NATURE OF WASTE: GENERATION AND DISPOSAL

Historians who have studied human development note that there has not always been a refuse problem, at least of the magnitude of modern times. Refuse is primarily an urban problem, exacerbated by limited space and dense populations. It must also be perceived to *be* a problem—understood to have a negative effect on human life—or else it will be viewed as an annoyance rather than as a health or environmental problem. That transition of perception occurred in the United States between 1880 and 1920, when the "garbage nuisance" was first recognized. City dwellers could no longer ignore the piles of garbage and the manure from horsecars that covered sidewalks and streets and polluted local waterways. A sense of community responsibility evolved as citizens developed an awareness of doing something about the problem. Garbage was seen not only as a health issue, but also as an aesthetic one, as it detracted from the overall attractiveness of city living. Gradually, municipal governments developed street cleaning and disposal programs (controlled by health officials and representatives of civic organizations) to begin to deal with the massive wastes generated by a growing industrial society.[3]

Just before the turn of the century, the United States imported one of the most common European methods of waste disposal, the "destructor," or garbage furnace. The British, with insufficient cheap land or water as dumping areas, had turned to incineration, which was hailed as a waste panacea. Cities throughout the United States quickly installed incinerators, while researchers continued to experiment with other European technologies such as extracting oil and other by-products through the compression of city garbage. During the first quarter of the twentieth century, the emphasis was on waste elimination, with little thought given to controlling the generation of waste. After World War I, however, the growth of the American economy changed the refuse situation with a dramatic increase in the manufacture of packaging materials—plastics, paper, and synthetics—which became a part of the waste stream. This not only increased the amount of waste, but posed new collection and disposal problems for local governments. One researcher estimates that solid waste increased about five times as rapidly as population increased after World War I. The most dramatic change in the composition of waste was the massive increase in the proportion of paper, which by 1975 accounted for nearly half of all municipal refuse. This increase is attributed to rampant consumerism during the 1970s, which fostered a boom in the packaging industry.[4] An even more pervasive waste problem emerged after World Wars I and II with the tremendous increase in chemical products, which were being discharged into the air, water, or land.

The Universe of Wastes

Waste is a generic term used to describe material that has no obvious or significant economic or other benefit to humans. Waste includes five major categories of materials that differ in their physical properties and origins.[5]

The largest component of the waste stream is industrial waste, which is nonhazardous and is generated by activities such as manufacturing, mining, coal combustion, and oil and gas production. It makes up nearly 94 percent of the waste universe. The second largest segment—about 5 percent—is hazardous waste, which is primarily generated by industry and which meets a specific legal definition. It comes under federal regulations because it poses a serious threat to human health or the environment if not handled properly. Sometimes the terms *toxic waste* and *hazardous waste* are used interchangeably, but this is not technically correct. *Toxicity* refers to a substance's ability to cause harm, and thus all waste could conceivably come under that definition. Since some wastes present only a minimal amount of harm if stored or disposed of properly, they are not considered hazardous. To be considered hazardous, waste must meet four criteria: the potential to ignite or cause a fire; the potential to corrode; the potential to explode or generate poisonous gases; and the capability to be sufficiently toxic to health. Federal regulations also classify as hazardous any other wastes mixed with hazardous waste, as well as by-products of the treatment of hazardous waste. According to the EPA, 65 percent of all hazardous wastes produced in the United States in 1993 was generated in five states: Texas, Tennessee, Louisiana, Michigan, and New Jersey.[6]

The problem of handling hazardous waste has become acute because waste generating industries in the past were often unaware or unconcerned about the potential toxic effects of hazardous waste. Dangerous chemicals may percolate from holding ponds into underlying ground water or wash over the ground into surface water and wetlands. Some hazardous waste evaporates into the air or explodes, other types soak into the soil and contaminate the ground, and some forms bioaccumulate in plants and animals that might be consumed later by humans. Typical hazardous wastes include dioxin, petroleum, lead, and asbestos.

The third element of waste, composing about 1 percent, is municipal solid waste (MSW), the garbage and trash generated by households, offices, and similar facilities. Americans deserve their reputation for being a "throwaway society" since they produce more than twice the consumer trash of any other industrialized nation. Much of our waste comes from the packaging of products that we use daily such as aluminum cans, cardboard boxes, cellophane, plastic jugs, and glass bottles, but it also includes less obvious waste such as abandoned appliances, junked automobiles, and used tires.

The EPA's estimates of the amount of municipal solid waste likely to be generated in the future are staggering. Without source reduction (reducing the volume of waste material before it enters the waste stream initially), the amount of waste generated by the year 2000 will be 216 million tons, or 4.4 pounds per person per day. By 2010, the figure jumps to 250 million tons, or 4.9 pounds per person per day.[7]

The last two types of waste are medical and radioactive wastes, each of which make up less than one-tenth of one percent of the waste stream. Hospitals and other medical and dental facilities generate more than a half million tons per year of waste that must be specially managed. This type of waste gained considerable attention in the late 1980s when miles of beaches in New Jersey and New York had to be closed when improperly handled syringes and vials of blood began washing ashore. There was considerable media attention on the problem because it became linked to fear about the spread of the acquired immunodeficiency syndrome (AIDS).

Radioactive waste includes fuel used in nuclear reactors, spent fuel from weapons production, and mill tailings from the processing of uranium ore. This category also includes substances that have become contaminated by radiation, either directly or accidentally. There are various levels of radioactive waste and regulations on its handling.

Americans produce more solid waste than do people in other wealthy countries. The average American produces just over 4 pounds per day of waste. The number of kilograms of waste produced per person per year in industralized countries ranges as follows:

1. United States   730[8]
2. Canada   660
3. France   470
4. Japan   410
5 Switzerland   400
6. Germany   360
7. Great Britain   350
8. Italy   350

Disposing of the Problem

Primitive cultures had an easy answer to disposal—they simply left it where they created it. Leftover or spoiled food and excrement were allowed to rot on the ground, where they naturally decomposed and returned to the earth as fertilizing compost, completing the naturally occurring ecological cycle. Aside from odors and foraging wildlife, waste did not pose much of a problem until it got in the way of other human activities. As the population grew, people began to burn their waste or bury it in the ground—practices that have remained unchanged throughout most of our history. The method of disposal now used depends in large part on what type of waste is being managed, as the following overview indicates.

Burial and Landfills   Dumping and burial have been among the most common ways of disposing of municipal waste, although communities have developed sanitary landfills as a way of avoiding the environmental problems caused by burial. The number of landfills declined as the federal government began regulating waste disposal in the 1960s and dropped further in 1979 when the EPA issued minimum criteria for landfill management. One of the biggest concerns over landfill operation has been pollution; since most landfills accept whatever household garbage is collected by waste haulers, there is often little screening of what gets dumped. As a result, landfills may contain a variety of substances, including paints, solvents, and toxic chemicals, that residents routinely put into their curbside trash. In older landfills, leachate (formed when water from rain or the waste itself percolates through the landfill) sometimes seeps into the ground, polluting the surrounding groundwater. Today's sanitary landfills, in contrast, are located on land where the risk of seepage is minimal, and most facilities are lined with layers of clay and plastic. A complex series of pipes and pumping equipment collects and distills the leachate and vents flammable methane gas, which is formed by the decomposition of waste. Many landfills now recover the gas and distribute it to customers or use it to generate electricity.

In the 1980s, there was considerable attention focused on the problem of landfill capacity. Projections warned that only 20 percent of the landfills in operation in 1986 would be open in the year 2008, despite increasing amounts of waste. As a result of this shortage of landfill space, the cost of disposal rose astronomically. The shortage occurred because the criteria for what becomes an acceptable disposal site changed, making it difficult to increase either the number or capacity of burial facilities. Historically, the key criterion for landfill operation was accessibility, but that gradually changed to a goal of minimizing health risks. By the 1930s, the United States switched from open dumping to sanitary landfills, which involves the compaction and burying of waste. Most cities established their landfills in the most inexpensive and accessible land available, which typically was a gravel pit, or wetland, with little attention given to environmental considerations. With the advent of the environmental movement in the 1960s and 1970s, planners began to consider whether a proposed site was near a residential area, was susceptible to natural phenomena such as earthquakes or flooding, or was a potential threat to water quality; they also considered the hauling distance from where the refuse was collected. Disposal costs today increase by as much as a dollar per ton for every mile the garbage is transported. Today's landfill operations are tightly regulated by federal restrictions that govern the location, design, operating and closure requirements, and cleanup standards for existing contamination. It is important to note that many of those restrictions were added only because of the political pressure of environmental organizations. An example is a 1994 settlement between the EPA and the Sierra Club.

The number of municipal solid waste landfills declined from more than 16,000 in 1976 to about 3,500 in 1995, as small facilities have been closed or consolidated. However, the capacity of landfills has increased, and by the mid-1990s, some reports began to identify surplus waste disposal capacity, as the competition for lucrative contracts increased the supply of facilities. There are even occasional conflicts between local recycling programs and efforts to maintain waste volumes in solid waste facilities to protect profits.[9]

Incineration   Many European nations have been successful at instituting waste incineration programs to deal with municipal waste. Their modern facilities produce minimal levels of visible emissions and have the added advantage of generating electricity as a by-product. The United States, in contrast, since the first garbage furnace was installed in 1885 on Governor's Island, New York, has been unsuccessful in convincing either policymakers or its citizens of the acceptability of incineration as a disposal method.

Incineration was initially accepted as a disposal method because it was considered the most sanitary and economical method available. Modifications of the European technology proved ineffective, however, for U.S. needs. Sanitation engineers became critical of the facilities, which often produced gas and smoke emissions because the waste was not completely burned when furnace temperatures were lowered to save on fuel consumption. Beyond design and operational problems, many of the incinerators were built by unscrupulous or inexperienced companies, and by 1909, 102 of the 180 furnaces erected between 1885 and 1908 had been abandoned or dismantled. Later adaptations of English technology produced a second generation of incinerators, and the facilities flourished until the 1960s. At that point, concerns about air pollution surfaced, and cities such as Los Angeles began to legislate against incinerators, setting standards so high that they virtually outlawed the plants. Although the technology was available to increase efficiency and reduce polluting emissions, the cost of upgrading equipment was high in comparison to disposal in sanitary landfills.[10]

There is still some support for incineration as a concept, especially among those who note the advantage of reducing the volume of waste or view the capacity of the incinerator as an energy generator. Critics argue that, even with improved technology, many facilities have suffered from mechanical breakdowns and costly repairs, and attempts to transfer European incineration technology to the United States have often been unsuccessful because American trash contains considerably more plastic that, when burned, produces toxic gases and leads to corrosion of equipment. Even plants that run efficiently are being closely scrutinized for adverse health effects. Environmental groups have raised questions about the toxicity of both the gases and the ash produced by the combustion process.

Despite these objections and problems, officials are taking a second look at waste-to-energy plants for MSW. Most of the plants are called "mass burn" facilities because they use unsegregated waste as a fuel, producing electricity that can then be sold to customers. Refuse-derived fuel plants remove materials that can be recycled from the waste stream, such as plastics and glass, and shred the remaining components, which are then burned in boilers. They have several advantages over other municipal disposal options because they require no change in waste collection patterns, their management can be turned over to a private owner if desired, low-cost financing mechanisms are available, and the market for the electricity they produce is guaranteed under the 1978 Public Utilities Regulatory Policies Act.[11]The EPA projects that combustion will increase significantly as a waste management strategy, accounting for over half of the disposal of MSW by 2000.[12]

Public opposition to incineration has proved to be the most formidable barrier to siting any new facilities,[13] ending projects throughout the United States, from the LANCER facility in Los Angeles to the Brooklyn Navy Yard, where opponents promised to block a proposed incinerator with their bodies. New Jersey residents even rejected a referendum on the state's ballot over an incinerator that had been planned and approved for a decade. Political leaders have found the topic so volatile that it has created an acronym of its own—NIMTOO—for "Not In My Term of Office." The phrase refers to the virtual paralysis over waste management decision making that keeps municipal officials from approving incineration projects in favor of more expensive disposal solutions.[14] The situation is different from that of Europe, where incineration has been more widely accepted. The difference lies perhaps in the contrast of political systems. Nations such as Denmark and Germany have a strong history of centralized decision making, which precludes the kinds of public participation and access to the legal system that allows citizens in the United States to have such an impact on decisions such as siting of hazardous waste facilities.

Ocean Dumping   The dumping of wastes into the ocean is one of the few disposal methods that has received almost universal condemnation. The initial objections to the practice were not necessarily environmental—too much of the garbage dumped off the New York coast in the early 1900s floated back to shore. The practice was also considered too costly, since barges had to tow the garbage to deep water to keep it from floating back to the surface and washing up on local beaches. As downstream cities filed lawsuits against upstream cities, the legal ramifications of dumping municipal waste into waterways limited the practice as well. Burial of waste seemed much more attractive and inexpensive to early sanitation engineers by the 1920s. In 1933, New Jersey coastal cities went to court to force New York City to halt ocean dumping. A ruling was affirmed by the U.S. Supreme Court in 1934, when the practice of ocean dumping of MSW ceased as a major means of disposal.

The Supreme Court ruling applied only to municipal waste, and the ocean dumping of industrial and commercial waste continued unabated. By the end of the 1960s, an estimated fifty million tons of waste were dumped into the ocean, most of it off the East Coast, where the rate doubled between 1959 and 1968. In the mid-1970s, there were nearly 120 ocean sites for waste disposal supervised by the U.S. Coast Guard. Of particular concern has been the use of ocean dumping for toxic wastes.[15] Not until passage of the Marine Protection, Research, and Sanctuaries Act in 1972 was there a federal effort to stop the practice, followed by the Ocean Dumping Ban Act in 1988, which restricted offshore dumping of sewage sludge and other wastes.

The ocean depths have also been considered as sites for the burial of radioactive waste, and for more than a dozen years, the United States was part of an eight-nation, $100 million research effort that had considerable scientific support. But the issue was so politically sensitive that the research program was cut off as Congress focused on geological storage instead.[16]

Recycling   The terms *recycling* and *recovery* refer to the reuse of materials, and most waste management analysts believe recycling represents one of the most underused yet promising strategies for waste disposal.[17] There are two aspects of recycling: primary recycling, in which the original material is made back into the same material and is also recyclable (such as newspapers back into newspapers); and secondary recycling, in which products are made into other products that may or may not be recyclable (such as cereal boxes made out of waste paper). Recycling gained acceptance in the early 1970s as the public became more aware of the garbage crisis, the need to conserve natural resources, and the shortage of landfill space. About 7 percent of the MSW was recovered in the 1960s and 1970s, and then increased gradually during the 1980s to about 17 percent today, although the rate varies from one community to another.

Recycling is actually less an environmental issue than it is an extremely volatile economic supply and demand issue. A shortage of markets for recycled goods represents the biggest obstacle to this waste management approach. During the early 1970s, recycling gained acceptance not only in the public's mind but economically as well. Rising costs of land disposal and incineration made recycling a booming business. Junked autos, worthless a few years before, were bringing up to $50 each, and prices for copper scrap rose 100 percent. Lead batteries became profitable recycling targets when the price of battery lead rose fourfold. Under President Richard Nixon, the federal government considered providing tax credits and direct cash subsidies to encourage the sale of recycled materials, but a 1974 EPA report recommended that such incentives were unnecessary because demand for recycling was high and prices were rising. Some states sought their own forms of monetary incentives, for example, Oregon, which pioneered a bottle-deposit law in 1972. The federal subsidy and incentive concepts never gained acceptance in Congress, however, and were not revived by President Gerald Ford when he assumed office after Nixon's resignation. Unfortunately for the future of recycling, prices collapsed in 1974 as quickly as they had risen, with waste paper prices dropping from $60 per ton in March 1974 to $5 by mid-1975.[18]

During the late 1980s and early 1990s, supplies of newspapers, cans, plastic, and glass began to pile up when communities and individuals believed they might be able to squeeze cash from trash, even when there were few markets for recycled goods. As demand for recycled goods increased, in some communities "recycling bandits" were taking newspapers out of curbside containers in the middle of the night or yanking it out of landfills. By 1995, 43 percent of all the paper consumed in the United States that was suitable for recycling made its way back to paper mills for reuse. The recycling of plastics, however, has not been nearly as successful. In 1994, the Society of the Plastics Industry announced it was phasing out the symbols it had used on plastic containers to help consumers understand what types were recyclable because most plastic cannot be recycled back into more plastic. Usually, the plastic must be shredded and used in other products. When a drought in China and India severely reduced cotton production, waste companies found a market for plastic fiber because overseas firms and American clothing manufacturers liked the fiber and continued to use it, causing the price of used plastic bottles to rise.[19] One clothing manufacturer, Patagonia, manufactured a polyester sweater completely made from used soda bottles, and Deja Shoe makes casual footwear from used tire rubber and plastic soda bottles.

Some analysts believe that there may be a link between recycling and the economy, termed the recycling-bin index. In 1995, for example, prices for scrap paper soared, peaking at $240 a ton as a result of confidence about the economy and a strong market for finished paper products. But by 1996, the price was about $35 per ton, with many paper makers cutting back production.[20] The problem is compounded further by consumer reluctance to absorb the higher cost of recycled materials and fears about a slumping economy, which reduces paper sales and makes manufacturers reluctant to build new mills capable of processing used paper and cardboard.

There are several ways in which recycling can be made more attractive to both consumers and recyclers. The most obvious is to boost the demand to create an appetite for the swollen supply of materials, or apply sanctions against those who use virgin material. In 1992, for example, the Bush administration took the incentive route by directing all federal agencies to purchase environmentally sound supplies, including those made of recycled materials, and several states have enacted similar legislation. Other approaches have included providing tax incentives for new recycling operations, mandating commercial recycling, recycling organic waste, and inverting rate structures for residential waste collection, with the price increasing with the number of trash cans collected at curbside. Nearly every state requires newspaper publishers to use some recycled fiber in their paper. Others have invested money into facilities that turn old newspapers into usable pulp in a process called de-inking,[21] so publishers have pushed their suppliers to increase demand.

Is recycling a viable waste disposal alternative in the United States? Recycling programs in America have not been nearly as successful as programs in other parts of the world. Even though other countries do not produce nearly the amounts of waste as does the United States, recycling is much more commonly used in other countries. Deposits on beverage containers are almost universally used, and more reverse vending machines (where returned containers are accepted) are common in Europe. Source separation programs are in place throughout Western Europe and Japan, and even in developing nations like Egypt and Thailand, institutionalized scavenging and recycling programs are fully operational.[22] The effectiveness of recycling in the United States appears to be largely dependent upon the way in which the programs are implemented. A national survey of 450 municipal recycling programs found several characteristics common to successful recycling efforts. The most successful voluntary efforts were in cities with clear, challenging goals for recycling a specific proportion of their waste stream, curbside pickup, free bins, private collection services, and compost programs. Mandatory recycling programs were most successful when they included the ability to issue sanctions or warnings for improper separation. In both types of programs, the highest participation was in cities that employed experienced recycling coordinators.[23] What all this means is that there are still a number of obstacles to be overcome before recycling—despite its inherent attractiveness—can be considered more than a supplemental answer to the solid waste dilemma.

Storage   There are two conditions in which storage tends to become the most viable alternative to managing waste. Some reclamation facilities will keep material until market conditions improve. Many of the companies that collect newspaper for recycling will hold their supplies in warehouses until demand increases and prices recover, perhaps when exports go back up or supplies at paper mills dwindle. For example, four Long Island, New York, towns that were unable to find a buyer for their used newspapers stashed 1,200 tons into an airplane hanger until a fire marshal declared it a hazard.

Storage is also used for the handling of hazardous and radioactive waste, with the goal of isolating the material until it no longer poses a threat to humans or the environment. Among the more politicized waste management problems is the "back end" of the nuclear fuel cycle—the storage of solids, liquids, gases, and sludges, which must be treated to remove contaminants or diluted to reduce their toxicity and then stored.

Radioactive waste decays at varying rates, so different types of disposal are needed for different types of waste. Although low-level radioactive waste can safely be stored in containers that are buried in shallow trenches, researchers have looked at several alternatives for high-level radioactive waste. Under the provisions of the 1982 Nuclear Waste Policy Act, the Department of Energy (DOE) is required to assume ownership of the waste in 1998 and store it in a permanent underground repository or in a temporary, above-ground site to be used only until the permanent one is ready. After years of debate over where the repository would be located, in 1987 Congress directed that the DOE focus on one site, Yucca Mountain, Nevada. State officials and the Nevada congressional delegation have protested the siting ever since, joined by environmental organizations and some scientists who believe the location is unsafe. In March, 1996, the Senate Energy and Natural Resources Committee passed a bill that would have created an interim high-level nuclear waste facility next to Yucca Mountain, Nevada. The Clinton administration and Nevada Senators opposed the legislation. The administration preferred instead the selection of a permanent site in Yucca Mountain but believed that site requires additional testing that will not be completed until 1998 or 1999.[24] The DOE expects that the waste will remain dangerous for ten thousand years, and its own staffers admit that there could be a massive leakage of radioactivity as a result of any number of factors, ranging from leaking storage containers to volcanic activity. Overwhelming public and political opposition (including passage of a 1989 bill by the Nevada legislature forbidding any government agency from storing high-level radioactive waste anywhere in the state) is compounded by reports that Yucca Mountain's facility cannot be ready before 2010, despite that over $4 billion has been spent thus far simply studying the site.[25] For the short term, utility companies are storing spent fuel at existing nuclear power plant sites (which are nearing capacity) while DOE looks for military bases and nuclear weapons factories for temporary storage to comply with the law.

Source Reduction   The reduction of the amount of toxicity of garbage, more commonly known as source reduction, is now viewed as the most likely contribution to the solution of the global waste problem. Source reduction's benefits are twofold. It decreases the amount of waste that must be managed and preserves natural resources and reduces pollution generated during the manufacturing and packaging process. The Pollution Prevention Act of 1990 required the EPA to develop and implement a strategy to promote source reduction. All the states have some kind of pollution prevention program, but only a few states have adopted source reduction goals while almost all have recycling goals.[26]

Source reduction relies largely on behavioral changes, and some corporations have begun to reduce the amount of waste they generate, as models for residential consumers. AT&T, for example, reduces office paper waste by promoting double-sided copying; the Seattle-based Rainier Brewing Company began buying back and refilling its beer bottles in 1990; Toyota Motor Manufacturing switched to standardized reusable shipping containers, which save the company millions of dollars each year.[27] While business works actively to promote source reduction, consumers are gradually showing retailers that they are interested in purchasing products with reduced packaging.

THE POLITICAL RESPONSE

Unlike some environmental protection issues where the federal government has assumed primary responsibility, waste management regulations are usually locally enacted and implemented. The issue is complicated by the fact that neither policymakers nor the public initially considered waste to be a serious problem, especially hazardous waste, making it difficult to push the issue onto the policy agenda. Some observers believe that the problem is not garbage per se, but improper management of hazardous waste, litter, and uncontrolled dumping.[28]

There are three major pieces of federal legislation that underscore the government's "hands off" policy toward waste that has dumped the problem in the hands of local government. Initially, the focus of regulation was on the problem considered the most visible—solid waste. In 1965, Congress passed the Solid Waste Disposal Act (SWDA), designed to offer financial and technical assistance to local governments rather than for regulatory purposes. The federal Bureau of Solid Waste Management, housed in the Department of Health, Education and Welfare, had jurisdiction over solid waste, but shared responsibility with the Bureau of Mines in the Department of the Interior. The agencies were underfunded and suffered from heavy personnel turnover, with the Bureau of Solid Waste Management moving its headquarters three times in five years. Creation of the Environmental Protection Agency in 1970 led to a consolidation of agency responsibilities, coinciding with the passage of amendments to the SWDA—the Resource Recovery Act of 1970. The legislation authorized a fourteenfold increase in funding, from $17 million to $239 million, for demonstration grants for recycling systems and for studies of methods to encourage resource recovery. The 1970 legislation also provided the foundation for the development of state waste management programs, and by 1975, forty-eight states had developed some form of program, with budgets ranging from zero to $1.2 million. Most of the state waste management programs were minimal, structuring themselves around the federal support programs rather than using federal assistance to help them develop a more comprehensive effort, and the statute remained essentially nonregulatory.[29]

With the passage of the Resource Conservation and Recovery Act in 1976 (RCRA) Congress intruded into what had been essentially local and state jurisdiction.[30] The RCRA required states to develop solid waste management plans and mandated the closing of all open dumps. The only disposal methods allowed under the legislation were sanitary landfills or recycling, with little attention paid to other potentially effective options such as a bottle deposit or waste recovery facilities. Another portion of the RCRA dealt with hazardous waste management, but gave the EPA the responsibility of determining what waste was solid and what part was hazardous—a task that is not as easy as it might have seemed to Congress at the time the legislation was enacted.

One of the problems faced by some local officials is that there simply is not enough landfill space available in their area to dispose of wastes properly, and despite the RCRA legislation, many states were slow to develop alternatives. In other states, there is a surplus of landfill capacity. As a result, communities turned to exporting their waste to other states. In a 1978 case involving Philadelphia and New Jersey, the U.S. Supreme Court ruled that attempts by the states to restrict interstate transfers of waste violated the Commerce Clause of the Constitution.[31] The Supreme Court reiterated that position in two 1992 cases, and as a result, there was little that states with plenty of landfill space—such as Indiana and New Mexico—could do to stop other states' dumping. Under the court's ruling, state and local governments cannot ban, impose restrictions on, or place surcharges on solid waste simply on the basis of its origin. Publicly owned facilities, however, can restrict the solid waste that they accept to waste generated within the state.[32]

In the 1980s, Congress seemed to have difficulty developing hazardous waste legislation that was acceptable to both the industries that produced the waste and environmental group supporters who believed the issue was not receiving appropriate attention from federal and state regulators. The 1980 amendments to the RCRA allowed for broad exemptions to what was considered hazardous waste, and another set of amendments in 1984 still failed to remedy earlier deficiencies in the law. The RCRA expired in 1988, with several states still unable to complete the solid waste management plans required by the 1976 law. Congress chose to rely upon the EPA to "regulate solutions" to hazardous waste while Congress itself seemed more interested in dealing with MSW problems.[33]

Congressional attempts to pass a sweeping reauthorization of RCRA have been unsuccessful, as the continuing legislative gridlock over solid waste demonstrates Congress has repeatedly rejected a national bottle deposit system, avoided the issue of industrial wastes from manufacturing and mining, and rolled back industry wide recycling rates for paper and plastic. Both business and environmental groups have opposed most reauthorization efforts thus far because proposed legislation neither promotes enough recycling nor creates markets for recycled materials.

Policymaking is often triggered when specific events capture the attention to both the media and the public, and this is especially true of hazardous waste. As discussed in Chapter 1, disclosure of massive contamination at Love Canal in New York and at a site near Louisville, Kentucky, was the catalyst for a change in the regulatory focus. Citizens began contacting their representatives in Congress, demanding that some form of action be taken, and Congress turned toward the EPA for guidance on what type of legislative remedies might be available. Both Congress and the EPA did an environmental policy about-face by shifting their attention from solid to hazardous and toxic waste. Shortly after the RCRA's passage in 1976, the EPA's Office of Solid Waste, facing political pressures from citizens' groups and public concerns for immediate action, abruptly changed focus, and with the election of Ronald Reagan, the federal solid waste effort was completely eclipsed by hazardous waste concerns. The EPA's solid waste budget was reduced from $29 million in 1979 to $16 million in 1981 to $320,000 in 1982, while staff was reduced from 128 to 74 in 1981, with 73 of those 74 positions eliminated in 1982.[34] The RCRA's hazardous waste provisions require permits for companies storing, treating, or disposing of hazardous waste and gives EPA the authority to levy fines or hold individuals criminally liable for improperly disposed waste. This created a "cradle to grave" program by which EPA regulates hazardous wastes from the time they are generated to the time of disposal. However, attempts to amend the RCRA to require private developers and government officials to prepare "community information statements" to deal with the environmental justice issues related to the demographics of the communities in which hazardous waste sites are located have failed.[35]

Abandoned waste sites became an extremely visible problem that forced Congress to revamp the regulatory provisions of the RCRA with the enactment in 1980 of the Comprehensive Environmental Response, Compensation and Liability Act (CERCLA), more commonly known as Superfund. The CERCLA legislation initially included a $1.6 billion appropriation to clean up abandoned toxic and hazardous waste sites throughout the United States.[36] But further research indicated that the number and magnitude of site cleanups was much larger than originally estimated. Realizing the long-term nature of waste cleanup, Congress reauthorized the program for another five years under the 1986 Superfund Amendments and Reauthorization Act (SARA). Legislators were dissatisfied with the slow pace of cleanup (only six sites had been cleaned up since 1980), so the SARA added $8.5 billion to the fund, and in 1990, Congress voted to continue the program an additional five years with another $5.1 billion. Oil and chemical companies were also taxed to augment the Congressional appropriation, but that provision of the law was allowed to expire at the end of 1995, further reducing the program's operating budget. Members of Congress were unable to decide the thorny issue of how to finance the program, with debate over how much of a site's cleanup costs should be paid for by government and how much should be paid for by private companies.[37]

Under Superfund, the EPA established a National Priorities List (NPL) of targeted sites, a relatively small subset of a larger inventory of tens of thousands of potential hazardous waste sites. Cleanup projects vary considerably from site to site, ranging from an abandoned steel mill to small parcels of land where toxic waste was once stored and leaked into the ground. The majority of sites are landfills, industrial lagoons, and manufacturing sites. Most of the nation's hazardous waste is treated or disposed of on-site with only a small percentage transported off-site for treatment, storage, or disposal. This avoids the problems associated with transporting waste and trying to find a place to take it once it has been removed. Congress also dealt with the cleanup problem under the corrective action program of the RCRA amendments. The legislation requires companies who are permitted to operate a hazardous waste treatment, storage, or disposal facility to also be responsible for the cleanup of that facility. Unlike Superfund, where the federal government must find the responsible party, RCRA permittees must themselves submit a cleanup plan.

Underground storage tanks present an additional hazardous waste problem because they may leak and contaminate drinking water supplies. The United States is estimated to have over two million underground tanks that store petroleum and other chemicals, and the EPA estimates 20 percent of the regulated tanks are leaking or have the potential to leak. Many of the tanks were installed during the 1950s, and the average lifetime use is only fifteen to twenty years. The EPA began regulating the tanks in 1984 under the RCRA amendments, requiring owners and operators to meet strict requirements for design, construction, and installation, including repair or closure of systems that do not meet federal guidelines. The EPA estimates that $50 billion will be spent on underground storage tank cleanup, called the "sleeping giant," by the end of the decade, far more than the cost of cleaning up Superfund sites.[38] In 1986, Congress established a $500 million Leaking Underground Storage Tank Trust Fund to be used by states for cleanup costs. The fund is supported by a one-tenth of a cent federal tax on certain petroleum products, primarily motor fuels. Tanks were also covered under a section of SARA that requires owners to maintain sufficient financial reserves or insurance to cover damages stemming from accidental leaks.[39]

The Superfund program has come under tremendous criticism ever since its inception, giving Congress ample reason to avoid or delay reauthorization and providing justification for cutting the program's budget. The implementation of the law has been much slower than originally anticipated as a result of budget cuts, so fewer sites have been cleaned up than the EPA had planned. In 1995 there were about 1,300 sites on the NPL, based on the quantity and toxicity of the wastes involved, the number of people potentially or actually exposed, the likely pathways of exposure, and the importance and vulnerability of the underlying supply of groundwater, with about 100 sites added to the NPL each year. Only about 350 of the sites had actually been cleaned up, although remediation was under way at more than 90 percent of the NPL locations. The remediation cost per site has soared, with an average of $30 million spent on each one in recent years. No one really knows how much the program will eventually cost, with estimates ranging from a half billion dollars to as much as one trillion dollars over the next fifty years.[40]

Another criticism relates to who ought to be responsible for paying for the cleanup. Congress has been divided on the issue of whether to revise the "polluter pays" concept, which involves extensive research and often costly litigation as to who originally created the waste. Industry has balked at one of the key components of the legislation, known as joint and several retroactive liability, which makes polluting companies responsible for the entire cost of cleaning up sites where wastes were dumped decades ago, even if they were responsible for only a portion of the contamination or before dumping was made illegal. Some legislators have sought to exempt small businesses from cleanup liability, arguing that Superfund regulations place an unfair burden on those firms that are least able to afford cleanup costs.[41]

Compensation for individuals seeking to recover damage claims has been equally contentious. Congress continues to be heavily lobbied—a lobbying effort led by the Chemical Manufacturers' Association (CMA)—to make it difficult for an individual to bring legal action against a company believed to be responsible for the improper storage or handling of hazardous waste. Proving that a site caused health problems leads to a complex legal maze from which few plaintiffs successfully emerge. A number of obstacles face those victims seeking compensation because of toxic waste problems, including that many chemical-caused illnesses have a long latency period (perhaps twenty to thirty years), making the assessment of the effects of exposure difficult. Some state laws provide that the statute of limitations begins with the first date of exposure, limiting claims by those exposed over long term. In addition, hazardous waste injuries require potential claimants to submit to (and pay for) sophisticated and expensive medical and toxicological testing and to pay legal fees that may extend for years. Class-action suits are difficult to pursue because, even if a group of workers were exposed to a chemical hazard, the effects on one worker, a forty-year-old male, is likely to be considerably different from the effect on a twenty-four-year-old female of childbearing age. Not surprisingly, potential industrial defendants have opposed attempts to legislate ways of easing the compensation process.[42]

Other problems with CERCLA cleanups pose serious challenges. Many sites are operated by companies that go bankrupt before cleanup begins or are otherwise unable to pay for remediation. One estimate of the extent of this problem concluded that between 25 and 30 percent of the current land disposal facilities will enter bankruptcy during the next 50 years.[43] Another concern is that more and more cities and towns will become responsible for cleaning up hazardous waste sites. Incineration of hazardous wastes may pose serious health risks from the resultant emissions of hazardous air pollutants. The EPA has estimated that about 25 percent of the sites on the NPL involve waste sites owned or operated by municipalities.[44] This figure may eventually grow to 50 percent.[45]

In response to the criticism of the cost of the Superfund program, the Clinton administration prepared House and Senate bills that were introduced early in 1994. The Administration's bills would have set uniform standards for site cleanups; encouraged proportional distribution of costs; used arbitration rather than litigation in settling disputes; used federal funds to pay for cleanups when responsible parties could not be held liable, rather than making other parties pay the balance; and established a new fund to pay environmental insurance fund.[46] The bills had been fashioned in consultation with representatives from industry, environmental and community groups, and local governments under the National Commission on Superfund. The House Energy and Commerce Committee reported out the bill in May, with no major changes. The House Public Works and Transportation Committee added a requirement that cleanups using federal funds be governed by the Davis-Bacon Act, so that contractors were required to pay the prevailing wage rate. Senators threatened to refuse to join a conference committee if that provision remained, but House leaders were unable to remove the amendment or to deal with the more than 50 amendments offered to the bill, including major changes such as eliminating retroactive liability for companies that disposed of materials before Superfund was passed in 1980. Environmentalists pressured Congress to include groundwater decontamination requirements in the law. Advocates of cost:benefit analysis insisted that provision be added to the law as well. The Senate failed to take action, preferring to wait and see if the House would be able to pass a bill. The House stopped work on the bill a few days before adjournment in October 1994.

Superfund was a major target of reform by Republicans in the 104th Congress. Senate Republicans proposed repealing liability for dumping of hazardous wastes before 1987, modifying the liability system, limiting natural resource damages, capping the number of new sites added to the NPL, requiring cost:benefit and least cost tests for remediation standards, and delegating to states responsibility for cleanup of Superfund sites including those located on federal land. House Republicans had a similar set of proposals.[47] The House Commerce subcommittee reported a Superfund reform bill out in November 1993 that included new exemptions from liability for waste dumped at municipal landfills, a 50 percent rebate for cleanup costs incurred where wastes had been dumped before 1987, and other major changes.[48] Some progress was made in 1996 to fashion a bipartisan bill, but members were unable to resolve many of the contentious issues that had plagued Superfund reform for years.

Another difficult policy issue is how to handle the hazardous material produced by military bases, which often disposed of solvents, dead batteries, dirty oil, unexploded shells and bombs, and other wastes by dumping them on site and contaminating the underlying water or soil. In the 1980s, the Department of Defense was estimated to be generating five hundred thousand tons of toxic waste per year, more than the top five U.S. chemical companies combined. One agency report identified nearly twenty thousand sites at eighteen hundred military installations that showed varying levels of contamination, nearly a hundred of which warranted placement on the NPL. For years, under the guise of national security, the Department of Defense considered itself exempt from environmental legislation, even though President Jimmy Carter signed an executive order in 1978 demanding that all federal facilities comply with environmental regulations. That order was not enforced by the EPA during the Reagan administration when policy shifted toward a buildup of military strength and a relaxing of environmental standards. Although additional attempts at getting the military to comply were made by both George Bush and Bill Clinton during their administrations, the Department of Defense has been slow or reluctant to adhere to laws like the 1992 Federal Facilities Compliance Act as it applied to arms productions facilities and military bases. Some observers believe the sites may be too contaminated to ever be cleaned up.[49]

In addition, the country must find a way to dispose of five decades of waste produced by the seventeen principal and one hundred secondary weapons factories left over from the nuclear arms race. Observers have expressed shock at the lack of attention paid to the environmental impact caused by the United States's rush to produce nuclear weaponry before the collapse of the former Soviet Union.

From 1990 to 1996, the Department of Energy spent almost $35 billion on its environmental management program, with another $6.5 billion expected in fiscal 1997. Over two-thirds of the expenditures were spent on six major sites: Hanford, Washington; Savannah River, Georgia; Rocky Flats, Colorado; Oak Ridge, Tennessee; Fernald, Ohio; and the Idaho National Engineering Lab.[50]

Part of the difficulty involved in cleaning up military sites relates to jurisdictional disputes that are not uncommon in environmental politics. The EPA does not control or manage contaminated facilities; its role is regulation and enforcement. The intent of Congress was to make the agency independent so that compliance could be assured. At the same time, the Department of Defense operates under its own political agenda and direction, and thus environmental remediation is not always its highest priority. While staffers talk of a "partnership" arrangement between the two agencies, the reality is that there has been more study and discussion than actual cleanup.[51]

Another factor that affects the military cleanup is the activism of antinuclear environmental groups that have focused on the weapons dismantling process. The federal government must deal with more than fifty thousand nuclear warheads, with plans to dismantle one to two thousand weapons each year. Grass-roots organizations such as Save Texas Agriculture and Resources (STAR) have pressured the Department of Energy to reassess the safety and processing procedures at a site in the Texas panhandle, while the City of Amarillo, its chamber of commerce, and other groups are seeking an expansion of the facility.[52] The issue presents a dilemma for environmental groups, which on one hand celebrate the end of the Cold War and the stockpiling of nuclear warheads and support the dismantling process. On the other hand, protesters, concerned whether the components of the weapons can be handled, transported, and stored safely, often voice their distrust of the DOE's plans. As is typical of waste management issues, the activism is often localized, but when radioactive material is involved, opposition is considerably more vocal and visible, triggering protests and demonstrations that are not unlike the emotionalism more commonly associated with the logging of old growth forests.

THE GLOBALIZED WASTE PROBLEM

While most nations have dealt with their waste problems independent of one another, the issue has now become globalized as a result of various developments in the way waste is managed, especially when developed countries attempt to ship their waste abroad. The issue gained international prominence in 1988 when three thousand tons of a flaky black material was dumped on a Haitian beach. A barge carrying the substance had entered the port with a permit to unload "fertilizer," which later turned out to be Philadelphia municipal incinerator ash laced with toxic residue. The United States is a key stakeholder in global waste policy because of an agreement (which lapsed in 1988) that it would accept spent nuclear

---

Another View, Another Voice

NIMBY
When Nobody Wants Your Waste

The problem is simple. A city, or factory, or government has a lot of waste and nowhere to put it. The material might be solid waste that has been collected by municipal waste haulers, or it could be spent fuel rods from a utility company's nuclear plant operations. Regardless of the type or source, the United States and other nations have too much trash for too few places to get rid of it. The problem has become so extensive both here and abroad that an acronym was created to describe it: NIMBYism.

> NIMBYs are noisy. NIMBYs are powerful. NIMBYs are everywhere. NIMBYs are people who live near enough to corporate or government projects—and are upset enough about them—to work, stall, or shrink them. NIMBYs organize, march, sue, and petition to block the developers they think are threatening them. They twist the arms of politicians and they learn how to influence regulators. They fight fiercely and then, win or lose, they vanish.

NIMBY means "not in my backyard," and it accurately describes the perspective of those who do not want a project such as a waste incinerator or a landfill sited in their area. NIMBYism is related to the fears of property owners that property values will plummet if a home or business is located near an undesirable facility. It is also tied to the widespread distrust of corporations following major environmental crises and a generalized fear or "chemophobia" about substances that are complex and often unknown.

NIMBY has also taken on racial overtones, especially among minority group leaders who argue there is a tremendous racial disparity in the siting and cleanup of toxic waste sites. The protests began in 1982 in Warren County, North Carolina, when the residents, most of whom were black, discovered that their community had been selected as the location of a landfill for soil contaminated with highly toxic polychlorinated biphenyls (PCBs). Hundreds of demonstrators were jailed in an unsuccessful attempt to stop construction. That incident was followed by a landmark 1987 study by the United Church of Christ's Commission on Racial Justice, which found that three of every five black and Hispanic Americans lived in a community with uncontrolled toxic waste sites. Although the EPA responded that the charges of environmental racism were unfounded, a 1992 study found that the federal government did indeed give preference to white communities in cleaning up toxic waste sites and that it took longer for abandoned hazardous waste sites in minority areas to be cleaned up.

The NIMBY syndrome has had an especially strong impact on waste management. A 1994 study by the International City/County Management Association, for example, found that local opposition can add years to the time it takes to obtain a site and construct a solid waste facility. In Claremont, New Hampshire, it took nearly ten years to obtain a site for a waste-to-energy facility, with

the delay resulting in expenditures of $1.2 million in legal fees and contract ne-
gotiations and anger and distrust on the part of citizens. When Los Angeles
County officials decided to use unoccupied canyons as potential landfill sites,
their efforts were thwarted by environmental organizations that purchased land
on the canyon floors. New York City has been trying to build an incinerator in
the vacant Brooklyn Naval Yard since 1978; meanwhile, the preconstruction
cost of the project has run into the millions of dollars.

Some communities have tried to avoid NIMBY by shipping their waste
to other sites, often with a highly publicized lack of success. In 1986, Islip,
a community on New York's Long Island, closed its landfill to school and
commercial trash. The local hauler, Waste Alternatives, was paying $86 a
ton to cart the city's trash upstate, so when United Marine Transport Services offered to charge only $50 a ton to bale, load, and barge the trash and
ship it "somewhere down South," the company readily agreed. In March
1987, the barge Mobro 4000 attempted to tie up at the dock in Morehead
City, North Carolina. Officials there refused to allow the barge to unload,
and the trash odyssey began. For the next 164 days, the barge tried to dock
in Louisiana, Florida, New York, Mexico, Belize, and the Bahamas in an attempt to find someone, somewhere, willing to accept the city's trash. Mexico and Cuba even sent gunboats to make sure the barge stayed away from
their shores as well. Turned away from ports along the eastern and southern
seaboard, the trash was eventually burned in Brooklyn, with the ashes buried
where the journey had begun—back in Islip, New York.

As these examples indicate, finding a place for the nation's unwanted
trash—whether solid, hazardous, or radioactive—is not an easy task. More often than not, companies and communities are likely to run into intense public
opposition from those nearby, whether their resistance is for economic or racial
reasons. To deal with NIMBYism, local officials often try to come up with incentives to reduce waste, rather than relying upon command-and-control policies, which never really deal with the problem. King County, Washington, for
instance, was faced with a lack of landfill space and intense public opposition
to proposed incinerator projects. Nearly a half dozen NIMBY groups formed
to fight the siting of the plants, picketing meetings of the city council, and
protesting at hearings. Seattle's mayor chose an alternative to forcing the incineration issue by organizing solid waste citizen task forces. The groups coordinated their efforts with the state legislature to develop preferred options for
planning and implementing waste management procedures and were able to
find ways to increase recycling and therefore decrease the need for the incinerators.

Such "civic environmentalism" has been hailed as the new wave in environmental policymaking, and bringing citizens into the decision-making
process has worked well in many communities. Although its supporters admit
it is not a replacement for traditional regulatory policies, civic environmentalism can complement those policies and help transform public attitudes from

(continued)

NIMBY to one in which the public is better informed about the costs and benefits of specific waste management options.

For Further Reading
Denis J. Brion. *Essential Industry and the NIMBY Phenomenon.* New York: Quorum Books, 1991.
Robert D. Bullard. *Dumping in Dixie.* 2d ed. Boulder, CO: Westview, 1994.
William Glaberson, "Coping in the Age of 'Nimby.' " *New York Times,* June 19, 1988, Section 3, 1.
DeWitt John. *Civic Environmentalism: Alternatives to Regulation in States and Communities.* Washington, D.C.: Congressional Quarterly Press, 1994.
Riley E. Dunlap, Michael E. Kraft, and Eugene A. Rosa, eds. *Public Reactions to Nuclear Waste: Citizens' Views of Repository Siting.* Durham, NC: Duke University Press, 1993.
Jane Anne Morris. *Not in My Backyard: The Handbook.* San Diego: Silvercat Publications, 1994.
John O'Looney. *Economic Development and Environmental Control: Balancing Business and Community in an Age of NIMBYs and LULUs.* Westport, CT: Quorum, 1995.
Barry G. Rabe. *Beyond NIMBY: Hazardous Waste Siting in Canada and the United States.* Washington, D.C.: Brookings, 1994.

fuel from research reactors in twenty-eight other countries to deter nuclear proliferation. Added to the list of concerns is what to do about improperly handled waste produced by the nations of the former Soviet Union.

Most of the import and export of waste is between industrialized nations with restrictive (and costly) regulations on hazardous waste disposal and developing cash-poor countries in the Pacific, Latin America, the Caribbean, and Africa. Although they often lack adequate facilities or technology for accepting or disposing of hazardous waste, the financial incentives (often extralegal) for developing countries are often too tempting to pass up. The EPA estimates the cost of disposing of a ton of hazardous wastes in the United States at $250–$300 per ton; some developing countries charged as little as $40 to accept waste. For years there was an extensive waste trade arrangement among the members of the European Community (EC), and some experts believe that as much as 10 percent of the thirty million tons of hazardous waste generated each year passed between European countries, with a smaller amount of domestic refuse and recyclable materials traded.[53]

At the 1972 United Nations Conference on the Human Environment, delegates made a commitment to regulate waste trading, although it was not until 1984–1985 that a UN Environment Programme committee developed the Cairo Guidelines, implementing that pledge. The guidelines included notification procedures, prior consent by receiving nations, and verification that the receiving nation has requirements for disposal at least as stringent as those of the exporter. Despite those restrictions, a coalition of African nations argued that the agreement was tantamount to exploitation or "waste colonialism." In 1987, the United Nations attempted to devise an agreement that would satisfy the African nations (who sought an outright ban on exports) and exporters (still seeking inexpensive ways of disposing of their wastes). In 1989, two attempts were made to further restrict the international trade in wastes. A group of sixty-eight less-industrialized nations from Africa, the Caribbean, and the Pacific, collectively known as the ACP countries, joined with EC officials in signing the Lome Convention, which banned all radioactive and hazardous waste shipments from the EC and ACP countries. A second agreement, the Basel Convention on the Control of Transboundary Movements of Hazardous Wastes and Their Disposal, which took effect in 1992, did not ban waste trade but allowed hazardous wastes to be exported as long as there is "informed consent" or full notification and acceptance of any shipments. Even though members of the EC and other nations have pledged not to export their hazardous wastes regardless of the Basel Convention, twelve African states subsequently signed the Bamako Convention in 1991, banning the import of hazardous wastes from any country—a move that further emphasized their determination not to become a dumping ground for other countries.[54] The Clinton administration initially called for a ban on all hazardous waste exports to developing countries, even though the shipping of hazardous wastes is not a commonly accepted practice in the United States. The United States also supported a ban on exports to any country by 1999, with only a few exemptions granted for items that can be recycled, such as scrap metal and paper. But at a 1994 meeting of the parties in Geneva, which the United States attended only as an observer, there was a consensus agreement reached that banned all hazardous waste exports, including recyclables, by December 31, 1997.[55]

The development of such a strong regime without full U.S. support came about as a result of the efforts of not only the developing nations seeking to ban waste trade, but because of the pressure exerted by major environmental groups such as Greenpeace and its international affiliates. The organization made the issue one of the keystones of its activism, especially in developing countries. Calling efforts to ship waste abroad "toxic terrorism," Greenpeace members helped publicize the lack of monitoring and regulations over what materials were being transported, often under the guise of recycling.[56]

Waste management has also gained a more global focus as the nations of the former Soviet Union have appealed to the industrialized world for assistance in dealing with the phenomenal amount of toxic waste and radioactive materials produced from decades of military activity and inattention to environmental contamination. For decades, billions of gallons of liquid radioactive waste were secretly pumped underground near major rivers in Russia, and scientists have little information about the potential risk the practice now poses. Cleaning up nuclear power plants like Chernobyl is estimated to take as long as one hundred years and will cost billions more in assistance. Although the Clinton administration, its allies, and international financial institutions offered some support, the amount of money needed for cleanup in that region alone is virtually incalculable.[57] Although the area of the former Soviet Union continues to suffer from massive pollution of its water and air from manufacturing and other industrial processes, radioactive contamination is by far its most pressing, and most expensive, challenge. Existing international institutions are simply not prepared to deal with either the cost or the coordination of the legacy of the Communist regime.

POLICY STALLED: TOO LITTLE TOO LATE

Various agencies and analysts are exploring a number of waste management strategies from technological solutions, such as soil washing, chemical dechlorination, underground vacuum extraction, and bioremediation (the use of microbes to break down organic contaminants), to the use of price incentives and cost-based disposal fees.[58] Despite these proposals, the waste management issue has been called an environmental policy paradox. Even though officials have been aware of the shortage of landfill space for decades and could have anticipated the need for alternatives, they have been unable to develop a viable long-term policy to deal with the problem. Observers point to the lack of a publicly perceived crisis, the incentives that have caused policymakers to choose short-term, low-cost options, and the incremental nature of the policy process. With regard to hazardous waste, officials at the federal level have failed to follow through on policy development with an appropriate level of resources to clean up the thousands of identified sites in the United States. In addition, the involvement of organized crime in the disposal industry has been connected to illegal disposal, or "midnight dumping" of hazardous wastes—a problem not yet solved by government officials at any level.[59]

It is equally accurate to characterize America's waste management practices as the policy of deferral. The inability of policymakers now to plan for future disposal needs (whether the waste be solid, hazardous, or radioactive) simply means that they are putting off until tomorrow an inevitable, and growing, environmental protection problem. Future generations will be forced to deal with the mounting heaps of trash, barrels of toxic waste, and radioactive refuse that is already piling up in our cities, chemical companies, and at utilities all around the country. Other analysts note that there is a lack of information about the full costs of various disposal alternatives. Without sufficient research into the "true" costs of waste management strategies, it is impossible for the most efficient systems to be developed.[60] Meanwhile, it appears as if the future of American waste management will involve a combination of disposal methods, rather than any single strategy. Technological strategies and price incentives are of little value, however, until the legislative gridlock is broken and policymakers get serious about finding a solution, rather than just passing stopgap measures for short-term fixes. We know the problem is there, but no one seems willing to get down and dirty to tackle it.

SUMMARY

From the turn of the century, when Americans, especially city dwellers, first recognized the "garbage nuisance," public officials have been attempting to find ways to deal with the mountains of waste that have built up. Strategies ranging from burial to incineration to ocean dumping to recycling have been attempted, each with its own set of costs and benefits. The impetus for decision making is that America's landfills are rapidly reaching capacity or are being closed to comply with environmental regulations while the amount of waste spirals upward. Cities are simply running out of room for their trash and have turned to exporting their trash to other states whose landfills are not yet full. The federal government has generally had a "hands off" policy, leaving the problem to be solved by state and local officials. But neither the public nor politicians seem willing to make a decision to deal with solid waste. The policymaking process has stalled while the problem continues to grow. Meanwhile, the issues of radioactive waste disposal and toxic waste have eclipsed the solid waste problem and have become the focus of legislative interests. Waste policies are globalized, with international regimes that call for a total ban on waste trading. Still unresolved are the serious issues of how massive radioactive and hazardous waste contamination in the area of the former Soviet Union can be cleaned up, given the scale of the problem and the limited resources available from other nations.

NOTES

1. Gary Lee, "Toxic Waste Dump Site Awaits Cleanup as Government Fights over Tools, Hill Republicans in Tug of War on Power of 'Superfund' Law," *Washington Post,* May 25, 1996, A3.

2. Ibid.

3. Martin V. Melosi, *Garbage in the Cities: Refuse, Reform and the Environment, 1880–1980* (College Station, TX: Texas A&M University Press, 1981), 3.

4. Ibid., 189–192. In fairness to the industry, however, it should be noted that the development of packaging has some beneficial consequences. Packaging has extended the shelf life of many goods (especially produce and dairy products) that otherwise might have rotted or spoiled. Packaging also allows products to be stored and shipped in bulk and often results in lower pricing of goods.

5. For an expanded explanation of this typology of wastes and their disposal, see Travis Wagner, *In Our Backyard: A Guide to Understanding Pollution and Its Effects* (New York: Van Nostrand Reinhold, 1994), 126–183.

6. U.S. Environmental Protection Agency, *National Biennial RCRA Hazardous Waste Report* (Washington, D.C.: EPA Office of Solid Waste, 1995).

7. U.S. Environmental Protection Agency, *Characterization of Municipal Solid Waste in the United States: 1990 Update,* EPA/530-SW-90-042 (Washington, D.C.: U.S. Government Printing Office, June 1990), ES-3.

8. Council on Environmental Quality, *Environmental Quality: 25th Anniversary Report* (Washington, D.C.: Council on Environmental Quality, n.d.), 349.

9. Ibid., 348–350.

10. Melosi, 171–176, 217–218.

11. See Howard E. Hesketh, *Incineration for Site Cleanup and Destruction of Hazardous Waste* (Lancaster, PA: Technomic, 1990).

12. *Characterization of Municipal Solid Waste,* 75.

13. See, for example, Jon R. Luoma, "Trash Can Realities," *Audubon, 7* (March 1990): 86–97; and Neil Seldman, "Waste Management: Mass Burn Is Dying," *Environment, 31,* no. 7 (September, 1989): 42–44.

14. Michael Specter, "Incinerators, Unwanted and Politically Dangerous," *New York Times,* December 12, 1991, B-1, B-11.

15. See Bruce Piasecki, ed. *Beyond Dumping: New Strategies for Controlling Toxic Waste* (Westport, CT: Quorum Books, 1984).

16. Michael J. Satchell, "Lethal Garbage: Nuclear Waste," *U.S. News & World Report,* November 7, 1994, 64–66.

17. See Richard A. Denison, ed. *Recycling and Incineration: Evaluating the Choices* (Washington, D.C.: Island Press, 1990).

18. John C. Whitaker, *Striking A Balance: Environment and Natural Resources Policy in the Nixon-Ford Years* (Washington, D.C.: American Enterprise Institute, 1976), 113–116).

19. Margaret Webb Pressler, "The Recycling Boom Is More Than Just Trash Talk," *Washington Post National Weekly Edition,* February 20–26, 1995, 33.

20. Timothy Aeppel, "Recycler Woes May Signal Soft Economy," *Wall Street Journal,* April 22, 1996, A9A.

21. Whitaker, 199–120. See also Pressler, 33; U.S. Council of Mayors, *Recycling America* (Washington, D.C.: June 1991); and Anna Maria Gillis, "Shrinking the Trash Heap," *Bio-Science, 42,* no. 2 (February 1992): 90–93.

22. Cynthia Pollock, *Mining Urban Wastes: The Potential for Recycling* (Washington, D.C.: Worldwatch Institute, April 1987), 32–41.

23. David H. Folz and Joseph M. Hazlett, "Public Participation and Recycling Performance: Explaining Program Success," *Public Administration Review, 51,* no. 6 (November–December 1991): 526–532. See also David H. Folz, "Recycling Program Design, Management and Participation: A National Survey of Municipal Expertise," *Public Administration Review, 51,* no. 3 (May–June 1991): 222–231.

24. 104th Congress, S. 1271.

25. See generally, Kristin Shrader-Frechette, "High Level Waste, Low Level Logic," *The Bulletin of the Atomic Scientists, 50* (November–December, 1994): 40–45; Jeff Wheelwright, "For Our Nuclear Wastes, There's Gridlock on the Road to the Dump," *Smithsonian, 26* (May 1995), 40–48); Matthew L. Wald, "New Waste Dump Standard Is Recommended in Report," *New York Times,* August 2, 1995, A15; Wade Roush, "Can Nuclear Waste Keep Yucca Mountain Dry—and Safe?" *Science, 270* (December 15, 1995), 1761–1762; and Gary Taubes, "Yucca Blowup Theory Bombs," *Science, 271* (March 22, 1996), 1664.

26. U.S. General Accounting Office, *Pollution Prevention: EPA Should Reexamine the Objectives and Sustainability of State Programs* (Washington, D.C.: General Accounting Office, 1994).

27. Bette Fishbein and David Saphire, "Slowing the Waste Behemoth." *EPA Journal, 16,* no. 3 (July–August 1992): 46–49.

28. Patricia Poore,"Is Garbage an Environmental Problem?" *Garbage,* November–December 1993, 40–45.

29. Louis Blumberg and Robert Gottlieb, *War on Waste: Can American Win Its Battle With Garbage?* (Washington, D.C.: Island Press, 1989), 63.

30. See William L. Kovacs and John F. Klusik, "The New Federal Role in Solid Waste Management: The Resource Conservation and Recovery Act of 1976," *Columbia Journal of Environmental Law, 3* (March 1977): 205.

31. *City of Philadelphia v. New Jersey,* 437 U.S. 617 (1978).

32. United States General Accounting Office, Report to the Ranking Minority Member, Committee on Governmental Affairs, U.S. Senate, *Solid Waste: State and Federal Efforts to Manage Nonhazardous Waste* (Washington, D.C.: U.S. Government Accounting Office, February 1995), 14.

33. See "Recent Developments, Federal Regulation of Solid Waste Reduction and Recycling," *Harvard Journal on Legislation, 29* (1992): 251–254. For a more comprehensive analysis of the policy process as it relates to both the RCRA and Superfund, see Charles E. Davis, *The Politics of Hazardous Waste* (Englewood Cliffs, NJ: Prentice Hall, 1993).

34. Blumberg and Gottleib, *War on Waste,* 66–67.

35. For more on the environmental justice issue as it relates to waste siting, see for example, Evan J. Ringquist, "Environmental Justice: Normative Concerns and Empirical Evidence" in *Environmental Policy in the 1990s,* 3d ed., eds. Michael Kraft and Norman Vig (Washington, D.C.: Congressional Quarterly Press, 1997), 231–254.

36. See Richard C. Fortuna and David J. Lennett, *Hazardous Waste Regulation, The New Era: An Analysis and Guide to RCRA and the 1984 Amendments* (New York: McGraw-Hill, 1987). See also William Harris Frank and Timothy B. Atkeson, *Superfund, Litigation and*

Cleanup (Washington, D.C.: Bureau of National Affairs, 1985); and Mary Devine Worobec, *Toxic Substances Controls Guide* (Washington, D.C.: Bureau of National Affairs, 1989).

37. See John H. Cushman Jr., "Program to Clean Toxic Waste Sites Is Left in Turmoil," *New York Times,* January 15, 1996, A1; and Allan Friedman, "Superfund Negotiators Hope for Bipartisan Compromise," *Congressional Quarterly Weekly Report,* April 20, 1996, 1040–1041.

38. "Questions the Public is Asking: An Interview with Don Clay," *EPA Journal, 17,* no. 3 (July–August 1991): 18.

39. See Geoffrey Commons, "Plugging the Leak in Underground Storage Tanks: The 1984 RCRA Amendments," *Vermont Law Review, 11* (Spring, 1986): 267. See also Jack Lewis, "Superfund, RCRA, and UST: The Clean-Up Threesome," *EPA Journal, 17,* no. 3 (July–August 1991): 14.

40. For more on the progress of Superfund cleanup, see Daniel Mazmanian and David Morell, *Beyond Superfailure: America's Toxics Policy for the 1990s* (Boulder, CO: Westview, 1992); John A. Hird, *Superfund: The Political Economy of Risk* (Baltimore: The Johns Hopkins University Press, 1994); and Michael Kraft, "Searching for Policy Success: Reinventing the Politics of Site Remediation," *Environmental Professional, 16* (September 1994): 245–253.

41. See Katherine N. Probst, et al., *Footing the Bill for Superfund Cleanups: Who Pays and How?* (Washington, D.C.: Brookings, 1995).

42. Frank P. Grad, "Compensating Toxic-Waste Victims," *Technology Review,* October 1985, 48–50.

43. "Comment, A Congressional Choice: The Question of Environmental Priority in Bankrupt Estates," 9 *UCLA Journal of Environmental Law and Policy, 73,* (1990): 77–78.

44. Superfund Program: Interim Municipal Settlement Policy, 54 Fed. Reg. 51,071 (1989).

45. U.S. Congress, Office of Technology Assessment, *Superfund Strategy* (Washington, D.C.: U.S. Government Printing Office, 1985): 4–5.

46. HR 4916, H. Rpt. 103-582, parts I, II, and III, and S 1834, S. Rpt. 1003-349.

47. 104th Congress, S 1285.

48. 104th Congress, H.R. 2500.

49. See Michael Renner, "Military Mop-Up," *WorldWatch, 7,* no. 5 (September–October 1994), 23–29; and Seth Shulman, *The Threat at Home: Confronting the Toxic Legacy of the U.S. Military* (Boston, MA: Beacon, 1992).

50. Katherine N. Probst and Michael H. McGovern, "Cleaning Up the Nuclear Weapons Complex: A Herculean Challenge," *Resources, 124* (Summer 1996), 18–19.

51. For one government official's view, see Steven A. Herman, "Environmental Cleanup and Compliance at Federal Facilities: An EPA Perspective," *Environmental Law, 24* (July 1994): 1097–1109.

52. Tori Woodward, "The Hope and the Danger of Weapons Dismantling," *Groundwork, 4* (1994), 4–6.

53. Duncan Lawrence and Brian Wynne, "Transporting Waste in the European Community: A Free Market?" *Environment, 31,* no. 6 (July–August 1989): 14.

54. See C. Russell H. Shearer, "Comparative Analysis of the Basel and Bamako Conventions on Hazardous Waste," *Environmental Law, 23,* no. 1 (1993): 141.

55. Gareth Porter and Janet Welsh Brown, *Global Environmental Politics,* 2d ed. (Boulder, CO: Westview Press, 1996), 84–88.

56. For a summary of the Greenpeace view, see the statement of James Vallette, coordinator of the Greenpeace International Hazardous Exports-Imports Prevention Project in U.S. Congress, House, Committee on Energy and Commerce, Subcommittee on Transportation and Hazardous Materials, *Basel Convention on the Export of Waste,* hearing, 102nd Cong., 1st sess., October 19, 1991 (Washington, D.C.: U.S. Government Printing Office, 1991), 185–198. See also the Greenpeace publications *Toxic Trade* and *Waste Trade Update.*

57. For an overview of the problems involved, see Murray Feshbach, *Ecological Disaster: Cleaning Up the Hidden Legacy of the Soviet Regime* (Washington, D.C.: Brookings,

1995); James Stewart, "The Cloud Over Chernobyl," *Washington Post National Weekly Edition,* June 26–July 2, 1995, 6–7; Margaret Shapiro and Curt Suplee, "Russia's Buried Monster," *Washington Post National Weekly Edition,* December 5–11, 1994, 18; Michael Dobbs, "Sacrificed to the Superpower," *Washington Post National Weekly Edition,* September 20–26, 1993, 13; and John Massey Stewart, ed. *The Soviet Environment: Problems, Policies and Politics* (New York: Cambridge University Press, 1992).

58. See Congressional Budget Office, Federal Options for Reducing Waste Disposal (Washington, D.C.: U.S. Government Printing Office, October 1991); and Frank Ackerman, "Taxing the Trash Away," *Environment, 34,* no. 5 (June 1992): 2–5.

59. Zachary A. Smith, *The Environmental Policy Paradox,* 2d ed. (Englewood Cliffs, N.J.: Prentice Hall, 1995), 164–188.

60. See A. Clark Wiseman, "Impediments to Economically Efficient Solid Waste Management," *Resources* (Fall 1991): 9–11.

FOR FURTHER READING

John T. Aquino. *Recycling Times' Recycling Handbook.* Boca Raton, FL: Lewis Publishers, 1995.

Murray Feshbach. *Ecological Disaster: Cleaning Up the Hidden Legacy of the Soviet Regime.* Washington, D.C.: Brookings, 1995.

Matthew Gandy. *Recycling and the Politics of Urban Waste.* New York: St. Martin's Press, 1994.

John A. Hird. *Superfund: The Political Economy of Environmental Risk.* Baltimore: The Johns Hopkins University Press, 1994.

Arjun Makhijani, Howard Hu, and Katherine Yih, eds. *Nuclear Wastelands.* Cambridge, MA: MIT Press, 1995.

Don Munton, ed. *Hazardous Waste Siting and Democratic Choice.* Baltimore: Georgetown University Press, 1996.

Katherine N. Probst, et al. *Footing the Bill for Superfund Cleanup: Who Pays and How?* Washington, D.C.: Brookings, 1995.

CHAPTER 6

Energy Politics:
Old Debates and New Sources

The hard fact is that we now have no effective energy policy. We have a choice
between the many reasons to do nothing and looking for ways to get the job done.
— Former President Jimmy Carter, commenting on U.S. energy vulnerability after the
Persian Gulf Crisis[1]

In October 1973, media headlines trumpeted that America was in the throes of an
"energy crisis" when the nations of the Organization of Petroleum Exporting
Countries (OPEC) announced increases in the price of a barrel of oil. The price
in oil jumped from $3 a barrel to $11.65 in three months in 1973.[2] Suddenly the
United States, which for years had been a major importer of foreign oil, found itself lining up at the world pump like other nations that had become dependent
upon Middle Eastern resources. Political officials and consumers alike, who had
previously filled their tanks with little thought of where the oil was coming from,
were suddenly forced to take a long, hard look at our energy resources, both foreign and domestic. Automobile owners found that they could buy gas only every
other day of the week when the government instituted an "odd/even" purchasing
system, officials ordered the thermostats to be turned down in public buildings
and schools, and some communities even outlawed Christmas light displays as
an excessive use of energy. But as quickly as it had surfaced, concern about the
country's energy policies faded, and even a second energy crisis in 1979–1980
failed to ignite public interest. Americans assumed that there was an unlimited
supply of fuel available—it was simply a matter of turning on the spigot. In August 1990, when Iraq's Saddam Hussein ordered his troops into Kuwait, once
again threatening the world's oil supplies, few Americans showed much evidence
of concern about whether or not their local gasoline pumps would go dry. When
President Bush signed the Energy Policy Act of 1992—the first major legislative
attempt to curb U.S. oil dependence in more than a decade—his action failed to
generate more than a single day's media headlines.

While it may be difficult to get as emotionally involved in energy policy as
one could get involved emotionally with the destruction of the rain forest or the
protection of the blue whale, it nevertheless has produced strong feelings on both

sides. Anti-nuclear-power activists have been arrested as they protested the siting of nuclear waste facilities, and opponents of a geothermal project in Hawaii have been equally vociferous in their state. Representatives of electric utilities are just as adamant about the safety record of nuclear plants, and farmers have a hard time understanding why their state's hydroelectric facilities are unable to provide them with the water they need in deference to a fish. Energy has also been called a "transparent" sector of society because no one buys or uses energy as an end in itself. All demand for energy is indirect and derived only from the benefits it provides. People do not buy gasoline because they *want* gasoline, but because they need it for their cars to take them where they want to go. Similarly, a manufacturing plant has a need for electricity only to run the machines that make the products the company sells.[3]

Our growing electricity needs make the debate both timely and controversial. Although energy is an issue of global concern, a stable, affordable supply is acutely important to the United States, which has just 5 percent of the world's population, but consumes 26 percent of the world's energy. During the past two decades, U.S. energy consumption has increased by approximately 25 percent and is estimated to increase by about approximately 7 percent during the 1990s. Over the next 20 years, energy consumption is expected to increase by 20 percent.[4] This increased demand comes when the nation is responding to environmental regulations that call for reducing power plant emissions from fossil-fueled plants, a virtual halt to building any new facilities, and political controversy over siting and the perceived dangers of nuclear power. Coupled with that opposition is that the average lead time for building new power plants is ten years. If consumption continues to increase at current rates, the United States could be facing an energy shortage as early as the end of this decade.

This chapter examines the politics of energy, focusing on the United States. It reviews the various energy sources and the problems associated with them and chronicles the technological changes that are reducing our current dependence upon fossil fuels, revisiting the nuclear power debate. The chapter then looks at the political environment and actors by examining events that led to the 1973 oil crisis and the subsequent regulatory aspects of energy policy. Lastly, the chapter concludes with an overview of future trends and projections for changes in energy use and conservation.

THE ENERGY PIE

Energy is needed to produce goods and services in four basic economic sectors: residential (heat for rooms and hot water, lighting, appliances), commercial (including air conditioners in commercial buildings), industrial (especially steel, paper, and chemicals), and transportation (of both people and goods). The crux of the energy debate has been to find efficient, environmentally safe, economical and stable sources of supply to meet those needs. Historically speaking, the

United States has endured three global energy transitions, each separated by a sixty-year interval. In 1850, the United States derived nearly 90 percent of its energy needs from wood, which remained the dominant fuel into the late nineteenth century. In 1910, coal replaced wood as the dominant fuel, capturing 70 percent of all energy produced and consumed. Along with the transition from wood to coal came the migration from rural areas to the cities, the development of an industrial base, and the railroad era. In 1970, the third phase began when oil and gas reached the 70 percent level. Although there is no evidence that oil production will follow the same pattern as wood and coal, it is likely that there will be more changes in the relative percentages of each energy source.[5]

Edward Teller, the "father of the atomic bomb," once commented, "No single prescription exists for a solution to the energy problem. Energy conservation is not enough. Petroleum is not enough. Nuclear energy is not enough. Solar energy and geothermal energy are not enough. New ideas and developments will not be enough. Only the proper combination of all these will suffice."[6] Like a recipe for an "energy pie," which is essentially the situation in the United States today (see Figure 6.1), Teller suggests that the answer to our global energy needs must be found in a blend of energy sources and strategies, rather than in a single fuel. This concept seems relatively reasonable were the costs and benefits of various forms of energy equal, but that is far from the case. Some forms of energy are relatively inexpensive to produce but are not in abundant supply. Other sources are expensive but less polluting. Still others are considered unsafe but could be made available to consumers around the world for pennies a day, improving the standard of living for millions of people in developing nations. A brief survey of fuel types follows.

Figure 6.1   U.S. Energy Production by Source, 1994
(in quadrillion Btu)

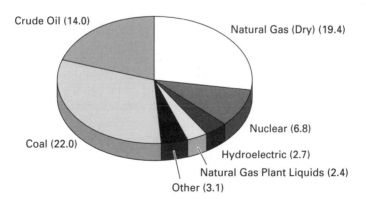

Source: U.S. Bureau of the Census, *Statistical Abstract of the United States* (Washington, D.C.: U.S. Government Printing Office, 1996): 578.

FOSSIL FUELS

Petroleum

In the two decades following World War II, the American life-style changed dramatically. In the postwar boom, Americans fell in love with the automobile, with the number of motor vehicles doubling between 1952 and 1972. Most cars were heavier and less mileage efficient than earlier models, further increasing the demand for petroleum. At the same time, new household appliances appeared — electric dishwashers, clothes driers, washing machines — that further expanded the demand for electricity. By the time the 1973 oil crisis hit, Americans had been repeatedly told that the global petroleum reserves were about to be depleted and that, as the supply dwindled, the cost of a barrel of oil would skyrocket. Both halves of that prediction were faulty. Prices did go up but then fell. The current world oil reserves are twice as large as they were in 1970, and in 1990, Saudi Arabia announced the discovery of new reserves that would allow the country to continue pumping oil at the current rate for at least another century. Why, then, is there still a perception of an oil crisis? The answer to that question is twofold. One, the United States is increasingly reliant upon imported oil, and 70 percent of known world oil reserves available for export come from the nations of the Persian Gulf, one of the most politically explosive regions in the world. Since crude oil provides 20 percent of America's energy production pie and more than 90 percent of the fuel used in transportation, the country is literally at the mercy of foreign nations as long as we continue to rely upon them for our energy needs. Two, the burning of fossil fuels such as petroleum contributes to poor air quality, acid rain, and greenhouse warming. As a result, the petroleum industry is being heavily regulated to reduce emissions into the air, water, and soil.

Coal

One of the ways in which the United States could reduce its dependence upon imported oil would be to use the fossil fuel in its own backyard — coal — which is found in thirty-eight of the fifty states. The United States is home to about one-quarter of the world's known coal supplies, and even exports more than one hundred million tons per year. There are a number of factors that have led to a reduction in coal's slice of the energy pie, which is now about one-third. One, new requirements under the 1990 Clean Air Act amendments (explained further in Chapter 8) are forcing coal-burning plants to reduce their emissions of sulfur dioxide, which contributes to acid rain, by installing costly technology or to use more expensive but less polluting low-sulfur fuels. Two, the average age of coal-burning plants in the United States is twenty-five years, and many facilities are outdated. Utility firms and potential investors are often hesitant to finance repairs or new controls on a facility that is ready for retirement. Still, the idea that coal will be the fuel of the future still exists, bound closely to the future of the electric utility industry and the possibility of political disruption of Middle Eastern oil supplies.[7]

Natural Gas

Another readily available source of energy is natural gas, which makes up about 31 percent of the energy pie in dry and plant liquid form. Domestic supplies are estimated at ten times the current annual production, with more reserves being discovered each year. The barrier to increased use of natural gas, which is a clean, virtually pollution-free source of energy, involves public opposition to new pipelines and offshore drilling. A proposal for a pipeline from Wyoming to California was derailed when researchers found that the proposed route passed through habitats of the endangered desert tortoise. An offshore drilling moratorium has brought an end to new exploration, even though two-thirds of the energy from offshore is natural gas. In February 1991, the Department of the Interior proposed opening up thousands of miles of the outer continental shelf for oil and gas exploration, including areas off the East Coast from central New Jersey to southern Georgia, along the eastern part of the Gulf of Mexico, and the California coast near Santa Barbara, which is believed to be the last large concentration of untapped oil and gas in the continental United States. The most controversial proposal involved the opening up of 1.5 million acres in the Arctic National Wildlife Refuge. In 1995, congressional Republicans made similar proposals. Intense opposition by groups such as the Natural Resources Defense Council and the Sierra Club blocked these plans, but these areas may be open to exploration and drilling at some point in the future.

RENEWABLE ENERGY SOURCES

When the 1973 oil crisis hit, the world turned to various forms of alternative, renewable energy as a potential replacement for fossil fuels. Although some of these sources have been used extensively in other countries, with the exception of hydroelectric power, the United States has only recently begun experimenting with them. Supporters of renewable energy point out that they produce no waste to be disposed of and no greenhouse gases. They generally do not deplete limited supplies of fuel, are safe for workers, and can be constructed more quickly than facilities using fossil fuels or nuclear power. Currently, these sources make up about 8 percent of the U.S. energy pie, although that figure is growing as the fossil fuel dependency is reduced. Their biggest drawbacks are their unreliability as a fuel source and the higher cost of producing and distributing electricity from them. The political process has greatly affected U.S. attention to alternative fuel sources, and the federal government's support for renewable energy research can be tied to both electoral cycles and to the cost of oil. Passage of the 1978 Public Utilities Regulatory Policies Act (PURPA), for example, required utilities to purchase power from nonutilities at an "avoided cost" rate (the rate of expense the utility would have incurred if it generated the energy itself). PURPA became an incentive for alternative sources like cogenerators (large industrial power users who produce steam and electricity for their own needs and sell the excess to local utilities) and small hydroelectric plants that were guaranteed a market for the electricity they generated and has increased the amount of energy that utility companies obtain from renewables.[8] In the wake of PURPA, the number of license applications for small hydropower projects soared from one hundred applications from 1976 to 1979 to forty-five hundred between 1980 and 1983. Passage of the Crude Oil Windfall Profits Tax in 1981, which provided an 11 percent investment tax credit for small hydropower facilities, also served as an important development incentive.[9] Funds for renewable fuel research reached $720 million at the end of the Carter administration in 1980 and dropped to $115 million during the Bush administration in fiscal 1989. The 1992 Energy Policy Act included provisions aimed at encouraging the development of renewable energy sources such as federal payments to public utilities that build or purchase facilities that generate electricity from renewable energy sources and joint ventures between the federal government and private companies to produce energy from renewable sources.

Critics of renewable energy point out that few places enjoy the right geography to make use of solar, wind, and geothermal energy, and as a result, these three types of energy sources make up less than 1 percent of the energy pie today. (California is one of the few states with the right combination of geography and weather.) Coal still remains the primary fuel for electricity in thirty-three states, with six eastern states depending mainly on nuclear power, five northeastern states on fuel oil, four West Coast states on hydroelectric power, and two on natural gas. This brief survey of alternative energy shows that some sources are more likely to be developed than others, and why.

Hydroelectric Power

As one of the world's oldest sources of renewable energy, the United States has maintained some reliance upon electricity produced from turbines at dams and other water sources for over a century. Hydroelectric power accounted for about 4 percent of the energy pie in 1994—a level that has changed only slightly since 1970, even with an increase in small hydro operations. Hydroelectric power is among the cheapest sources of energy available, although its use is becoming more limited, as environmental groups have lobbied Congress in opposition to the siting of new dams along waterways. In October 1986, passage of the Electric Consumer Protection Act required that environmental concerns be given "equitable treatment" with the development purposes of the Federal Water Power Act and provided protection for recreational value, water quality, and fish and wildlife.[10] There is also a limited growth potential to hydroelectric power, since most bodies of water that can be profitably dammed and developed are already in use. There is increasing concern about the environmental impacts of hydroelectric dams, particularly on fish. Still, hydropower remains a reliable, cost-effective source of electricity.[11]

Solar Power

Solar power is generally divided into two types: passive (such as siting a house on a lot to take advantage of the sun's natural warming effect) and active (which uses some kind of device to collect and store heat). Passive solar heating is usually built into the design of a home or office building, while active solar heating has the advantage of being retrofitted onto existing structures. Active solar devices have been used most often for small applications, such as heating swimming pools or heating hot water. Solar power was initially hailed as a prime alternative energy source because the sun's rays touch every portion of the planet (some areas more than others, of course) and the resource is free (although collecting it is not!). The technology is already available to provide between 20 and 25 percent of our energy needs from the sunshine, which naturally reaches the Earth.

Solar power got a big push from the Carter administration in the late 1970s when the federal government provided funds for private research and development and tax credits for individuals installing solar equipment in their homes. Under the Reagan administration, however, the federal research subsidies were drastically cut, and Congress voted to end the tax incentives in 1985. The 1992 Energy Policy Act permanently extended the 10 percent tax credit for solar and geothermal energy-powered business facilities. Since the federal grant dollars have been cut back, most of the solar power research has been conducted by western utility companies, most of whom are under pressure to fund less polluting energy sources. Research has been focused in two areas: large facilities producing electricity for commercial and residential customers, and smaller applications for home use. Thus far, large projects have not been especially successful, with the parent company of one of the world's largest facilities, Luz International, declaring bankruptcy in 1991.[12] In the smaller application category, Texas Instruments and Southern California Edison have teamed up in another venture to produce a solar panel that could be mounted on south-facing rooftops. The new technology uses photovoltaic cells produced from an impure form of silicon at a cost less than a fifth of those now on the market. The cells, wrapped in aluminum sheeting, would replace shingles on new housing at a cost of about $3,000 and would produce about one-third of the electricity used by an average household. The Solar Energy Research Institute projects that, by the year 2030, photovoltaics could supply half of America's electrical power. The technology works best in those areas with uniform sunshine and in regions where residents will not reject the building of solar facilities. Even in the Southwest, which receives more sunshine than any other region, about three square miles of land are required to collect from solar radiation the energy produced by a standard power station. Despite these innovations, solar power alone cannot meet all of the world's energy needs.

Wind Power

The U.S. government hailed wind as a promising energy source during the 1970s, since it has several characteristics that make it comparable to solar power. The wind is free and can be harnessed relatively easily and turned into electricity. Currently, about seventeen thousand wind turbines are in operation in the United States, most of them in California, where development was encouraged through generous tax incentives. The 1992 Energy Policy Act also gives utilities a Federal tax credit for electricity produced from wind turbines. One difference is that wind power is more geographically limited, with certain areas more likely to be used as collection points than others. But the biggest problem is the fickle nature of the wind—people cannot control when and where it will blow. In California, for example, the thousands of wind turbines at the Altamont Pass fifty miles east of the San Francisco Bay region deliver only one-quarter of the power they could theoretically generate. The cost of producing a kilowatt-hour of electricity of wind power has steadily dropped to about seven cents per hour, just slightly more than the cost of production from coal-burning facilities and less than nuclear plants.

Although it only generates less than 1 percent of global energy, wind power is the fastest growing energy source in the world. Capacity increased by 150 percent between 1990 and 1996.[13] Wind power has won acceptance in areas suffering from poor air quality such as Sacramento, California. There, the local utility has accepted a private firm's bid to build a wind farm, which will provide electricity at a cost of only 4.5 cents per kilowatt hour to replace capacity once provided by the Rancho Seco nuclear plant, which was closed down in a referendum. The overall goal is for the utility to receive 75 percent of its total energy needs from renewables and conservation by the year 2000.[14] Still, opposition to the sight of thousands of large metal structures on the landscape has limited wind power application to just a few sites in the United States, and it will require major attitudinal changes before such projects are widespread.

Geothermal Power

Tapping the reservoirs of energy under the Earth's surface is one of the unexplored sources of potential energy, advocates believe. Geothermal energy is produced when hot, dry rocks and water generate steam for electric power. Geothermal projects have been proposed at a number of locations, including northern California, home of the nation's largest geothermal field, and along the national park boundaries at Oregon's Crater Lake.[15] But support for geothermal power has diminished considerably because of a blowout at the drilling site on the Big Island of Hawaii in 1991 and extended controversy over threats to endangered species and the Hawaii rain forest.[16] Expansion of geothermal projects will require massive amounts of research and development dollars, which to date have not materialized.

Biomass Conversion/Synfuels

The burning of wood and other plant matter to produce electricity or fuel (such as ethanol and methanol) is referred to as biomass conversion, and it now accounts of about 4 percent of U.S. energy production. The transportation energy problem is an important aspect of the U.S. energy pie, since Americans are so reliant upon their automobiles. As a result, attempts to concoct nonpetroleum-based fuels (liquids and gases from coal, biomass and peat, oil shale and "unconventional" natural gas) were at one time an important element of U.S. strategy and seen as an alternative when oil reserves ran dry.[17] The technology has been available for decades, and Congress began subsidizing synthetic fuel development in 1944. The White House did not catch "synfuel fever" until late 1979 and the passage of the $20 billion Energy Security Act and creation of the U.S. Synthetic Fuels Corporation. Environmental groups have opposed synfuel production for a number of reasons, including concerns about possible violation of clean air laws, carcinogenic and toxic contamination, and land disruption and water pollution from synfuels plants. Funding for synfuels research ended in 1986 after funding only four projects, and this alternative energy source has had little federal support since that time.[18] Still, industry is pressing forward with attempts to find an environmentally safe method of biofuel production. In 1992, two U.S. firms announced plans to build a facility to produce ethanol from pulp and paper mill sludge. The plant is expected to initially produce ten million gallons of fuel per year, with a boost to one hundred million gallons annually within five years.[19]

The 1990 Clean Air Act requires states with high levels of carbon monoxide to sell oxygenated fuels—usually containing ethanol—to increase the oxygen content of fuels and cause them to burn cleaner and reduce emissions. The 1992 Energy Policy Act requires certain motor vehicle fleets to run on ethanol, methanol, or other gasoline substitutes. But there have been problems. Los Angeles abandoned its plan to use methanol-powered buses in 1993 after buses broke down and had engine failures nearly twice as often as diesel buses.[20]

Although a considerable amount of federal and private funds have been spent on researching and developing alternative energy sources, there are a number of factors that have made these technologies less attractive than they initially appeared in the 1970s. When oil prices stabilized during the 1980s, the rush to develop alternatives to foreign imports slowed down. The price of crude oil fell to

Another View, Another Voice

AMORY LOVINS

Amory Lovins is perhaps the leading proponent of energy conservation and the development of alternative energy sources in the world. From his home at the Rocky Mountain Institute (RMI) in Snowmass, Colorado, Lovins writes frequently about energy policy and travels throughout the world with his briefcase full of lighting fixtures and energy-efficient devices that he uses to illustrate his lectures. Lovins and his wife, Hunter, established RMI in the mid-1980s as a center for architects, engineers, policymakers, and others to come together and design solutions to energy and environmental problems. Amory Lovins is director of research, Hunter Lovins is president. The center is itself a model of conservation and construction in harmony with its environment. Perched in the Colorado mountains at an elevation of 7,100 feet, where temperatures drop to -45 degrees Fahrenheit, Lovins has had twenty-four successive banana crops in his solar greenhouse, with no central heat source, but with superinsulated construction. Lovins believes that technology is not only part of the problem but also part of the solution to environmental quality. He combines technical innovation with a commitment to market forces and capitalism in creating a greener, safer world. His studies conclude that cars waste 99 percent of the gasoline that they consume, that only 3 percent of the fuel burned in a power plant actually produces light in an incandescent bulb, and that the total waste of water, energy, mobility, and materials in the world may cost as much as $10 trillion a year. He argues that some 94 percent of the mass flow of materials used to produce American goods is jettisoned before manufacturing is completed, and about 80 percent of finished products are scrapped after just one use: "somewhere near 99 percent of all the original materials used to manufacture goods in the United States ends up as waste within six weeks of sale."

One of Lovins' projects is the design of hypercars: "vehicles that are fully recyclable, 20 times more energy efficient, 100 times cleaner, and cheaper than existing cars. These vehicles retain the safety and performance of conventional cars but achieve radical simplification through the use of lightweight, composite materials, fewer parts, virtual prototyping, regenerative braking, and very small, hybrid engines." There are no manufacturing facilities at Snowmass. Lovins and his colleagues serve as consultants and are looking for collaborative agreements with others to eventually produce the new vehicles.

Lovins began calling on policymakers to encourage more competition in the electric industry in the 1970s as a way to shift from large, inefficient, pollution-producing power plants to dispersed, small-scale, more environmentally friendly generators who would increasingly rely on alternative energy sources. His call for competition in the electric utility industry was used by some to support proposals in the mid-1990s for deregulation, but Lovins criticized proponents as "a curious coalition of large industries eager to grab the cheapest power at everyone else's expense, free-market ideologies with a limited knowledge of utility reality and history, anti-environmentalists who think 'retail wheeling' [opening a local utility company's transmission lines so retail customers can choose from competing electric generators] is a neat way of avoiding environmental accountability or expenditures . . . and consultants who see chaos as a profit opportunity."

For Lovins, the solution to efficient, sustainable resource use is in better design: "The essence of good or even great engineering is to do more with much, much less. Engineers ought to be rewarded for practicing elegant frugality. . . . The profession's contribution to efficient utilization of resources is probably the most important single need in our technical system today. It will have the most far-reaching benefits for society." For Lovins, improved energy efficiency means improved product quality, less pollution, more efficient human work, economic savings, and reduced dependency on foreign supplies of resources. It is also politically irresistible, argues Lovins. Efficiency is nonideological: everyone is in favor of it, and it can accommodate a wide diversity of views.

The Rocky Mountain Institute's home page on the world wide web is: <http://solstice.crest.org/rmi>

For Further Reading
Lee Goldberg, "Green Engineering: Designing for a Brighter Future, Part 1," *Electronic Design*, 45, no. 1 (January 6, 1997): 108.
Stuart L. Hart, "Beyond Greening; Strategies for a Sustainable World," *Harvard Business Review* (January 1997): 66.
Amory Lovins, *Soft Path* (New York: Basic Books, 1978).
Jonathan Weisman, "Drive to Open Power Industry to Competition Gains Steam," *Congressional Quarterly Weekly Report* (October 12, 1996): 2911–2917, at 2916–2917.

$13 a barrel in 1986, and plentiful supplies of cheap, imported oil reduced pump prices even more. The panic subsided that had driven the search for alternatives after the Arab oil embargo, and most policymakers returned to their love affair with oil and gas. Second, the public interest in new gadgets and gizmos faded as the nation became indifferent to energy issues generally. Many potential customers decided to wait until the new solar panels and home wind turbines were fine-tuned and the technology further refined. Alternative sources never gained public acceptance among mainstream America. And finally, pocketbook issues, as they often do, altered behavior. When the federal government offered tax incentives, companies and products flourished; when the incentives were removed, interest waned.

REVISITING NUCLEAR POWER

Unlike many environmental problems, it is possible to identify the exact place and moment in time when nuclear power became a political issue. That moment was 3:25 P.M. on December 2, 1942, and the place was a former squash court beneath the West Stands of Staff Field in Chicago. A group of scientists under the direction of Enrico Fermi created the first human-made self-sustaining nuclear reaction, followed two and a half years later by the explosion of a nuclear weapon beneath the sands of New Mexico. It became a political issue because the United States was in the midst of World War II, and nuclear weapons were considered the only way to bring about a swift conclusion to the war. Thus, nuclear power was first thought of not as an energy source but as a military weapon. Advances in technology were pushed through government agencies not to provide electricity but for their destructive capabilities. But the most important element of nuclear power development from the splitting of the atom through the first weapons testing and into the late 1960s was secrecy—a factor that slowed the evolution of the technology and limited its spread to only a handful of nations.[21]

Although the United States and the Soviet Union produced small amounts of electricity from experimental reactors in the early 1950s, the first full-scale commercial applications were at Calder Hall in the United Kingdom in 1956 and in France in 1962. But the English efforts were rapidly overtaken by the United States, then by France, then by Japan and Germany. The United States did not seriously consider sharing its fuel-enrichment technology with other nations until late 1970, leaving a major gap in global development. After the end of World War II, the federal government took several steps that bolstered nuclear power as a source of energy. In 1954, Congress enacted the Atomic Energy Act, which permitted private ownership of nuclear reactors and private use of nuclear fuels under lease arrangements. For the first time, an emerging private sector nuclear power industry could gain access to classified government information on nuclear fuels. The legislation was followed by the Power Demonstration Reactor Programs from 1955 to 1963 through which the federal government encouraged the construction of prototype nuclear power stations throughout the United States. By 1960, the Atomic Energy Commission (AEC), the federal agency charged with regulating the new facilities, announced its objective of making nuclear power economically competitive by 1968 in those parts of the country dependent on high-cost fossil fuels.[22]

The result of the government's policy was a massive expansion of nuclear-generating facilities, beginning with an announcement in 1960 by Southern California Edison of its plan to build a huge facility at San Onofre, California, and a similar announcement by Pacific Gas and Electric to build a privately funded plant at Bodega Bay, California.[23] In 1962, as an incentive to encourage the building of large-capacity nuclear plants, the AEC offered to pay part of the design costs, and the rush to build began. Nine nuclear power plants were ordered by American utility companies during 1965, twenty-two in 1966, and twenty-four in 1967. With the passage of the Air Quality Act in 1967 and its crackdown on polluting coal and oil-fired plants in urban areas, utility companies were convinced that nuclear power was the energy source of the future. Environmentalists had already begun to complain about the damage done by coal mining, and as one analyst puts it, coal's days seemed to be numbered. Orders for new nuclear plants continued: seventeen in 1970, twenty-eight in 1971, forty-two in 1973, and twenty-four in 1974. Yet all of the nuclear power plants ordered since 1974 have been either canceled or placed on an indefinite construction schedule.[24]

What happened to shorten the promising beginnings of nuclear power? There are several explanations as to why more than one hundred reactor projects since 1972 have been canceled or stopped in midcompletion. First, the growth of the environmental movement in the early 1970s, combined with zealous antiwar sentiment, led to a strong sense of public opposition to anything associated with nuclear weapons, including nuclear power as an energy source. Second, that same public pressure led to increased government sensitivity about the impacts of new projects, as seen in the history of legislation outlined in Chapter 1. In 1971, the U.S. Court of Appeals ruled that the AEC had failed to follow the provisions of the National Environmental Policy Act in licensing the Calvert Cliffs facility near Baltimore, Maryland, followed by a similar ruling on the Quad Cities nuclear power station on the Mississippi River in Illinois. Both decisions focused attention on the environmental impacts of nuclear facilities and led to increased scrutiny of license applications.

Third, media coverage of a malfunctioning cooling system at Three Mile Island in 1979 and the explosion of a nuclear reactor at Chernobyl in 1986 made utilities still considering nuclear power think twice about the effects of widespread public opposition to such projects. These attitudes are still prevalent today and account for the general reluctance of policymakers to even consider this power source as an option.[25] Fourth, economics played a key role in scuttling the building of new facilities. Government estimates on the growth in demand for electricity in the 1970s turned out to be overly optimistic, and as demand for energy decreased, the cost of building new plants rose, making them non–cost-effective. In 1971, the estimated cost of building a typical facility was $345 million, but by 1980 the figure had climbed to $3.2 billion. The federal government had spent nearly $18 billion in subsidizing the commercial development of nuclear power by 1980, and smaller utilities could not afford to build on their own.

In addition, construction and licensing of new plants were taking as long as ten years—delaying the point at which utilities could begin passing the costs on to consumers and recouping their investments. Financial horror stories began to proliferate. Of five nuclear reactors started in the 1970s by the Washington Public Power Supply System, only one has been completed, and the utility ultimately defaulted on $2.25 billion in bonds in 1983. When the Long Island Lighting Company began building its Shoreham plant in April 1973, the cost was estimated at $300 million. Delayed by protests from nearby residents and federally mandated design changes, the cost escalated to $5.5 billion by the time it was completed in December 1984. Suddenly plan for *all* types of power plants—not just nuclear—were being shelved, as they became too costly.

Although the United States has come to a halt in its construction of nuclear power plants, four other nations have pushed forward, with more than two-thirds of the world's facilities operating in France, Japan, the United Kingdom, and in the republics of the former Soviet Union. The United States is still the leader in the amount of commercial nuclear power generation, followed by France, Japan, Germany, and Russia.[26] Some regions have become almost totally dependent upon nuclear power, while others have been untouched by nuclear technology, including Australasia, Africa (except for South Africa), the Arab states of the Middle East, Southeast Asia, and most of Latin America (except Mexico, Argentina, and Brazil). For the most part, these nations have only traditional "poor country" energy sources—fuel wood, charcoal, and forage for animals, and there is almost a complete absence of nuclear power. Although the United States began to provide fissile material and millions of dollars in grants for research reactors in 1953, very few Third World countries have reached the point of having commercial nuclear power plants connected to their electricity supply networks.

There are several reasons why nuclear power has been limited to the most-industrialized nations. Prior to 1973, world oil prices were low enough to make nuclear power seem less attractive as an energy source than fossil fuels. In addition, most developing nations were too poor or too much in debt to develop nuclear plants, which are extremely capital-intensive. To do so would have meant sacrificing other priorities that were deemed more important. Lastly, concerns about the proliferation of nuclear weapons preoccupied those nations with the capacity for producing plutonium and uranium, limiting their desires to share the necessary raw materials. Despite international agreements, at least seven countries are believed to have developed nuclear weapons capabilities outside the safeguards of the International Atomic Energy Agency: Argentina, Colombia, India, North Korea, Pakistan, Israel, and South Africa.[27]

Will nuclear power ever be reconsidered as a major source of energy? The answer to that question has little to do with science or technology and much to do with politics. Some industry officials believe such a change can take place only if the regulatory framework for licensing facilities is streamlined by Congress. Other analysts feel that utilities would be more likely to gain public acceptance for new nuclear facilities if they were sited or expanded near existing plants rather than in new areas. Public opposition to nuclear facilities, although still strong, appears to have leveled off. Attempts to close down facilities or ban nuclear power altogether have not been successful in a number of states, suggesting that Americans may not be so disenchanted with nuclear power to close down the industry completely. But most observers believe that, unless Congress moves forward with a plan to store nuclear waste (see Chapter 5), and dismantles aging reactors,[28] the nuclear energy debate will remain at a standstill, with 113 nuclear reactors now in operation in the United States and none under construction.

THE HISTORY OF POLICY PARALYSIS

Historically, U.S. energy policy has been separated by types of fuel, with different institutional associations and interests for each type and few attempts at coalition building. Coal interests from the Northeast have dealt with the Bureau of Mines, while states with uranium were more likely to converse with the Atomic Energy committees in Congress and the Nuclear Regulatory Commission. Seldom did jurisdictional boundaries cross over from one fuel to another, and as a result, terms like *disarray, turmoil,* and *inertia* are often used to describe U.S. energy policy. Those terms are in part applicable because of the maze of legislative and regulatory obstacles that have developed, along with a profusion of competing interests. The result is an energy policy that is highly segmented and neither comprehensive nor effective. While many analysts have attempted to explain why U.S. energy policy has been so ineffective, the consensus appears to be that the government has intervened unnecessarily rather than allowing market forces to allocate scarce energy resources.[29] How did such a policy develop?

Before 1900, the U.S. government had an ad hoc approach to what was perceived to be an unlimited supply of energy resources. A sense of abundance and virtual giveaways of public lands resulted in many valuable resources coming under private ownership. Although there were early rumblings of competition among interests representing the various fuels, it was not until after the turn of the century that the government began to intervene. To assure a stable and competitive oil market, the government relied upon the Sherman Anti-Trust Act in 1911 to break up the Standard Oil monopoly, and during World War I, President Woodrow Wilson established the Petroleum Advisory Committee to allocate American supplies. After the 1921 Teapot Dome scandal, in which officials were convicted of leasing federal lands to oil companies in exchange for bribes, the Federal Oil Conservation Board was created to oversee the oil industry. By the 1930s, the federal government's role had changed to one of consumer protection, expanding its jurisdiction with the Natural Gas Act of 1938 and the creation of the Tennessee Valley Authority. There was never an attempt made to coordinate policy across fuel and use areas. Each area of energy supply—coal, gas, hydropower, oil, and nuclear power—was handled separately, as was each consumption sector—utilities, transportation, industrial, and residential. During the 1950s, as Congress approved a massive interstate highway system and transportation network, the Supreme Court ratified the Federal Power Commission's power to regulate natural gas prices, which held prices artificially low as gas consumption skyrocketed.[30]

As the environmental movement developed in the late 1960s and early 1970s, the process of developing energy policy became increasingly complex as more interests demanded to be included in the decision-making process. At the same time, the importance of energy as a political issue brought in congressional leaders who sought to respond to their constituents' demands that something be done about the long lines at the gas pumps and rising prices for fuels. One study of energy policy found eight distinct groups active in national energy politics.[31]

Between 1969 and 1973, a confluence of negative factors and events changed the history of American energy policy forever. First, predictions by a few officials about a dependence upon foreign oil came true. Although the United States first began importing oil as early as 1947, oil from Arab sources reached over a million barrels a day by 1973, more than double the amount imported eighteen months earlier and 30 percent of total U.S. demand. Second, domestic oil production decreased because of price disparities over foreign oil and increasing costs for exploration and recovery. Third, new environmental legislation discouraged production of coal and nuclear power and brought a delay in completion of the trans-Alaska pipeline at the same time that Americans were driving more miles than ever before. Finally, the highly publicized Santa Barbara oil spill in 1969 had led to a five-year moratorium on offshore drilling, further restricting American oil production. The result was a nation made vulnerable to the vagaries of Middle Eastern politics.

The Nixon administration's approach to energy policy in the 1970s was marked by a series of failed attempts to do something about the impending crisis. Initially, the government imposed an Economic Stabilization Program, which froze prices on crude oil and petroleum products for ninety days, and froze wages and prices nationwide. In early 1973, Nixon restructured the country's mandatory oil import quota plan, which had limited foreign oil imports and allowed an unlimited purchase of home heating oil and diesel fuel for a four-month period. This action was followed by the creation of a hand-picked Special Committee on Energy comprised of key Nixon advisers, who recommended steps be taken to cope with price increase and fuel shortages. The strategy was to increase energy supplies, with little concern for modifying demand or conserving energy. By midyear, the administration's mandatory fuel allocation program had led to the closure of hundreds of independent gasoline stations. Then the administration shifted its policies once again by proposing that $100 million be spent on research and development for new energy technology and creation of a Federal Energy Administration to coordinate policy.

In October 1973, OPEC members, resentful of United States aid to Israel, voted to cut their oil production and to end all petroleum exports to the United States, resulting in a sharp increase in world oil prices and forcing the Nixon administration to drastically revise its approach. Nixon responded with Project Independence to eliminate foreign oil imports by 1980, and Congress enacted the Emergency Petroleum Allocation Act to distribute fuel supplies evenly.

Analyses of the politics of energy during this period point out a number of lessons learned from the 1973 crisis. For example, a "cry-wolf syndrome" arose when the first warnings appeared about dependence upon foreign oil. One survey had even found that the majority of Americans were unaware that the United States imported any oil and were unable to understand how the most technically advanced nation in the world simply couldn't produce enough oil to meet demand. As a result, the concerns were often ignored or disbelieved. Decisions were often based on misleading or poor quality information, and confused and often contradictory policies resulted. A turnover in leadership (four different people held the position of White House energy policy coordinator in 1973) exacerbated the problem. The role of "energy czar" passed through the hands of seven men from 1971 to 1973, each of whom had a different concept of what U.S. energy policy should be. Some, such as Secretary of Agriculture Earl Butz, were given new titles and responsibilities, while others, such as George Lincoln, were made heads of agencies that were then abruptly abolished (Office of Emergency Planning).[32] Lastly, by treating each fuel source separately and allowing the disparate interest groups to be so deeply involved in the decision-making process, the government never really took control of the crisis.[33]

As a result of the 1973 crisis, a host of agencies took turns formulating energy policy. The Federal Energy Administration was created in May 1974, but the agency lacked direction and suffered from a lack of a clear sense of mission. It was designed to bring together smaller agencies that had historically been in conflict with one another and was caught between the competing objectives of regulating prices and expediting domestic resource development. After Nixon's resignation, Congress attempted to pick up the pieces by enacting the Energy Policy and Conservation Act of 1975, which levied a windfall profits tax on oil to control imports and gave the president the power to ration gas in an emergency. Other provisions included appliance standards, improved auto mileage standards, and authorized petroleum stockpiling.

The politics of energy took a different turn during the administration of President Jimmy Carter. The creation of a separate Cabinet-level Department of Energy in 1977 underscored the nation's crisis mentality, and Carter's campaign promise to reorganize government. The agency was charged with regulating fuel consumption, providing incentives for energy conservation, and research and development into alternative energy sources. In 1977, an acute natural gas shortage led Carter to propose his National Energy Plan (NEP), as he characterized the energy situation as "the moral equivalent of war." The NEP differed from the Nixon administration's strategies because it called for greater fuel efficiency and conservation rather than increased production. In 1977, Congress also replaced the Federal Power Commission, which had been created in 1920, with the Federal Energy Regulatory Commission (FERC), giving the agency responsibility for oversight of the electric power and natural gas industries.

By the time Congress passed the National Energy Act in October 1978, Carter's NEP had been gutted. In retrospect, it has been argued that the Carter proposal was doomed from the beginning. Members of Congress found that their constituents were unwilling to make sacrifices (like reducing the number of miles they drove yearly) because they didn't feel there really was an energy shortage. Voters made it clear that they believed the entire energy crisis was concocted by the big oil companies to force prices upward and generate bigger profits. In addition, the Carter administration was guilty of taking its case directly to the people, rather than developing a program in consultation with Congress.

The Reagan administration, in contrast, marks an eight-year period of amicable cooperation between the petroleum and coal industries and the administration and a dramatic shift in energy research and development.[34] Reagan's strategy, outlined in his 1981 National Energy Plan, was to limit governmental intervention as much as possible, especially with regard to regulatory agencies, while supporting nuclear power and cutting research funds for alternative energy sources. Renouncing the Carter administration's goal of meeting 20 percent of the nation's energy needs through solar power by the year 2000, Reagan even symbolically had his staff remove the solar panels Carter had installed at the White House. He was unsuccessful in dissolving the Department of Energy, which he viewed as indicative of Carter's "big government" approach, although his appointment of former South Carolina governor James Edwards signaled his intentions. The Reagan presidency was marked by a return to the strategies of the 1960s—including reliance on the free market to control prices, dependence on fossil fuels, tax benefits for oil producers, and little support for conservation.

George Bush continued the policies initiated by his predecessor. His 1991 national energy strategy sought to achieve roughly equal measures of new energy production and conservation. One of the cornerstones of that policy was to open up 1.5 million acres of the nineteen-million acre Arctic National Wildlife Refuge in northeast Alaska for oil and gas exploration. After the Persian Gulf Crisis in 1991, Congress seemed more inclined to move forward on energy policy, finally enacting the comprehensive Energy Policy Act of 1992 just prior to the November election. The new law restructures the electric utility industry to promote more competition, provide tax relief to independent oil and gas drillers, encourage energy conservation and efficiency, promote renewable energy and cars that run on alternative fuels, make it easier to build nuclear power plants, authorize billions of dollars for energy-related research and development, and create a climate protection office within the Energy Department. Critics point out that the bill does not address the issue of automobile fuel efficiency (one of the planks in Bill Clinton's environmental platform) and does not significantly reduce U.S. dependence on foreign oil, but rather caps existing levels of use. Still, it marks the first time in a decade that Congress has been able to compromise on the most contentious provisions—those dealing with alternative fuels and energy-related tax provisions.[35]

Early in his presidency, Bill Clinton proposed a broad tax on all forms of energy in order to raise federal revenue to reduce the budget deficit. The proposed tax, called a Btu tax because it was based on the heating ability of different fuels, as measured by British thermal units, would have raised the prices of gasoline, electricity, and other energy sources. Environmentalists supported the measure as a way to promote conservation and to begin to move away from fossil fuel consumption. The tax would have raised only approximately $22 billion per year, only a tiny fraction of the $6 trillion U.S. economy, but opposition from Democratic and Republican senators representing energy-producing states killed the idea.[36] The administration was successful in raising gasoline taxes by 4.3 cents per gallon in 1993 as part of its deficit reduction plan. During the 1996 campaign, when gas prices jumped 17 percent during the summer, Republican candidate Bob Dole called for a repeal of the gas tax, and President Clinton called for an investigation of the oil companies and ordered the release of 12 million barrels of oil from the nation's Strategic Oil Reserve to soften the price increase.[37] Increasing energy taxes sufficiently for significant conservation or revenue purposes requires more political skill than recent presidents and their congressional allies have been able to muster.

More politically popular have been proposals to deregulate the electric power industry, the last government-sanctioned monopoly. Deregulatory proposals have been made since the 1970s, as economists and power producers argued that increased competition would result in lower prices and improved efficiency. Large consumers such as industries are also active proponents of electricity deregulation. The agency responsible for regulating electricity production, the Federal Energy Regulatory Commission, issued in 1996 an order to utilities to open their transmission lines to any competing electric generator willing to pay fair transmission costs, paving the way for real competition in the industry. In 1996, two states, California and Rhode Island, enacted laws that brought competition into the industry, and almost every state was at least studying the idea. A number of deregulation bills were introduced in the 104th Congress and deregulation was a high priority of the Republican leadership's plan for the 105th Congress. The Clinton administration has promised its own plan. But the politics of energy policy is complicated: utilities want compensation for old investments such as nuclear power plants that will likely be unprofitable, the natural gas industry warns of increased profits to the electric companies and no benefits to consumers, westerners who enjoy cheap hydroelectric power fear national plans proposed by states whose residents have high electricity bills, and midwesterners want to burn more of their coal to produce power while northeasterners fear increased air pollution if they do. Environmentalists fear the deregulation will increase consumption and thereby increase fossil fuel emissions. As companies focus on the bottom line, they will be less willing to invest in research and production of more expensive renewable energy sources. Others argue that it is a mistake to tamper with the nation's electric power system when there is no pressing need to do so and the system is arguably the best in the world.[38]

It is important to consider U.S. energy policy in light of a global perspective, although this section provides only a snapshot view of what the future holds for the United States, rather than a region-by-region overview of what the energy picture looks like in other nations. Energy is considered to be a global issue for a number of reasons. It transcends the traditional boundaries of the nation-state and cannot be resolved by a single country. It is an issue that possesses a present imperative that forces nations to press for resolution (i.e., oil is a finite commodity and thus it is crucial that alternative sources be found). The resolution of the issues requires policy action—it will not resolve itself. Finally, energy is a global issue because of its persistence on the policy agenda—there is no consensus about how to solve the problems that have been identified.[39]

Energy consumption is closely tied to economic development, and future projections of energy use show a changing profile of fuels as we approach the next century, as seen in Figure 6.2. Total world consumption is projected to grow

steadily well into the next decade, on average about half as fast as world economic growth, as measured by gross domestic product. Oil will continue to be the
most important source of energy, but the growth in oil consumption is the slow-
est of all the major energy sources. The fastest-growing fuel is natural gas, which
will grow over one and one-half times as fast as oil. The most noteworthy pro-

Figure 6.2   World Energy Consumption, by Type, 1990–2010
(in quadrillion Btu)

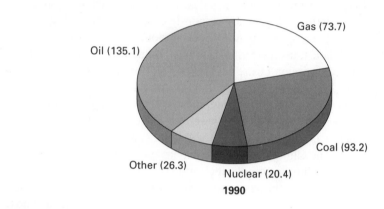

Gas (73.7)

Oil (135.1)

Coal (93.2)

Other (26.3)   Nuclear (20.4)
1990

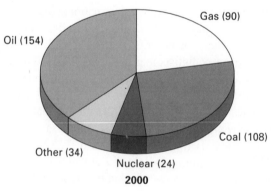

Gas (90)

Oil (154)

Coal (108)

Other (34)   Nuclear (24)
2000

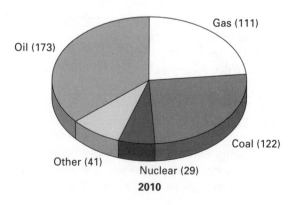

Gas (111)

Oil (173)

Coal (122)

Other (41)   Nuclear (29)
2010

jection, however, is that energy consumption in the developing countries will grow about twice as fast as energy consumption in industrial countries. The growth of urban areas and industrial activities that accompany development bring with them increased demands for transportation, electrification, and all the energy-using appliances and amenities associated with modernization.

The U.S. energy pie looks somewhat different from the energy use of other countries. Western Europe, for example, has become heavily dependent upon imported energy since World War II and the switch from native coal resources to oil imported from the Middle East. A vocal antinuclear power lobby in several European nations has limited the development of facilities in parts of France and in the United Kingdom, Germany, and Sweden. In Eastern Europe and the republics of the former Soviet Union, coal has been the predominant energy source, although nuclear energy has been used in those regions far from coal reserves. Japan, with virtually no indigenous fossil fuels, has become a leader in both energy conservation and nuclear power, but still imports nearly 90 percent of its energy in the form of oil. China, in contrast, has sufficient hydroelectric power and coal reserves to last well into the twenty-second century at current levels of output, but has been unable to develop an adequate distribution system to get power to consumers. South Korea and Taiwan have been able to vigorously develop their nuclear power programs with little public opposition and significant government support. Most developing nations are heavily dependent upon traditional fuels (coal, timber) and must import oil, although Latin American countries are now expanding their hydroelectric power. The sources of energy vary throughout the globe, depending upon a nation's resources and, to some extent at least, political forces. In absolute terms, the United States, Western Europe, the republics of the former Soviet Union, and China consumed the most energy in the 1990s and will remain the largest consumers through 2010.

FUTURE ENERGY TRENDS

If the past is indicative of the future, the American energy pie may look different by the year 2000. Over the past forty years, the U.S. outlook has changed somewhat as new sources have become more competitively priced and traditional sources of fuel—primarily crude oil and coal—have become less reliable or polluting. Coal production has increased since 1960, while production of oil has been reduced following the Arab oil crisis in the early 1970s. The most dramatic change has been the increase in the production of energy from nuclear sources, despite the political barriers and a virtual end to construction of new facilities. Projections for the future indicate nuclear power will be surpassed by natural gas as the second largest source of U.S. electricity generation. Similarly, renewable energy use is expected to increase sharply by 2010 as new technologies are developed and the prices of other energy sources increase. The most significant market penetration is expected from geothermal installations, the use of municipal solid waste as fuel, and various biomass applications, with nonhydropower sources increasing to as much as 39 percent of the energy pie near 2010.[40]

But it is the consumption side of the equation that raises concern among many decision makers. Although total energy use almost doubled since 1970 and increased by 4 percent between 1990 and 1994, the resumption of normal economic growth (at a rate of 2–3 percent per year) and the prospect of relatively low energy prices (compared to the peaks of the 1970s) are projected to raise total energy use in all sectors in the next twenty years. Where will the additional energy come from? Domestic oil production is gradually decreasing, while the demand for petroleum is increasing, leading to projections that the amount of imported petroleum will jump from about 42 percent in 1990 to between 53 and 69 percent by 2010. The United States will continue its reliance upon Middle Eastern oil (source of the majority of proven reserves), as will other producing nations whose supplies are beginning to be exhausted. Some analysts believe that this will lead to a competition for Saudi Arabian oil at a time when political pressures in the Gulf region continue to simmer.

There are two basic scenarios of what the next decade will bring to the politics of energy. One of the most prevalent views—the so-called conservation alternative—is that we must dramatically change our consumption patterns. Proponents believe the way to satisfy the world's energy appetite is simply to go on an energy diet; rather than looking for new sources of power, we should be conserving what is available and getting more out of it. Advocates of this strategy point to the fact that Western Europeans use only half as much energy as Americans to maintain their life-style—evidence that energy conservation does not mean a starvation diet.

Can Americans simply agree to use less energy to reduce the need for new power plants? That question has already been answered as a result of the oil crises of the 1970s. Despite that the American economy grew by more than 40 percent from 1973 to 1986, the amount of power consumed by the United States during that same period remained stable. Residential fuel use, for example, dropped appreciably after the 1979–1980 crisis when thermostats were voluntarily lowered. One way in which we could make a serious impact on our dependence on foreign oil would be to require that automobiles be more energy efficient. The federal government took the initial steps in this direction in 1975 when Congress enacted Corporate Average Fuel Economy (CAFE) standards, which specified targets for miles per gallon. Although the Reagan administration later weakened those standards, the average new car in the United States today is rated at twenty-eight miles per gallon, twice as high as the 1974 average—a difference that saves four million barrels of oil per day. Increasing CAFE standards and encouraging Americans to cut down their driving by 25 percent could reduce oil consumption for cars by half and eliminate the need for Middle Eastern oil imports. Other researchers have pointed out that only economic incentives for public utilities will provide the impetus that the country needs to develop a full conservation effort.[41]

Although representatives of both political parties have given their support for energy conservation as a key element in future energy planning, their rhetoric has failed to result thus far in any substantial conservation legislation. Four explanations for this gap between appearance and substance have been offered. First, despite the prevailing myth that predatory oil and gas producers have blocked or resisted price controls (the most effective conservation incentive), there is evidence that public interest groups have failed to exert much influence in protecting consumer interests. The kinds of consumer advocates who pressed states for electric rate reform during the 1970s have been largely silent since that time. Second, public opinion, often said to be the driving force behind legislative decision making, has not reached consensus on energy issues. The public appears caught between a desire to avoid energy exploitation while at the same time showing little willingness to support federal control of industry. Third, energy policies have been filtered through localized interests and congressional blocs (Western-Eastern, oil-gas, Democrats-Republicans, etc.), making it difficult for Congress to come up with a national sentiment on energy conservation. Lastly, energy policy is but one example of several policy issues symptomatic of a larger pathology—periodic institutional immobilism, or, as it is more commonly known, policy paralysis. Like civil rights legislation in the 1950s, or budget debates in the 1980s, energy has bogged down in a complex political system that is short on leadership and long on intense political convictions.[42]

A second, more controversial scenario for the future begins with the premise that the events of 1973–1974 were not an energy crisis, but rather the beginning of a New Energy Era—a time of uncertainty and volatility, which decision makers must learn to face, and with which they must struggle over the coming decades. That view believes energy decisions are made in the private sector rather than by the government, since governments are neither producers nor consumers of energy. Advocates of this view believe that the United States has blundered in its approach to energy policy in the past by relying upon outdated and inappropriate ideas about the role of the public and private sectors. They support an Integrated Energy System (IES) approach, which involves fuel sources that are clean, secure and reliable, safe, economic, and robust. More simply, IES would involve using existing renewable fuel sources but take advantage of improvements in technology and better ways to put the pieces together to improve system efficiency and social acceptability. For example, IES might involve greater reliance upon cogeneration and combined cycle systems, as well as newer technologies such as carbon dioxide recovery from combustion processes.[43] Are the kinds of legal and institutional barriers that exist to implementing IES surmountable? Supporters of IES believe that the public (and public officials) will accept a fine-tuning of the energy pie recipe rather than a complete change in its ingredients. So far, however, there has been little incentive for decision makers to even look at the menu, and they are unlikely to do so until the next energy crisis intrudes.

SUMMARY

Political events such as the 1973 Arab oil embargo, the passage of the 1990 Clean Air Act, the 1991 Gulf War, and the 1992 Energy Policy Act have been milestones in the development of U.S. energy policy, since they forced policy-makers to confront U.S. dependence upon foreign oil. After the 1973 oil crisis, for example, research and federal support for alternative energy sources flourished, and serious energy conservation measures were enacted. But during the 1980s, as the price of oil dropped and supplies stabilized, Americans began using more oil than ever before. Recent air quality legislation is now beginning to force technological advances and is likely to lead to a gradual decrease in the use of fossil fuels to produce electricity. In the regulatory arena, energy policy has been characterized as the politics of disarray, focused upon only in times of crisis. There are two ways of looking at the world's energy future. One view is that rather than looking toward new sources we must go on an energy diet and conserve existing resources. A second scenario assumes that the world entered a New Energy Era in the early 1970s and argues that most decisions about energy will not be made in the political arena but in the marketplace. Supporters of this view recommend that the world continue its reliance upon fossil fuels but implement an Integrated Energy System based on evolving technology to better use those resources. Given the historical record, however, it is unlikely that there will be great strides made in global energy policy until another crisis is upon us. In the meantime, the way we produce and consume energy in the world will have tremendously important consequences for air pollution and environmental quality.

NOTES

1. Quoted in Keith Melville, ed., *Energy Options: Finding a Solution to the Power Predicament* (New York: McGraw-Hill, 1992), 4.

2. To put those figures in perspective, the reader should keep in mind that the price rose from $13 to $34 per barrel following the cutoff of Iranian oil in 1979. The price in 1992 had declined to $21 per barrel.

3. This view of energy is presented in Thomas H. Lee, Ben C. Bell, Jr., and Richard D. Tabors, *Energy Aftermath* (Boston, MA: Harvard Business School Press, 1990), 1.

4. U.S. Bureau of Census, *Statistical Abstract of the United States 1996* (Washington, D.C.: U.S. Government Printing Office, 1996): 578–579.

5. Barry B. Hughes et al., *Energy in the Global Arena: Actors, Values, Policies and Futures* (Durham, NC: Duke University Press, 1985), 10–11.

6. Edward Teller, *Energy from Heaven and Earth* (San Francisco, CA: W.H. Freeman, 1979), 2.

7. For an analysis of coal policies, see Walter Rosenbaum, *Energy Politics and Public Policy,* 2nd ed. (Washington, D.C.: Congressional Quarterly Press, 1987), 161–187.

8. Keith Lee Kozloff, "Renewable Energy Technology: An Urgent Need, A Hard Sell," *Environment, 36,* no. 9 (November 1994): 4–9, 25.

9. Constance Elizabeth Hunt, *Down by the River* (Washington, D.C.: Island Press, 1988), 200–201.

10. Ibid., 215–243.

11. See John D. Echeverria, Pope Barrow, and Richard Roos-Collins, *Rivers at Risk: The Citizen's Guide to Hydropower* (Washington, D.C.: Island Press, 1989).

12. See Christopher Anderson, "The Future Is Now (Again)," *Nature, 354* (December 5, 1991): 344–345.

13. Christopher Flavin, "Windpower: Small, but Growing Fast," *WorldWatch* (October 1996): 35–37.

14. Peter Asmus, "A Fresh Breeze: New Technologies Revitalize Wind Power," *California Journal, 23,* no. 8 (August 1992): 413–415.

15. See Richard A. Kerr, "Geothermal Tragedy of the Commons," *Science, 253,* no. 5016 (July 12, 1991): 134–135; and "Developer Drills at Crater Lake Border," *National Parks, 64,* nos. 1–2 (January–February 1990): 9–10.

16. See Ian Anderson, "Blowout Blights Future of Hawaii's Geothermal Power," *New Scientist,* July 20, 1991, 17; and Mark Mardon, "Steamed Up over Rainforests," *Sierra, 75,* no. 3 (May–June 1990): 80–82.

17. See Daniel Sperling, *New Transportation Fuels: A Strategic Approach to Technological Change* (Berkeley: University of California Press, 1988).

18. See Daniel Sperling, ed., *Alternative Transportation Fuels: An Environmental and Energy Solution* (Westport, CT: Quorum Books, 1989).

19. Otis Port, "Turning Paper-Mill Sludge into Clean Burning Fuel," *Business Week,* October 19, 1992, 61.

20. Mark Katches, "Cleaner methanol-fuel buses revealed as mechanical lemons," *The Oregonian* (December 26, 1993): B2.

21. For a comprehensive history of the development of atomic power, see Margaret Gowing, *Reflections on Atomic Energy History* (Cambridge: Cambridge University Press, 1978).

22. See Peter R. Mounfield, *World Nuclear Power* (New York: Routledge, 1991).

23. That project was later canceled by the company.

24. Mounfield, 73.

25. See Paul Slovic, Mark Layman, and James H. Flynn, "Risk Perception, Trust, and Nuclear Waste: Lessons from Yucca Mountain," *Environment, 33,* no. 32 (April 1991): 6.

26. U.S. Bureau of the Census, *Statistical Abstract of the United States 1996:* 576.

27. Mounfield, 48.

28. See Bill Breen, "Dismantling Nuclear Reactors," *Garbage, 4,* no. 2. (March–April 1992): 40–47.

29. See, for example, Walter J. Mead, *Energy and the Environment: Conflict in Public Policy* (Washington, D.C.: American Enterprise Institute, 1978).

30. James Everett Katz, *Congress and National Energy Policy* (New Brunswick, NJ: Transaction Books, 1984), 5–7.

31. John E. Chubb, *Interest Groups and the Bureaucracy: The Politics of Energy* (Stanford: Stanford University Press, 1983), 14–15.

32. See John C. Whitaker, *Striking a Balance: Environment and Natural Resources Policy in the Nixon-Ford Years* (Washington, D.C.: American Enterprise Institute, 1976), 66–68.

33. There are a number of highly readable accounts of this period, including Lester A. Sobel, ed., *Energy Crisis, Vol. 1, 1969–1973* (New York: Facts on File, 1974); and Robert J. Kalter and William A. Vogely, eds., *Energy Supply and Government Policy* (Ithaca, NY: Cornell University Press, 1976).

34. See Claude E. Barfield, *Science Policy from Ford to Reagan: Change and Continuity* (Washington, D.C.: American Enterprise Institute, 1982); and Don E. Kash and Robert W. Rycroft, *U.S. Energy Policy: Crisis and Complacency* (Norman, OK: University of Oklahoma Press, 1984).

35. Holly Idelson, "National Energy Strategy Provisions," *Congressional Quarterly,* November 28, 1992, 3722–3730.

36. Susan Dentzer, "R.I.P. for the Btu tax," *U.S. News and World Report* (June 21, 1993): 95.

37. Howard Gleckman, "Gas pump politics," *Business Week* (May 13, 1996): 40–41.

38. Jonathan Weisman, "Drive to Open Power Industry to Competition Gains Steam," *Congressional Quarterly Weekly Report* (October 12, 1996): 2911–2917.

39. For a comprehensive explanation of this approach, see Hughes et al, *Energy in the Global Arena,* xii–xviii.

40. Energy Information Administration, *Annual Energy Outlook 1992* (Washington, D.C.: U.S. Government Printing Office, January, 1992), viii–ix.

41. See, for example, Peter N. Nemetz, *Economic Incentives for Energy Conservation* (New York: Wiley, 1984); and John C. Sawhill and Richard Cotton, eds., *Energy Conservation: Successes and Failures* (Washington, D.C.: Brookings Institution, 1986).

42. These four explanations were developed by Pietro S. Nivola, *The Politics of Energy Conservation* (Washington, D.C.: Brookings Institution, 1986), 252–85.

43. A summary of the IES approach is found in Thomas H. Lee, Ben C. Ball, and Richard D. Tabors, *Energy Aftermath* (Boston, MA: Harvard Business School Press, 1990), 219–250.

FOR FURTHER READING

Hans H. Bass et al., eds. *Energy and Sustainable Development.* Boulder, CO: Westview Press, 1994.

Timothy J. Brennan et al. *A Shock to the System: Restructuring America's Electricity System.* Washington, D.C.: Resources for the Future, 1996.

Robert Hill, Phil O'Keefe, and Colin Snape. *The Future of Energy Use.* New York: St. Martin's Press, 1995.

Leslie McSpadden Wenner. *Energy and Environmental Interest Groups.* New York: Greenwood Press, 1990.

Ed Smelof and Peter Asmus. *Reinventing Electric Utilities.* Washington, D.C.: Island Press, 1996.

Vaclav Smil. *Energy in World History.* Boulder, CO: Westview Press, 1994.

Richard Wolfson. *Nuclear Choices: A Citizen's Guide to Nuclear Technology.* rev. ed. Cambridge, MA: MIT Press, 1993.

CHAPTER 7

Managing Water Resources

It is time to realize that one major, overwhelming reason
why we are running out of water is that we are killing
the water we have.

—William Ashworth, author[1]

The scarcity and availability of water, and the ways in which it is being used, are at issue not only in the United States but by governments in virtually every region of the globe. What makes water management interesting from a political perspective is that the officials and agencies that make water policy often labor in relatively obscure agencies and speak a language all their own. The terms to measure water, the science of keeping it clean, and the economics over who controls water resources are not the sort of thing most of us think about or talk about in our everyday conversation. "Waterspeak" includes references to acre feet, maximum contaminant level goals, interflow zones, and calichefication. And yet the prize of the "water wars" that this chapter chronicles is absolutely critical to our existence. Without water, we cannot live.

The basic political issue is that there is a continual shortage of fresh water for 40 percent of the world's population, with only one-half of 1 percent of the world's total water supply easily and economically available for human use. The rest is "locked up" in oceans, polar ice caps, surface collectors such as lakes and rivers, in clouds, or under Earth's surface yet too deep to be drilled in wells. Coupled with the problem of supply is the planet's expanding population and the basic human need for water, along with increased agricultural and industrial demand. In some areas of the world, natural causes such as climate change and drought have led to shortages.

This chapter examines the world's management of its water resources, beginning with an overview of the reasons behind Earth's water shortages. The chapter then goes on to look at the results of those shortages from a global perspective and offers a survey of the proposed solutions and their successes and failures. The discussion then turns to a key water issue, the protection of wetlands. It concludes with an examination of the challenges posed by water pollution in the United States and throughout the world.

WHY DON'T WE HAVE ENOUGH WATER?

Human use of water has increased more than thirty-five-fold over the past three centuries, with most of the increase in the developing nations worldwide. There are three basic reasons why, despite significant outlays of funds, there is a shortage of fresh water for almost half of the world's population. The first reason deals with personal water use and an increasing global population. Each individual consumes only about two quarts of water per day, but there are dozens of other daily uses, such as washing clothing, taking baths or showers, cooking meals, flushing toilets, and watering lawns, as seen in Table 7.1. For example, the average American's personal water use averages ninety gallons per day, and another six hundred gallons per day are used in the manufacturing, chemical, and industrial processes that create the goods and services we take for granted as a part of modern life. That includes water used, for example, by utility power plants, breweries, steel makers, and mining operations. Agricultural use accounts for an additional eight hundred gallons per person per day, for a total of almost fifteen hundred gallons per person per day.

How much water do we need, and how much do we have? That question is at the heart of the water management debate. Unfortunately, the United States does not have an up-to-date assessment of its existing water supply, so many of the political decisions that are being made are based largely on speculation rather than on science. A similar problem exists internationally. As a result, political decisions about water management are often made in a scientific vacuum, based largely on the claims of competing interest groups and users.

But personal water consumption is just part of the water management problem. The world's population is growing at such an alarming rate (see Chapter 13) that existing sources of fresh water are insufficient to meet the human demand. Researchers predict that over the next three decades, global population is expected to grow by nearly two-thirds, from about 5.5 billion to 8.5 billion. Even more important is the increasing urbanization of the world's population, and the demands placed on natural resources and the existing infrastructure. Currently, the population of the industrialized world is about three-fourths urban, compared

Table 7.1   How Much Water Does It Take . . .

to brush your teeth?	2 gallons
to flush a toilet?	5–7 gallons
to shave with water running?	10–15 gallons
to run a dishwasher?	12 gallons
to wash dishes by hand?	20 gallons
to take a shower?	25–50 gallons
to wash a load of clothes?	59 gallons
to wash a car with a hose?	150 gallons

with about one-third in the developing world, with complex regional differences. By the year 2005, half of the world's people will live in an urban area; by 2025, that number will be two of three. Many of those urban enclaves are in areas with minimal rainfall or severe shortages already, such as Los Angeles, New York, Mexico City, and Calcutta. In northern China, for example, where 300 cities are already experiencing water shortages, finding new sources of water will be a difficult task. Although the government has considered massive water transfers and has encouraged water conservation, existing supplies are almost fully utilized by agricultural users.[2]

The second cause of water scarcity is the increased demand for industrial, commercial, and agricultural use of water. Almost every industrialized nation is relying more and more on water for manufacturing, oil refineries, and utility power plants. There is also a considerable amount of water used in commercial settings, such as office air-conditioning systems, which use water to cool air for employee and customer comfort. These industrial and commercial needs are greatest in urban areas, where the population base already places its own demands on the water system.

Agricultural water use is also behind the scarcity issue. Irrigation is the answer to how to grow crops in areas where there is insufficient natural rainfall. Piping systems and wells transfer water from natural sources (lakes, streams, or aquifers) to fields, basically altering the natural hydrological cycle. It takes nearly one thousand gallons of water to grow each pound of food we consume, making agricultural irrigation a major water consumer, although consumption varies considerably from one country to another. In the Middle East, where high birthrates combine with a lack of rainfall, irrigation is a massive undertaking. Egypt, for example, irrigates 100 percent of its cropland, while Israel irrigates almost two-thirds. Jordan anticipates a 50 percent increase in its water needs by 2005, and several nations are considering the need to shift water usage away from agriculture in order to satisfy demands for drinking water.[3] In the years after World War II, especially the 1960s and 1970s, irrigated land tripled worldwide to 160 million hectares, mostly in China, India, and Pakistan. Currently, 250 million hectares of land are being irrigated. The least-irrigated acreage (less than five million hectares) is in the sub-Saharan region of Africa. Most of this increase came largely at the urging of international donors hoping to increase food production — a generally accepted justification. The United Nations Food and Agriculture Organization estimates irrigation will have to increase by 40 percent over the next twenty years to meet expected food supply demands. The largest planned increase in irrigated acreage will come in India, Pakistan, China, Mexico, and Brazil.[4]

The pressure to grow more and more food to meet the needs of the growing population is faced globally. The republics of the former Soviet Union have slowly drained the Aral Sea by diverting water for crop irrigation. The Aral Sea, located in central Asia, was once the fourth-largest lake on Earth, but has now shrunk to two-thirds its original size.[5] In the United States, there are signs that too many farms are trying to irrigate too much land with too little water. Of the 165 billion gallons of water used in states west of the one-hundredth meridian (a line stretching north to south from North Dakota through Texas), 145 billion gallons, or 88 percent, will go to irrigation. Areas to the west of the meridian generally receive less than twenty inches of rain per year, while those to the east have a problem of too much water in some states.[6] Despite the political costs of doing so, a shift in water priorities from agriculture to other uses would help to alleviate the scarcity problem in this country.[7]

There are, however, many political considerations that make irrigation controversial throughout much of the developing world. Critics of massive irrigation projects point out that such schemes often involve massive relocation efforts as new dams and reservoirs are built. The building of the Aswan Dam in Egypt, for example, involved the relocation of over one hundred thousand people,[8] and between 1979 and 1985, the World Bank approved financing for forty hydropower projects that resulted in the resettlement of at least six hundred thousand people in twenty-seven countries.[9] Critics of massive irrigation projects also argue that they benefit only wealthy farmers, not the population as a whole, and may lead to public health problems from waterborne diseases and parasites.[10]

Lastly, natural causes are also responsible for water shortages. The United States has had several recent periods of severe drought that have made water management a critical political issue in almost every state. In 1977, Californians began using "gray water"—kitchen sink and bathtub drainage—on their lawns when a severe drought hit the state. Signs were posted in college and university bathrooms urging conservation ("Is this trip necessary?"), and one of the most popular bumper stickers seen throughout the state reminded drivers, "Save Water: Shower with a Friend." Severe drought conditions in New York in 1985 led to a ban on watering lawns, and in 1986, drought in the southeastern United States led to massive crop and livestock losses. California, Oregon, and Washington declared drought conditions from 1986 to 1992, with the impact of water shortages affecting everything from ski resorts to forest fire conditions. Several of California's endangered bird populations were considered at risk from the drought, as were winter-run Chinook salmon because of diversion of water for human use.[11] The severe drought in western states had additional environmental impacts. Hydroelectric capacity in these regions has been greatly reduced, causing California utilities to rely more on fossil fuels, which have increased emissions of carbon dioxide by more than 25 percent. These increased emissions also affect air quality in urban areas where pollution is already severe.

The same situation is true internationally. Drought in north-central and western Africa from 1968 to 1973 had devastating consequences for a region that already suffered from growing population and diminishing resources. India faced a massive drought in the mid-1980s, even though the nation's monsoon rains produce significant amounts of water. The Indian government has attempted to capture the runoff in large dams, but deforestation has led to massive flooding, and some streams and rivers now dry up for parts of the year.

THE AMERICAN WATER WARS

American water policy is among the most politicized in the world, colored by political appointments and powerful industry lobbies, as this overview indicates. It is a policy that has recently changed as political clout has shifted from the farm and agricultural lobby, which controlled policy at the turn of the century, to urban interests who now dominate Congress. Water management in the United States has primarily been the responsibility of two federal agencies, although that responsibility is shared with a large number of public and private entities ranging from local sewage companies and irrigation districts to state water boards. The Corps of Engineers was originally created in 1802 under the Department of the Army and became the main construction arm of the federal government. In 1824, Congress gave the corps authority over navigational operations, and the agency gained additional jurisdiction through the Flood Control Act of 1936. Just four years after Franklin Roosevelt began his New Deal, the corps was embarking upon a reservoir construction program that erected ten large dams a year, on average, for fifty years. The authority was expanded further in 1972 with passage of the Clean Water Act, which brought its jurisdiction into wetlands permits.

The Reclamation Service (later renamed the Bureau of Reclamation) was authorized by Congress in 1902 with responsibility for aiding western settlement in a seventeen-state area.[12] One of the factors that made the bureau popular among western farmers is that it was chartered with a limitation that it serve only those landowners who held title to 160 acres or less, and thus the agency rapidly came to be influenced by local interests. During its early years, the bureau constructed massive water development projects, canals, and public works programs, such as Washington's Grand Coulee Dam (the largest single-purpose peacetime appropriation in U.S. history) and California's Central Valley Project. Between them, the two federal agencies quickly established a reputation as the home of the pork barrel—congressionally approved water projects that benefited a single district. Projects such as dams and flood control channels brought a visible product (and jobs) to the home base of a member of Congress, paid for by liberal cost-sharing formulas and substantial federal financing. In 1920, the Federal Water Power Act created the Federal Power Commission, which was replaced in 1977 by the Federal Energy Regulatory Commission. The commission was initially responsible for regulating the nation's water resources, but its charter was eventually redirected to oversee the electric power and natural gas industries.

There has always been a closely knit relationship between the congressional committees that had oversight responsibility for the agencies, the two agencies, and local water interest lobbies. Decisions on which projects to fund, and at what level, were frequently made by those leaders with the most political clout, or because of pressure from campaign contributors, rather than on the merits of good water management. Around 1900, for example, the National Rivers Congress, comprised of powerful business figures, contractors, and members of Congress (who were honorary members of the group) began monitoring Corps of Engineers projects. They were extremely successful at convincing Congress to continue authorizing funds for projects that had long since been completed. The water lobby became so powerful that in its heyday in the early 1960s, the chair of the House Appropriations Committee would boast that "practically every Congressional district" was included in the omnibus public works bills and that "there is something here for everybody."[13]

For the most part, America's growth spurt continued unabated after World War II, and few questioned the advisability of the corps and bureau's massive undertakings. New water technology, modern farming and cropping techniques, and widespread pesticide use made agricultural expansion a key element of the postwar boom, with cheap, government-subsidized water the key. Land irrigated with government-financed water grew from 2.7 million acres in 1930 to more than 4 million acres after the war and nearly 7 million acres by 1960. But during the late 1950s and mid-1960s, water resource planning changed from an emphasis on economic development to municipal, industrial, and recreational purposes. The water lobby was forced to make some concessions to environmental groups, outraged when projects began to infringe upon scenic or preserved areas, such as a proposal to build Echo Park Dam in Dinosaur National Monument.[14] The Sierra Club mobilized its members when a plan to build a hydroelectric plant in the Grand Canyon surfaced, and in so doing, lost its federal tax-exempt status. The bureau "compromised" by agreeing instead to expand the coal-fired power plant at Mojave, near the four corners area, and environmentalists believed that they had saved the Grand Canyon. In an ironic twist, the Mojave facility later became the center of a totally different environmental issue when its emissions were thought to be the source of air pollution and haze over the Grand Canyon.

There is another clear pattern to U.S. water policy: the regional nature of the dispute. Growing urban development in California once led to a call by some members of Congress for the state to import water from its water-rich neighbors in the Pacific Northwest. Frostbelt state representatives bristled at the idea that all the federal money was going to their sunbelt colleagues. And although the tug-of-war over rights to the Colorado River between Arizona and California is essentially over, the dispute created more legal documents (by weight) than any other in the history of U.S. litigation, on any subject.

By the mid-1970s, environmental groups turned their attention to water issues, becoming a potent force in policymaking. Groups such as the Sierra Club, the American Rivers Conservation Council, the National Wildlife Federation, and the Natural Resources Defense Council pressured Congress to follow the requirements of the National Environmental Policy Act and used litigation as a tool of forcing compliance with new legislative initiatives. Bolstered by environmental support during his campaign, President Jimmy Carter began his administration in 1977 by developing a "hit list" of nineteen water projects that were to be deleted from the federal budget, including the Central Arizona Project. Carter underestimated the powerful water industry lobby, however, which was able to convince Congress to restore all nineteen appropriations.

Water industry officials cheered the 1980 election of Ronald Reagan, believing his appointment of Robert Broadbent, a Nevada legislator, as head of the Bureau of Reclamation was a positive omen. It turned out to be a conflicting sign, however, as Reagan continued Carter's cost-sharing requirements on water projects (the portion of a water project to be borne by the federal government). As state and local governments began to realize that they might have to pay a larger share of the cost for many of the projects, they became less attractive, and in some cases, financially burdensome. Part of the shift in policy can be traced to the growing clout of urban political interests over those of agriculture, as city politicians began to question why farmers were getting all the cheap water.[15]

Equally important was the discovery of dead waterfowl at the Kesterson National Wildlife Refuge in California's San Joaquin Valley. Ducks and geese were dying of a mysterious sickness that not only killed them, but resulted in birth deformities in their chicks. The eventual cause was found to be selenium, a trace element that can be toxic in high concentrations. The selenium was carried by the San Luis Drain from the politically powerful Westlands Water District in Fresno and Tulare counties. In 1985, Secretary of the Interior Donald Hodel called for a halt in the drainage by June 30, 1986, but the public had by then had just about enough of the Bureau of Reclamation's projects and its negligence.[16] By 1987, the policy change became clear when James Zigler, the Department of the Interior's assistant secretary for water and science, announced that the bureau was changing its mission from an agency based on federally supported construction to one based on resource management. The empire-building days of the corps and the bureau were over, replaced by an administration that was paying more attention to urban needs for a stable water supply than to agricultural interests seeking cheap water for their fields.

Pricing inequities continue to be at the heart of the battle over water management in the United States. The "real" cost of providing and distributing water is often impossible to determine, and historically, municipalities have been reluctant to try to pass those costs on to developers and commercial interests. City leaders often avoided charging a new business the true cost of water delivery for fear it would discourage economic growth. As a result, the rate structure has often allowed large users to benefit because of a system that charges the user less the more water is used. Favored customers often receive preferential pricing, and some cities served by the same water district often unknowingly subsidize the water costs of other cities in their area through complex pricing arrangements. Residential users tend to subsidize industrial users throughout most of the United States today.

Another new wrinkle has been the development of "water markets"—transactions ranging from transfers of water rights to the sale and lease of those rights or the land above the water source. Market transfers are dependent upon the concept of reallocating water supplies, rather than coming up with new sources of water. Part of the affection for the market concept was purely economic—new capital projects were becoming increasingly expensive and politically unpopular in much of the West. One group even began purchasing water rights in Colorado as an investment, with the expectation that, as supplies diminished, the rights could be sold for tidy profit. Cities such as Phoenix and Scottsdale have also been active in the water market, buying thousands of acres of farmland outside their city limits to have a water source as their population increases and water within city boundaries runs short. Reallocation is gradually being looked upon as an alternative to finding a new allocations as the primary mode of water development.[17]

One of the more recent battles in the water wars has involved the rights of Native Americans to water resources. In 1908, in a far-reaching U.S. Supreme Court case,[18] the Winters Doctrine granted Native Americans the right to all waters that arise under, border, traverse, or underlie a reservation and requires that these waters must continue to be made available to serve the current and future needs of the reservation. Historically, Native American claims to water rights were ignored by the Bureau of Reclamation and the Army Corps of Engineers, but a 1963 Supreme Court case[19] reinforced Native American authority over their land and water. Several nations explored the possibility of marketing their water rights, but the issue leaves open the question of what the real value of water is.[20]

The American water wars have also touched our southern border with Mexico, where the Colorado River flows on its way to the Gulf of California. In 1922, Congress approved the Colorado River Compact, which divided up the river's resources, giving the three lower basin states (California, Arizona, and Nevada) and the four upper basin states (Wyoming, Colorado, New Mexico, and Utah) 7.5 million acre-feet for each region (an acre-foot is the volume of water that covers one acre to a depth of one foot, or 325,851 gallons). It should be noted, however, that the actual flow of the river is closer to fourteen rather than fifteen million acre-feet. Congress also authorized the building of Hoover Dam in 1928, giving the United States total control over the Colorado River—a situation that understandably made our Mexican neighbors nervous. Seeking to keep Mexico as a wartime ally, the United States signed a treaty in 1944 that assigned 1.5 million acre-feet to Mexico and created the International Boundary Water Commission to administer the treaty. In the early 1960s, a combination of population growth, the drilling of wells on the U.S. side, saline runoff from drainage projects, and construction of the Glen Canyon Dam in Utah began affecting both the quantity and quality of Mexico's water allocation. It took nearly ten years for the two sides to reach an agreement that in 1973 guaranteed Mexico a fair share of the Colorado in usable form—a turning point in the region's development. Twenty years later, the treaty has still not been fully implemented, in part because the United States has not held up its end of the bargain to operate a desalination plant in Yuma, Arizona.[21.]

IMPACTS AND SOLUTIONS

The growing pressure to tap more and more of the Earth's water resources is having a number of negative impacts on a global scale. More urban communities are tapping into underground aquifers, drying them up as residential and agricultural demand increases. In cases such as Mexico City and Phoenix, water levels are dropping as a result of heavy pumping, leading to subsidence—literally, the sinking of the city. In addition to a reduction in the availability of a valuable commodity, it is unlikely that the water in the aquifers will ever be fully replaced.

Among the most important consequences of poor water management are soil erosion and desertification, which threaten nearly a third of Earth's surface. Desertification refers to the process by which the land gradually becomes less capable of supporting life and nonproductive. In one 1992 study, the UN's Global Assessment of Soil Degradation found that three billion acres of land have sustained moderate to extreme degradation since 1945, accounting for 10.5 percent of the planet's fertile land. Of that land, 740 million acres are severely degraded and considered useless unless a major international financial and technical campaign is launched to reclaim it. The vast majority of the damaged land is in Asia, with 1.1 billion acres, and Africa, with 792 million, where most of the world's subsistence farmers live. Central America has the highest proportion of damaged land—24 percent of its total, followed by Europe (17 percent), Africa (14 percent), Asia (12 percent), and North America (4.4 percent). More than fifteen million acres worldwide (an area the size of West Virginia) are claimed by desertification every year, primarily as a result of four causes: overgrazing on rangelands, overcultivation of croplands, waterlogging and salting of irrigated lands, and deforestation.[22]

At least one-sixth of China's land is believed to have been ravaged by soil erosion to the extent where it is no longer productive, with another one-sixth ruined by desertification. Deserts there are expanding at the rate of more than six hundred square miles a year, and by the year 2000 are expected to have doubled in size. China lost 3 percent of its croplands between 1986 and 1992 to human settlements and plans to nearly double the size of its urban areas by 2012. Water tables are also dropping in many areas. As a result, China moved in 1994 from being a grain exporter to the world's second largest grain importer in 1995.[23]

In Africa, a 1991 UN study found that the area of land classified as arid or hyperarid has increased by nearly fifty-four million hectares since 1931. Some scientists believe that there is a link between desertification and drought, pointing to a 30 percent reduction in rainfall in the African Sahel, the semi-arid region on the southern edge of the Sahara.[24] This zone is characterized by high temperatures and a short rainy season that begins and ends abruptly. The ground is flat and the vegetation consists of strips of steppe interspersed with ruined soil. The scanty resources of the Sahel are the home of a nomadic population who graze cattle, moving their livestock to the areas where water is available. As the area's population has grown, the nomads have increased their herds, which have stripped the soil of its meager vegetation.[25] According to meteorologists, a reduction in vegetative cover resulting from desertification may reduce rainfall because of an increase in the albedo, the share of sunlight reflected back from Earth. According to the hypothesis, developed by Jule Charney of the Massachusetts Institute of Technology, less of the sun's radiation is absorbed at Earth's surface as albedo increases, so surface temperatures drop, causing a sinking motion in the atmosphere. Since the sinking air is dry, rainfall declines, and a degraded, higher-albedo area begins to feed on itself and become more desertlike.[26] Desertification, may, in turn, have an effect on global warming. Overgrazing and deforestation are thought by one researcher to be responsible for increasing temperatures in the Northern Hemisphere over the past century, although other scientists believe it is too premature to make such conclusions.[27]

Adding to the desertification process are increasing levels of salt in the water. An additional one hundred million acres, mostly in India and Pakistan, is estimated by the UN Environment Programme to suffer from salinization, which occurs in dry regions when evaporation near the soil surface leaves behind a thin salt residue.[28] Salinity also affects water quality in Peru and Mexico, where the annual loss of output as a result of salinization is estimated at one million tons of food grains, or enough to provide basic rations to five million people.[29]

Water diversion has also led to the destruction of valuable wildlife habitats, as is the case in California. In 1940, the state's Division of Water Resources granted the Department of Water and Power (DWP) of Los Angeles a permit to divert virtually all of the flow from four of the five streams that flow into Mono Lake, the second-largest lake in California. The diversion represents about 15 percent of Los Angeles's total city water supply. The lake is located at the base of the Sierra Nevada near Yosemite National Park, and although saline, its brine shrimp population is the food source for millions of migratory birds and 95 percent of the state's nesting gulls. As a result of DWP's diversion through its Owens Valley aqueduct, the level of the lake has dropped and increased salinity levels, which threaten the entire food chain. The lake's surface level has been diminished by one-third, exposing gull rookeries to predators, and future diversions are expected to reduce the lake even further. The receding lake waters have exposed a lake bed composed of an alkali silt, which when dry becomes airborne and becomes a health hazard.

In 1983, the National Audubon Society filed suit against Los Angeles to stop the diversions,[30] arguing that the state had an obligation to protect the public trust embodied by the lake. The California Supreme Court agreed and sent the case back to the state's Water Board to determine whether and to what extent DWP ought to reduce its diversions. Despite nearly a decade of environmental studies, reports, investigations, and litigation, a solution to Mono Lake's dwindling water level still is not forthcoming.[31]

There are two basic solutions to the water scarcity and management problem: conservation and technology. The first is relatively straightforward—convince users to use less. The second involves a wide range of options from ancient to modern technological solutions. Water conservation is being implemented in many regions, ranging from urban communities to irrigation improvements in an attempt to reduce residents' dependency upon existing sources. Some of the easiest conservation efforts have been accomplished by metropolitan water districts that have enacted consumption ordinances or made water-saving showerheads and low-flow toilets available.[32] These efforts are not temporary responses to drought—studies indicate that by 2010 southern California will have enough water to fulfill only 70 percent of its needs, making demand management practices a more likely strategy for reducing consumption.[33]

Conservation is not limited to urban areas. One of the most obvious strategies used to reduce seepage from agricultural irrigation was the replacement of unlined ditches with piping. Thousands of miles of earth-wall feeder ditches have been replaced in the United States, saving as much as 25 percent of the water in each one thousand feet of ditch. Improvements in furrow irrigation have resulted in irrigation efficiency improvements of approximately 10–40 percent, and lowhead sprinkler systems have reduced loss to evaporation to almost zero. Through such methodologies, farmers can achieve water savings from 25 to 40 percent, leading to a stabilization of the underlying groundwater table in many areas.[34]

There are also a number of innovative solutions designed to increase shrinking supplies. One of the oldest methods involves desalination, long considered as one way in which communities could attempt to keep up with the explosive growth common to coastal regions.[35] There are two basic methods of desalination: distillation (heating ocean water and distilling the vapor) and filtering water through a membrane in a process called reverse osmosis. Distillation produces water that is more pure, but reverse osmosis is more energy efficient and the facilities are smaller and more compact. More than two-thirds of the thousands of desalination plants currently in operation worldwide use distillation, with more than half of all desalination facilities located in the Middle East. Israel, one of the pioneers in desalination technology, opened its first plant in 1965 for the new desert town of Eilat. The first U.S. facility opened in Key West, Florida, in 1967, and over one hundred plants have opened to serve other coastal cities. Although there was widespread interest in desalination during the 1960s,[36] public and government interest (and federal funding for research) seemed to go on hiatus during the 1970s and 1980s. The worldwide drought of the late 1980s, however, rekindled interest, especially in California. In 1992, officials dedicated a plant on Catalina Island, twenty-six miles off the coast of Los Angeles, which will provide 130,000 gallons of water a day, enough for a third of the island's needs. Similar plants are being built or considered in Santa Barbara and Morro Bay, California.

Cloud seeding is another strategy that has historically been used to increase rainfall. Airplanes release tiny crystals of silver iodide into clouds with the potential to release water by forming a base of ice crystals, which eventually fall as ice or snow. Cloud seeding, when successful, can lead to a 5–15 percent increase in rainfall. Researchers are also considering the use of dry ice, a type of bacterium, and ground-based seeding programs using propane to trigger precipitation.[37]

There are also several "megaprojects" being considered to transfer resources from water-rich areas to those most in need. In the Middle East, water is far more rare and precious than oil, and scarcity is a growing problem. Turkey proposed in 1991 a "peace pipeline," a $20 billion project to pump water from its Seyhan and Ceyhan rivers to more arid lands, but the project's estimated price of more than $20 billion has kept the project on the drawing board.[38] In China, the government began construction in 1994 on the Three Gorges Dam, a massive project that will cost from $17 billion to $30 billion by the time it is finished in 2009. The dam is anticipated to increase China's electrical generating output by 10 percent and protect millions of people downstream from flooding. But it will also require more than 1.1 million people to relocate before the 400-mile-long dam can be created and threatens to destroy a number of national cultural treasures.[39] Chinese engineers are also preparing to build a canal from Zhenjiang, on the Yangtze to Tianjin, following the path of the Grand Canal, built in the sixth century C.E. The original canal was built to transport grain; this twenty-first-century version will supply Chinese urban centers and provide water for irrigation.[40]

Restoring degraded land is a much more complex problem, however. Efforts are being concentrated on stabilizing soil, diversifying crops, and focusing agricultural production on regions that are the most fertile and least erodible. In China and Ethiopia, for example, researchers are experimenting with ways to trap soil in shallow dams or terrace crops to increase productivity and hasten land reclamation. Other projects include the planting of soil-trapping grasses that form vegetative barriers, and alley cropping, which involves the planting of food crops between hedgerows of trees—a strategy that has been extensively used in tropical regions. Other UN projects are aimed at reducing the harvest length of certain crops or improving species productivity so that the land can be double- or triple-cropped.

Many of the proposals seem farfetched if not downright silly, such as towing icebergs from the Arctic to California to provide fresh drinking water for thirsty Los Angeles residents. Others get serious consideration from policymakers desperate for innovation. For example, Canada's Medusa Corporation proposed solving California's scarcity problem with floating vinyl water balloons, each the size of twenty football fields. The storage bags (up to twenty-four hundred feet long, six hundred feet wide, and eighty feet deep) would cost $6 million each and would hold a million tons of water from Alaska. The idea would be to tow the balloons, which would be partially submerged like an iceberg, down the coast to water-short cities. The concept was eventually termed "not viable" by representatives of the Metropolitan Water District of southern California, which estimated that the region would need at least five balloons a day.

Such fanciful solutions are evidence of the desperate straits many regions are in as they seek an answer to the question of where the water is coming from. Although it is obvious to most that water conservation is the most obvious choice among these strategies, it is also one of the most difficult to implement as long as residents (especially those in the United States) are used to simply turning on the tap. Only when drought conditions force cities to adopt restrictive measures does conservation finally hit home. In summer 1992, for example, the city of Portland, Oregon, banned all use of water for watering lawns and gardens and washing cars when its Bull Run reservoir began to dry up. The city's Water Bureau established a special late-night patrol to catch flagrant violators—those sprinkling their lawns while the rest of the city slept. A "snitch line" allowed residents to inform the patrols of alleged violations, and some neighbors even turned to vigilante tactics— one woman's new lawn was attacked by vandals who accused her of violating the city's conservation ordinance. She awoke one July morning to find rows of sod neatly rolled up on her porch.

THE WETLANDS ISSUE

While the water resource debate has focused primarily on the issue of supply, water quality is an equally enduring problem for policymakers in both the United States and abroad. Historically, legislative efforts at reducing pollution at the source have been ineffective, as will be seen later in this chapter. More recently, scientists have looked at wetlands restoration as another strategy for improving water quality. Wetlands are sensitive ecological areas that serve as breeding grounds for migratory birds and as plant habitats. They also serve as natural flood and storm control systems, and some communities are experimenting with using wetlands as a way of treating wastewater.[41]

Wetlands have become an increasingly important topic on the environmental protection agenda as scientists monitor the numbers of acres of wetlands lost to development. A 1991 study conducted by the Department of the Interior found that of an original 221 million acres of wetlands in the lower forty-eight states, only 103.3 million acres of wetlands remained intact, with losses continuing at the rate of about two hundred to three hundred thousand acres each year. The greatest loss of acreage is occurring in Florida, Louisiana, Texas, Arkansas, Minnesota, and Illinois.[42]

In addition to concerns about wetlands losses from an ecological perspective, the issue has become highly politicized. The Clean Water Act of 1992 included provisions that required anyone seeking to build or otherwise conduct business that would alter the landscape of wetlands to first obtain a permit from the Army Corps of Engineers. Of particular interest in the act is Section 404, which makes it unlawful to put dredged or fill material into navigable waters—the term *wetlands* was never mentioned in the legislation. But in 1975, a Washington, D.C. Court of Appeals decision held that the Clean Water Act applied not only to rivers but also to wetlands that drain into rivers, and eventually, the statute was applied to isolated wetlands with no connection to rivers or waterways. Four agencies—

Another View, Another Voice

THE EVERGLADES

The Everglades National Park in Florida provides a sobering example of how difficult it is to preserve wetlands and how the failure to understand the ecological functioning of wetlands can have tremendous consequences. Once environmental damage is done, it is difficult and usually expensive to remedy it. The Everglades is actually a slow-moving river, some 50 miles wide and only approximately six inches deep, that flows to an estuary at Florida Bay, and, in the process, creates the largest freshwater marshland in the world. The Everglades plays a critical role in the Florida panhandle ecosystem in recharging its aquifer and in fostering rainfall and is home to 14 endangered or threatened species. About half of the Everglades has been lost to development. The Everglades National Park was created in 1947 to protect about 20 percent of the remaining wetlands. Development has caused the Everglades to be the most endangered national park.

Diversion of water from the North is a major threat to the viability of the park. In the 1960s, the Army Corps of Engineers converted the Kissimmee River, a 103-mile-long meandering river, into a 56-mile-long canal, to provide flood control. The construction drained water from wetlands and the land was used for grazing cows. Cow manure flowed down the canal into Lake Okeechobee, where the increased nutrients fueled the growth of algae that depleted the oxygen in the water. Water flowing into the Florida Bay has become warmer and more salty, which, along with the increased nutrients, stimulated the growth of algae blooms in the bay that threaten the diving and fishing industries. Nutrients from sugarcane and vegetable fields also contribute to the damage to the park and bay. As more and more water has been withdrawn from the area to meet Miami's growing water demands, salt water has moved inland to fill the void and has contaminated drinking water supplies. The impact has been dramatic in some areas. Nesting bird populations, for example, have declined by 90 percent in the park during the past 60 years.

State and federal officials and property owners have been slow to remedy these problems. After twenty years of discussion, officials devised a plan to undo the damage to the Kissimmee, and Congress authorized the Army Corps of Engineers in 1993 to restore 52 miles of the river to its natural course, a 15-year project that is projected to cost at least $370 million. In 1993, after a decade of delays from legal challenges launched by industries, sugarcane and vegetable growers agreed to contribute one-third of the initial cleanup costs, estimated to be $700 million, as long as they were immune from the balance of the cost, expected to be at least $1.3 billion over twenty years.

In November 1996, Florida voters rejected a ballot initiative to impose a tax of one penny on each pound of raw sugar grown in the Everglades region. The money would have been used for conservation and protection of the Everglades. Robert H. Buker, vice president of the United States Sugar Corporation in Clewiston, Florida, the state's largest sugar producer, commented on the election: "Floridians clearly said no to higher taxation. Everyone has a desire for a cleaner environment, but there is a heavy antitax sentiment here. The sugar tax would have put many of Florida's sugar producers out of business. They could not have competed with producers in other states and foreign countries." Rindy M. O'Brien, vice president of the Wilderness Society, countered: "The sugar industry poured a lot of money into this campaign. Advertising determined the outcome, persuading voters to go in and vote against the initiative. If we had been able to match the industry dollar for dollar, the outcome would have been different."

For Further Reading

Steve M. Davis and John C. Ogden, *Everglades: The Ecosystem and Its Restoration* (Delray Beach, FL: St. Lucie Press, 1994).

Lance H. Gunderson, et al. Eds. *Barriers and Bridges to the Renewal of Ecosystems and Institutions* (New York: Columbia University Press, 1995).

Thomas E. Lodge, *The Everglades Handbook: Understanding the Ecosystem* (Delray Beach, FL: St. Lucie Press, 1994).

G. Tyler Miller, Jr. *Living in the Environment* (Belmont, CA: Wadsworth, 1996): 475–477.

Robert Pear, "The 1996 Elections: The States—The Initiatives," *New York Times,* November 7, 1996): B7.

Douglas R. Porter, *Collaborative Planning for Wetlands and Wildlife* (Washington, D.C.: Island Press, 1995).

United States Government Accounting Office, *Restoring the Everglades: Public Participation in Federal Efforts* (Washington, D.C.: U.S. Government Accounting Office, 1995).

the Department of Agriculture, the EPA, the Department of the Interior, and the Army Corps of Engineers—have developed regulations to implement the law and to designate which areas are defined as wetlands, with an estimated 77 million acres of wetlands privately owned. Since each of the agencies has its own interpretation of the wetlands designation, the importance of wetlands preservation has collided with private property rights and become one of the most contentious water management issues in the United States.

At the height of his campaign for president in 1988, George Bush announced on the shores of Boston Harbor that there would be "no net loss" of the nation's remaining wetlands—a concept that was the brainchild of then-Conservation Foundation president William K. Reilly (later Bush's nominee to become administrator of the Environmental Protection Agency). During the 1992 presidential campaign, the term came back to haunt Bush as one of the major failures of his administration, eliciting criticism from both environmental groups and property owners.[43]

Farmers have been among the most vocal critics of federal wetlands policies. Their concerns were brought to the attention of the president by a group called the National Wetlands Coalition led by farming, oil and gas, and housing industry representatives, who had formed in 1989 to oppose sections of the wetlands program implementation. The organization asked the White House Council on Competitiveness, chaired by Vice President Dan Quayle, to develop a less restrictive wetlands definition.[44] The result was the release of the *Federal Manual for Identifying and Delineating Jurisdictional Wetlands* in August 1991. Under the new directive, the definition of wetland was expanded and an additional fifty million acres of land came under federal protection.

More than eighty thousand formal comments, most of them highly critical of the proposed manual, were sent to the EPA. Critics of the proposed rules change argued that millions of acres of previously protected land would be open to development, and environmental groups called upon Congress to study the problem further.[45] In contrast to the president's policy, a December 1991 report by the National Research Council recommended that the United States embark upon a policy of wetlands restoration, with a goal of a net gain of ten million acres of wetlands by 2010, a program that went far beyond the Bush administration's policy of "no net loss." Failure to implement such a policy, the report warned, would lead to permanent ecological damage that would reduce the quality of American life.[46]

While Congress held hearings over the wetlands designations, each agency charged with implementing the Clean Water Act interpreted President Bush's proposals in a different way. The Army Corps of Engineers used a 1987 version of a wetlands manual, the EPA and Fish and Wildlife Service used another developed in 1989, the Soil Conservation Service had its own slightly different criteria, and some federal agencies adopted the 1991 manual's proposed rules.[47]

The Clinton administration reexamined federal wetlands policies almost immediately, in large part due to court rulings that questioned whether the government had the authority to place sanctions on those who failed to meet wetlands permit criteria. In 1993, both the EPA and the Army Corps of Engineers reverted back to the use of the 1987 manual, abandoning the proposed rewriting of the law spearheaded by President Bush. While environmental organizations believe loopholes in the Clinton administration policy would lead to the loss of designation of half of the nation's remaining wetlands,[48] critics of federal involvement have argued that wetlands protection is best accomplished by private organizations like Ducks Unlimited.

In 1995, the debate resumed as the Republican controlled Congress sought to rewrite a Clean Water Act that would have established another new classification scheme for wetlands. Under the proposal, the least valuable lands would no longer be protected by the federal government, and less protection would be given to the remaining wetlands. The measure would also have required government agencies to compensate landowners for any loss in property values of 20 percent or more resulting from wetlands regulations, but the proposals failed to obtain sufficient bipartisan support.[49]

One of the most interesting aspects of the wetlands controversy, however, is the politicization of the entire designation process. During the Bush administration, it became clear to most observers that the development of a new wetlands criteria would deteriorate to a battle between developers and property rights activists against environmental groups. The scientific community, with years of detailed reports and field testing, was gradually squeezed out of the process, with the result being a policy that satisfied neither side.[50] Opposition to wetlands regulations continues, fueled by enforcement actions taken against landowners that have been widely criticized by private property activists and by policies that are still being tested in federal courts.[51]

THE NATURE AND CAUSES OF WATER POLLUTION

In 1965, when he signed the Water Quality Act, President Lyndon Johnson predicted that Washington's Potomac River would be reopened for swimming by 1975.[52] Yet the Potomac's Tidal Basin, with its Japanese cherry trees, has been called "the best decorated sewer in the world," making LBJ's prediction premature and unrealistic, as is the case of most of the legislative attempts to improve the quality of America's water supply. A number of factors have contributed to make the nation's waterways and drinking water as polluted now as they were in the 1960s. The debate over how best to improve water quality focuses on two issues: first, pollution of surface waters (rivers, streams, lakes, wetlands, and even drainage ditches), largely from discharges directly into waterways, and second, the pollution of groundwater, which flows beneath Earth's surface and is the source of nearly half of the nation's drinking water. Sources of groundwater contamination include landfills, biocide applications[53] on farmland and urban lawns, underground storage tanks, leakage of hazardous waste, and waste disposal wells.

The current level of water pollution is largely a result of massive industrialization and inadequate waste disposal strategies that took place in the United States during the mid-to- late nineteenth century. At that time, local officials were generally reluctant to antagonize industry and to try to stop the widespread practice of simply dumping industrial wastes into the closest waterway. Most of the early government concerns dealt with navigational hazards rather than health. In 1886, Congress prohibited the dumping of waste into New York harbor, followed by the 1899 Refuse Act, which prohibited the dumping of solid waste into commercial waterways. Not until the U.S. Public Health Service was formed in 1912 was there serious consideration given to monitoring pollution levels. Today, much of what is known about trends in surface water quality comes from the U.S. Geological Society, which monitors waterways through its National Ambient Stream Quality Accounting Network, or NASQUAN, which began collecting information in 1974. Groundwater quality, in contrast, must be monitored from wells, or at the tap.

Basically, water contaminants can be divided into the following categories:

Organisms: Biological contaminants including bacteria, parasites, and viruses are included in this category. These occur in most water sources, although there are usually fewer in groundwater than in surface water. Human and animal wastes carry fecal coliform and fecal streptococcus bacteria, which may enter the water source from improper sewage treatment, cattle feedlots, or through failing, leaching septic tanks.

Suspended and Totally Dissolved Solids: Soil particles, inorganic salts, and other substances may make water brown or turbid (cloudy) and may carry bacteria and other harmful substances that pollute water. The problem is particularly acute in areas with significant erosion, including logged watersheds, construction sites, and abused rangelands. Agricultural practices are thought to be the largest single source of unregulated water pollution.

Nutrients: Some contaminants, such as phosphorous, iron, and boron, can be harmful when ingested in excess quantities. Nitrates, which are not harmful in limited concentrations, occur naturally in some vegetables such as beets and cabbage, and are used in the meat-curing process.[54]

Metals and Toxics: A wide spectrum of heavy metals are commonly found in drinking water, among the most dangerous of which is lead. In 1991, the Environmental Protection Agency issued new regulations requiring municipal water suppliers to monitor lead levels, focusing on households at high risk (those with lead service pipes) and at the location where lead content is likely to be the highest—at the consumer's faucet. In areas where water quality standards are not met, suppliers must add bicarbonate and lime to lower the water's acidity chemically. Other contaminants include radioactive minerals and gases. Toxic concentrations usually come from sources such as pesticides and chemical solvents used in a variety of manufacturing processes.

Municipal Wastewater Discharges: Domestic sewage accounts for a large percentage of the materials handled by municipal wastewater treatment plants, but other substances also routinely enter the wastewater stream, including hazardous chemicals dumped down drains and sewers by individuals, industries, and businesses.

THE POLITICS OF WATER QUALITY

Like many environmental issues, the politics of water quality is not linked to a single act of legislation. One of the factors that makes water policy somewhat difficult to understand is that Congress has given regulatory responsibility for water quality to EPA under a number of legislative mandates. The Resource Conservation and Recovery Act (RCRA), for example, gives the EPA the authority to regulate the treatment, transport, and storage of both hazardous and nonhazardous waste. The Comprehensive Environmental Response, Compensation, and Liability Act, (CERCLA) more commonly known as Superfund, gives the EPA responsibility when groundwater is contaminated by inactive waste sites or accidental chemical releases. The Toxic Substances Control Act (TSCA) gives the EPA regulatory authority over the manufacture, use, and disposal of toxic chemicals, and the Federal Insecticide, Fungicide, and Rodenticide Act (FIFRA) regulates certain pesticides, which can also enter groundwater. Despite the overlap of these regulatory mandates, Congress has also enacted legislation specifically targeting surface and groundwater pollution.

Surface Water

The process of placing surface water on the political agenda has been a long one. Before World War II, only a few environmental organizations seemed interested in the deteriorating condition of America's lakes, rivers, and streams. The Izaak Walton League was among the first to draw attention to the contamination problem, noting in a report published in the late 1920s that 85 percent of the nation's waterways were polluted and that only 30 percent of all municipalities treated their wastes, many of them inadequately. Industrial interests like the American Petroleum Institute, the American Iron and Steel Institute, and the Manufacturing Chemists Association insisted "streams were nature's sewers" and convinced key legislators that industrial dumping posed no environmental threat.[55]

The initial attempts to regulate surface water pollution were weak and ineffective. In 1948, Congress passed the first Water Pollution Control Act, which established the federal government's limited role in regulating interstate water pollution. The law also provided for studies and research and limited funding for sewage treatment. It also authorized the surgeon general to prepare or adopt programs for eliminating or reducing pollution in cooperation with other agencies and the industries involved. The emphasis on a cooperative approach, coupled with provisions that were both cumbersome and often unworkable, gave the law little impact. In 1952, a report to Congress indicated not a single enforcement action had been taken, and Congress began to hold hearings on a revision to the legislation. The 1956 amendments to the act eliminated many of the difficulties of the 1948 law, but still limited Congress's role to interstate waters and allowed Congress to delegate much of its authority to implement the law to the states. It did, however, condition federal funding of sewage treatment facilities on the submission of adequate water pollution plans by the states. This provided an incentive for states to write water quality standards to meet state goals for surface water pollution. Still, only one enforcement action was filed under this authority over the next fifteen years.

During the 1960s, Congress, led by Senator Edmund Muskie of Maine, became restless over the slow pace of water pollution control, since it was obvious that states were doing an inadequate job. In 1965, passage of the Water Quality Act established a June, 1967 water quality standard for interstate waters and streamlined federal enforcement efforts. A year later, the Clean Water Restoration Act provided $3.5 billion in federal grants for the construction of sewage treatment plants and for research on advanced waste treatment.[56] These early attempts at water quality legislation were weak and ineffective. They allowed the states to classify waterways within their jurisdiction, so a state could decide that a particular stream was best used for industrial use rather than for swimming. The use designation of the Cuyahoga River in Ohio, for example, was waste disposal—a fact that did not seem to bother most residents until the river caught fire in 1969. From an enforcement standpoint, the initial pollution laws were meaningless. For the two decades before 1972, only one case of alleged violation of federal water pollution control law reached the courts, and in that case over four years elapsed between the initial enforcement conference and the final consent decree.[57]

President Richard Nixon's February 1970 message to Congress on the environment called for a new water pollution bill, which eventually became the 1972 Federal Water Pollution Control Act. The main emphasis of the legislation was on technological capability. In addition to establishing a regulatory framework for water quality, the bill gave the EPA six specific deadlines by which it was to grant permits to water pollution sources, issue effluent (wastewater) guidelines, require sources to install water pollution control technology, and eliminate discharges into the nation's waterways to make them fishable and swimmable.[58] A key component of the legislation was the establishment of the National Pollution Discharge Elimination System (NPDES), which made it illegal to discharge anything at all unless the source had a federal permit to do so. The NPDES had a historical basis in the 1899 Refuse Act, which had previously been thought to apply only to discharges that obstructed navigation. But the U.S. Supreme Court broadened the interpretation of the act in two cases that made it applicable to any industrial waste.[59]

Water quality continued to capture media interest when consumer advocate Ralph Nader publicized contamination along a 150-mile stretch of the Mississippi River between Baton Rouge and New Orleans known as the "petrochemical corridor." A public outcry after a February 1977 spill of carbon tetrachloride (a potential carcinogen) into the Ohio River contaminated Cincinnati's water supply further fueled the legislative fires, although Congress took no action to strengthen the 1972 law. Although the act was amended in 1977, it was not until the mid-1980s that there was general agreement among policymakers and environmental groups that the 1972 legislation had been overly optimistic in setting target dates for the standards to be met. Little progress had been made in improving the overall quality of the nation's waterways, although given the pace of the country's population growth and economic expansion, the argument could be made that at least the situation did not get much worse, or worse as fast. In 1987, Congress enacted a new legislative mandate—the Water Quality Act—over two vetoes by President Ronald Reagan. The new legislation expanded congressional authority to regulate water pollution from point sources—a confined conveyance, such as a pipe, tunnel, well, or floating vessel (such as a ship) that discharges pollutants—as well as from nonpoint sources, which is basically anything else. The Water Quality Act also required every state and territory to establish safe levels of toxic pollutants in fresh water by 1990.

Congress considered but failed to pass a new Clean Water Act in 1995 and 1996. Dubbed the "Dirty Water Act" by critics, the proposed legislation would have given states the option to develop their own runoff control programs and would have relieved some industrial polluters from having to pretreat wastes before discharging them into publicly owned treatment facilities.[60]

Groundwater and Drinking Water

The main groundwater source of drinking water is aquifers—layers of rock and earth that contain water or could contain water.[61] For most of this century, groundwater was thought to be a virtually unlimited natural resource, constantly filtered and replenished and available for human use and consumption. Currently, about half of all drinking water is supplied through groundwater.[62]

As a policy issue, water quality has often suffered from differences of opinion over where the regulatory responsibility ought to lie, with regulatory authority divided between drinking water and groundwater. Federal authority to establish primary drinking water standards (those applying to materials that are human health standards) originated with the Interstate Quarantine Act of 1893, which allowed the surgeon general to make regulations covering only bacteriological contamination. But the first U.S. primary drinking water standard was not set until 1914 by the U.S. Public Health Service, whose main concern was the prevention of waterborne diseases. The federal standards were applicable only to systems that provided water to an interstate common carrier. From 1914 to 1974, the standards were revised four times—in 1925, 1942, 1946, and 1962—and were gradually extended to cover all U.S. water supplies.[63]

Groundwater regulatory authority was treated somewhat differently from the way drinking water regulatory authority was treated. There were those who felt that the federal government should not hold the responsibility for regulating and cleaning up groundwater. President Dwight Eisenhower, for example, believed water pollution was a "uniquely local blight" and felt that the primary obligation for providing a safe drinking water supply ought to rest with state and local officials, not with the federal government.[64] But with the creation of the Environmental Protection Agency in 1970, the federal government reaffirmed its policy-making authority for water quality. With passage of the 1974 Safe Drinking Water Act, the EPA was authorized to identify which substances were contaminating the nation's water supply and set maximum contaminant levels, promulgated as the National Primary Drinking Water Regulations. The act was amended in 1986 to accelerate the EPA's regulation of toxic contaminants, and included a ban on lead pipe and lead solder in public water systems. It mandated greater protection of groundwater sources, and set a three-year timetable for regulation of eighty-three specific chemical contaminants that may have an adverse health effect known or anticipated to occur in public water systems.[65]

During the summer of 1996, Congress and the Clinton administration, anxious to provide some evidence to voters that they were able to address pressing national issues, enacted amendments to the Safe Drinking Water Act. The amendments gave more discretion to states and local governments to determine what contaminants pose a threat to human health. The new law emphasized controlling the greatest risks for the most benefit at the least cost. It required local water agencies to issue annual reports disclosing the chemicals and bacteria in tap water. The reports must be written in simple, accessible language and sent to residents enclosed with their utility bills. Agencies must notify the public when water contaminants pose a serious threat. The law also authorized a $7.6 billion revolving fund to loan money to local water agencies for construction of new facilities. Small water systems can get waivers from compliance with the federal regulations. The measure was criticized some Democrats for including water-related projects in states where Republicans were in tight reelection campaigns and by environmental groups for weakening national water quality standards.[66]

But passage of the 1996 amendments did not eliminate concern over water quality. One organization, the Environmental Working Group, released a report in 1996 analyzing EPA data that concluded that one in six Americans—45 million people—receive water from a utility that has had recent pollution problems, including fecal matter, parasites, disease-causing microbes, radiation, toxic chemicals, and lead. More than 18,500 public water suppliers reported at least one violation of a federal drinking water standard in 1994 and 1995. The report urged water providers to supply more information to consumers about water quality. Representatives of the American Water Works Association subsequently criticized the study as an exaggeration of sporadic incidents that were unfairly described in the study as chronic problems.[67]

THE TOXICS LEGACY

Until the early 1960s and the publication of Rachel Carson's *Silent Spring*, Americans paid little attention to the millions of gallons of toxic chemicals that were routinely being poured into waterways or dumped onto remote sites or even stored on private property. The dangers posed by the storage and handling of toxic chemicals were either unknown or ignored. Only a series of highly publicized incidents and disclosures moved the toxics legacy onto the political agenda as a water quality issue.

Groundwater can be contaminated from a variety of human sources, from dumping to runoff from agriculture use. Homeowners, for example, may unknowingly pour products down their kitchen drains or toilets, contaminating the sewage stream. Some toxic contamination has been deliberate, while in other cases the groundwater was accidentally polluted long before researchers and officials even knew contamination was possible, or the extent to which it could be cleaned up.[68] In Los Angeles, for example, California's Department of Health Services requested that all major water providers conduct tests for two hazardous substances, trichloroethylene (TCE) and perchloroethylene (PCE), both routinely used in dry cleaning, metal plating, and machinery degreasing. The survey found hazardous levels of the two substances in several water production wells and traced them to the period between 1940 and 1967 when disposal of large quantities of chemical wastes was unregulated.[69]

Other forms of toxic contamination are legal and permitted by officials. The nation's pulp and paper mills have been targeted by environmental groups as among the biggest polluters of U.S. waterways, with bleaching plants the source of millions of pounds of chlorinated compounds annually. Among the compounds identified in bleach effluent are dioxins (a generic term applied to a group of suspected carcinogens that are the by-products of other substances or processes), which have been shown to cause reproductive disorders in animals and immune system suppression and impaired liver function in humans.[70]

The pace at which toxic contamination has been regulated and enforced, both at the federal and state levels, has been uneven and decidedly sluggish. The Clean Water Act of 1972 required the EPA to impose the best available pollution control technology standards on industries that discharge toxic waste into rivers, lakes and estuaries, or sewage treatment facilities. The agency did not take action to implement the law until 1976, when a lawsuit forced it to agree to regulate twenty-four of more than fifty industrial categories, including organic chemicals, pharmaceuticals, and pulp and paper industries. In 1987, Congress amended the legislation and ordered the EPA to update the old standards and to begin regulating additional categories by February 1991. When the congressional deadline passed, the Natural Resources Defense Council (NRDC) filed suit in U.S. District Court to force the agency to comply with the 1987 law. In its suit, the NRDC noted that the EPA had not developed rules for four of five, or fifty thousand of the seventy-five thousand, industrial plants that dump toxic substances directly into surface waters. In 1992, the EPA agreed to settle the lawsuit and extend federal standards to sixteen additional industry categories between 1996 and 2002, including industrial laundries, pesticide manufacturers, and hazardous waste facilities and incinerators.

Similarly, the states have failed to comply with the 1987 Water Quality Act provisions, which required them to impose limits on toxic pollution in their waters by 1990. In 1991, the EPA announced that it would impose federal rules on the twenty-two states and territories that had not set their own standards to reduce levels of 105 toxic compounds, including pesticides, solvents, and heavy metals. Most states are now in the process of working to complete regulations, but the EPA's announcements hastened their pace.[71]

Why has water pollution taken so long to gain policymakers' attention, and why has the EPA been so reluctant to move forward on the legislative mandates? There are several reasons that may explain the current status of water pollution control. One, EPA officials site staff and budgetary constraints that virtually crippled the agency during the 1980s, especially under President Reagan, that put many water quality initiatives on hold. Two, the federal government had delegated much of its responsibility to the states, which are required to issue permits to industries that discharge pollution onto surface water. The permit limits vary from state to state and have generally been much more lenient than federal controls. Three, water quality issues have tended to take a back seat to air quality issues when it comes to the political arena. Congressional committees have focused on the more politically visible issues of smog and auto emissions rather than water quality. Although the 1972 law eliminated the gross pollution that cause rivers and lakes to look or smell bad, the more invisible but nevertheless hazardous toxic pollutants have been largely ignored until recently. Four, the overlapping of jurisdictions and responsibilities between the federal and state governments has led to a competition among agencies. Five, both environmental groups and public officials reluctantly admit that the compliance deadlines of the 1972 legislation were extremely unrealistic, forcing the EPA to scramble to come up with new rules that even the agency leadership knew were not attainable. Lastly, despite attempts at innovative conservation strategies and protection of existing sources, one of the compelling factors in water quality policy today is cost. Many of the new federal requirements place a severe burden on small communities that cannot afford expensive water treatment plants on budgets that are already stretched thin. The EPA is thus exploring more affordable and innovative technologies, although the cost of bringing public water systems into full compliance is estimated at $1–2 billion per year. Small communities may not be able to take advantage of some treatment technologies, for example, and may not have access to alternative water supplies. Thus, many of the proposed solutions may benefit large urban areas, leaving smaller, rural communities with few alternatives.[72]

INTERNATIONAL PERSPECTIVES ON WATER QUALITY

As one of the world's most industrialized countries, the United States has the advantage of technology and monetary resources to ensure a safe supply of drinking water. To most Americans, water quality is as much a matter of aesthetics as it is health. Around the globe, however, the concerns and attention paid to the issue are quite different. First, in most developing countries water policy has been almost totally health based, with little attention paid to the recreational or scenic value of waterways — values considered luxuries in economies struggling to fund any type of environmental program at all. What minimal environmental resources there are must be spread thinly between air and water pollution, with groundwater contamination receiving the bulk of funds.[73] Despite the fact that the United Nations designated the decade of the 1980s as the International Drinking Water Supply and Sanitation Decade, millions of Africans still do not have access to water resources considered a necessity in the industrialized world. Two of the most painful and debilitating parasitic diseases, guinea worm and schistosomiasis, which affect millions of residents in sub-Saharan Africa, are caused by poor sanitation and unsafe water supplies.

Second, a lack of a regulatory framework has allowed decades of industrial and household discharges to continue almost unabated. Some of the effluent problems are a result of ignorance about pollution, while in other cases, substances are simply dumped into rivers and streams because it is the least expensive and easiest method of disposal and because it has always been done that way. Typical is the case of a rubber-processing facility in Malaysia that discharged its wastewater into the Malacca River, forcing urban residents to transport water from rural areas, while villagers were forced to dig wells or collect rainwater to supplement emergency water rations distributed by local authorities.[74]

A historical pattern of wastewater dumping exists in the former Soviet Union and in most of eastern Europe, where water quality problems are the result of decades of forced industrialization and unmitigated surface water pollution. The "growth at any cost" mentality that was pervasive since the 1920s left environmental concerns off the Communist political agenda. Most environmental problems were state secrets, and before the dissolution of the USSR, there was little public discussion of what most Soviet citizens already knew—the country was killing its lakes and rivers. American researchers have harsh criticisms for what took place throughout much of this century, noting that no other great industrial civilization so systematically and for so long poisoned its air, land, water, and people.[75] The entire region is marked with water quality tragedies.

The Black Sea, formerly home to the *dachas* and beach resorts of wealthy citizens of the former Soviet Union, is perhaps the best example of what is happening to the environment on a global scale. This body of water has an immense excess of marine nutrients that has resulted in massive eutrophication—the growth of algae and bacteria that create clotted mats that block sunlight and upset the entire ecosystem. The Black Sea also served as a convenient dumping ground for the military during the Cold War, filling it with toxic chemicals from factories and municipal waste. The oxygen supply has now been virtually depleted, leading to a decline in the number of species and losses to tourist-dependent communities. Some scientists believe that the Black Sea has 10 to 15 years to live, others say 40 years, but all agree that this once beautiful body of water is choking to death.[76] Similar conditions exist in the regions of the Aral, Caspian, and Baltic Seas, as well as chemical waste pollution of rivers and streams in Poland, Lithuania, and Lake Baikal.[77]

Many countries have only marginal enforcement operations to handle water pollution, and legislation to control and punish polluters is weak where it exists at all. There is a shortage of lawyers with expertise in environmental law, and even fewer judges who are informed or sympathetic. Enforcement of water quality regimes is made more difficult by the fact that water pollution ignores international boundaries, with many nations often sharing the same waterways. In Europe, for example, the problem was first recognized as early as 1868, when nations along the Rhine River agreed to a treaty that required vessels transporting toxic substances on the river to bear the word poison in French and German. The 1963 Berne Convention and the 1977 Rhine Chemical Convention dealt with deliberate discharge of pollutants, but neither document had effective enforcement mechanisms.

Third, environmental organizations in the United States have been much more successful than their counterparts in other countries in raising the public's awareness about water quality. In many developing nations, polluted waters have always been a way of life, and there is little knowledge of the care and advantages of clean water. As a result, there have been fewer grassroots efforts to demand stronger enforcement and less media attention to gross violations and health risks. As a result of these factors, 31 percent of the people in the developing world lack access to safe drinking water, and 44 percent lack sanitation facilities. Waterborne diseases and illnesses are the cause of high mortality and morbidity rates as well as diminished economic prospects.[78]

Although efforts are being made to transfer American technology to both developed and developing nations to improve water quality, most observers believe the best that can be done for now is to buy time. Early efforts at providing assistance in the former Soviet Union were often poorly thought out or were abandoned before fulfillment, leading some governments to rethink their aid plans. As one researcher notes, "What the West needs at this point is not a detailed blueprint for future action, but a new intellectual framework for approaching the problem: patience is necessary. More importantly, policymakers must think in terms of multiyear time frames, collection action, mechanisms for developing joint strategies, and coordination.[79]

SUMMARY

As the global population continues to grow, water scarcity and water quality have become critical environmental issues. The problems have been exacerbated by the increased demand for industrial, commercial, and agricultural use of water, and by natural causes such as drought. Water scarcity is not limited to the United States but is shared by countries in north-central and western Africa. American water policy is highly politicized, with the power shifting from the farm and agricultural lobbies at the turn of the century to urban legislators and industrial interests now. Water diversion has also destroyed valuable wildlife habitats, with wetlands among the most severely affected areas. Massive industrialization and inadequate waste disposal practices that began in the mid-nineteenth century have led to massive water problems around the globe. Although the United States has made efforts at reducing wastewater discharges, legislation has been ineffective, especially in response to the problem of pollution of groundwater by toxic chemicals. From an international perspective, the United States has a considerable advantage over other nations in terms of funding and technology, coupled with the fact that water quality issues in developing nations vary considerably from region to region.

NOTES

1. William Ashworth, *Nor Any Drop to Drink* (New York: Summit Books, 1982), 19–21.

2. World Resources Institute, *World Resources 1994–95* (New York: Oxford University Press, 1994): 2, 73.

3. Sandra Postel, "Emerging Water Scarcities," in *The World Watch Reader on Global Environmental Issues,* ed. Lester R. Brown (New York: Norton, 1991), 127–143.

4. Montague Yudelman, "Sustainable and Equitable Development in Irrigated Environments," in *Environment and the Poor: Development Strategies for a Common Agenda,* ed. H. Jeffrey Leonard et al. (New Brunswick, NJ: Transaction Books, 1989), 61–85.

5. See William S. Ellis and David C. Turnley, "A Soviet Sea Lies Dying: The Aral," *National Geographic, 177* (February 1990): 70–94. See also Peter Rogers, "The Aral Sea," *Environment, 33,* no. 1 (January–February 1991): 2.

6. For an overview of agricultural water use issues in the United States, see Ashworth, *Nor Any Drop to Drink,* 55–68.

7. See Ernest A. Englebert, *Water Scarcity: Impacts on Western Agriculture* (Berkeley, CA: University of California Press, 1984).

8. See Gilbert White, "The Environmental Effect of the High Dam at Aswan," *Environment, 30,* no. 7 (September 1988): 5–28.

9. Yudelman, "Sustainable and Equitable Development," 71.

10. Ibid., 62.

11. See "Drought Threatens California Bird Populations," *Nature, 350* (March 21, 1991): 180.

12. See George Wharton James, *Reclaiming the Arid West: The Story of the United States Reclamation Service* (New York: Dodd, Mead, 1917).

13. Robert Gottlieb, *A Life of Its Own: The Politics and Power of Water* (New York: Harcourt Brace Jovanovich, 1988), 48.

14. See Wallace Stegner, *This Is Dinosaur* (New York: Knopf, 1955). At that time, the Bureau of Reclamation also had the proposed Glen Canyon Dam near the Arizona-Utah border on the drawing boards; the project was eventually built after the Echo Park controversy.

15. See Constance Elizabeth Hunt, *Down by the River* (Washington, D.C.: Island Press, 1988), 11–14.

16. See Tom Harris, *Death in the Marsh* (Washington, D.C.: Island Press, 1991).

17. Gottlieb, *Life of Its Own,* 270–271.

18. *Winters v. United States,* 207 U.S. 564 (1908).

19. *Arizona v. California,* 373 U.S. 546 (1963).

20. See Marc Reisner and Sarah Bates, *Overtapped Oasis: Reform or Revolution for Western Water* (Washington, D.C.: Island Press, 1990), 92–98. See also Lloyd Burton, *American Indian Water Rights and the Limits of Law* (Lawrence, KS: University of Kansas Press, 1991).

21. See Jose Trava, "Sharing Water with the Colossus of the North," in High Country News, *Western Water Made Simple* (Washington, D.C.: Island Press, 1987), 171–81. See also Gottlieb, *Life of Its Own,* 223–282.

22. See David D. Kemp, *Global Environmental Issues: A Climatological Approach* (London: Routledge, 1990), 37–67.

23. Gary Gardner, "Asia Is Losing Ground," *WorldWatch* (November/December 1996): 19–27.

24. See Brett Wright, "Colder Winters for Northern Africa as Deserts Expand," *New Scientist,* January 18, 1992, 20. See also William Langewiesche, "The World in Its Extreme," *The Atlantic, 268* (November 1991), 105–128.

25. For an analysis of the problems of the Sahel, see Malin Falkenmar and Gunnar Lindh, *Water for a Starving World* (Boulder, CO: Westview Press, 1976), 70–74.

26. Postel, "Emerging Water Scarcities," 32.

27. Brett Wright, "Does Overgrazing Make the World Warmer?" *New Scientist,* January 11, 1992, 21.

28. Postel, "Emerging Water Scarcities," 25–42.

29. Yudelman, "Sustainable and Equitable Development," 70.

30. *National Audubon Society v. Superior Court (Mono Lake),* 33 Cal.3d 419 (1983).

31. See Daniel B. Botkin et al. *The Future of Mono Lake* (Riverside, CA: Water Resources Center of the University of California, 1988).

32. William H. MacLeish, "Water, Water, Everywhere, How Many Drops to Drink?" *World Monitor,* December 1990, 54–58.

33. See Benedykt Dziegielewski and Duane D. Baumann, "Tapping Alternatives: The Benefits of Managing Urban Water Demands," *Environment, 34,* no. 9 (November 1992): 6–11.

34. Reisner and Bates, *Overtapped Oasis,* 111–122.

35. See William Fletcher, *The Marine Environment* (New York: Academic Press, 1977), and K.S. Spiegler, *Salt-Water Purification* (New York: Plenum Press, 1977).

36. See, for example, the publications of the U.S. Office of Saline Water, such as its *Research and Development Progress Report,* published annually from 1954 to 1972 by the U.S. Government Printing Office, Washington, D.C.

37. See Elizabeth Schaefer, "Water Shortage Pits Man against Nature," *Nature, 350* (March 21, 1991): 180–181.

38. Alan Cowell, "More Precious Than Oil, and Maybe as Volatile," *New York Times* (March 17, 1991): IV: 3.

39. Patrick E. Taylor, "Dam's Inexorable Future Spells Doom for Yangtze Valley's Rich Past," *The New York Times* (October 6, 1996): A12.

40. Robert Delfs, "The Canal's Siblings," *Far Eastern Economic Review,* March 15, 1990, 23–25.

41. See, for example, Gerald A. Moshiri, ed. *Constructed Wetlands for Water Quality Improvement* (Boca Raton, FL: Lewis Publishers, 1994).

42. U.S. Department of the Interior, U.S. Fish and Wildlife Service, *Wetlands Status and Trends* (Washington, D.C.: U.S. Government Printing Office, 1991).

43. See Frank Graham, Jr., "Of Broccoli and Marshes," *Audubon,* 7 (July 1990): 102.

44. Keith Schneider, "Administration Proposes Opening Vast Protected Areas to Builders," *New York Times,* August 3, 1991, 1.

45. Warren E. Leary, "In Wetlands Debate, Acres and Dollars Hinge on Definitions," *New York Times,* October 15, 1991, C-4.

46. William K. Stevens, "Panel Urges Big Wetlands Restoration Project," *New York Times,* December 12, 1991, A-16.

47. Jon Kusler, "Wetlands Delineation: An Issue of Science or Politics?" *Environment,* 34, no. 2 (March 1992): 7–11, 29–37.

48. Led by the Environmental Defense Fund, numerous mainstream groups testified in opposition to the policy. See Marguerite Holloway, "High and Dry," *Scientific American,* 265 (December 1991): 16–17, and Stephen M. Johnson, "Federal Regulation of Isolated Wetlands," *Environmental Law 23,* No. 1 (1993): 1.

49. 104th Congress, H.R. 961, S. 851.

50. Kusler, "Wetlands Delineation," 8.

51. See, for example, Karol J. Ceplo, "Land Rights Conflicts in the Regulation of Wetlands," in Bruce Yandle, ed. *Land Rights: The 1990s Property Rights Rebellion* (Lanham, MD: Rowman and Littlefield, 1995), 106; Todd Shields, "Judge Fines Developers $4 Million," *Washington Post* (June 18, 1996): D-1, and "EPA's Most Wanted," *Wall Street Journal* (November 18, 1992), A20.

52. "Remarks at the Signing of the Water Quality Act of 1965, October 2, 1965," *Public Papers of the President: Lyndon B. Johnson* (Washington, D.C.: Government Printing Office, 1966), 1035.

53. The term *biocide* is a more inclusive definition and describes pesticides, fungicides, and herbicides; the term *pesticides* generally refers to the use of chemicals on insect pests only.

54. The health effects of nitrates are outlined by M.H. Ward, et al., "Drinking Water Nitrate and the Risk of Non-Hodgkin's Lymphoma, *Epidemiology* 7 (1996): 465–471.

55. Robert Gottlieb, *A Life of Its Own: The Politics and Power of Water* (New York: Harcourt, Brace, Jovanovich, 1988), 163.

56. See J. Clarence Davies III, *The Politics of Pollution* (New York: Pegasus, 1970).

57. Zygmunt J. B. Plater, Robert H. Abrams, and William Goldfarb, *Environmental Law and Policy: Nature, Law, and Society* (St. Paul, MN: West, 1992), 827.

58. See Alfred A. Marcus, *Promise and Performance: Choosing and Implementing an Environmental Policy* (Westport, CT: Greenwood Press, 1980), 141–149.

59. The Court's interpretation is outlined in *United States v. Republic Steel Corporation,* 362 U.S. 482 (1960) and *United States v. Standard Oil Company,* 384 U.S. 224 (1966).

60. 104th Congress, H.R. 961.

61. The science of groundwater analysis is a complex one. See, for example, Domy Adriano, Alex Iskandar, and Ishwar Murarka, *Contamination of Groundwaters* (Delray Beach, FL: St. Lucie Press, 1995); Martin Jaffe and Frank DiNovo, *Local Groundwater Protection* (Washington, D.C.: American Planning Association, 1987), and T. R. Crompton, *The Analysis of Natural Waters* (New York: Oxford University Press, 1993).

62. For an overview of drinking water issues, see Colin Ingram, *The Drinking Water Book* (Berkeley, CA: Ten Speed Press, 1996).

63. See Charles D. Larson, "Historical Development of the National Primary Drinking Water Regulations," in *Safe Drinking Water Act: Amendments, Regulations, and Standards,* ed. Edward J. Calabrese, Charles E. Gilbert, and Harris Pastides (Chelsea, MI: Lewis Publishers, 1989), 3–16.

64. James Ridgeway, *The Politics of Ecology* (New York: E.P. Dutton, 1970), 51.

65. See Joseph A. Cotruvo and Marlene Regelski, "Overview of the Current National Primary Drinking Water Regulations and Regulation Development Process," in *Safe Drinking Water Act: Amendments, Regulations, and Standards,* ed. Edward J. Calabrese, Charles E. Gilbert, and Harris Pastides (Chelsea, MI: Lewis Publishers, 1989), 17–28.

66. David Hosansky, "Drinking Water Bill Clears, Clinton Expected to Sign," *Congressional Quarterly Weekly Report* (August 3, 1996): 2179.

67. *U.S. Water News Online* (June 1996).

68. See William Ashworth, *Nor Any Drop to Drink* (New York: Summit Books, 1982).

69. Rogene A. Buchholz, "Groundwater Contamination: A City with Problems," in *Managing Environmental Issues,* ed. Rogene A. Buchholtz, Alfred A. Marcus, and James E. Post (Englewood Cliffs, NJ: Prentice Hall, 1992), 106–120.

70. See Mark Servos, Kelly Munkittrick, John Carey, and Glen Van Der Kraak, *Environmental Fate and Effects of Pulp and Paper Mill Effluents* (Delray Beach, FL: St. Lucie Press, 1996).

71. Keith Schneider, "U.S. Pushing States to Curb Water Pollution," *New York Times,* November 7, 1991, A-23.

72. For an overview of water quality successes and failures, see Robert W. Adler, Jessica C. Landman, and Diane M. Cameron, *The Clean Water Act 20 Years Later* (Washington, D.C.: Island Press, 1993); Susan Hunter and Richard W. Waterman, *Enforcing the Law: The Case of the Clean Water Acts* (New York: M.E. Sharpe, 1996).

73. The difficulties in funding pollution control programs are outlined by Philip R. Pryde, ed., *Environmental Resources and Constraints in the Former Soviet Union Republics* (Boulder, CO: Westview, 1995), and by Robert Mendelsohn, ed., *The Economics of Pollution Control in the Asia Pacific* (Brookfield, VT: Edward Elgar, 1996).

74. Doug Tsuruoka, "Back on Tap," *Far Eastern Economic Review,* March 26, 1992, 53.

75. See, generally, Murray Feshbach, *Ecological Disaster: Cleaning Up the Hidden Legacy of the Soviet Regime* (New York: Twentieth Century Fund Press, 1995); John Massey Stewart, ed., *The Soviet Environment: Problems, Policies and Politics (New York: Cambridge University Press, 1992);* Murray Feshbach and Alfred Friendly, *Ecocide in the USSR* (New York: Basic Books, 1992, and Joan DeBardeleben, ed., *To Breathe Free: Eastern Europe's Environmental Crisis* (Washington, D.C.: Woodrow Wilson Center Press, 1991).

76. Anne E. Platt, "Dying Seas," *WorldWatch,* 8 (January–February 1995), 10–12.

77. See, for example, Fred Pearce, "Poisoned Waters," *New Scientist,* October 21, 1995, 29–33; Peter Rogers, "The Aral Sea," *Environment,* 33 (January–February 1991): 65–68; John Pomfret, "Black Sea, Strangled by Pollution, Is Near Ecological Death," *Washington Post,* June 20, 1994, A1.

78. Kenneth D. Frederick, "Managing Water for Economic, Environmental and Human Health," *Resources,* 106 (Winter 1992): 22.

79. Feshbach, *Ecological Disaster,* 106.

FOR FURTHER READING

Robert W. Adler, Jessica C. Landman, and Diane M. Cameron. *The Clean Water Act 20 Years Later*. Washington, D.C.: Island Press, 1993.

Sarah Bates, David H. Getches, Lawrence J. MacDonnell, and Charles F. Wilkinson. *Searching Out the Headwaters*. Washington, D.C.: Island Press, 1993.

Robin Clark. *Water: The International Crisis*. Cambridge: MIT Press, 1993.

Peter H. Gleck, ed. *Water in Crisis: A Guide to the World's Fresh Water Resources*. New York: Oxford University Press, 1993.

Diane Hillel. *Rivers of Eden: The Struggle for Water and the Quest for Peace in the Middle East*. New York: Oxford University Press, 1995.

Susan Hunter and Richard W. Waterman. *Enforcing the Law: The Case of the Clean Water Act*. New York: M.E. Sharpe, 1996.

Alice Outwater. *Water: A Natural History*. New York: Basic Books, 1996.

Peter Rogers. *America's Water: Federal Role and Responsibilities*. Cambridge: MIT Press, 1993.

CHAPTER 8

Air Quality and Environmental Health Concerns

Los Angeles Mayor Fletcher E. Bowron announces at a press conference that the city's smog will be entirely eliminated within four months.
—August 14, 1943[1]

Air quality was a problem long before the mayor of Los Angeles made his optimistic prediction. There are references to the fumes produced at the asphalt mining town of Hit, about one hundred miles west of Babylon in the writings of King Tukulti around 900 B.C.E. In 61 C.E. the philosopher Seneca reported on the "heavy air of Rome" and its "pestilential vapors and soot." Marco Polo refused to use coal as a fuel because of its smoky odors. Foreigners traveling to Elizabethan England were astonished and revolted at the filthy smoke produced by domestic fires and workshops.[2] In the United States, concerns about air pollution increased in almost direct proportion to the nation's growing industrialization. In 1881, the Chicago City Council adopted an ordinance that prohibited dense smoke emissions, and in 1905, Los Angeles enacted a similar measure aimed at emissions of dense smoke from flues, chimneys, and smokestacks in the city.[3] The history of cleaning up urban air pollution is marked by small successes on what has proven to be a much longer road than most early municipal officials ever anticipated.

There are three characteristics that can be used to describe global attempts to improve air quality: one, in the United States, local government historically has been given most of the responsibility for pollution control; two, policy efforts have been split between those wishing improvement because of impaired visibility and those who recognize the health effects of pollution; and three, in most other parts of the world, the national government, rather than municipalities, has taken the initiative for improving air quality, with varying degrees of success. This chapter reviews these characteristics and the challenge of developing policies to control urban air pollution both in the United States and in other urban centers and explores the ways in which the problem has been expanded to other concerns such as visibility and toxic air pollution. The chapter then turns to the problems of indoor air pollution and the challenges of reducing these risks to health.

WHAT IS AIR POLLUTION?

Until well into the twentieth century, the components of pollution were thought to be primarily smoke and soot (suspended particulate matter) and sulfur dioxide — waste products from home heating, industrial facilities, and utility power plants. With industrialization and the advent of the automobile, that list has expanded to include a broad range of emissions.

As Table 8.1 indicates, today the term is usually applied internationally to the six conventional pollutants identified and measured by the Environmental Protection Agency: carbon monoxide, lead, nitrogen oxides, ozone, particulate matter, and sulfur oxides. Of more recent scientific study are air toxics, such as lead and benzene, regional and global pollutants, such as acid rain and carbon dioxide, and atmospherically reactive gases, such as chlorofluorocarbons. The conventional, or "criteria," pollutants are found in the atmosphere, and although most are human-made, some, like particulate matter, include the fine particles of dust and vegetation that are natural in origin and small enough to penetrate the most sensitive regions of the respiratory tract. There are three primary categories of sources for conventional pollutants: stationary or point sources, such as factories and power plants, mobile sources, including cars, trucks, and aircraft, and domestic sources, such as home heating or consumer products.

The EPA sets standards of pollution exposure, and federal legislation sets a target date by which regions must meet those standards. The federal government has a variety of sanctions, ranging from fines to shutting down facilities, which can be levied for noncompliance. During the past two decades, U.S. levels of sulfur dioxide, carbon monoxide, particulate matter, and lead have all been reduced, in some cases sharply. Between 1970 and 1995, carbon monoxide emissions fell by 28 percent; volatile organic compounds (precursors of urban ozone), by 25 percent, particulate pollution, by 79 percent, and sulfur dioxide emissions, by 41 percent. However, nitrogen oxide emissions increased by 6 percent. During the same period of time, the U.S. population increased by 28 percent, the total number of vehicle miles traveled increased by 116 percent, and the gross domestic product grew by 99 percent. When the Clean Air Act Amendments were passed in 1990, 274 areas were designated as nonattainment for at least one of the criteria pollutants. By 1996, only 174 areas were not in attainment. Improving air quality is one of the great environmental policy success stories. However, despite the progress, the EPA found that in 1995 nearly 80 million Americans still lived in areas that violated at least one of the national air quality standards. Ozone pollution continues to be the most widespread problem: in 1995, 71 million Americans lived in areas that exceeded the ozone standard.[4]

THE RESPONSIBILITY DILEMMA

For most of the twentieth century, air pollution has been considered a local problem, and as a result, most of the efforts to do something about it have been

Table 8.1   Components of Air Pollution

Criteria Pollutant	Sources	Health Effects
Carbon monoxide (CO)	Motor vehicles	Interferes with ability of the blood to absorb oxygen; impairs reflexes
Lead (Pb)	Motor vehicles, lead smelters	Affects kidneys, reproductive and nervous systems; accumulates in bones; hyperactivity in children
Nitrogen oxides (NOx)	Electric utility boilers, motor vehicles	Causes increased susceptibility to viral infections, lung irritation
Ozone	Formed by a chemical reaction of NO_2 and hydrocarbons	Irritates respiratory system; impairment of lung function; aggravates asthma
Particulate matter (PM10)	Combustion from industry, forest fires, windblown dust, vehicles	Organic carcinogenic compounds can migrate into lungs, increasing respiratory distress
Sulfur oxides (SO_2)	Utility plant boilers, oil and chemical refineries	Aggravates symptoms of heart/lung disease; increases respiratory illnesses and colds

accomplished by municipal governments. By 1912, industrial smoke, the hallmark of urban growth after the turn of the century, was regulated in twenty-eight U.S. cities with populations of two hundred thousand or more. Smoke was the prime target of most ordinances because it was visible, but there was little attention paid to controlling the problem.[5]

The federal government up until the passage of the Clean Air Act in 1963, took only passing interest in the problem. The Bureau of Mines conducted research on smoke control (which at the time was considered to be the only form of pollution) in 1912, and in 1925, the Public Health Service began to study carbon monoxide in automotive exhaust, but for the most part, the federal role was minor. A six-day smog siege in Donora, Pennsylvania, in 1948, which resulted in the deaths of twenty persons and illness for six thousand residents, focused national attention on a problem that up until then had been considered to be limited to Los Angeles. The Donora incident was followed in December 1952 by a similar sulfurous smog episode in London, and in 1953 in New York, resulting in two hundred deaths.[6] All three events lent some urgency to the problem. As city officials began to realize the irrelevance of political boundaries to pollution control, they began to coordinate their regulatory efforts.

The discovery in 1949 that automobiles were a prime source of pollution forestalled statewide controls on industrial sources, and local government stepped in to fill the void left by federal inaction. In 1955, Los Angeles officials began to coordinate their efforts with the nation's top automakers, and Congress appropriated $5 million for research into motor vehicle emissions—the beginning of federal intervention in urban air pollution regulation. Research in the early 1960s debunked the idea that pollution was a problem only in the area immediately adjacent to the source or in urban areas. Studies began to show that pollution was being transported over long distances, causing environmental damage in regions far removed from the actual source. Long-range transport of sulfur and nitrogen compounds across international boundaries—a phenomenon known as acid rain—made air pollution a global problem (see Chapter 9).[7] These findings made air quality much more than a simple local question and focused problem solving on Congress.

During the 1960s, four members of Congress did attempt to bring the federal government back into the air pollution policy debate: Edmund Muskie, senator from Maine; Abraham Ribicoff, former secretary of the Department of Health, Education, and Welfare (HEW); Kennedy Roberts, member of Congress from Alabama; and Paul Schenck, member of Congress from Ohio. Their efforts were largely responsible for the passage of the pioneering 1963 Clean Air Act, which expanded research and technical assistance programs, gave the federal government investigative and abatement authority, and encouraged the automobile and petroleum industries to develop exhaust control devices. In November 1967, President Lyndon Johnson signed a second air quality bill, which left the primary responsibility for air pollution control with the state and local governments, suggesting that the federal agencies study, but not establish, national automobile emission standards.

Meanwhile, environmental groups were pressuring Muskie to produce a new federal bill, and the senator, an early contender for the 1972 Democratic presidential nomination, felt the sting of their criticism. A 1970 report by consumer activist Ralph Nader referred to "the collapse of the federal air pollution effort" and laid the blame squarely on Muskie's shoulder.[8] Muskie and the members of his Public Works Committee staff, relying on estimates provided by the National Air Pollution Control Administration (a part of HEW), proposed tough new federal standards for air quality and a timetable by which the standards had to be met through the filing of state implementation plans (SIPs). The 1970 Clean Air Act required the newly created Environmental Protection Agency to 1) develop national air quality standards; 2) establish emission standards for motor vehicles, effective with fiscal 1975; and 3) develop emission standards and hazardous emission levels for new stationary sources. The legislation went further than ever before by giving the EPA responsibility for regulating fuels and fuel additives, for certifying and subsidizing on-the-road inspections and assembly-line testing of auto emission control systems.[9] States faced a formidable task when the 1970 act gave them responsibility for preparing emission reduction plans. In addition to facing tight deadlines for plan preparation, neither the states nor the newly created EPA knew very much about translating federal standards into emission limits on sources. Therefore, relatively crude rules—like requiring all sources to diminish emissions by some specified percentage—were often employed.[10]

Critics charge that the 1970 law had several major faults. First, there was some ambiguity over the intent of the act with regard to the setting of auto emission levels. The legislation provided automakers with a one-year extension if they made a good-faith effort to comply but found technology was not available to meet the new standards. Second, Congress appropriated only minimal amounts for research for development of control devices that were in some cases required but that did not yet exist. Third, stationary sources such as steel mills and utility power plants faced serious problems because control devices were either prohibitively expensive or technologically unfeasible.[11]

Five major automakers (Chrysler, Ford, General Motors, International Harvester, and Volvo) responded in early 1972 by filing for an extension of the requirement that they meet emission standards by 1975, arguing that they needed additional time to comply with the law. Their request for an extension was denied by EPA administrator William Ruckelshaus, so the automakers appealed to the federal court, which ordered Ruckelshaus to review his original denial.[12] The automobile manufacturers argued that the necessary catalyst technology would not be available in time to meet the federal deadline, and Chrysler and American Motors testified that, even if the vehicles could be mass-produced in time, they would break down.[13] Ruckelshaus redenied the request of extension, then reconsidered and granted the automakers what they were seeking, setting interim standards that the automobile companies did not appeal.

Implementation of the 1970 law was further hampered by what one observer has called "the enduring reluctance of the public to make significant sacrifices for the sake of healthy air."[14] The nation was locked into a pattern of rapid inflation and high unemployment, which was coupled with the imposition of an oil embargo by the Organization of Petroleum Exporting Countries (OPEC) in October 1973. With rising concern over energy supplies, in March 1974, President Nixon proposed a package of thirteen amendments to the 1970 Clean Air Act, which froze the interim 1975 auto emission standards for two more years. In 1975, the automakers applied for another one-year extension, which was granted by new EPA administrator Russell Train, largely as a result of claims that the catalysts produced a sulfuric acid mist.[15]

In 1977, industry pressure to relax the emission standards on automobiles resulted in the passage of new Clean Air Act amendments. The legislation suspended the deadlines for automakers and extended the deadlines by which states were to have attained federal standards to 1982. If a state's implementation plan made all reasonable attempts to meet the standards but was unable to do so, the state had to submit a second plan, which would bring the area into compliance no later than December 1987, an issue that primarily affected California. A key element of the 1977 law was a provision, shepherded through Congress by the Sierra Club, that states be required to show that any new sources of pollution would not worsen existing pollution conditions. This complex concept, known as prevention of significant deterioration (PSD), required businesses to install the best available control technology (BACT) to ensure that any potential pollution was minimized.

The concept had first been outlined in a 1972 Sierra Club suit again EPA administrator William Ruckelshaus[16] in which the organization argued that the EPA's guidelines under the 1970 Clean Air Act would permit significant deterioration of the nation's clean air, violating congressional intent. The federal district court agreed, ruling that EPA could not approve state implementation plans that degraded existing air quality even if the region still met national air quality standards. The EPA appealed, but the U.S. Supreme Court's 1973 4–4 ruling upheld the district court. The EPA proposed new regulations to implement the Court's ruling in 1974.

The EPA showed more flexibility toward industry with the introduction in 1979 of a "bubble" policy, which allowed businesses to find the least expensive method of reducing pollution from an entire plant or series of plants, rather than from an individual source (as if the entire facility were under a regulatory "bubble"). The policy allowed companies to choose how to reduce emissions and to use more innovative strategies than was previously required.[17]

The Clean Air Act was scheduled for reauthorization in 1981, but a change in policy direction came with the Reagan administration, and as a result, the 1970 legislation remained virtually unchanged until 1990.[18] Chief among the congressional barriers to a new law were Representative John Dingell, a Democrat from Michigan, chairman of the House Energy and Commerce Committee, who stalled efforts to enact legislation that would impose new standards on automakers, and Senate Majority Leader Robert Byrd, a Democrat from West Virginia, who protected the interests and jobs of coal miners in his region affected by acid rain proposals.

Clean air legislation regained its place on the policy agenda in the late 1980s partly as a result of changes taking place in Congress. Restless Democrats in the House were openly expressing their hostility to Dingell and Henry Waxman of California, members of the House Energy and Commerce Committee, whose personal battles were perceived as holding up the reauthorization. The result was the formation of the Group of Nine—moderate Democrats hoping to break the legislative logjam over urban smog. In the Senate, Byrd was replaced as majority leader by George Mitchell of Maine, who promised an end to the deadlock. Both houses had the opportunity to end the deadlock when the Bush administration unveiled its own clean air proposal, forcing the key players to resolve their differences.[19]

The resulting legislation, signed by President Bush in 1990, contained several far-reaching proposals that went far beyond the 1970 and 1977 acts. The bill established five categories of cities, termed nonattainment areas (marginal, moderate, serious, severe, or extreme), and set new deadlines by which they must meet federal standards. Only one region, the Los Angeles/South Coast Air Basin, was classified as extreme by the EPA and was given twenty years to meet federal standards. In contrast, serious nonattainment areas have fifteen years from November 1990 (the date of the enactment of the amendments), moderate areas have six years to comply, and marginal areas have three years. Plants emitting any of 189 toxic air pollutants are required to cut emissions and would be forced to shut down by 2003 if these emissions posed more than a one in ten thousand risk of cancer to nearby residents. Chemicals that harm Earth's protective ozone layer are to be phased out more rapidly than under the Montreal Protocol, to which the United States is a signator. One of the most contentious portions of the bill dealt with acid rain, requiring an annual reduction of sulfur dioxide emissions by 10 million tons by the year 2000 and annual nitrogen dioxide emission reductions of 2.7 million tons by that same date. The cost of the legislation was hotly debated, ranging from $25 to $35 billion dollars. Much of that burden falls on coal-fired utility power plants, many of them in the East and Midwest, which are required to reduce SO_2 emissions. Automakers estimate the costs of compliance will add hundreds of dollars to the price of new cars, and small businesses will also feel the pinch with controls on dry cleaners, gasoline service stations, and other sources.[20]

President Bush called passage of the 1990 Clean Air Act "the cornerstone of our environmental agenda." But the battle was far from over. The implementation of the 1990 act has been just as controversial as its development. Congressman Waxman has charged, "We'll never see clean air in large parts of the country."[21] There are a number of factors that make implementation difficult. Among the most difficult hurdles that the EPA faces is the regulatory time frame of the seven-hundred-page legislation. The law ordered the EPA to complete 150 regulatory activities, including 100 rule makings, in only two years. To put the process in perspective, consider that in the past the EPA has issued seven or eight major regulations *per year* on all phases of environmental law—from pesticides to solid waste to air and water pollution.

Second, the implementing regulations are among the most complex that the agency has ever issued. While the issue of nitrogen oxide emissions (one of two acid-rain-causing chemicals) took only two pages of the 1990 act, the regulations crafted by the EPA took hundreds of pages. Because of the large volume and complexity of the rules, the EPA has been forced to rely upon outside consultants for many of its rule makings and on its advisory committees for assistance in prioritizing what rules to tackle first. Many of those advisory groups, such as the Acid Rain Advisory Committee, which has forty-four members, are packed with industry members and few representatives of environmental groups.[22] Among the most complex provisions of the law are those dealing with air toxics, an area in which EPA staff members are notoriously short on expertise.

Within a year of passage of the 1990 law, Congress began to step back from the thrust of the 1990 amendments. One portion of the legislation, for example, was designed to require state and local planners to adhere to air quality goals when formulating transportation projects. Theoretically, the intent was to force municipalities to look for alternatives to increased use of single-occupancy vehicles. But in 1991 President Bush proposed, and Congress accepted, plans for a 185,000-mile national highway system that would increase auto use—at odds with the intent of the air quality act—by giving the most funds under the program to those with the highest gasoline use.[23]

Industry's political clout managed to reduce the impact of the law. Under Vice President Dan Quayle, the Council on Competitiveness, created by Executive Order during the Reagan administration as the Task Force on Regulatory Relief, reviewed the EPA's rulings "to reduce the regulatory burden on the free enterprise system." In 1991, the council rejected one EPA regulation that would have prohibited incineration of lead batteries and another that would have required that recyclables be separated from trash before burning. Both rules had been strongly supported by environmental groups, but were quashed by the council. Congressman Waxman accused the council of "helping polluters block EPA's efforts,"[24] while the Sierra Club called it "a pipeline into the federal regulatory apparatus for corporate interests."[25]

That view was reinforced by President Bush's 1992 State of the Union message in which the president announced a 90-day freeze on all federal regulations, and then extended it another 120 days after that. The freeze affected several clean air regulations, including the Pollution Prevention Act, which required polluters to report on the amount of toxic chemicals they generate before they were released. Later that year, the president overruled an EPA regulation that required industries to obtain permits that include limits on the pollution emitted by each plant. Industry had originally sought the right to exceed the limits after minor changes in plant operations, without going through the costly and time-consuming process of obtaining a new permit. Citizen groups considered the permit process an important opportunity for public participation, and the EPA, which drafted the regulation, agreed. Bush then overturned the regulation as a part of his emphasis on deregulation.

In November 1993, the Senate Environment and Public Works Committee issued a "report card" on the implementation of the Pollution Prevention Act. It gave the EPA A grades for its acid rain and stratospheric ozone programs, a B− for its small business assistance program, a C for its management of the state implementation plan process, and a D both for development of air toxic standards and for the implementation of the California Low Emission Vehicle Program.[26] The Senate study trumpeted the success of the acid rain program in devising a market-based approach to environmental regulation and emphasized the importance of environmental quality-based performance standards that create incentives for the development of new technologies.

These shortcomings in implementation were serious, but seemed manageable, until the dynamics of implementation underwent a fundamental change with the election of Republicans in statehouses and Republicans as the new majority party in Congress in November 1994.[27] During the first years of implementation, regulations focused on industrial polluters. But when the focus shifted to people's driving habits, opposition to clean air action skyrocketed. Disgruntled citizens generated considerable opposition to state implementation plans, joined by industry groups who saw a political opening to gain some regulatory relief. Governors, in response, began challenging EPA. As long as Congress was there to back up the EPA and reopening the act to weaken its provisions was not an option, the EPA could hold firm. Once the new Congress took office in 1995, however, and amending the act was a real possibility, the EPA had to scramble to accommodate state demands. Much of the criticism of the Clean Air Act in the states focused on the enhanced inspection and maintenance system, developed to replace the traditional tail-pipe test required under the Clean Air Act. The system was to be implemented through centralized locations to ensure quality control and to separate clearly the testing and repairing of motor vehicles. The EPA required that states with ozone nonattainment areas include the enhanced program as part of their effort to reduce pollution, but in the fall of 1994, several states balked. Groups representing service station owners who could perform the original testing and motorists began criticizing the enhanced inspection and maintenance program; California was the first state to be permitted to develop an alternative system of testing at both centralized locations and traditional service stations. Additional states then began pressing the EPA for exemptions.[28] Other programs aimed at reducing vehicle emissions have been just as controversial. Illinois officials complained in early 1995 that the EPA had failed to provide guidance on how states were to require car pooling in companies with more than 100 employees. Pennsylvania officials excused employers in the Philadelphia area from complying with the car pool requirement.[29]

Some two dozen bills were introduced during the first months of the 104th Congress to amend the Clean Air Act. One House bill would have repealed the entire 1990 Clean Air Act; two House bills provided that the employer commuting program be optional; a Senate bill would have made car-pooling voluntary options for states; and two Senate bills called for making auto inspections voluntary.[30] While Congress made no major changes in the Clean Air Act in 1995 and 1996, it passed several laws that made significant changes. A 1995 budget bill that cut fiscal year 1995 spending prohibited the EPA from spending any money to force states to comply with vehicle inspection and maintenance and commuter vehicle trip-reduction programs.[31] In November 1995, Congress passed a highway bill that included some clean air provisions: it ordered the EPA to give states full credit in determining their compliance with the law for noncentralized inspection and maintenance programs and abolished federal regulation of speed limits, which the EPA estimated would increase nitrogen oxide emissions by about 5 percent per year, as vehicles traveled faster and burned more fuel.[32] The following month, Congress passed a bill making the commuter vehicle trip-reduction program optional, so states with highly polluted areas would not be forced to require employers to require employee car pooling.[33] Throughout the

Another View, Another Voice

THE LOS ANGELES SOLUTION
TO AIR POLLUTION

California has always been a leader in the United States in regulating air pollution. Californians have faced first and with more intensity all of the policy challenges facing the nation in reducing air pollution. Southern California's air pollution problems are the worst in the nation. The state's air pollution regime has usually been far ahead of other states and even the federal government in the development of regulatory responses to its persistent pollution problem. One of the earliest efforts tying air pollution to health was that of the Los Angeles County Medical Association, which supported an ordinance in 1907 that regulated smoke discharges from industrial sources and called for the appointment of the nation's first smoke inspector. The gray haze became known as "smog"—erroneously thought of as a combination of smoke and fog—and it became a hallmark of California living. As industrialization increased, so too did the need to do something about the "pall of haze" that during World War II was once mistaken for Japanese gas attacks. A particularly heavy layer of smoke on September 8, 1943, called the "daylight dimout," was blamed on Southern California Gas Company's synthetic rubber plant, and the firm spent $1.5 million on corrective equipment. Yet the pollution continued, and city officials began to realize that the plant was not the sole source of the problem. Two years later, Los Angeles passed an ordinance limiting smoke emissions from any single source, but it was limited to the city's boundaries and did not apply to the other 45 incorporated cities or unincorporated areas surrounding the city. In 1949, A.J. Haagen-Smit, a biochemist at the California Institute of Technology, announced that his research showed that the automobile, which was rapidly becoming a fixture in southern California, was a prime cause of smog. This delighted refineries and utility companies, who were being painted as the air pollution villains. The Western Oil and Gas Association, one of the leading industry lobbies, hired Stanford Research Institute to confirm Haagen-Smit's studies, and they reported that automobiles, not incineration or refineries, were 95 percent responsible for smog.

The mid-1950s mark the search for a technological solution to pollution, since it was obvious that Californians were not about to give up their cars. Local newspapers published dozens of ideas on how best to rid the basin of smog, including circulating the air with helicopters, creating "smoke umbrellas" (huge parasols to block the sun), seeding the clouds for rain, and blowing the smog out to the desert through huge tunnels. Similarly, in 1959 California gave the state's Department of Public Health the authority to determine air quality and motor vehicle emission standards necessary to protect health, avoid interference with visibility, and avoid damage to crops and vegetation. In 1961, California began an aggressive air pollution control program requiring automakers to install crankcase devices to reduce pollution and in 1963 began to require exhaust control devices. In 1966, the state legislature established the first state auto emission standards—two years before federal efforts to do so.

In 1977, the state legislature gave the South Coast Air Quality Management District (SCAQMD) the authority to develop air quality control regulations from stationary sources in the basin, which encompasses an area of 13,350 square miles, the four California counties surrounding Los Angeles, and a population of more than 12 million people. In 1979, SCAQMD and the Southern California Association of Governments (SCAG) adopted the first Air Quality Management Plan (AQMP), which eventually became part of California's attainment plan required under the federal Clean Air Act. The proposal was revised in 1982 with a provisions to meet all federal air quality standards by 2002, but the plan was challenged by a group of citizens and then rejected by a federal court, which ordered EPA to disapprove the AQMP because it did not demonstrate attainment by the federal law's 1987 deadline. The court's action forced the SCAQMD and SCAG to develop one of the most comprehensive air quality attainment plans in the United States. The new AQMP, adopted in 1989, proposed attainment by 2010 (arguing that there was no way to comply any earlier) by adopting stringent pollution control measures on nearly every conceivable source of pollutants. In addition to requiring that all known control technologies be implemented within five years (affecting coatings and solvents, petroleum refining, industrial and commercial processes, and other sources), the plan also called for significant advancements in new technology, including switching 40 percent of passenger vehicles and 70 percent of freight vehicles to clean fuels, such as methanol or electricity, reducing emission from planes, ships, trains, construction equipment, solvents, coatings, and consumer products by half; and maintaining the number of vehicle miles traveled at 1985 levels through car pooling and other measures.

The 1989 AQMP, which was heavily criticized by labor, business, and industry interests before its adoption, has had mixed success. The media has ridiculed many of its control provisions, such as a ban on charcoal lighter fluid, which prompted one politician to print up bumper stickers saying "Use a barbecue, go to jail." Industry groups argued that the cost of implementing the plan was disproportionate to the small improvement in air quality that might accrue. Many companies have argued that they are unprepared to deal with the confusing and detailed control provisions of the plan, which is constantly under revision. Some regulations have already proven to be unworkable. A requirement in the 1989 AQMP that the region's 8,000 employers with 100 workers or more submit annual ride-sharing plans to reduce the number of cars driven (and the pollution they cause) became an implementation nightmare. Many business owners claimed that they did not have the staff or expertise to comply. Labor unions claimed that the ride-share regulation infringed upon collective bargaining agreements, and the agency later modified the requirement.

In January 1994, the SCAQMD put in place an innovative emissions trading program called the Regional Clean Air Incentives Market (RECLAIM) to

(continued)

achieve some of the goals of the AQMP, especially to reduce emissions of the two major precursors of ozone: hydrocarbon or reactive organic compound (ROC) emissions by 85 percent and nitrogen oxide emissions by 95 percent. Under the plan, oil refiners and other large industrial polluters are to reduce their emissions by a fixed percentage each year for different pollutants. Sources that reduce their emission below their allowances earn credits that can be sold to other sources. The plan calls for the allocation of allowable emissions to each regulated source (for hydrocarbons, those that emit more than four tons a year). Sources would be required to reduce emissions by 5 percent per year from their baseline. The marketable permit plan, according to district officials, "will provide an equivalent or greater pollutant emissions reduction than existing and proposed command control type rules." Emissions cannot exceed 1990 levels and sources cannot remove existing control devices. Stationary sources may, under certain conditions, obtain credits from mobile sources, by purchasing and retiring older model cars to extend compliance deadlines or increasing average vehicle ridership among employees.

In 1995, the SCAQMD reported that Los Angeles had made significant improvements in air quality. In 1960, ozone levels exceeded the national standard four of every five days; in 1995, the standards were exceeded only every two of five days. These reductions were achieved despite a threefold increase in motor vehicle traffic and population and the construction of new industries throughout the air basin. Los Angeles continues to have the worst air pollution in the nation, and its residents suffer more adverse effects than anyone else. Air pollution results in an estimated $10 billion in health costs and 1,600 premature deaths each year. But some officials began expressing optimism that national air quality standards could be met by 2010.

Despite the setbacks and modifications, the AQMP has become a model of regional cooperation and innovation, and there has been improvement in air quality over the last decade, despite substantial increases in population and the number of vehicles. Other states and air quality districts consider the Los Angeles proposals, particularly the emissions trading scheme, to be on the cutting edge of air pollution regulation and have adopted many of the rules to meet their own attainment needs. Initially proposed as "a living document" that would be altered as technology and policies change, the AQMP may be the region's blueprint for clean air in the twenty-first century.

For Further Reading

B. Drummond Ayres, Jr., "California Smog Cloud Reveals a Silver Lining." *The New York Times,* November 3, 1995, A7.

James E. Krier and Edmund Ursin, *Pollution and Policy* (Berkeley, CA: University of California Press, 1977), 93–94.

South Coast Air Quality Management District, "Regional Clean Air Incentives Market, Establishing the Foundation" (Spring 1992): 2–2 to 2–3, 3–4.

South Coast Air Quality Management District, "Regional Clean Air Incentives Market, Summary Recommendations" (Spring 1992).

Richard W. Stevenson, "Trying a Market Approach to Smog," *The New York Times,* March 25, 1992, C1.

Wyn Grant, *Autos, Smog and Pollution Control: The Politics of Air Quality Management in California* (Brookfield, VT: Edward Elgar, 1996.

budget process in 1995, Congress included additional riders to appropriations and balanced budget bills that would have restricted EPA's implementation of the Clean Air and other acts, but President Clinton's vetoes blocked those measures, and Congress abandoned them in 1996.

The Clean Air Act has contributed to great reductions in air pollution. But the health effects associated with current levels of pollution are serious. Even EPA officials admit that Americans will wait years to see cleaner air as a result of the 1990 legislation. Full implementation of the law will not take place until 2005.[34]

ASSESSING THE IMPACT OF URBAN POLLUTION

Why has there been such a concern over the impact of urban pollution? There are five types of environmental damage attributable to air pollution: 1) damage to vegetation, including crops and forests;[35] 2) damage to animals, birds, and insects; 3) damage to synthetic materials, including painted surfaces, rubber, nylon, and metals; 4) soiling of materials, such as clothing and buildings; and 5) weather and climatic changes, including visibility deterioration, surface temperature increases, and reduced solar radiation.[36] But the most serious impact that concerns policymakers is one of health. It is difficult to pinpoint exactly when concerns about health effects of air pollution made their way to the policy agenda. Smoky chimneys and smokestacks were considered part of the price urban dwellers paid for living in an industrialized society, and most people were probably unaware of any damage to their health.

One factor that made it difficult for policymakers to reach consensus on what to do about air pollution was the lack of a consensus about its sources. States had primary responsibility for regulating air pollution, and their responses were as varied as the sources of the problem. Eventually, air pollution disasters in Pennsylvania, New York, and London focused public attention on the hazards.

The emphasis on the health effects of pollution was largely a result of the role of the U.S. Public Health Service, which was given responsibility for air pollution legislation from 1959 until the passage of the Clean Air Act in 1963. Although there was little policy initiation before 1963, the surgeon general did convene the First National Conference on Air Pollution in 1958. Since 1970, research has shown that many Americans are affected by air pollution. A 1981 study found that asthmatics are especially sensitive to sulfur dioxide, and EPA researchers have discovered that otherwise healthy, exercising individuals show significant effects after six to eight hours of breathing ozone at levels even below the threshold of the current health standard. Still remaining to be answered are the long-term effects of repeated exposures to smog. The American Lung Association, one of the leading organizations to call for more regulation to reduce the health impacts of air pollution, estimates the annual health cost of air pollution at $50 billion.[37] Cost estimates include days lost from work as a result of pollution-related illnesses, as well as the actual cost of care.

More than one hundred studies have been published that have identified the health effects of urban ozone pollution. People breathing ozone, even at concentrations below the national standards, appear to be susceptible to increased respiratory hospital admissions, frequent and severe asthma attacks, inflammation of the upper airways (in healthy children), coughing and breathing pains, reaction to irritants, sensitivity to allergens, and decreased lung function much like smokers suffer from. Epidemiological studies show a strong correlation between increased mortality and ozone pollution. Research published in the 1990s also focused attention on the health effects of particulate pollution, and many scientists became convinced that fine particles were the most serious public health threat from air pollution. The health effects of particulate matter at levels below the national air quality standards (as well as when air quality exceeds the standards) include increased respiratory hospital admissions, increased frequency and severity of asthma attacks, increased school absences, increased respiratory symptoms such as wheezing and coughing, increased hospitalization for cardiovascular problems, and increased mortality. In two major studies of particulate pollution, the risk of early death was estimated to be from 17 to 26 percent higher in areas with high levels of PM10. The research focused on the health effects of fine particles, released during combustion, that were not easily expelled by the respiratory system's normal safeguards when breathed by humans.[38]

The goal of air quality standards, as Congress provided in the Clean Air Act, was to "protect the public health" with an "adequate margin of safety."[39] In the face of compelling research in peer-reviewed scientific scientific publications concerning the health effects of particulates and ozone, in November 1996 the EPA proposed new, tighter standards for ozone and proposed a new PM2.5 standard to regulate fine particles. The agency argued that the new particulate standards would result in 60,000 fewer bronchitis cases, 9,000 fewer hospitalizations for respiratory problems, fewer visits to doctors, less use of medication, less suffering by those with respiratory disease, improved visibility in national parks and wilderness areas, and prevention of as many as 20,000 premature deaths a year. The proposed ozone standards would result in 1.5 million fewer cases of breathing problems where lung function declines by at least 20 percent, fewer hospitalizations and visits to emergency rooms, less school and work absenteeism, and reduction of crop damage by $1 billion. The EPA also argued that every dollar spent on emissions reductions from 1970 to 1990 resulted in $15–20 worth of reduced health care cost. Critics, like the U.S. Conference of Mayors and the Air Quality Standards Coalition, comprised of industry executives, testified in congressional hearings that the proposed standards were too expensive and urged the EPA to do more research before finalizing the regulations. But in June 1997, President Clinton endorsed a compromise proposal and promised the EPA would be flexible in implementing the regulations.[40]

The government's concern over public health has also focused on the control of toxic air contaminants. Five metals found in air—beryllium, cadmium, lead, mercury, and nickel—are known to pose various hazards to human health. With the exception of lead, most of these substances pose a risk primarily to those living adjacent to the source, such as a waste dump or factory. Lead, however, is much more widely dispersed as a component of vehicle fuels and paints. Lead poisoning is characterized by anemia and may lead to brain dysfunction and neurological damage, especially in children. The elimination of lead from automobile fuels in the United States, Japan, and Canada have reduced emissions significantly, but few developing countries have made an attempt to phase out lead in gasoline. The problem is compounded by a lack of emission controls on lead smelters, battery manufacturing plants, and paint production facilities.[41]

Little is known about the health risk posed by the tens of thousands of synthetic chemicals available today. Although research is ongoing, many of the effects of toxic contamination, such as cancer, are not apparent until decades after exposure. Although many of these substances are produced by factories and industrial processes, such as pulp and paper processors, smaller sites, such as municipal waste dumps, dry cleaners, and print shops are also responsible for toxic emission releases. Pesticides and herbicides used in agricultural application also are released into the atmosphere.

As is often the case in policy development, government regulation of toxics has typically come on the heels of crisis, and in this case, events outside the United States. In July 1976, an explosion at a herbicide manufacturing facility in Sevesco, Italy, released a toxic cloud of dioxin and other chemicals that spread downwind. Dioxin is a generic term applied to a group of suspected cancer-causing substances that are known to cause severe reproductive disorders as well as immune system problems and impaired liver function. Although no deaths were directly attributed to the incident, within two weeks plants and animals were dying and residents were admitted to local hospitals with skin lesions. More than seven hundred persons living near the plant were evacuated, and five thousand others in the surrounding areas were told not to garden or let their children play outside. It took two weeks for local authorities to discover that a toxic chemical had been involved and to implement effective safeguards.[42] The incident resulted in the Sevesco Directive in 1984—an agreement by members of the European Community that plants using hazardous chemicals must inform residents of the nature and quantity of the toxics they use and the risks they pose. Later that year, the accidental release of forty tons of isocyanate at a Union Carbide facility in Bhopal, India, refocused attention on the need to require safeguards in developing nations as well. The incident resulted in death or injury to hundreds of thousands of residents near the plant.

Two landmark pieces of U.S. legislation, the Federal Insecticide, Fungicide and Rodenticide Act (FIFRA) of 1972 and the 1976 Toxic Substances Control Act (TSCA), which regulates how toxic chemicals are to be used, were a result of such incidents. The laws allow the EPA to regulate chemicals that pose an unacceptable health risk, such as polychlorinated biphenyls (PCBs), which were first regulated in 1978. In addition, the Emergency Planning and Community Right-to-Know Act of 1986 now provides communities with access to information about toxic chemicals in their region. The law calls for extensive data collection and for the creation of state emergency response commissions to plan for chemical release emergencies. The federal government also conducts the Toxics Release Inventory, an annual inventory of toxic releases and transfers of about three hundred toxic chemicals from over twenty thousand manufacturing facilities nationwide. As information about the health effects of each substance is gathered, chemicals of little or no toxic concern are removed from the list, while others are added. Before a new pesticide may be marketed or used in the United States, it must first be registered with the EPA after a series of health, economic, and cost: benefit studies. If the studies indicate that the risks outweigh the benefits, the EPA can refuse to register the product or regulate the frequency or level of application. This process was used to ban the pesticide DDT in 1972 and to cancel registrations for thirty-four other potentially hazardous pesticides.[43] In 1996, Congress passed a new pesticides law that created a single standard for regulating pesticides in food, rather than having different rules for raw and processed food. Only pesticides that pose a "reasonable certainty of no harm," understood to mean resulting in a risk of no more than one-in-one million lifetime risk of cancer, are permitted.[44]

Yet some observers believe that the United States's progress toward controlling toxic air pollutants has been glacially slow. Before the passage of the 1990 Clean Air Act, the EPA had completed regulations for only seven toxic chemicals,[45] and no information is available on the toxic effects of nearly 80 percent of the chemicals used in commerce.[46] Information generated from the Superfund Right-to-Know rule indicates that more than 2.7 billion pounds of toxic air pollutants are emitted annually in the United States. EPA studies indicate that exposure to such quantities of air toxics may result in one thousand to three thousand cancer deaths each year.[47] The 1990 legislation, however, does offer a comprehensive plan for reducing hazardous air pollutants from major sources and includes a list of 188 toxic air pollutants for which emissions must be reduced. In addition to publishing a list of source categories that emit certain levels of these pollutants, the EPA must develop standards for pollution control equipment to reduce the risk from the contaminants. Based on information from the Toxics Release Inventory as well as additional estimates of emissions from mobile sources and dispersed or area sources such as residential wood-burning stoves, the EPA reported in 1995 that 4.4 million tons of toxics are released into the air each year. The mobile and area sources account for 70 percent of hazardous air pollutant emissions. (Motor vehicle and wood-burning stoves alone account for 47 percent of all toxic emissions.) Efforts to reduce air toxic emissions may also reduce levels of PM and ozone, since many sources emit several different kinds of pollutants.[48]

The Clinton administration proposed in 1996 expanding the requirements of the Toxic Release Inventory to get better data on what pollutants were being released into the environment. The new requirements would increase the number of facilities required to report their emissions to 30,000, up from the 23,000 required to report under the old system. The EPA also won in 1996 an important court victory that permitted it to add 286 new chemicals to the inventory of those that must be reported.[49] It is difficult to know whether air toxic emissions are increasing or decreasing because of the numerous problems that have plagued monitoring and reporting efforts. But some sectors of the economy, such as the chemical industry, have committed to reducing dramatically their emissions through pollution prevention programs. Publication of toxic emissions appears to have created a powerful incentive for companies to reduce emissions; companies have also frequently found that reducing emissions also reduces production costs and increases profits.[50]

Reductions in the EPA's budget and costly and time-consuming studies of the health effects of toxics are still barriers to effective regulation of hazardous air pollutants. Some toxics, such as mercury and lead, last a long time in the atmosphere before they are deposited in bodies of water where they are ingested by fish or plants, later harvested for human consumption. The Clean Air Act calls for studies by the National Academy of Sciences and the EPA that will review and recommend improvements to current techniques for estimating risks to public exposure to air toxics. The Council of Economic Advisers estimated the cost to industry of the air toxics program would be as much as $6–7 billion in 2005. It is impossible to quantify, however, the potential health benefit costs, since the results of reducing the damage may not be seen for many years.[51]

INTERNATIONAL AIR POLLUTION EFFORTS

Much of what is known about air pollution in nations other than the United States comes from the Global Environmental Monitoring System (GEMS) established under the auspices of the World Health Organization (WHO) and the United Nations Environment Programme (UNEP). GEMS/Air is active in more than fifty countries representing different climatic conditions, levels of development, and pollution situations. Data are available for five pollutants: sulfur dioxide, suspended particulate matter, nitrogen dioxide, carbon monoxide, and lead.

One GEMS report found that, worldwide, an estimated six million people live in urban areas where average SO_2 levels exceed recommended levels of exposure. Particulate levels are unacceptably high in most cities, and residents in rapidly industrializing countries are being exposed to higher levels of NO_2. Although the data are not complete, there is evidence that people living in as many as half the cities in the world may be exposed to excessive carbon monoxide levels, with one-third of the world's city dwellers exposed to marginal or unacceptable lead concentrations.[52] Smog can travel for hundreds of miles and last for many days, growing as it passes over new sources of pollutants. As a result, "modern" smogs frequently cross international boundaries, such as a 1976 smog that began in central Europe and was tracked several days later crossing the shores of Ireland from the Atlantic Ocean.[53]

The air quality issue has been approached differently between developed and less developed nations throughout the world, although the United States is considered to be at the vanguard of pollution control.[54] Great Britain has been at the forefront of European regulatory programs, enacting the Alkali Acts in 1863, which required that 95 percent of the emissions from industrial alkali facilities be controlled. In 1956, the Clean Air Act granted local authorities power to regulate "smoke control areas" and a 1968 law expanded those powers. Pollution episodes in London in 1972 and 1974, caused largely by fuel oil emissions, resulted in legislation in 1974 that reduced the sulfur content of fuel.[55] In other developed regions, environmental deterioration emerged as a political issue more or less simultaneously in the late 1960s, when many countries introduced similar protective legislation, although success has varied from one nation to another.[56] Japan, for example, which has traditionally been a pioneer in requiring industrial pollution controls, has made progress, but it is being countered by emissions of pollutants from household energy consumption and the transportation sector. A study by Japan's Environment Agency found that, although industrial emissions had dropped considerably over the past twenty-five years, increased electricity use (from air conditioning and household appliances) and diesel truck emissions (which are not controlled by Japan's strict automotive exhaust regulations) increased dramatically.[57]

In eastern Europe and the republics of the former Soviet Union, industrialization that went unchecked for decades has led to a continuing air quality nightmare. Strict Soviet emission standards established in the 1950s were virtually ignored, and figures on emissions were kept secret during the Communist regime. Local leaders often had no idea how much pollution was being emitted by factories in their area, and in Poland, the electrostatic precipitators installed on factory chimneys to control dust were often switched off at night to save electricity.[58]

Even though air pollution is almost as serious in the urban areas of less developed countries—Mexico City, Sao Paulo, Cairo, Beijing, Bangkok—the problem has taken a backseat to efforts to increase economic development. Attempts by international organizations such as the United Nations to encourage more restrictive air pollution controls are often met by skepticism in Third and Fourth World countries where leaders have a less global view. They argue that attention to environmental matters should follow the attainment of a higher standard of living for their people.[59]

Private cars and geography are the primary culprits in Mexico City, where residents are crammed into a valley ringed by mountains—the same conditions responsible for Los Angeles's notorious smog. Vehicles at the high altitude burn fuel inefficiently, releasing unburnt hydrocarbons, which are then trapped at street level, especially during the winter. In 1990, the city suffered from the most polluted conditions ever, and the nation's ecology ministry twice declared an emergency, requiring industries temporarily to cut their operations by half. In response, Mexico's president announced a five-year, $4.6 billion program to clean up dirty industries or move them out of the city entirely. In addition, the city enacted a mandatory program restricting automobile use and forced the government-owned petroleum company to reduce the lead content in gasoline and shut down its city refinery, the largest single source of industrial pollution. Hundreds of trees were also planted in a companion effort to create a green belt.[60]

Air pollution in developing countries is approached differently than in industrialized nations for a number of other reasons. In China, pollution was long considered a problem of capitalist societies that exploited workers and resources. But the expansion of the Chinese population has outgrown its attempts at environmental management, and most of its air pollution control policies have had only limited success. China's reliance upon coal as a fuel source, for example, has resulted in high levels of suspended particulates and tremendous visibility impairment. Although China has relatively few privately owned vehicles, cars there are considerably more polluting (estimates indicate that they produce from fifteen to fifty-five times the amount of hydrocarbon emissions as comparable Japanese models), so any increase in vehicles within the cities will sharply affect pollution levels.[61] Indonesia, which suffers from a variety of air pollution sources common to developing nations, faces unique challenges because of its large geographic coverage and fragmentation of land masses. In addition to traditional sources of urban pollution such as poorly tuned vehicles and uncontrolled rubbish burning, the country's air is also poisoned by clouds of dust and fumes from erupting volcanoes.[62]

While the United States can accurately claim credit for major reductions in air pollution over the last five decades, the international perspective is one of mixed success. Industrialized nations in western Europe come close to matching the U.S. record in curbing pollutants, while the problems facing eastern Europe are still being identified. In developing nations, attempts to control emissions are often thwarted by policies that encourage economic growth at the expense of the environment. Like many other environmental protection policies, there is no "one-size-fits-all" solution for this problem, and very limited resources to use for policy implementation.

ENVIRONMENTAL HEALTH CONCERNS

While ambient, or outdoor, air pollution, has been one of the world's most visible environmental concerns, the last two decades have seen increased attention focused on a variety of other environmental problems of equal or greater health risk. Although these health issues are dissimilar in terms of source and degree of potential hazard, they share a common characteristic in that they are exemplary of policy avoidance.

One report by the Environmental Protection Agency has suggested that indoor air pollution risks, for instance, are higher than most other environmental risks—a problem made even more serious because, on average, an employed person spends 28 percent of the day indoors at work and 63 percent indoors at home. Conceivably, this would make indoor air pollution a high priority for policymakers, and if so, would warrant some form of government intervention and regulation.[63]

Like other environmental problems, concern about indoor air quality surfaced because of individual events, which then begin to capture the public's attention, and subsequently, policymakers' interest. In 1968, an epidemic of illness characterized by fever, headaches, and muscular pains affected nearly 150 people in a building in Pontiac, Michigan, but no source could be found and the incident was simply called "Pontiac fever." In 1976, twenty-nine people attending an American Legion convention in Philadelphia died from a previously unknown pneumonia-like illness that affected nearly two hundred people. The cause was later traced to a bacterium, now identified as *Legionella pneumophila* (Legionnaire's disease), found in a defective air-conditioning system. These two events began to call attention to indoor air pollution—a term applied to environmental illnesses caused by a wide spectrum of substances found in residential and commercial buildings. Generally, these pollutants are divided into fourteen primary pollutant types emanating from fifteen major sources, as seen in Figure 8.1. Classifications such as those found in the figure are not totally satisfactory, since some pollutants, such as environmental tobacco smoke, are both particulates and gases, and passive smokers may also be exposed to various types of volatile organic compounds. Prolonged exposure from a multiplicity of these sources may lead to sick building syndrome, a term applied to situations where 20 percent of more of a building's occupants exhibit symptoms, such as headaches, nausea, dizziness, sore throats, dry or itchy skin, sinus congestion, nose irritation, or excessive fatigue. The World Health Organization has estimated as many as 30 percent or all new and renovated office buildings emit some type of toxic contaminant, exposing millions of workers to potential health risks.[64]

Other types of environmental health concerns have found their way to the policy agenda when media coverage focuses on a problem and brings it to the public's attention. Such is the case with radon, first discovered in 1900 by Friedrich Dorn, a German physicist who described the "emanations" of radon from the decay of uranium-238. Radon is an inert, colorless, tasteless, odorless gas found in more than 150 types of rocks found throughout North America and in various regions in Europe. Radon gas decays and emits radiaoctive particles called radon progeny which are hazardous when inhaled directly or when attached to dust particles that are lodged in the lungs. In 1971, the EPA issued federal guidelines limiting exposure for uranium miners after numerous studies showed a causal link between radon exposure and an increased incidence of lung cancer. Other researchers, however, have concluded that radon may not be an important cause of lung cancer, raising questions about the risk posed by low level exposure.[65]

In 1990, *The New Yorker* magazine published an article on radon by writer Paul Brodeur[66] that launched a flurry of environmental health scare stories. Some authors meshed science fact and fantasy, calling on the federal government to "do something" about problems that were still relatively unknown to researchers, or where research was often conflicting. The topics ranged from the health risks posed by environmental tobacco smoke (ETS), to asbestos, to electromagnetic fields (EMFs).

In the case of ETS, the health debate has been heavily polarized. On the one side, the tobacco industry argues that smoking is like a lot of other risky activities that individuals freely and knowing undertake. On the other side is a great

Figure 8.1 Sources of Indoor Air Pollution

SOURCES / POLLUTANTS	Respirable Particles	Environmental Tobacco Smoke	Radon	Asbestos	Volatile Organics	Pesticides	Formaldehyde	Polycyclic Hydrocarbons	Carbon Monoxide	Nitrogen Dioxide	Sulfur Dioxide	Ozone	Lead	Biological Agents
AC Systems	X	X												X
Outdoor Air	X								X			X	X	X
Building Materials	X		X	X	X	X	X							
Copying Machines					X							X		
Earth/Ground	X		X		X	X		X					X	X
Furnishings					X		X							
Kerosene Heaters	X				X			X	X	X	X			
Gas Stoves					X				X	X				
Gas Heaters	X				X			X	X	X				
Consumer Products	X				X	X	X							
Insulation	X			X			X							
Moist Materials														X
Tobacco Smoke	X	X			X			X	X					
Vehicle Exhaust	X				X		X	X	X	X			X	
Wood Stoves	X				X	X		X	X					

Source: Dennis F. Naugle and Terrance K. Pierson, "A Framework for Risk Characterization of Environmental Pollutants," *Journal of the Air Waste Management Association, 41,* no. 10 (October 1991): 1299.

body of literature that shows ETS may be responsible for a wide range of health effects, including reduced pulmonary function, age at menopause, cardiovascular disease, and prenatal development and birth weight.[67] In 1997, after decades of litigation and legislation aimed at warning consumers about the dangers of smoking and ETS, the tobacco industry agreed to a settlement that would require them to contribute billions of dollars towards health care and increased regulation of tobacco advertising.

Sometimes, environmental health concerns have made the policy agenda even though the health risk was overstated or easily controlled. Asbestos, a mineral once called the "wonder fiber" because of its multiplicity of uses, has historically been used in construction (acoustic ceilings, roofing and flooring felt, shingles, and thermal insulation) and in automotive parts such as drum brake linings and disc break pads. There were few concerns about health risk from asbestos use until the 1930s, when asbestosis, a disease caused when the mineral fibers scar delicate lung tissue, became classified as an occupational disease. The illness potentially could affect a myriad of workers, from school custodians working in buildings insulated with asbestos to more than one million U.S. workers doing brake repair work.[68]

During the 1980s, policymakers responded to what some have called an "asbestos panic" in their attempts to solve what was at the time perceived as a crisis. Fueled by media hype, asbestos removal programs were undertaken throughout the United States, especially in public schools where children were believed to be at risk. Many schools rushed to remove the substance without seeking expert advice or consultation, even though removal was not always necessary as long as the asbestos was not friable (crumbling) and capable of releasing fibers into the air.[69]

Of more serious concern now are the millions of workers exposed to asbestos on the job for decades before the adverse health effects were known. Workers who were exposed while working on pipes under New York's Grand Central Terminal once were so covered by asbestos powder that they became known as the "snowmen of Grand Central." They worked without protective devices until the late 1980s and have been told by their physicians that they face statistically significant increased risks of dying from asbestos-related diseases. Others have sued the nation's 20 million asbestos producers in a class action lawsuit, while an estimated 300,000 cases remain in the federal and state courts, with the number of new cases growing by almost 5,000 a month in 1995.[70]

The debate over the environmental risk posed by electromagnetic fields continues to be waged in the media and, less frequently, in the legislative arena, with policymakers undecided as to what action, if any, needs to be taken to protect public health. Scientists have been studying artificial and naturally occurring electric and magnetic fields since the nineteenth century. In the United States and Canada, utility power plants produce electricity, which is sent out at a frequency of 60 hertz (Hz), which means that the current in the circuit reverses direction (called alternating current, or AC) sixty times each second. Nations in other parts of the world generally use 50-Hz-power. The term electromagnetic fields (a combination of electric and magnetic fields) usually refers to extremely low frequencies (ELFs)—the portion of the electromagnetic spectrum from 0 to 100 Hz, as opposed to x-rays at the other end of the spectrum, with radio, television, and microwave frequencies between. There is an ambient or natural magnetic field that surrounds us, and humans are exposed to additional electromagnetic radiation depending upon the kind of life-style we lead and the number of household appliances we use.

The controversy is over what effect EMFs have on human beings, if any, and if so, what dose presents a risk to human health. The U.S. Department of Energy has supported EMF research since the mid-1970s, as have a number of electric utilities, the National Cancer Institute, the National Institutes of Health, and the U.S. Navy. Most studies are generally of two types: those that measure the potential health risk of EMF exposure within the home, and those that are primarily occupational, based on the exposure of those working directly with power sources, such as lineworkers or electricians. So far, the studies have been controversial, contradictory, or inconclusive. One 1982 study, for example, found that men whose occupations required them to work in electric or magnetic fields died from leukemia proportionately more often than did men in ten of eleven occupations studied.[71] Other studies linked EMF exposure and brain tumors.[72]

Of particular health interest has been the relationship of children and EMFs, with several early studies showing no adverse relationship and a 1991 study showing an increased chance of getting leukemia for a child who lives close to high-voltage powerlines. The issue was complicated further when a 1997 study funded by the National Institutes of Health and the University of Minnesota's Children's Cancer Research Fund found no association between magnetic field strength from powerline and wiring patterns and leukemia rates in children.[73]

It is not unexpected that public officials would have difficult coming up with EMF policies given the conflicts within the scientific community. At the same time, they are facing mounting pressures from constituents who have read of the potential dangers in popular magazines, and from industry groups like the Electromagnetic Energy Policy Alliance, which has characterized many of the studies as "alarmist."[74] The issue has, however, affected utility operations, contributing to delays or failures in attempts to site new transmission and distribution facilities in one out of three cases. Residents worried about the potential lowering of their property values by transmission lines have led some utilities to change the design of their distribution circuits and placing more lines underground, measures that may increase costs by as much as $1 billion per year.[75] There is however, unanimous agreement that more research is needed to determine the nature and extent of any environmental health risk posed by EMFs. Even if a risk is determined to exist, decisions still remain as to whether that risk is significant, whether the risk can be reduced, and if so, at what costs.

POLICY AVOIDANCE AND NON-DECISION MAKING

The characteristic that each of these environmental health concerns has in common is that they are exemplary of "policy avoidance"—a subject most public officials have managed to finesse for decades without being forced to make policy.[76] This tendency has also been called "non-decision making"—the ways in which problems are kept off the policy agenda, often before they even have a chance to be heard, a problem common to many public policy issues.[77] Why is this so?

First, despite that the adverse health effects of many of these environmental hazards were identified decades ago, the hazards themselves have never been systematically monitored. This is especially important for substances like asbestos that have a long latency period (the period between first exposure and the manifestation of any health effects). It may take as many as forty years for there to be evidence of any risks from exposure, and evidence may be hidden in interacting causes of disease, such as smoking.[78] The difficulties of identifying the nature and extent of the problem allow it to remain unresolved. In other cases, such as radon and EMFs, it is difficult to reach scientific consensus on the risk factor.

Second, these issues have often been lumped along with a host of other problems routinely labeled as "occupational health" rather than as environmental problems. As such, they may have captured the interest of health professionals, but not the mainstream environmental groups that have been responsible for bringing other issues to the top of the policy agenda and to the attention of the media. On an already crowded environmental agenda, a topic like indoor air quality has been edged aside by more publicly or politically salient issues.

Third, these environmental health concerns lack the graphic visibility that initially focused attention on urban air quality. There are no tall smokestacks spewing smoke, nor dirty emissions from automobiles and city buses. They cannot be seen, nor, for the most part, smelled, touched, or tasted. Victims do not die overnight, and it is often hard to link their deaths to a specific source for years. Many homeowners may be reluctant to admit that radon or asbestos have invaded their residences, preferring to believe that they are safe there. As a result, policymakers have not been forced to confront angry constituents, allowing issues to languish at the bottom of the policy pile, overwhelmed by more "dirty" pollution sources.

Fourth, ambient or outdoor air is generally thought of as common property, meaning there is a justification for regulation because all of society benefits from cleaner air. Cleaning up emissions from one factory improves the air all of us breathe. Not so with most environmental health problems like radon or asbestos, however, except in "public" spaces. An argument can be made that it is the responsibility (financial and moral) of the homeowner or landlord or building owner to maintain whatever interior atmosphere he or she chooses. For that reason, there is less public acceptance of either government intervention or promulgation of standards of what constitutes acceptable levels of contamination.

Lastly, there is a political challenge for leaders to avoid succumbing to the hysteria that has often permeated the media, allowing them to jump into the fray before sufficient evidence has been gathered. Policymakers have several options before them:

- Do nothing at this point, waiting for the scientific evidence to be more clearly defined.
- Continue scientific investigation and allow the public to make exposure decisions on their own.
- Seek voluntary compliance based on the best available data.
- Adopt regulations anyway based on a lack of scientific evidence.

Unfortunately, many legislators and regulators have chosen the last option, believing that administrative convenience (based on evidence that has a questionable scientific basis) is preferable to the political pressures that they face from constituents. Some political leaders prefer to take immediate and dramatically visible action, even if it is wrong.

SUMMARY

Even though efforts to improve air quality have been made for decades, researchers have continued studying the causes and effects of air pollution. Most regulations have focused on mobile sources such as automobiles and trucks, and stationary sources, such as factories and other industrial emission sources. There have also been shifts in the reasons why policymakers are concerned about pollution. At some decision points, the concern has been health, and at others, aesthetics. As the cost of controlling pollution has risen, attention is now being paid to more innovative control measures, such as for paints, solvents, and consumer products. In the United States, air quality legislation has been fine-tuned over the past forty years, with the 1990 Clean Air Act amendments providing a comprehensive regulatory framework. On the international front, the United States is far ahead of most other nations in controlling air pollution, while in Third and Fourth World counties, the desire for industrial progress, coupled with limited resources, has made air quality less of a priority. More recently, environmental health concerns have begun to surface, although most policymakers have chosen to deal with more visible pollutants. Hazards such as indoor air pollution, environmental tobacco smoke, radon, asbestos, and electromagnetic radiation are the subject of limited and often conflicting research to determine the nature of risk for human exposure. Mainstream environmental groups, however, have paid little attention to these problems, allowing environmental health issues to slip further down the policy agenda.

NOTES

1. Ed Ainsworth, "Fight to Banish Smog, Bring Sun Back to City Pressed," *Los Angeles Times,* October 13, 1946, 7.

2. For examples of the earliest awareness of air pollution, see Donald E. Carr, *The*

Breath of Life (New York: Norton, 1965), 28–34; and Arthur C. Stern et al., *Fundamentals of Air Pollution* (New York: Academic Press, 1973), 53–59.

3. For a chronology of the early air pollution control efforts, see James E. Krier and Edmund Ursin, *Pollution and Policy* (Berkeley, CA: University of California Press, 1977), 46–47.

4. U.S. Environmental Protection Agency, *National Air Quality and Emissions Trends Report, 1995* (Research Triangle Park, NC: U.S. EPA, 1996): 1–4.

5. Krier and Ursin, *Pollution and Policy,* 47.

6. For a description of the London episode, see Peter Brimblecombe, *The Big Smoke* (London: Methuen, 1987), and Fred Pearce, "Back to the Days of Deadly Smogs," *New Scientist,* December 5, 1992, 25–28.

7. Derek Elsom, *Atmospheric Pollution* (New York: Basil Blackwell, 1987), 4–5.

8. John C. Esposito, *Vanishing Air: The Ralph Nader Study Group Report on Air Pollution* (New York: Grossman, 1970), vii.

9. John C. Whitaker, *Striking a Balance: Environment and Natural Resources Policy in the Nixon-Ford Years* (Washington, D.C.: American Enterprise Institute, 1976), 94.

10. Marc K. Landy et al., *The EPA: Asking the Wrong Questions* (New York: Oxford University Press, 1990), 205.

11. See Alfred Marcus, "EPA," in *The Politics of Regulation,* ed. James Q. Wilson (New York: Basic Books, 1980), 267–303.

12. *International Harvester v. Ruckelshaus,* District of Columbia Court of Appeals, February 10, 1973.

13. Whitaker, *Striking a Balance,* 100.

14. Alfred A. Marcus, *Promise and Performance: Choosing and Implementing an Environmental Policy* (Westport, CT: Greenwood Press, 1980), 123.

15. Whitaker, *Striking a Balance,* 104.

16. *Sierra Club v. Ruckelshaus,* 344 F.Supp. 253 (1972). For an analysis of the case, see Thomas M. Disselhorst, "Sierra Club v. Ruckelshaus: On a Clear Day . . .", *Ecology Law Quarterly,* 4 (1975): 739–780.

17. For examples of how the "bubble" policy has affected industry, see Elsom, *Atmospheric Pollution,* 176–177.

18. See Arnold W. Reitze, Jr., "A Century of Air Pollution Control Law: What's Worked; What's Failed; What Might Work," *Environmental Law, 21,* no. 4:II (1991): 1549–1646.

19. For a detailed chronology of these events, see Richard E. Cohen, *Washington at Work: Back Rooms and Clean Air* (New York: Macmillan, 1992).

20. See Norman W. Fichthorn, "Command-and-Control vs. the Market: The Potential Effects of Other Clean Air Act Requirements on Acid Rain Compliance," *Environmental Law, 21,* no. 4:II (1991): 2069–2084; and Alyson Pytte, "A Decade's Acrimony Lifted in the Glow of Clean Air," *Congressional Quarterly Weekly Report,* October 27, 1990, 3587–3592.

21. Michael Weisskopf, "Writing Laws Is One Thing—Writing Rules Is Something Else," *Washington Post National Weekly Edition,* September 30–October 6, 1991, 31; see also Henry Waxman, "An Overview of the Clean Air Act Amendments of 1990," *Environmental Law, 21,* no. 4:II (1991): 1721–1816.

22. Henry V. Nickel, "Now, the Rush to Regulate," *The Environmental Forum, 8,* no. 1 (January–February 1991): 19.

23. Mark Mardon, "Last Gasp Next 185,000 Miles?" *Sierra, 76,* no. 5 (September–October 1991): 38–42.

24. "Quailing over Clean Air," *Environment, 33,* no. 6 (July–August 1991): 24.

25. "Industry's Friend in High Places," *Sierra, 76,* no. 5 (September–October, 1991): 42.

26. U.S. Senate Committee on Environment and Public Works, "Three Years Later: Report Card on the 1990 Clean Air Act Amendments," (November, 1993).

27. For a discussion of the implementation of the Clean Air Act, see Gary Bryner, *Blue Skies, Green Politics: The Clean Air Act of 1990 and Its Implementation* (Washington, D.C.: Congressional Quarterly Press, 1995), chapters 5–6.

28. Alex Daniels, "Tempest in a Tailpipe" *Governing* (February, 1995): 37–38.

29. *Greenwire* (February 2, 1995).

30. *Greenwire* (January 20, 1995; January 23, 1995; and February 2, 1995).

31. P.L. 104–19.

32. P.L. 104–59.

33. P.L. 104–70.

34. "Questions and Answers: An Interview with William G. Rosenberg," *EPA Journal, 17,* no. 1 (January–February 1991): 5.

35. See James J. Mackenzie and Mohamed T. El-Ashry, *Air Pollution's Toll on Forests and Crops* (New Haven, CT: Yale University Press, 1989).

36. Elsom, *Atmospheric Pollution,* 13.

37. John R. Garrison, "Will the New Law Protect Public Health?" *EPA Journal, 17,* no. 1 (January–February 1991): 58.

38. Douglas W. Docker et al., "An Association Between Air Pollution and Mortality in Six U.S. Cities," *The New England Journal of Medicine, 329,* no. 24 (December 9, 1993): 1753–1759); C. Arden Pope III et al., "Particulate Air Pollution as a Predictor of Mortality in a Prospective Study of U.S. Adults," *American Journal of Respiratory Care Medicine, 151,* (1995): 669–674.

39. 42 U.S.C. 7409(b)(1).

40. For an overview of these issues, see Natural Resources Defense Council, *Breath Taking* (New York: Natural Resources Defense Council, 1996); U.S. EPA, "Review of the National Ambient Air Quality Standards for Particulate Matter: Policy Assessment of Scientific and Technical Information," (Research Triangle Park, NC: U.S. EPA, April 1996).

41. Alan J. Krupnick, "Urban Air Pollution in Developing Countries: Problems and Policies," *Discussion Paper QE91-14* (Washington, D.C.: Resources for the Future, 1991), 8.

42. Elsom, *Atmospheric Pollution,* p. 58. See also Angela Liberatore and Rudolf Lewanski, "Environmental Disasters and Shifts in Italian Public Opinion," *Environment, 32,* no. 5 (June 1990): 36.

43. "Chemicals," *EPA Journal, 16,* no. 5 (September–October 1990): 27.

44. "Bipartisan Agreement Reached on Pesticides," *The New York Times,* July 17, 1996, A16.

45. The EPA has set standards for arsenic, asbestos, benzene, beryllium, mercury, radionuclides, and vinyl chloride.

46. Walter A. Rosenbaum, *Environmental Politics and Policy,* 2d ed. (Washington, D.C.: Congressional Quarterly Press, 1991), 149.

47. U.S. Environmental Protection Agency, *The Clean Air Act Amendments of 1990: Summary Materials* (Washington, D.C. November 15, 1990), 4.

48. U.S. Environmental Protection Agency, *National Air Quality and Emissions Trends Report, 1995* (Research Triangle Park, NC: U.S. EPA, 1996): 49–58.

49. H. Joseph Herber, "Utilities, Incinerators, Mines to Make Reports," *Washington Post,* June 27, 1996, A13.

50. Stuart L. Hart, "Beyond Greening: Strategies for a Sustainable World," *Harvard Business Review* (January 1997): 66.

51. Lydia Wegman, "Air Toxics: The Strategy," *EPA Journal,* 17, no. 1 (January–February 1991): 32–33.

52. "Monitoring the Global Environment: An Assessment of Urban Air Quality," *Environment, 31,* no. 8 (October 1989): 6–37.

53. Pearce, "Back to the Days of Deadly Smogs," 28.

54. For an overview of global/urban air quality efforts, see, for example, Derek Elsom, *Smog Alert: Managing Urban Air Quality* (London: Earthscan, 1996), and Jorge E. Hardoy, Diana Mitlin, and David Satterthwaite, *Environmental Problems in Third World Cities* (London: Earthscan, 1993).

55. Elsom, *Atmospheric Pollution,* 194–208.

56. Elsom, *Atmospheric Pollution,* 6–7.

57. See David Swinbanks, "Pollution on the Upswing," *Nature,* 351 (May 2, 1991): 5.

58. See, for example, Philip R. Pryde, ed., *Environmental Resources and Constraints*

in the Former Soviet Republics (Boulder, CO: Westview, 1995); Joan De Bardeleben, *To Breathe Free: Eastern Europe's Environmental Crisis* (Washington, D.C.: Woodrow Wilson Center Press, 1991).

59. Elsom, *Atmospheric Pollution,* 9.

60. See "Smog City," *The Economist,* May 18, 1991, 50. See also Stephen Baker, "Mexico's Motorists Meet the Smog Patrol," *Business Week,* June 25, 1990, 100–101; Christine Gorman, "Mexico City's Menancing Air," *Time,* April 1, 1991, 61; and Mark A. Uhlig, "Mexico City: The World's Foulest Air Grows Worse," *New York Times,* May 12, 1991, 1.

61. See Barbara J. Sinkule and Leonard Ortolano, *Implementing Environmental Policy in China* (New York: Praeger, 1995); and Elsom, *Atmospheric Pollution,* 235.

62. Robert Cribb, "The Politics of Pollution Control in Indonesia," *Asian Survey, 30,* no. 12 (December 1990): 1123–1135.

63. See U.S. Environmental Protection Agency, *Comparing the Risks and Setting Environmental Priorities* (Washington, D.C.: Office of Policy, Planning, and Evaluation, 1989), and W. R. Ott, "Human Exposure to Environmental Pollutants" (Paper presented at the Eighty-first Annual Meeting of the Air Pollution Control Association, June 1988).

64. For an overview of indoor air pollution hazards, see Richard B. Gammage and Barry A. Barven, eds., *Indoor Air and Human Health* 2d ed. (Boca Raton, FL: Lewis Publishers, 1996); Jonathan M. Samet and John D. Spengler, eds., *Indoor Air Pollution: A Health Perspective* (Baltimore, MD: The Johns Hopkins University Press, 1991); and Shirley J. Hansen, *Managing Indoor Air Quality* (Lilburn, GA: Fairmont Press, 1991).

65. See David Bodansky, Maurice A. Robkin, and David R. Stadler, eds., *Indoor Radon and Its Hazards* (Seattle, WA: University of Washington Press, 1987); "New Study Questions Radon Danger in Houses," *New York Times,* July 17, 1996, A11.

66. Paul Brodeur, "Annals of Radiation," *The New Yorker,* July 9, 1990, 38.

67. For the industry view, see Robert D. Tollison, ed., *Clearing the Air: Perspectives on Environmental Tobacco Smoke* (Lexington, MA: D.C. Heath, 1988). The book was supported by Philip Morris, Inc. In contrast, see Donald J. Ecobichon and Joseph M. Wu, eds., *Environmental Tobacco Smoke* (Lexington, MA: D.C. Heath, 1990), and U.S. Public Health Service, "The Health Consequences of Involuntary Smoking," *Surgeon General's Report* (1986).

68. See Barry I. Casteleman, *Asbestos: Medical and Legal Aspects* (Englewood Cliffs, NJ: Prentice Hall, 1990).

69. For various views on the potential risk of asbestos exposure and how to deal with the problem, see, for example, Paul Brodeur, *Outrageous Misconduct: The Asbestos Industry on Trial* (New York: Pantheon Books, 1985); Diana Goodish, "Asbestos Exposure in Schools," *Journal of School Health, 59,* no. 8 (October 1989): 362–363; Louis S. Richman, "Why Throw Money on Asbestos?" *Fortune,* June 6, 1988, 155; and Jay Mathews, "To Yank or Not to Yank?" *Newsweek,* April 13, 1992, 59.

70. Linda Greenhouse, "High Court Agrees To Hear Two Cases on Asbestos Exposure," *New York Times,* November 2, 1986: A8.

71. Samuel Milham, Jr., "Mortality from Leukemia in Workers Exposed to Electric and Magnetic Fields," *New England Journal of Medicine, 307,* no. 4 (July 22, 1982): 249.

72. See, for example, R. S. Lin et al., "Occupational Exposure to Electromagnetic Fields and the Occurrence of Brain Tumors: An Analysis of Possible Associations," *Journal of Occupational Medicine,* 27 (1985): 413–415, and T. L. Thomas, et al., "Brain Tumor Mortality Risk among Men with Electrical and Electronics Jobs: A Case-Control Study," *Journal of the National Cancer Institute,* 799 (1987): 233–236.

73. See, for example, J. Fulton et al., "Electric Wiring Configurations and Childhood Leukemia in Rhode Island," *American Journal of Epidemiology,* 11 (1980): 292–296; Stephanie London et al., "Exposure to Residential Electric and Magnetic Fields and Risk of Childhood Leukemia," *American Journal of Epidemiology,* 134 (1991): 923–937; and Charles Petit, "Power Line Cancer Link Discounted," *San Francisco Chronicle,* July 3, 1997, A–1.

74. For the popular view, see Robert O. Becker, *Cross Currents: The Promise of Electromedicine, the Perils of Electropollution* (Los Angeles, CA: Jeremy P. Tarcher, 1990). For an overview of the positions of environmental groups, health experts, and industry analysts,

see U.S. Congress, House, Committee on Interior and Insular Affairs, Subcommittee on General Oversight and Investigations, *Electric Powerlines: Health and Public Policy Implications,* hearing, 101st Cong. 2nd sess., March 8, 1990 (Washington, D.C.: U.S. Government Printing Office, 1990).

75. "Utilities Agree: The EMF Issue Is 'Very Serious,'" *Electrical World,* 256 (September 1991):14.

76. See, for example, Charlotte Twight, "From Claiming Credit to Avoiding Blame: The Evolution of Congressional Strategy for Asbestos Management," *Journal of Public Policy,* 2, no. 8 (September 1991).

77. See Peter Bachrach and Morton S. Baratz, *Power and Poverty* (New York: Oxford University Press, 1970).

78. In the workplace, for example, it is extremely difficult to determine which illnesses can be attributed to a specific agent or source. This problem is explained by Laura Punnett, "Airborne Contaminants in the Workplace," in *To Breathe Freely: Risk, Consent, and Air,* ed. Mary Gibson (Totowa, NJ: Rowan and Allenheld, 1985): 31–51.

FOR FURTHER READING

Gary C. Bryner. *Blue Skies, Green Politics: The Clean Air Act of 1990 and Its Implementation.* Washington, D.C.: Congressional Quarterly Press, 1995.

Eric Chivian et al., ed. *Critical Condition: Human Health and the Environment.* Cambridge, MA: MIT Press, 1993.

Leonard A. Cole. *Element of Risk: The Politics of Radon.* New York: Oxford University Press, 1994.

Richard B. Gammage and Barry A. Barven, eds., *Indoor Air and Human Health.* 2d ed. Boca Raton, FL: Lewis Publishers, 1996.

Robert Gottlieb, ed. Reducing Toxics: *A New Approach to Policy and Industrial Decision-making.* Washington, D.C.: Island Press, 1995.

Wyn Grant. *Autos, Smog, and Pollution Control.* Brookfield, VT: Edward Elgar Publishing, 1995.

CHAPTER 9

Regulating Transboundary Pollution and Protecting the Global Commons

> Pollution from the United States creates health hazards, and it does kill. Their legislation stops at the border, as if the air will ask for a visa.
> —Canadian Environmental Minister Sergio Marchi[1]

Priva Uniones is a patch of land fifty to two hundred yards that contains thirty homes, made mostly of plywood and corrugated tin, surrounded by chemical plants and an abandoned pesticide waste pit. Residents have been exposed to a constant barrage of hazards, including a chemical leak that killed most of their dogs and chickens, a chemical cloud that sent ninety of them to the hospital, and an ammonia leak and explosion that broke windows and TV screens. The colonia is located in Mexico, just across the Rio Grande River. The nearby chemical company is a Mexican-owned affiliate of Stepan Chemical, headquartered in Illinois. The Coalition for Justice in the Maquiladora produced a film documenting the health effects of the chemicals, the dumping of wastes into an open pit, and the deplorable conditions in which the residents of Priva Uniones live. Ross Perot even used the video as a prop in his debate on the North American Free Trade Agreement (NAFTA) with Al Gore in 1993. The plight of the occupants of the maquiladoras has been covered by journalists from throughout the world, but there is little will on the part of the Mexican and American governments, and those corporate officials responsible, to remedy the problems caused by decades of companies coming to the tariff-free trade zone along the border, hiring workers at minimal wages, and ignoring environmental laws. The maquiladoras are somber symbols of the challenges in making effective environmental policy for problems that cross political boundaries.[2]

Environmental politics now require countries to consider how human activities affect the entire planet, rather than only what is happening in their own back yard. Pollution is now thought of in global terms; the phrase often used to describe the phenomenon is the transnationalization of pollution problems. Acid rain is an example where there has been policy successes in negotiating international agreements. Similarly, climate change is an issue on which there has been some degree of global cooperation, especially after the Earth Summit in 1992 and the signing of the Framework Convention on Climate Change. This chapter focuses on these two issues, as well as several others, in exploring the nature of transboundary pollution and international collaborative efforts to protect the biosphere.

TRANSBOUNDARY POLLUTION

There are several reasons why nations cooperate in addressing problems of transboundary pollution. It may be in their own self-interest to support cooperative pollution reduction agreements in order to protect the quality of life within their own boundaries. It is advantageous to them to help establish dispute resolution mechanisms so they can pressure their neighbors to comply with environmental accords. Nations may recognize that collective benefits such as a stable climate and healthy oceans are in everyone's interest and compel some sacrifice of the freedom to engage in polluting activities. International organizations, norms, and laws play an important role in reflecting that self-interest. Cooperative efforts are bolstered through scientific research that clearly and compellingly identifies collective threats and offers feasible solutions. As scientific consensus develops over an environmental problem, nations are encouraged to participate in solutions. Some countries seek to be leaders in the global community, while others simply wish to avoid the criticisms of others. Domestic politics plays a critical role, and environmental activists demand that their own governments comply with their global commitments and contribute to collective solutions. Political leaders may see global environmental leadership as central to their own political prospects or part of their personal policy agenda. Industries that must comply with domestic environmental regulations have a strong incentive to urge their governments to pressure other countries to enforce similar standards on their industries. In some cases, economic powerhouses like Japan and the United States can compel compliance by other nations who want to continue trade with them or otherwise benefit through cooperative relations.[3]

However, there are significant challenges to making effective international environmental agreements. International law recognizes the sovereignty of each nation, and countries guard that sovereignty jealously even as they participate in global environmental conventions and agreements. Environmental preservation is often a public, global good: the protection of clean air and water and the preservation of forests, lands, and biodiversity produce benefits that are available to others whether or not they help pay the costs of preservation. Countries, like individuals, are tempted to be free riders when others will provide benefits and bear the burdens. Environmental issues are intertwined with economic, national security, and other concerns that complicate agreement making. Negotiators seek to fashion international rules that are consistent with their own form of national regulation. Powerful domestic interests may also resist any kind of environmental regulation, global or domestic. Agreements are a complex product of scientific consensus, the relative power of participant nations, the costs of international transactions, and other variables that are difficult to balance.[4]

Given the inevitable domestic economic and political barriers, for example, the international community must create incentives to ensure that participating nations implement programs that achieve the goals given them in global agreements. If there is no means of encouraging and pressuring nations to implement the agreements, then implementation will constantly be threatened by calculations that some countries can avoid the compliance costs and perhaps gain competitive advantage for domestic industries. Some countries will comply with agreements as a means of demonstrating leadership or as a result of farsightedness on the part of their leaders. To bolster such motivations, agreements will need to include several kinds of provisions. They must provide for a global reporting system so that emission levels can be compared with limits included in the agreements. An international body will be required to monitor reporting data and to impose sanctions when compliance agreements are not satisfied. Economic sanctions must be imposed when implementation failures occur. They may range from cutoffs of foreign assistance to import barriers on goods produced in noncomplying countries. An international body will have to be empowered to decide disputes. As indicated above, financial and technological assistance must be provided to the poorer countries to encourage compliance and to make it even possible. These sanctions and incentives are of limited power, since they require unparalleled cooperation and unity on the part of the nations of the world. The process of formulating global agreements itself will be critical in building support for the measures agreed to by ensuring that all parties believe that their interests were considered and share a commitment to make the agreement work.[5]

Water disputes between the United States and Mexico provide an illuminating example of the challenges in dealing with transboundary pollution. To both regions of both countries, no resource is more critical than the waters of the Rio Grande/Rio Bravo and the Colorado rivers, and the broader watersheds, that the two countries share. Disputes over water quality have been the traditional problem, as Mexicans complain that U.S. residents withdraw too much water before the rivers reach the thirsty Mexican towns and lands. More recently, disputes have focused on the impact of water withdrawals on groundwater basins that are pumped out faster than they are replenished. A growing concern is water quality and pollution. The area is plagued by periods of severe drought and highly variable surface flows. As economic development grows in the region as a result of NAFTA as well as the Mexican government's maquiladora policy that encourages industry to develop along the border by giving them tax advantages, the demand for water skyrockets. The United States developed its water resources first and has been able to preserve its initial advantage through the general principle of prior appropriations—first in time, first in right—and in treaties. Two dams were jointly built in the 1950s and 1960s on the Rio Grande. The International Boundary and Water Commission was established in 1944 to plan and construct flood control and hydroelectric facilities and resolve disputes.[6]

The twin desert communities of Ambos Nogales that straddle the border between Arizona and Sonora, Mexico, provide a fascinating case study of how difficult it is to combine water policy and international relations. The Nogales Wash wanders across the valley, crisscrossing the international boundary. It is dry much of the year and is then often flooded during the summer and winter rainy seasons. The most serious flooding occurs downstream on the U.S. side, but the best place to build structures to prevent that is upstream, in Mexican territory. The water available to residents of the Mexican community is more polluted and in lower quantities than that available to the Arizonans, exacerbating border tensions. The incentives that local residents have to come together, in grass-roots fashion, to solve their problems, is largely prohibited by international barriers to such agreements. A study of the area has argued that the solution to the problem is to create new local institutions, where both countries give up some of their sovereignty in order to permit communities to devise more rational solutions to their common concerns and to build the capacity of local environmental and municipal water agencies to deliver improved water quality and quantity.[7]

Despite major cultural and economic differences, Mexico and the United States have been able to resolve most of their water differences peacefully. The biggest barrier appears to be that of centralized, bureaucratic power, inherent in national sovereignty; the solution lies in breaking those barriers through the creation of local, binational institutions that bring the affected residents together to solve their common problems and pursue their shared interests. Optimists argue that the increasing economic ties of the two nations have helped generate new environmental pressures, but they have also opened new opportunities for environmental cooperation in solving problems facing communities like Ambos Nogales.

NAFTA AND GATT

Critics of the establishment of the North American Free Trade Agreement, primarily labor and environmental groups, argue that the agreement promotes industrial flight to Mexico because of lax environmental and labor protection laws. They fear the undermining of U.S. regulations that can be characterized as indirect ways of protecting domestic industries and rejected by international tribunals as trade restrictions. They point to the 1991 decision by a panel established by the General Agreement on Tariffs and Trade (GATT), which found that a U.S. embargo of Mexican tuna caught in drift nets that also trapped dolphins was a nontariff trade barrier. The 1972 U.S. Marine Mammal Protection Act (MMAP) authorized the federal government to embargo tuna from other nations caught by any means that results in the incidental killing of or injury to ocean mammals beyond what is permitted under U.S. standards.[8] Tuna fishing boats often follow dolphins to locate the tuna and then cast nets on the dolphins to harvest the fish. Amendments enacted in 1984 required nations from which the United States imports tuna to demonstrate that they have a dolphin conservation program comparable to the U.S. program.[9] Amendments in 1988 imposed a limit for foreign nations operating in the tropical Pacific Ocean a dolphin take of no more than 125 percent of what U.S. vessels took and required the federal government to impose an intermediary embargo on tuna from countries that import tuna from nations subject to a primary embargo by the United States.[10] The 1992 amendments (also called the International Dolphin Conservation Act) authorized the lifting of primary embargoes for countries that commit to a five-year moratorium on using nets on dolphins in catching tuna, and the amendments banned the sale of or importation into the United States of tuna that is not "dolphin safe"—requiring, among other things, that dolphin nets not be used in harvesting tuna.[11]

In September 1990 the U.S. Customs Service banned tuna imported from Mexico, Panama, and Equador. Mexico challenged the ban in 1991 and a GATT panel was convened to hear Mexico's claims. The United States acknowledged that the MMPA violated the GATT prohibition against quantitative limits on imports, but argued that it was a domestic standard that nevertheless satisfied GATT's standard that imported products not be treated less favorably than domestically produced ones. The panel found that the U.S. action violated GATT because: 1) it did not qualify as an internal regulation applying equally to imports or fall within any of the general exemptions, 2) it constituted a quantitative restriction, and 3) regulated land was a unilateral action on the part of the United States.[12] U.S. fishing companies complained bitterly that Mexican companies could harvest tuna much more cheaply than the Americans who complied with U.S. laws protecting dolphins. The Mexican government, however, responded to the public outcry by voluntarily adopting some measures to protect dolphins.

Like GATT, NAFTA is primarily an effort to reduce trade barriers and offers only some procedural protection for the environment. The North American Agreement on Environmental Cooperation (NAAEC) created two public advisory bodies, one to advise the Committee on Environmental Cooperation, and a second to assist the Border Environmental Cooperation Committee (BECC). The environmental commissions are to monitor the environmental conditions affected by increased trade. While the agreement encourages nations to improve food safety and technical standards and to not reduce environmental standards in order to attract investment, there is little recognition of the importance of internalizing environmental costs and the challenges for less developed countries in competing in global markets without further compromising environmental quality and natural resources.

Under NAFTA, parties can establish levels of protection of human health and ecology based on "legitimate" objectives.[13] The only trade regulations permitted are those that affect "product characteristics or their related processes and production methods."[14] But NAFTA does not expressly provide for that; environmental laws can be challenged as discriminatory and can be reviewed by dispute panels. One problem is that states may not be able to impose more stringent environmental standards than the federal government can, because only the participating nations can impose more stringent standards. If, for example, California had more stringent pesticide residue standards than the rest of the nation, Mexican exporters of food who failed to meet the California standards could challenge them as "arbitrary or unjustifiable distinctions." California itself could not appear before the NAFTA panel but would have to be represented by the federal government. Mexico could argue that the California standard is a "disguised restriction" on trade, aimed at protecting domestic producers, since no other state had felt compelled to provide that level of safety.[15] Another NAFTA provision, concerning energy, might conflict with environmental protection efforts. Parties are free to "allow existing or future incentives for oil and gas exploration, development, and related activities."[16] But such provisions could be used to restrict efforts to reduce fossil fuel combustion in response to the threat of global climate change.[17]

Opponents of NAFTA fear that stimulating the Mexican economy will increase pollution levels and resource damage; proponents believe that a healthier economy will translate into greater environmental protection. One of the most important provisions of NAFTA is that environmental standards should be "harmonized upward," that parties should use "international standards . . . without reducing the level of protection of human, animal, or plant life or health."[18] NAFTA requires that a party "should not waive or otherwise derogate" from environmental and health standards in order to encourage investors."[19] But the language is the hortatory "should" rather than the obligatory "shall." And trade agreements have been criticized for encouraging standards that satisfy the lowest common denominator.[20] In sum, the environmental provisions in NAFTA appear to be significantly greater than those proposed in the current round of GATT negotiations: parties are more free to choose their own appropriate level of protection, the least-trade-restrictive test is eliminated, harmonization of standards is aimed upward, there is deference to the three major international environmental treaties, and the language discourages the relaxing of standards in order to entice investors. Despite these strengths, NAFTA does not list explicit environmental goals, it fails to recognize subnational governments, many provisions are vague, parties are not obligated to comply with environmental treaties, and no mechanism exists to develop regional environmental agreements or to establish common standards for protecting shared air and water. Perhaps the greatest test of NAFTA will be the possibility it provides for devising solutions to transboundary problems and solutions that are tailored to the environmental, social, and political contexts in which they occur.

ACID RAIN

Acid rain (or acid deposition, as it is also known) is invisible and cannot be smelled or tasted. For many years, it had been undetected because in its early stages there was little evidence of its impact. It did not become a potent policy issue in the United States until the late 1970s, and now researchers are finding that many other regions of the world also face an acid rain problem.

There are three primary components of acid rain: sulfur dioxide, nitrogen oxides, and volatile organic compounds (VOCs). The most common of the pollutants, sulfur dioxide, comes primarily from the combustion of coal, which reacts with oxygen in the air. The sulfur content of coal varies considerably with the geographic region in which it is mined, so not all areas experience acid deposition to the same degree. Coal from the western portion of the United States, for example, typically has a sulfur content of about 0.5 percent, which is considered to be very low. In contrast, coal mined in the northern region of Appalachia and some midwestern states has a sulfur concentration of 2 to 3 percent.

Coal has become an increasingly significant source of energy in the United States ever since the oil embargo of the early 1970s and Americans' fear about dependence on foreign sources of fuel. Fuel burned in utility power plants is responsible for about two-thirds of the nation's sulfur dioxide emissions, followed by industrial processes (16 percent), noutility fuel combustion from stationary sources (14 percent), and transportation sources (4 percent). Acid rain also becomes an issue for those regions or countries that import coal, since they may, in effect, be importing the resultant sulfur emissions as well.

Acidity is measured on a pH scale from 1 to 14, with lemon juice measured at 1, vinegar a 3, and "pure" (nonacid) rain at 5.6. Readings below 7.0 are acidic; readings above 7.0 are alkaline. The more pH decreases below 7.0, the more acidity increases. Because the pH scale is logarithmic, there is a tenfold difference between one number and the next one to it. Therefore, a drop in pH from 6.0 to 5.0 represents a tenfold increase in acidity, while a drop from 6.0 to 4.0 represents a hundredfold increase. Rain with a pH below 5.6 is considered "acid rain."

Acid rain causes several types of environmental damage, and because its effects are not merely localized, it becomes a critical transboundary pollution issue. In regions where coal is used heavily, acid rain contributes to increased acidity levels in bodies of water that are fed by rainfall, damaging entire ecosystems and showing up along the entire food chain. Researchers in the United States, for example, have found reduced yields of crops attributable to acid rain, and studies show it also contributes to health problems.[21] The long-term impact also includes damage done to our cultural heritage, since there is evidence that acid rain has damaged some of the most beautiful historical artifacts in the world. In Greece, Rome, and Venice, stonework, palaces, and frescoes have been discolored and destroyed by acid deposition.

One of the reasons why acid rain has become such a critical international issue is that it knows no political boundaries, so any attempts at solutions must be made multilaterally. Emissions from facilities in Eastern Europe, for example, have been traced throughout the continent, with acidic particles borne on the prevailing westerly winds. Although there was a considerable amount of evidence that electric utilities were responsible for acid rain emanating in the United States that had damaged as many as sixteen thousand Canadian lakes, there was little progress on the political front until 1990.[22] For the first time, the passage of the Clean Air Act amendments went beyond simply appropriating more funds to study the problem. Title IV of the law required significant reductions in sulfur dioxide emissions, with industry required to install monitoring equipment to ensure compliance. In 1991, President George Bush went a step further by signing an accord with Canada which committed both nations to further reduce sulfur dioxide emissions.[23] The treaty foreshadowed a 1996 agreement among the United States, Canada, and Mexico that established common scientific standards for calibrating equipment and measuring pollution. The Commission for Environmental Cooperation, an offshoot of NAFTA, places jointly monitored equipment at strategic locations in all three nations to begin studying transboundary pollution patterns.[24]

One of the most ambitious international efforts to control acid rain has taken place in Europe. Two organizations have been leaders in the negotiations: the UN Economic Commission for Europe (ECE), and the nations of the European Community (EC). In 1979, the members of the UN body enacted the Convention on Long-Range Transboundary Air Pollution, which served as a declaration of intent for development of an acid rain control strategy. However, it left up to each member nation the decision as to what the "best" strategy for control might be. Yet it did establish a framework for further scientific cooperation and consultation.[25] Some progress was made in Helsinki in 1985 with the adoption of a protocol reducing sulfur emissions by 30 percent no later than 1993—a document signed by thirty nations, known as the "30 percent club." It is a political, rather than science-based target, and several nations refused to participate. Although acid rain has traditionally been associated with the industrialized nations of Europe and the United States, there is some evidence that damage is also being done in other regions of the world. A survey conducted by the International Union for Conservation of Nature and Natural Resources found acid rain-related threats in Brazil, Australia, Thailand, and South Africa, while similar problems have developed in Asia and Japan.[26] Meanwhile, scientific research on acid rain continues, with some studies indicating that the acidification of some bodies of water may result not only from acid rain, but from large accumulated stores of sulfur compounds in deep soils.

The bottom-line environmental protection question really remains unresolved, however. Since the acid rain problem is not shared equally by all regions of the United States (or the world, for that matter), should the financial burden of solving it be borne only by those sources that contribute to it? This is the approach taken by the 1990 Clean Air Act amendments, and somewhat grudgingly agreed to by utilities and coal producers. But when the issues involve the global commons, rather than one or two nations, the problems of environmental protection become much more complex and interrelated.

PROTECTING THE GLOBAL COMMONS

Three-quarters of the planet's surface is covered with seawater, causing one observer to suggest that "Planet Water" is a more accurate name than "Planet

Earth." For centuries, the oceans and their resources have played a central role in human development, serving as a transportation network, as a food source, and as a spiritual element in many cultures. But the oceans have also served as humanity's dumping ground, and except for the past thirty years, we have ignored the results of our actions. Because the world's oceans are so vast, the common belief was that they could assimilate waste without significant harm. "The solution to pollution is dilution"—dispose of wastes far enough from shore, and dilution would make them disappear.

The oceans and the atmosphere are also what is commonly known as a common pool resource, a term used by biologist Garrett Hardin in his 1968 essay, "The Tragedy of the Commons."[27] Using as an analogy the medieval practice of grazing cattle on an open pasture, Hardin theorized that each individual livestock herder would graze as many cattle on the pasture (the commons) as possible, acting purely from economic self-interest. The result, of course, would be overgrazing of the commons to the point where all the herds would starve.

The metaphor is applicable to the marine environment and to the atmosphere. For years, waste and chemicals have been dumped into the ocean with little thought about the eventual result for all who use it as a resource. The marine environment that makes up the oceans of Earth is not a static one, but rather an ever-changing, dynamic system. It is affected by both physical and chemical changes as substances are added to it, intentionally and otherwise. The ocean environment is also affected by another common pool—the atmosphere—so that changes in one affect the other. In this cycle, water evaporates from the surface of the ocean, is carried by the winds over the continents, where it falls to earth as rain, which then enters the oceans again from streams and rivers. Pollution of the atmosphere thus becomes a common pool problem as well.[28]

Implicit in Hardin's metaphor is the idea of common-property resources, which share two characteristics. The first is that the physical nature of the resource is such that controlling access by potential users is costly, and in some cases, virtually impossible. The second characteristic is that each user is capable of subtracting from the welfare of other users.[29] This concept is especially applicable to the oceans and their resources, raising difficult ethical and legal questions about ownership and access. The remainder of this chapter focuses on the issues surrounding the protection of the two primary global commons—the oceans and the atmosphere.

MARINE POLLUTION: SOURCES AND EFFECTS

The small coastal town of Minamata, Japan, brought worldwide attention to marine pollution in the early 1950s. Starting about 1953, the town's cats began to die of a mysterious ailment, and residents contracted severe neurological diseases. Between 1953 and 1968, thousands of citizens suffered severe permanent nerve damage or died, with the cause later traced to the consumption of seafood contaminated with dimethyl mercury. A manufacturing plant on the shores of the bay was suspected as being the source of the mercury poisoning, but tests revealed that it discharged only modest quantities of inorganic mercury, which was relatively safe. It took fourteen years for Swedish scientists to conclude that fish and shellfish in the bay had somehow stored mercury from the facility in their flesh, which had then been eaten by the residents and their cats. The Japanese government, in what became its most notorious environmental disaster, agreed to award compensation to the victims.[30]

The incident led to a global call for a more complete understanding of the oceanic food web and the human-made pollution that threatens the marine environment. Since then, oceanographers, biologists, meteorologists, and politicians have developed a different perspective on the ocean, viewing it as one large ecosystem. Some environmental issues affect the "blue water" deep oceans, while others affect coastal zones, which include estuaries, deltas, reefs, and the continental shelf. Marine pollution consists of a variety of components, including the following.

Floating Debris

The incidence of pieces of plastic, fishing nets, bottles, and other non-biodegradable materials is alarming many marine biologists. Studies have shown that many marine species have become entangled and then choked and drowned on human debris that is discharged into the ocean, such as plastic rings from six packs of soda or beer. Indiscriminate discharges by fishing vessels as well as beachgoers pose a significant threat to marine mammals and birds.

Petroleum

An estimated four million tons of petroleum products are discharged annually into the ocean, partially from shipping operations or bilge washings, although a significant amount also comes from land-based industrial discharges that find their way to the sea and some natural seepage. Nearly 70 percent of the world's petroleum output is transported by sea, making tanker spills an additional source of oil pollution worldwide.

Nutrients

One of the most difficult coastal pollution problems to deal with comes from an overload of nutrients, primarily nitrogen and phosphorous from sewage, agricultural runoff, and erosion, which overfertilize an area. The problem grows along with the world's population. The resulting algal blooms deplete oxygen as they decay, leading to mass kills of fish and other marine invertebrates and making beaches unsafe for swimming.

Heavy Metals and Trace Elements

These pollutants are usually found in coastal zones and include lead, mercury, aluminum, copper, and zinc. The source is usually local industrial facilities. Excessive concentrations can lead to a variety of health ailments.

Radiation

From 1946 to 1970, the United States was among the nations that routinely dumped steel drums of low-level radioactive waste off the Atlantic and Pacific coasts. A legacy of weapons-testing, radioactive isotopes have been found in fish harvested from open oceans, although levels of radiation have declined as the testing programs ended. A more contemporary concern is the danger of radiation leakage into coastal zones adjacent to nuclear power plants, although this has not been shown to be a problem at U.S. power plants.

Dredged Materials

To keep maritime shipping lanes open, ports and harbors are regularly dredged of their natural sand and sediments, which are dumped in deeper waters. The dredged spoil, as it is known, may be contaminated by toxic metals and chemicals, which then contaminate the marine life where they are dumped.

Toxic Chemicals

Synthetic organic compounds pose a threat when they are taken up through the food chain and become a human health hazard when accumulated in food fish. Those most affected are coastal residents who depend upon fish as a primary food source.

Marine pollution poses a number of serious environmental policy issues that are complicated by the nature of the oceans themselves. First, there is much uncertainty about the short- and long-term effects of ocean pollution. Scientists are still not sure of the potential impact on human health or of the ability of the oceans to adapt to change. Much evidence suggests that the marine food chain is easily disrupted and that any major changes could affect the chemical balance that exists between marine organisms and seawater. A study published in 1996 by the U.S. National Oceanic and Atmospheric Administration reported on monitoring of fourteen elements and compounds in mussels and oysters at 154 sites along the U.S. coastline. While contamination levels had declined overall, there were still significant levels of many of the substances, such as DDT, polychlorinated biphenyls (PCBs), and lead, whose discharge into waterways is illegal. The study provides a sobering example of how difficult it is to rid the oceans of pollution.[31]

Second, many policymakers are grappling with the issue of what to do about waste generally. Is it better to dispose of human-made waste on land, which is expensive but where it can be confined, or dump it in the ocean, which is free but where the effects are unknown? Or is it better yet to minimize the generation of waste by changing industrial processes or recycling? As the volume of waste grows, and as land-based disposal becomes less acceptable and costly for urban residents (see Chapter 5), ocean dumping begins to look somewhat more attractive, although eventually it may be the most costly alternative.[32]

Third, marine pollution is not just what is dumped into the oceans, but also the effect it has on coastal zones and beaches and the thirty-five major seas of the world, some coastal and some enclosed by land. Millions of dollars of tourist business are estimated to be lost every time beaches are closed because of pollution when debris washes ashore. Seven of these great bodies of water—the Baltic, Mediterranean, Black, Caspian, Bering, Yellow, and South China Seas—are suffering from combinations of human activity, causing many of their ecosystems to be on the verge of collapse.

OVERFISHING

The fish that inhabit the world's oceans are a critical renewable resource, serving as both a food source and as a source of income for much of the developing world. It is estimated that a sixth of the world's people now derive more than a third of their animal protein from the sea, compared to a world average of about 16 percent. Fishing and the processing of the ocean's catch employ nearly 200 million people worldwide.[33]

There are thirty thousand species of fish in the world's oceans, and their numbers are estimated to be in the billions. At one time, the great sea fisheries were considered to be inexhaustible, and statistics on the number of fish caught each year have been rising, in some decades dramatically. In 1900, for example, the world catch was four million metric tons; between 1950 and 1970, the figures rose from twenty-one million metric tons to seventy million annually. But by the late 1960s and 1970s, scientists began to realize that the catch levels were just barely increasing, even with technological advances such as fish-finding instruments and improved gear.

In 1990 the total global fish catch declined for the first time in thirteen years. The UN's Food and Agriculture Organization (FAO), which monitors world fishing harvests, reported a total catch of 99.6 million metric tons of fish, crustaceans, and mollusks in 1989, but only 95.2 million in 1990. The FAO reported that most traditional fish stocks had reached full exploitation, meaning that an intensified fishing effort is unlikely to produce an increase in catch. The FAO study divided the ocean into seventeen major fishing areas and found that between 1988 and 1990 the fish catch declined in nine areas, remained stable in three, and increased in five. Four of the areas were classified as overfished. The largest decreases occurred in the Southeast Pacific, which is heavily influenced by the anchovy catch off Peru, and in the Northeast Atlantic off Europe, where the most commercially valuable species are found.

In the United States, the National Marine Fisheries Services, which regulates fishery resources, has described the situation as a crisis. The problem is especially acute in New England, where the stock of fish has been declining for the last twenty years. The New England Fishery Management Council instituted measures in 1994 to reduce fishing efforts by 50 percent over five years for groundfish species such as haddock, cod, and yellowtail flounder. The measures included a moratorium on new commercial entrants into the marketplace, restrictions on how many days companies could fish, closing of areas, and the requirement that net mesh sizes be increased. The Clinton administration attempted to help by issuing a $30 million aid package for the New England fishing industry to offset expected losses, and the governor of Massachusetts declared the collapse of the industry a natural disaster. In September 1996, Congress passed legislation to revamp management of fisheries and move toward sustainable fishing of the nation's waters, one of three environmental laws passed in the closing days of the 104th Congress.

The consequences of overfishing are perhaps even greater in the developing world. In the early 1970s, for example, there was a "collapse" of the anchovy industry in Latin America, defined as an event when the catch undergoes an abrupt and continued drop, often drastic, from which the stocks may or may not recover. Peru, whose anchovy catch, minimal in the early 1950s, became the world's largest fishery by the 1960s, was one of the first nations to experience a massive economic loss. In the 1970s more than twelve million metric tons of anchovy were captured in Peruvian waters, representing nearly a fifth of the world's total fish catch. Peru capitalized on the anchovy catch (which was used as high-protein feed for poultry and pigs) and made it the nation's number one export. Environmental groups pressed for a 9.5-million-ton limit on the yearly catch, but by 1972 the catch plummeted to less than half that amount and by 1980 dropped to only three-quarters of a ton. Part of the blame was placed on El Nino—changes in the weather and currents off the Pacific Coast in 1972–1973 that caused a mild winter, warm spring, and water shortages in the Pacific Northwest—but overfishing was a key element of the decline.[34] No significant recovery of fish (or the Peruvian economy) has taken place since then. Similar fates are behind the loss of the Pacific sardine fishery in the 1940s and the halibut catch in the mid-nineteenth century.[35]

There are a number of factors that contribute to the loss of marine stock and diversity, not all of them human-caused. Much of the blame for declining stock can be traced to natural factors that vary from year to year. For example, the conditions under which larval fish develop are considered especially important. A small percentage increase in the survival rate of larval fish can result in a severalfold enhancement in the number of fish that eventually survive. Survival rates are affected by natural predation by other fish, the amount of nutritional organisms available for the larval fish to feed upon, water temperature, and even factors such as the turbulence of the water in which the fish live.

In the Pacific Northwest, salmon productivity appears to be correlated with long-term changes in the intensity of a persistent barometric feature of the area, called the "Aleutian low." Salmon catches are highest when the atmospheric pressure is persistently low, which suggests that there may be a possible physical linkage between fish stocks and natural changes in the environment. During the 1970s, when there was the most recent intensification of the Aleutian low, there was also a substantial increase in the abundance of the floating aquatic animals called zooplankton, in squids, and in Hawaiian monk seals. If further investigation reveals that long-term climatic changes affect the productivity of fisheries, then management of marine resources needs to be viewed in the context of natural cycles.[36]

One of the most controversial of the methods used to catch fish is the use of drift nets, nets that hang vertically like curtains in the open ocean and stretch for twenty to forty miles, sweeping an area the size of Ohio. The nets are suspended by floats at the ocean's surface and catch fish by their gills as they attempt to swim through. In addition to being extremely efficient at catching fish, the drift nets also capture marine mammals, birds, and nontarget fish. The Sierra Club estimates that seven million dolphins were killed between the 1960s and 1980s when drift nets were commonly used. They were also blamed for a 1988 crash in the Alaska pink salmon fishery, when only twelve million fish, rather than an expected forty million, were taken by Alaskan trawlers.[37]

A number of factors led to an increase in the use of drift nets in the mid- and late 1980s within the Asian fishing industry. Initially, many of the trawlers used a seine in search of squid, but as supplies dwindled, the boats ventured further into the Pacific to catch salmon and tuna and began using drift nets. The fishing industry worldwide was caught in a cost crunch as seafood demand rose but prices plummeted, and crews demanded higher wages at a time of labor shortages. By the end of the decade, there was a glut on the seafood market, and many large companies found that they had overextended themselves by investing in massive cannery operations.[38]

The United Nations attempted several times during the late 1980s and early 1990s to encourage restricted drift-net usage, and both the United States and the European Economic Community imposed bans on the use of drift nets within their own waters. But real political pressure came from American environmental organizations that urged a boycott in 1990 of any tuna that was caught in drift nets because of the damage done to the dolphin population—an action that led to the labeling of cans as "dolphin safe" when several companies began to comply. With the 1995 Panama Declaration, the United States and ten other fishing nations agreed that there would be a move towards dolphin-safe fishing practices so that their catch would be allowed into the U.S. market.

But a year later, the Clinton administration proposed reversing the ban that allowed only dolphin-safe tuna into the U.S. marketplace and allowing the use of purse seining methods once again. In an unusual division among environmental organizations, groups such as Greenpeace, the World Wildlife Federation, the

Another View, Another Voice

PROTECTING THE WHALES
A Clash of Cultures

There are many cases in environmental politics where science confronts culture head-on—situations where facts and figures have less meaning than deeply
held social or spiritual beliefs. An example of that type of confrontation involves one of the most visible efforts at endangered species protection over the
last fifty years—protection of whales. While today, the vast majority of nations
within the global community have recognized the importance of these species
to the overall ecological health of the oceans, this view has not been universally accepted.

Although the establishment of the International Whaling Commission (IWC)
in 1946 set up the political regime for the mammals' protection, there has been
less success at changing the attitudes of various cultures and nations. The United
States, for example, granted an exemption from the 1972 Marine Mammal Protection Act to Alaska's Inupiat Eskimos, who hunt bowhead whales. This
species is considered to be one of the most endangered, with four thousand estimated to still exist. For the Inupiat, the issue is one of cultural significance, and
they do not believe their kills significantly affect survival of the species. The
Makah have also sought to kill up to five California gray whales, which have
not been hunted in American or Canadian waters for nearly forty years. They
argue that a whale hunt would provide focus for a people whose unemployment
rate is 50 percent and whose fishing fleet has been hit hard by declining salmon
runs. For them, whaling would be for subsistence and ceremonial purposes, not
part of a commercial operation. A similar situation exists among the Inuit of
Greenland, who are subsistence hunters and who have resisted attempts to restrict whaling in their region. These groups have gained some degree of acceptance among environmentalists, if not support, for their position.

The public has reacted differently, however, to the attitudes of those nations
that have sought to continue whaling for reasons considered more economic
than cultural. Japan, Norway, and Iceland initially refused to abide by the
moratorium on commercial whaling which had been proposed by the United
States in 1972 at the Stockholm Conference. Instead, the nations began con-
ducting what they termed "scientific" whaling, although done by commercial
ships, and even threatened to quite the IWC. Norway announced in 1993 that
it planned to resume modest commercial whaling despite threatened boycotts,
and Japan went to some expense to conduct a worldwide public relations campaign arguing that the whales it was harvesting were not really endangered after all.

Japan has defied the IWC by harvesting minke whales, whose numbers are
estimated to be over 760,000 in the Antarctic alone. Minke whales are small in
comparison with other species, reaching twenty feet in length and weighing an

average of seven tons. In recent years, Japan has killed about 500 minke whales, an amount it considers minuscule in comparison with the overall minke whale population. The Japanese also consider it hypocritical for the United States to allow Native Americans to kill whales that are in much greater danger of becoming extinct than the minke, while at the same time putting pressure on Japanese whalers who have been plying their trade for nearly two thousand years.

Whaling presents a situation where culture and politics often clash. One veteran Japanese harpooner, for example, voiced his frustration with the criticism his country has faced over scientific whaling. "I feel I can't trust foreigners because they just force their opinions on us," he said. To him, whales are no different than tuna, trout, or any other marine resource. Whale meat was traditionally a staple in Japanese school lunch programs and a major source of protein for many coastal communities.

For the Norwegians, who also decided to hunt minke whales, there is a similar cultural conflict. Even those considered the most politically progressive within Norway's environmental community believe that hunting whales is a traditional part of the country's seafaring economy. As one observer put it, whales are just cows that roll in the surf and hunting them is no more immoral than hunting deer or elk.

Greenpeace and other environmental organizations disagree, arguing that the scientific data on the number of minke whales is incomplete, and the resumption of whaling by even a handful of nations puts the species at risk. The Sea Shepherd Conservation Society—one of the more radical environmental groups—has threatened to use force to stop the Makah hunt. They believe that only pressure from the rest of the international community will bring an end to scientific whaling—a step they believe is needed to responsibly manage marine resources.

The key issue, some believe is over sustainable development and whether or not the planet's resources can be used in such a way as to allow it to reproduce and not be diminished for the next generation. Some environmental group members argue that killing whales is immoral as an animal rights issue, rather than one that deals with the demographics of whale populations or sustainability. The bottom line for many is whether hunting whales to provide a culture with subsistence or to continue its spiritual traditions is more important than the moral issue of killing itself. International treaties and debates at the IWC have yet to find answers to that dilemma.

For Further Reading
Donald Day, *The Whale War*. San Francisco, CA: Sierra Club Books, 1987.
D. Donovan, ed., "Aboriginal/Subsistence Whaling." *Report of the International Whaling Commission,* Special Issue 4 (1982), 1–86.
Timothy Egan, "A Tribe Sees Hope in Whale Hunting, But U.S. Is Worried," *The New York Times,* June 4, 1995, A-1.
Nicholas D. Kristof, "Japan's Whales Start to Take on a Hunted Look," *The New York Times,* June 24, 1996, A-4.
Fred Pearce, "When Killing Things Is a Livelihood," *New Scientist, 148,* October 28, 1995, 51–52.
Langdon Winner, "Kill the Whales?" *Technology Review, 97,* November–December 1994, 74.

National Wildlife Federation, and the Environmental Defense Fund agreed with Vice President Al Gore's proposal to reinstitute drift-net use. Their position was that the fishing industry has improved the methods by which tuna are caught and that there has been a 90 percent drop in dolphin mortality since 1990, with only about 4,000 dolphins killed each year. But the proposal was strongly opposed by the Sierra Club and the Earth Island Institute, which called Gore's plan "the dolphin death act."[39] In 1996, the administration and allies in Congress pushed legislation that would have weakened protection for dolphins in U.S. law in order to avoid trade sanctions.[40] As discussed at the beginning of the chapter, Mexico successfully challenged the U.S. Marine Mammal Protection Act before the World Trade Organization.

Environmental groups are also seeking increased scrutiny of bycatch—the nontarget fish that are too small or less valuable species that are routinely thrown overboard. It is estimated that bycatch now accounts for about 27 tons of fish per year, or about a third of the amount that is kept. In some commercial fishing operations, the fraction can exceed by far that which is kept. Little is known of the possible disruptions that take place when so much of the ocean's ecosystem is discarded and returned to the sea as waste.[41]

PROTECTING THE MARINE ENVIRONMENT

The United States has entered into more international agreements pertaining to marine life than it has for any other type of wildlife, beginning with a 1923 agreement with Canada to protect the Pacific halibut fishery. Current agreements focus on the management of a particular fishery to achieve its maximum sustainable yield. The overriding legislative basis for regulating overfishing, however, is the Fishery Conservative and Management Act, passed in 1976, which gives the United States exclusive management authority over not only fish but other forms of marine animal and plant life other than marine mammals, birds, and highly migratory species. One of the key provisions of the legislation is a requirement that each of the eight Regional Fishery Management Councils, comprised of both state and federal officials, develop comprehensive species management plans for the fish in its region. Foreign fishing is prohibited in all areas where the United States claims jurisdiction, unless there is an international agreement in effect. This obligates foreign nations and their vessels to abide by U.S. regulations, including permit fees, catch limits, and inspections. But it also requires the secretary of state, upon a request from the secretary of commerce, to initiate agreements with other nations to secure American fishing fleets "equitable access" to the fishery conservation zones established by other countries.[42]

A number of international agreements have been developed to protect the ocean environment from pollution, with varying degrees of effectiveness. Initially, these agreements were focused on oil spills, a visual marine pollution problem. In the 1950s and 1960s, eight of nine multilateral agreements signed involved oil pollution; from 1970 to 1985, only thirteen of thirty-six dealt with oil.[43] Oil tanker spills have attracted environmental interest even though they account for only 12 percent of global marine pollution. But it is the image of oil-soaked birds and tar on beaches that captures the public's (and the policy-makers') attention much more than statistics. The environmental damage caused by highly publicized spills such as the *Torrey Canyon* in 1967, the *Amoco Cadiz* in 1978, or the *Exxon Valdez* in 1989 often pales in comparison with less publicized ones such as the 1972 *Sea Star* spill in the Gulf of Oman and an incident off South Africa's coast involving the supertanker *Castello de Belver* in 1983.

One of the first agreements was the 1954 International Convention for the Prevention of the Pollution of the Sea by Oil, which was limited to a zone fifty miles from any coast and had no enforcement capabilities. It was replaced in 1973 by the International Convention for the Prevention of Pollution by Ships, also known as the MARPOL Convention, which set limits on discharges from land and at sea for various pollutants. An addition to the MARPOL Convention, Annex V, prohibited the discharge of plastics by ships effective in January 1969. In 1972, the Convention on the Prevention of Marine Pollution by Dumping of Wastes and Other Matter, more commonly called the London Dumping Convention (LDC), set limitations on the disposal of many pollutants at sea, including high-level radioactive waste. In 1988, the accord was modified to prohibit ocean incineration of toxic substances by 1994. The agreement is administered by the International Maritime Organization (formerly called the Intergovernmental Maritime Consultative Organization, or IMCO). The LDC prohibits the dumping of certain hazardous substances and establishes a five-tier permit system for other types of ocean dumping and keeps records of all dump sites throughout the world. In the United States, the permit process is administered by the Environmental Protection Agency under the Marine Protection, Research, and Sanctuaries Act of 1972.

In 1974, the United Nations Environment Programme prioritized oceans through the creation of the Regional Seas Programme. The program covers ten regions and involves more than 120 coastal states, one of the few regional approaches to solving common pool problems. Typically, a group will begin with a framework convention (as was the case with East Asia and South Asia), followed by progressive agreements to establish scientific cooperation and monitoring efforts. The model is the Mediterranean Action Plan (MedPlan), adopted in 1975 in Barcelona, to prevent, abate, and combat pollution of the Mediterranean Sea and to enhance the marine environment of the area. The MedPlan includes participation by all eighteen Mediterranean nations (including Israel and Lebanon), which coordinate their pollution control practices and sponsor joint research programs. The accord includes oil and marine dumping as well as land-based sources of marine pollution, such as agricultural spraying and municipal and industrial wastes.

Despite that such agreements often take years to negotiate, they are an important part of the political process because those involved have managed to overcome intense animosities among individual countries to form alliances, as seen in agreements formed by the United States and Cuba, Iran and Iraq, and Israel and Syria.[44]

By far the most important of the marine regimes is the United Nations Convention on the Law of the Sea, considered by some to be one of the most notable achievements in international diplomacy of the twentieth century. The Convention was completed in 1982 after fifteen years of negotiation and drafting that began in Geneva in 1958. What makes this agreement so important is its comprehensiveness, establishing more equitable relationships among the member states, and distinct zones of sovereignty and jurisdiction for coastal nations. Its 320 articles and nine annexes include rules for the high seas and the rights and duties of members with respect to navigation, protection of the marine environment, and research. It lays down rules for drawing sea boundaries, transit passage for international navigation, and the establishment of a 200-nautical-mile exclusive economic zone (EEZ) over which coastal states have sovereign rights with respect to natural resources and economic activities.

The Law of the Sea agreement provides the legal framework to govern the oceans and their resources, and, for the first time, recognizes that the resources of the deep seabed are part of the world's common heritage. The Convention did not enter into force until 1994, a year after it obtained the necessary 60 ratifications. A key feature of the convention is an elaborate system of dispute settlement mechanisms, including compulsory procedures entailing binding decisions by the International Tribunal for the Law of the Sea and the Commission on the Limits of the Continental Shelf. Land-locked and geographically disadvantaged nations have the opportunity, under the agreement, to participate in exploiting part of the zones' fisheries on an equitable basis, with special protection given to highly migratory species of fish and mammals.[45]

The United States refused to ratify the Convention until 1994, when Secretary of State Warren Christopher announced that the United States would accept changes that made the agreement more acceptable to business interests. One of the more controversial issues dealt with the mining rights to the seabed floor, which President Ronald Reagan had rejected in 1982, saying it clashed with free-enterprise principles by requiring mining companies to pay substantial royalties and to share sophisticated technology with developing countries.[46] American negotiators eventually developed an acceptable provision that allows the United States and other industrial countries to have an effective veto over the convention's administrative body, the International Seabed Authority.

The treaty is typical of the kinds of disputes that are becoming increasingly more common between rich and poor countries in dealing with common pool resources. Wealthy nations such as the United States resent being asked (or forced) to share their more advanced technology with newly developing or poorer countries. There is additional antagonism when poorer countries demand some form of redistribution of wealth in the belief that the oceans and their resources should be more equitably shared. Although the Law of the Sea is now in force, there will undoubtedly be continuing ethical and economic disputes as the convention is fully implemented.[47]

Although political agreements are one way to deal with problems such as pollution, overfishing, and drift-net use, there is some evidence that treaties alone are not enough. The United States is using satellites to monitor compliance with the drift-net restrictions as part of bilateral agreements with Japan and South Korea. Fishing boats using drift nets are required to carry radio transmitters so their movements can be tracked to detect fishing in waters that are off limits. Coast Guard officials are given authority under various agreements to board and detain suspicious ships if necessary, a system that has proved successful in preventing fishing by pirate vessels.[48]

Making policy also means going beyond the political realm and into that of science to better manage resources. Scientists have explored using the large marine ecosystem (LME) approach as one of a variety of ways in which the ocean environment can be better understood and managed. An LME is a broad geographic region distinguished by a self-contained food web and by oceanographic properties such as currents and surface temperatures. LME management involves the collection of a vast amount of data on the number of species in the region, the effects of pollution, the nature of the food chain, and what oceanographic factors influence marine animals and plants. LME management has already been used successfully in the Southern Ocean by the nations that are signatories to the convention for the Conservation of Antarctic Marine Living Resources (CAMLR) signed in 1982. The parties who have signed the CAMLR have agreed to regulate fishing to maintain all ecological relationships and have set up a structure to obtain data on Antarctic species. The ecosystem approach is considered the wave of the future by many experts in international law, despite obstacles such as a lack of funds for gathering information.[49] UNESCO's World Heritage Committee has identified coral reef regions for protection as world heritage sites, prompted by the work of nongovernmental organizations dedicated to preserving underwater environments.

Still, political and economic realities influence the effectiveness of monitoring systems and multilateral agreements. For example, a nation might decide not to comply with the provisions of a particular treaty, such as the Basel Convention, allowing an area to become contaminated by toxic wastes. But that nation might also not have the resources necessary to implement a cleanup plan, effectively leaving the responsibility to the international community or not solving the problem at all. Even the United States, with its advanced technology, has been unable to effectively deal with the cleanup of its hundreds of Superfund waste sites, and the problem would be magnified with a marine cleanup, especially if it were caused by or near a less affluent nation. But countries do attempt to comply with global environmental treaties, usually out of self-interest, but also out of a sense that they are part of a web of international economic and political relationships. They understand that protecting the oceans and their resources is almost always best served by living up to their obligations, rather than risking isolation or expulsion from the club of nations.[50]

CLIMATE CHANGE

Ever since the 1860s, when British scientist John Tyndall first described a phenomena we now call the greenhouse effect, the public has been alerted to imminent doom caused by climatic change. Unfortunately, researchers have been unable to agree whether our future is tied to an impending ice age that will result in continental glaciation or a warming trend that will melt the glaciers and send coastal cities into the sea. The debate flourished around the turn of the century when Nobel Prize-winning Swedish scientist Svante Arrhenius calculated that a doubling of the carbon dioxide in the atmosphere would raise the average surface temperature of Earth. His calculations were confirmed by American geologists Thomas Chamberlain and C. F. Tolman, who studied the role that the oceans play as a major reservoir of carbon dioxide. In the 1930s, after three decades of warming temperatures and the development of a massive dust bowl in the central United States, other scientists warned of the dangers of rising temperatures, which had already been tied to increasing levels of carbon dioxide in the atmosphere. But between the 1940s and 1970s, global temperatures fell, and many reputable scientists prophesied a new ice age rather than a warming trend.[51] The global warming forecast was resurrected again in June 1988 when Dr. James Hansen, director of the National Aeronautics and Space Administration's (NASA) Institute for Space Studies told a Senate Committee, "The greenhouse effect is here."

Humans' ability to cause changes in the atmosphere is a relatively recent phenomenon—primitive peoples did not have the technology to alter the environment as we do today. With the Industrial Revolution came technological devices such as the steam engine, electric generator, and internal combustion engine, which have forever altered the planet, the water we drink, and the air we breathe. That ability to alter the environment is threatening to some, but considered a natural part of the evolutionary process by others. Some believe that Earth exists as a living organism in which internal control mechanisms maintain the stability of life—a theory called the Gaia hypothesis.[52] According to this theory, environmental problems such as ozone depletion will be brought under control naturally by the environment itself, which will make the necessary adjustments to sustain life. Critics of the theory, however, refer to policies built on such optimism as "environmental brinksmanship" and warn that we cannot rely upon untried regulatory mechanisms to protect the planet from large-scale human interference. This section looks at two issues with obvious global dimensions: global warming and stratospheric ozone depletion. It provides an overview of the scientific controversy and identifies the ways in which the two issues differ politically.

Global Warming

Although global warming is ostensibly a subject for scientific debate, it has become one of the most politicized environmental issues of this decade.[53] It is also part of the evolution of environmental concerns from pollution in the 1960s to energy (beginning with the oil crisis of 1973) to the more global concerns of the 1980s. It became the focus of attention at the Earth Summit in Rio de Janeiro in June 1992 and is likely to remain near the top of the political agenda well into the twenty-first century.

Global warming refers to the process by which solar radiation passes through Earth's atmosphere and is absorbed by the surface or reradiated back into the atmosphere. The phenomenon is also called the "greenhouse effect" because some heat in but keeping some of it from going back out.

There are about twenty so-called greenhouse gases that make up Earth's atmosphere, with the five major sources identified in Table 9.1. Changes in the volume of these gases affect the rate at which energy is absorbed, which then affects Earth's temperature. Greenhouse gases are emitted or absorbed by virtually every form of human activity, as well as by oceans, terrestrial plants, and animals, which contribute to the carbon dioxide cycle. Scientists are primarily concerned about increases in levels of carbon dioxide, since it is difficult to quantify the exact cause and effect of other greenhouse gases. The more carbon dioxide builds up, the more heat is trapped near Earth. The buildups have been monitored since 1958 at facilities on Mauna Loa on the big island of Hawaii.

Although researchers began studying the effect of carbon dioxide on climate in the early part of this century, the implications of such changes were not seriously considered until the early 1970s. A World Climate Conference in Geneva in 1979 was one of the first efforts at organizing international research, followed by a series of studies and conferences over the next ten years. One of the most re-

Table 9.1   Major Greenhouse Gases

Gas	*Where It Comes From*
Carbon dioxide	Fossil fuel sources including utility power plants, refineries, automobiles
Chlorofluorocarbons (CFCs)	Solvents, foam insulation, fire extinguishers, air conditioners
Halons	Compounds used in fire extinguishers
Methane	Natural sources such as decaying vegetation, cattle, rice paddies, landfills, oil field operations
Nitrogen oxides	Fertilizers, bacteria

spected reports was published in 1987 by the World Commission on Environment and Development, which recommended a global approach to a broad spectrum of environmental problems, including greenhouse warming.[54] In December 1988, the UN General Assembly unanimously passed a special resolution calling for a framework convention on climate change, which was implemented through the Intergovernmental Panel on Climate Change (IPCC). The IPCC was formed to develop a scientific consensus on the danger of greenhouse warming stemming from the use of fossil fuels.

Researchers have relied upon a variety of tools to help them understand the impact of climate change, with general circulation models (GCMs) the most commonly used ways of forecasting the results. The models allow scientists to predict what would happen when carbon dioxide levels are increased to specific levels, but the models are not foolproof.[55] They are limited by a number of factors, including our incomplete knowledge of atmospheric and ocean processes, heat transfer in the atmosphere, details of the effects of clouds, and the nature of ocean currents. Any one of these factors could alter the results reached by the modeling process.[56]

Other models show that certain types of human activities, such as sulfur emissions from the burning of fossil fuels, may increase the rate of cloud condensation and clouds' reflecting power may actually cool Earth, offsetting any predicted temperature increases. Other researchers believe that temperature increases, which began around 1880, are not the onset of greenhouse warming but rather a retreat from the "Little Ice Age," which is a part of an interglacial interval, with the onset of the next glacial cycle near.[57] Scientists acknowledge that it is difficult to use GCMs to predict regional changes that may occur, rather than global ones, and when they are used to "hindcast" (look backward to analyze trends in temperature that have already occurred) the models are notoriously inaccurate.[58]

There is little controversy over the scientific evidence that the levels of carbon dioxide have increased by about 50 percent since the late 1700s, 25 percent over the past century, and are now increasing at the rate of 0.5 percent each year. Most of the studies agree that continued emissions of greenhouse gases will lead to a warming of Earth's temperature between 1.5 and 4.5 degrees Celsius (or 2.7 to 8.1 degrees Fahrenheit). So far this century, global average temperatures have risen between 0.5 and 1 degree Fahrenheit, consistent with the GCM predictions.

Why should we be concerned about what seems like relatively small changes in temperature? There are a number of possible scenarios attributed to global climate change. One of the most respected scientists who has studied the issue, Dr. Stephen H. Schneider of the National Center for Atmospheric Research, believes that the temperature increases would lead to a rise in sea levels through the heating of the oceans, and possibly higher levels from the melting of polar ice as well. Drought and prolonged heat would be expected to lead to a greater likelihood of fire damage, more severe air pollution and air stagnation, and increased energy use leading to a need for more power production. Some of the changes forecast to occur might not be as negative. Global warming might lengthen the growing season for grain in Siberia, allowing some nations to increase their food production. The flip side of the equation, however, would be a loss to U.S. farmers, who are currently the world's leading grain exporters, with an accompanying impact on our economy.[59]

Other scientists using case studies of climate-related events such as rising levels of the Great Lakes and the Great Salt Lake, are attempting to predict how society might react to global warming using "forecasting by analogy."[60] Some analysts, however, believe that people can adapt to climate change and that such apocalyptic predictions are unwarranted. They believe that there are ways in which we can reduce dependence upon fossil fuels without taking the kinds of draconian measures that would damage our standard of living.[61] Some studies show that, even if temperatures rise as predicted, the effect will be more subtle, with gradual adaptation by humans and other species. For example, the more industrialized nations such as the United States, Great Britain, and Japan will be better able to adapt to rising sea levels than will, for example, Bangladesh.[62]

Are the models of doom correct? Despite human advances and technological breakthroughs, weather and climate remain elements of the environment that remain imperfectly understood and uncontrolled by humankind. The uncertainty over global warming comes from three sources: predicting future climate, predicting future impacts, and assessing costs and benefits of policy responses.[63] The polarization among the members of the scientific community has spilled over to the political arena, where policymakers are trying to decide which view is the most reliable. The debate is joined by industry representatives (primarily electric utilities) who argue that it is foolhardy to make costly changes in technology or life-style changes until all the evidence is in. They seek support and funding for further study and analysis until there is a general scientific consensus.

Nonetheless, there is a growing body of scientific evidence that, given the various scenarios, it is imperative that steps be taken immediately to avoid the devastating effects of climatic change being forecast, with general agreement of a need for a major reduction in carbon dioxide emissions. Such a strategy would require substantive (and costly) changes in the way we live, and not only in the United States. Although the burden of cost is likely to fall disproportionately on the industrialized nations of the North, developing countries in the South will be asked to make drastic changes in their current patterns of energy use. This raises a whole host of policy questions. Will industrialized nations share their technology and expertise with the less developed countries? If so, will they also give their financial support to those nations to help them reduce their dependence upon fossil fuels? Could developing countries, already facing massive foreign debt, afford to switch to alternative fuels without aid from the North? Is the United States willing to set an example with its policies and rely more on energy conservation and non-fossil fuel sources?

The answers to those questions are at the heart of the international debate over global warming. Though industrialized countries have been dealing with the issues for over a decade through bodies such as the IPCC and are aware of the ramifications of the problem, developing nations are less likely to perceive global warming as a potential risk. They are less represented on various international study boards and have devoted fewer resources to research on the potential impact of global climate change. As a result, they are understandably less concerned and less anxious about finding a solution.[64]

Despite these uncertainties, one compelling argument is for an "insurance policy" approach to greenhouse warming. Such a strategy calls for reductions in energy consumption and enhanced conservation—policies that would benefit the United States by reducing the nation's dependence upon foreign oil. The energy savings would have spillover effects as well, such as reducing the need to drill for oil in environmentally sensitive areas and reducing the emissions that contribute to acid rain. Such policies would not solve global warming, advocates say, but would buy more time for additional research and the opportunity to find better solutions.[65] Even though most scientists admit that additional research is needed to predict the timing and magnitude of global warming, there is a growing consensus that some initial steps such as those to reduce carbon dioxide emissions can be taken now without a major economic disruption. This view appears to be gaining more acceptance. A 1991 study by the National Academy of Sciences marked a decided shift in policy. The group, which had previously concluded that additional research into greenhouse warming was needed, recommended that, "despite the great uncertainties, greenhouse warming is a potential threat sufficient to justify action now."[66]

Implementation of the global climate change convention has been slow. Some parties have delayed their expected compliance date from 2000 until 2005. Others have changed the base date from which reductions are to be made in order to reduce required cuts, promised only to freeze emissions beginning in the year 2000, and proposed that emissions be stabilized on a per capita basis, thus permitting increased emissions as population grows, and some have disregarded the treaty. One of the challenges confronting the United States has been to reduce energy consumption in the face of declining prices. The American Petroleum Institute released a study in 1995 that concluded that the price of gasoline, after adjusting for inflation, was the lowest it has ever been since gas prices were first recorded 75 years ago. A gallon of gas cost $1.17 in 1994 and $2.21, in comparable dollars, in 1920. Since 1967, the cost of gas has risen more slowly than any other consumer product.[67] Many of the less developed countries are doing even less to comply with the global climate convention. Less developed countries contribute only about one-third of total CO_2 emissions while they make up 80 percent of the world's population. Emissions are increasing there by more than 5 percent per year, in contrast with a 1-percent increase in the more developed world. Emissions from China represent one-half of all emissions in Asia, and plans call for dramatic increases in emissions as China's coal resources are increasingly used. North-south tension over who is responsible for global warming and where the greatest future threats lie poses a serious challenge to collective action. Industrial nations are responsible for the vast majority of emissions, and they control the technology that can solve the problem, but cooperation from the developing countries is essential.

The First Conference of the Parties to the Rio Climate Change Convention met in Berlin in March and April 1995. Representatives from 120 countries agreed to begin negotiations, to be completed by 1997, for reducing greenhouse gas emissions after the year 2000. The Berlin conference recognized that the commitments made by the developed world to stabilize emissions at 1990 levels would be insufficient to achieve the convention's goals. For the first time, the developing countries took the lead in demanding more aggressive global action for climate change. The Alliance of Small Island States, 36 nations that are threatened by a rise in sea level, were joined by India, Brazil, Egypt, China, and other developing countries who have come to believe that their development efforts might be undermined should significant changes in climate occur. Some seventy less developed countries (excluding the major oil-producing nations) joined in a "green paper" that called for major reductions in industrial nations' emissions of greenhouse gases. Many observers noted that developed countries led by the United States, Australia, and Canada, fought against the proposal.[68]

In 1996, after a new report by the IPCC concluded that human activity had clearly begun to affect the biosphere, the United States and other nations shifted their position. The Second Conference of the Parties, held in Berlin in July 1996, resulted in a commitment to negotiate legally binding targets and timetables for reducing greenhouse gas emissions from the more developed world. The targets and timetables are to be negotiated in time to be signed at the Third Climate Summit to be held in Kyoto, Japan, in December 1997.[69]

Stratospheric Ozone Depletion

Ozone is an element of Earth's atmosphere caused by a photochemical reaction of hydrocarbons (produced mainly from the burning of fossil fuels) and sunlight. In one sense, there is "bad" ozone and "good" ozone. At the surface of Earth, ozone is one of the major components of smog, but higher up in the stratosphere (between six and thirty miles above Earth's surface), the ozone layer provides a filtering layer of protection against the harmful effects of ultraviolet radiation. Without such protection against ultraviolent radiation, medical experts believe that there would be a substantial increase in skin cancers and genetic changes in some types of plants and animals.

In the early 1970s, scientists warned that the exhaust gases from high-flying supersonic transport planes could damage the ozone layer. Studying components of the high-altitude atmosphere, they discovered that CFCs, which are synthetic, reacted with ultraviolet light when released into the atmosphere, forming chlorine. Chlorine is known to attack ozone molecules, and the researchers warned that, unless steps were taken to reduce CFC production, between 7 and 13 percent of the Earth's protective ozone layer would be destroyed.[70] CFCs are found in thousands of synthetic products and are used primarily in air conditioning and refrigeration, foam packaging, and insulation. They are also used in cleaning the sides of the space shuttles, in sterilizing whole blood, and as a solvent in cleaning computers. Congress responded in 1977 by including provisions in the Clean Air Act amendments, which authorized the EPA administrator to regulate substances affecting the stratosphere, and in 1978, the EPA banned the use of CFCs in most aerosols. At the time, scientists were unable to measure the damage to the ozone layer, but on the strength of the theoretical evidence alone, Congress responded.[71]

With the election of Ronald Reagan in 1980, research into CFCs came to a standstill and the search for substitute compounds subsided. Even though the United States had banned CFCs in aerosols, the nonaerosol use grew to record levels with the United States producing about one-third of the world total.[72] The issue gained new prominence in 1985 when a group of British scientists in Antarctica, who had been monitoring ozone levels for thirty years, found a "hole" in the ozone layer approximately the size of North America above the continent that lasted nearly three months each year.[73] The National Science Foundation sent its own team of researchers to Antarctica later that year, and, although they could not agree on an exact cause, they concluded that chlorine chemistry was somehow involved and that the hole was getting larger. In 1992, one study by the European Ozone Secretariat and another by NASA concluded that the ozone shield had also thinned markedly over the Northern Hemisphere. Although researchers were unable to discover a similar ozone hole over North America like that over the Antarctic, they warned that the increased levels of ozone-destroying chemicals were cause for alarm. As the scientific evidence of stratospheric ozone depletion mounted, the environmental protection wheels began to turn in the political arena.

Balancing the Options

Even though the evidence that CFCs are responsible for ozone depletion is not irrefutable, there were a number of differences in the response of the government and industry from that of global warming. First, the issue of stratospheric ozone depletion was perceived as a more "manageable" problem than global warming, which is a much more complex and multifaceted problem than developing substitutes for CFCs. While industry officials called for more research into global warming before they were willing to accede to costly changes in production and technology, CFC manufacturers almost immediately agreed that CFC production should be reduced, even in the absence of proof that CFCs were damaging the ozone layer.

In 1988, the DuPont Company, the inventor and world's largest user of CFCs, announced that it was phasing out production of two types of CFCs altogether. Other manufacturers and users of CFCs followed suit, and competition began to find replacement products and processes. The significance of the CFC strategy, from a political standpoint at least, is that the United States and its industry leaders were willing to take action even before all of the scientific evidence was in. This "preventive action on a global scale" was a unique approach to environmental protection. Rather than bucking the trend and refusing to cooperate, companies such as DuPont immediately began researching alternatives and substitutes for CFCs. And rather than stalling for time, the U.S. government took a leadership role and sought the strongest action possible—a complete ban on CFCs. The cost of finding replacements for the estimated thirty-five hundred applications where CFCs are used could reach $36 billion between now and 2075, according to the EPA.[74] As a result, what might initially be seen as an unreasonable cost of compliance is now being viewed as a new marketplace by many in the chemical industry. Forced to find substitutes for products and processes, some companies anticipate higher profits, while others fear that substitute substances will have their own complications. For example, one substitute—hydrochlorofluorocarbons, or HCFCs—is being criticized by environmentalists because HCFCs still contain ozone-damaging chlorine. But they are less damaging than CFCs and may prove to be a valuable transitional substitute while industry research continues.

Second, the U.S. government accepted the premise that a unilateral phaseout of CFCs was not acceptable for solving such a global problem. The United States initiated an international agreement to phase out CFC production within ten years, a move that led to the signing in September 1987 of the Montreal Protocol on Substances That Deplete the Ozone Layer. The document set a strict timetable of step-by-step reductions in CFCs and other ozone-depleting substances, leading to a complete production ban by 2000. Developing nations were given a ten-year grace period before full compliance is required, but many have refused to sign the treaty because of the expense involved in switching to new technology.

After scientists warned that the 50 percent reduction was not adequate to reduce the destruction of the ozone layer, the United States enacted even more stringent domestic legislation with passage of Title VI of the Clean Air Act amendments of 1990.[75] The legislation required an accelerated phase-out of the compounds that pose the greatest threat to the ozone layer: CFCs, halons, carbon tetrachloride, and methyl chloroform, with elimination as soon as possible and no later than 2002. Under the terms of the amendments, the EPA now requires the mandatory nationwide recycling of CFCs in motor vehicle air conditioners, the biggest user of CFCs in the United States. The American efforts were not designed to replace a stronger version of the Montreal Protocol, but instead were expected to serve as a model for future international agreements. Subsequent negotiations among the parties to the protocol in London in 1990 and Copenhagen in 1992 led to a speeding up of the CFC phase-out. Delegates in Copenhagen also agreed to reduce HCFCs by 35 percent by 2004, by 99.5 percent by 2020, and to a total ban by 2030. The parties also added methyl bromide, which may be responsible for 10 percent of the ozone lost so far, as a "controlled substance," which means emissions would be frozen at 1991 levels. Methyl bromide is used to fumigate soils and crops in some less industrialized countries. The Copenhagen amendments are expected to reduce deaths resulting from the thinning of the ozone layer by forty thousand.[76]

In 1994, the protocol's scientific assessment panel concluded that the single largest action to reduce the threat to the ozone layer would be to phase out methyl bromide emissions; in a 1995 Vienna meeting, the parties agreed to phase out its use by 2010 in the developed nations and freeze its use in the developing world at 1995–1998 levels by the year 2002. As of October 1995, 159 countries had ratified the original protocol, 111 had agreed to the 1990 London amendments, and 61 had acquiesced to the 1992 Copenhagen agreement.[77]

Ozone-depleting substances (ODS) are largely a problem emanating from the North, but the efforts to raise living standards in the South could have a tremendous impact on emissions levels. The participation of the developing countries is critical, since increased use of CFCs in China and India could largely negate reductions in emissions throughout the rest of the world. The Montreal Protocol gave developing countries an additional ten years to comply with the production bans and also included promises from the North to help fund the transition in the South to ODS alternatives: the developing countries agreed to freeze CFC use by 1999 and phase it out by 2010.[78] One of the most important elements of the ozone protection agreements was the creation of a multilateral fund to help developing countries finance their implementation of the international commitments. The budget during the three-year pilot phase of the fund, from 1991 to 1994, was $1.3 billion. Twenty-five countries contributed $860 million to the core fund, and $420 million came from individual countries for parallel funding or cofunding of specific projects. Thirty-four countries contributed to the replenishment of the fund in 1994, including thirteen recipient countries. In exchange for the new round of financial support, the eighty countries participating in the fund agreed on a restructuring of the governing process. Actions by the thirty-two member governing council now require support from 60 percent of the members; these members must also have contributed at least 60 percent of the funds.[79]

Only a few countries have implemented laws and regulations to ensure reduction in the manufacturing or use of CFCs. Despite the consensus concerning the threat of ozone depletion, the relatively small number of CFC producers, and other factors that should have led to rapid effective international action, the Protocol was still slow in coming (the agreement was signed thirteen years after publication of the first article that suggested the ozone layer was threatened) and slow in being implemented. We may have acted too late to prevent widespread harm from a weakened ozone layer. Global consumption of CFCs have decreased from a peak in 1987, but ozone depletion is still proceeding twice as fast as expected over parts of the Northern hemisphere; 200,000 additional deaths from skin cancer in the United States alone could occur during the next 50 years as a result.

The United States has not pursued a similar strategy with regard to greenhouse warming.[80] While the United States took a leadership position with ozone depletion, the United Nations has been the vanguard for development of an international regime to address global climate change.

Third, media coverage of the ozone-depletion issue kept attention focused on the U.S. efforts to develop an international agreement and prevented the administration negotiators from weakening the proposed CFC controls. For example, on May 29, 1987, the media published reports that Secretary of the Interior Donald Hodel was attempting to revoke the authority of the U.S. delegation to negotiate significant reductions in ozone-destroying compounds. After newspaper headlines reading "Advice on Ozone May Be: 'Wear Hats and Stand in Shade'" and "Administration Ozone Policy May Favor Sunglasses, Hats; Support for Chemical Cutbacks Reconsidered," the public outcry over the apparent change in the U.S. position created a backlash that virtually guaranteed the imposition of stringent controls.[81] Media coverage of global warming, in contrast, has been colored by the lack of scientific consensus on the rate of onset and the potential magnitude of the problem. The attention given to global warming has not been as focused, if only because the potential impacts are more uncertain, less tangible, and less immediate than those of ozone depletion. Global warming lacks an equivalent to the ozone hole upon which the media and public can focus their attention.[82]

It is this lack of scientific consensus that is perhaps the most important difference in how the policy debate has developed. At least initially, concerns about global warming were dominated by scientists who debated the consequences of human interference in the environment. There were many more attempts to measure the nature of global climate change before taking action than had been the case with CFCs. Increased production of carbon dioxide and rising atmospheric turbidity were recognized as two important factors capable of causing climate change, but there was uncertainty whether the result would be a warming or a cooling of the atmosphere. There have been dozens of scientific congresses and meetings, but the task of building consensus among scientists has been formidable.

Equally difficult has been the task of agreeing on what should be done about greenhouse warming. For example, the National Academy of Science report made several recommendations to Congress, including a phase-out of CFCs and other halocarbon emissions and the development of substitutes that minimize or eliminate greenhouse gas emissions; enhanced energy conservation and efficient development of a new generation of nuclear reactor technology that is designed to deal with safety, waste management, and public acceptability; and reduction of global deforestation, initiation of a domestic reforestation program, and support for international reforestation efforts to restore the cleansing capacity of forests.

Critics argue that, while several of these proposals may have some merit, others do not. For example, a UN Environment Programme study has noted that, while reforestation is probably a good idea on its own merits, it probably cannot do much to slow the accumulation of carbon dioxide in the atmosphere. A much larger area than France would have to be reforested annually to "mop up" the carbon dioxide released from the burning of fossil fuels.[83] The most likely option is to reduce source production of greenhouse gases through energy conservation and a switch to cleaner-burning fuels such as natural gas and nuclear energy (see Chapter 6). If the experts cannot agree on the nature and extent of the problem, it is unlikely that they will agree on solutions as well.

Lastly, the global warming issue lacks the support of major actors in the political arena, including the United States. In order for an international agreement to be effective, it must also have the support of the developing countries, which are becoming dependent upon fossil fuels. This was not the case with CFCs and the Montreal Protocol. In that instance, sufficient concessions could be made outside the fishbowl of media publicity to allow room for negotiation and compromise. Global warming does not have a similarly low profile.[84] What that means is that the process of reconciling differences among developing and industrialized nations to produce a global warming agreement will be much more politicized and therefore much more difficult.[85] Until there is sufficient scientific consensus on the problem itself, there is little foundation for future policymaking.

SUMMARY

The transnationalization of environmental pollution now requires policymakers to identify problems and solutions in global terms, rather than as localized issues. Historically, acid rain was one of the few issues where international agreements were successfully negotiated, as in the case of treaties between the United States and Canada. Now, nations are realizing the importance of supporting cooperative pollution reduction agreements in order to protect the quality of life within their own boundaries, exemplified by the North American Free Trade Agreement. There are significant challenges to these regimes, however, since international law recognizes the sovereignty of nations and environmental issues are closely intertwined with economic, national security, and other concerns that complicate negotiations. More attention is now being paid to common pool resources, a term applicable to the marine environment and to the atmosphere. Scientists have developed a more complete understanding of the ways in which pollution affects oceans and marine life, and the world community has responded with notable diplomatic achievements, such as the Convention on the Law of the Sea. In the case of climate change, the debate has been more highly polarized, with political and scientific disagreement on the nature and extent of global warming. Implementation of the global climate change convention has been slow and marked by delays in compliance and tension over which nations should be responsible for emissions reduction. In comparison, the issue of stratospheric ozone depletion has been perceived as being a more manageable problem, and there has been international consensus that only a global approach would be successful, rather than unilateral action by the United States.

NOTES

1. Howard Schneider, "North American Air Monitoring System Planned," *The Washington Post,* August 3, 1996, A10.

2. Bruce Selcraig, "Border Patrol," *Sierra* (May/June 1994): 58–64, 79–80.

3. For an in-depth discussion of international cooperation, see Oran R. Young, *International Governance: Protecting the Environment in a Stateless Society* (Ithaca, NY: Cornell University Press, 1994).

4. For a helpful summary of these issues and an application to one environmental problem see Juliann Allison, "Following the Leader: The Role of Domestic Politics in U.S.-Canadian Air Quality Negotiations," paper prepared for the annual meeting of the Western Political Science Association (March 14–16, 1996).

5. A.O. Adede, "International Environmental Law from Stockholm to Rio—An Overview of Past Lessons and Future Challenges," *Environmental Policy and Law* (22/2 1982): 88–105, at 99.

6. Helen Ingram, Lenard Milich, and Robert G. Varady, "Managing Transboundary Resources: Lessons from Ambos Nogales," *Environment, 36,* no. 4 (May 1994): 6–9, 28–38.

7. Ingram, Milich, and Varady, 34–37.

8. 16 U.S.C. sec. 1361–1421h, at sec. 1371.

9. 16 U.S.C. Sec. 1371.

10. 16 U.S.C. 1371(a)(2)(B)(II), 1371(1)(2)(C).

11. 16 U.S.C. 1415.

12. Steve Charnovitz, "Dolphins and Tuna: An Analysis of the Second GATT Panel Report," *Environmental Law Reporter, 24* (October 1994): 10567–10587.

13. NAFTA, Art. 904.2.

14. NAFTA, Art. 915.

15. Steve Charnovitz, "NAFTA: An Analysis of Its Environmental Provisions," *Environmental Law Reporter, 23* (February 1993): 10069–10072.

16. NAFTA, Art. 608.1.

17. Charnovitz, "NAFTA: An Analysis of Its Environmental Provisions," at 10071.

18. NAFTA, Arts. 713.1, 714.1.

19. NAFTA, Art. 1114.2.

20. Charnovitz, "NAFTA: Analysis of Its Environmental Provisions," at 10071.

21. There are numerous studies which identify the ecological damage caused by acid rain. See, for example, "Acid Rain Affects Coastal Waters Too," *Environment,* 30 (June 1988): 22; Philip Shabecoff, "Acid Rain Is Called Peril for Sea Life on Atlantic Coast," *New York Times,* April 25, 1988, A1; Robert A. Mello, *Last Stand of the Red Spruce* (Washington, D.C.: Island Press, 1987); Jon R. Luoma, "The Human Cost of Acid Rain," *Audubon,* 90 (July 1988): 16–27; and John McCormick, *Acid Earth: The Global Threat of Acid Pollution* (Washington, D.C.: International Institute for Environment and Development, 1985).

22. For an account of the U.S.–Canadian negotiations, see Jurgen Schmandt, Judith Clarkson, and Hilliard Roderick, eds., *Acid Rain and Friendly Neighbors: The Policy Dispute between Canada and the United States* (Durham, NC: Duke University Press, 1988). The Eastern European situation is assessed in Jon Thompson, "East Europe's Dark Dawn," *National Geographic,* June 1991, 36–68.

23. See Norman W. Fichthorn, "Command-and-Control vs. The Market: The Potential Effects of Other Clean Air Act Requirements on Acid Rain Compliance," *Environmental Law,* 21, no. 4:II (1991): 2069–2084; and Glen Allen, "Savoring Victories," *Maclean's,* March 25, 1991, 14–15.

24. Howard Schneider, "North American Air-Monitoring System Planned," *Washington Post,* August 3, 1996, A20.

25. See Marc Pallemaerts, "The Politics of Acid Rain Control in Europe," *Environment,* 31, no. 2 (March 1988): 42–44.

26. See Anna La Bastille, "The International Acid Test," *Sierra,* May–June 1986, 54; and Clayton Jones, "Acid Rain Looms as Newest Threat to Japan's Island of Kyushu," *The Oregonian,* November 8, 1992, A–14.

27. Garrett Hardin, "The Tragedy of the Commons," *Science, 162* (December 13, 1968): 1243–1248.

28. For a more extensive discussion of the common pool resource theory, see Susan J. Buck, "No Tragedy on the Commons," in *Green Planet Blues,* eds., Ken Conca, Michael Alberty, and Geoffrey D. Dabelko (Boulder, CO: Westview Press, 1995), 46–52; and Zachary A. Smith, *The Environmental Policy Paradox,* 2d ed. (Englewood Cliffs, NJ: Prentice Hall, 1995), 4–5.

29. See David Feeny, et al., "The Tragedy of the Commons: Twenty-two Years Later," in *Green Planet Blues,* eds. Ken Conca, Michael Alberty, and Geoffrey D. Dabelko (Boulder, CO: Westview Press, 1995), 54.

30. See "Japan's Green Tinge," *The Economist,* February 2, 1991, 32.

31. William J. Broad, "Survey of 100 U.S. Coastal Sites Shows Pollution Is Declining," *The New York Times,* January 21, 1997, B10.

32. See Michael A. Champ and Iver W. Duedall, "Ocean Waste Management," in *Marine Pollution,* ed. J. Albaiges (New York: Hemisphere, 1989), 305–345; and Steven J. Moore, "Troubles in the High Seas: A New Era in the Regulation of U.S. Ocean Dumping," *Environmental Law, 22,* no. 3 (1992): 913–952.

33. Brian J. Rothschild, "How Bountiful Are Ocean Fisheries?" *Consequences, 2* (1996), 15.

34. See D. H. Cushing, *The Provident Sea* (Cambridge, MA: Cambridge University Press, 1988), 253–256.

35. See Anne W. Simon, *Neptune's Revenge: The Ocean of Tomorrow* (New York: Franklin Watts, 1984), 32–33.

36. Rothchild, "How Bountiful Are Ocean Fisheries?" 20–21.

37. Nicholas Lenssen, "The Ocean Blues," in *The Worldwatch Reader on Global Environmental Issues,* ed. Lester R. Brown (New York: W.W. Norton, 1991), 53.

38. Lincoln Kaye, "A Quest for Net Profits," *Far Eastern Economic Review,* September 28, 1989, 138–139.

39. Gary Lee, "Tuna Fishing Bill Divides Environmental Activists," *The Washington Post,* July 8, 1996, A–7.

40. 104th Congress, H.R. 2823 and H.R. 2856.

41. Rothschild, "How Bountiful Are Ocean Fisheries?" 23.

42. See U.S. Executive Office of the President, Council on Environmental Quality, *The Evolution of National Wildlife Law* (Washington, D.C.: U.S. Government Printing Office, 1977), 423–443.

43. Peter M. Haas, *Saving the Mediterranean: The Politics of International Environmental Cooperation* (New York: Columbia University Press, 1990), 11.

44. World Resources Institute, *World Resources 1992–93* (New York: Oxford University Press, 1992), 181.

45. "Sea Law Convention Enters into Force," *UN Chronicle, 32* (March 1995), 8–12.

46. Steven Greenhouse, "U.S. Having Won Changes, Is Set to Sign Law of the Sea," *The New York Times,* July 1, 1994, A1.

47. See Ian Townsend-Gault and Michael D. Smith, "Environmental Ethics, International Law, and Deep Seabed Mining: The Search for a New Point of Departure," in *Freedom for the Seas in the 21st Century,* eds. Jon M. Van Dyke, Durwood Zaelke, and Grant Hewison (Washington, D.C.: Island Press, 1993), 392–403.

48. Hilary E. French, *After the Earth Summit: The Future of Environmental Governance,* Worldwatch Paper 107 (Washington, D.C.: Worldwatch Institute, March 1992, 30.

49. T.M. Hawley, "Managing the Oceans," *Technology Review, 92,* no. 2 (February–March 1989): 18.

50. For more on why nations comply with their treaty obligations, see Lawrence E. Susskind, *Environmental Diplomacy: Negotiating More Effective Global Agreements* (New York: Oxford University Press, 1994).

51. See, for example J.D. Hays, John Imbrie, and N.J. Shackleton, "Variations in the Earth's Orbit: Pacemaker of the Ice Ages," *Science, 194* (December 10, 1976): 1121–1131.

The authors conclude, "A model of future climate based on the observed orbital-climate rela-tionships, but ignoring anthropogenic effects, predicts that the long-term trend over the next several thousand years is towards extensive Northern Hemisphere glaciation."

52. See James E. Lovelock, *Gaia* (Oxford, England: Oxford University Press, 1979).

53. See U.S. Congress, Senate, Committee on Commerce, Science and Transportation, *Policy Implications of Greenhouse Warming,* hearing, 102nd Cong., 1st sess., 25 April 1991 (Washington, D.C.: U.S. Government Printing Office, 1991).

54. World Commission on Environment and Development, *Our Common Future* (Ox-ford, England: Oxford University Press, 1987).

55. See John R. Luoma, "Gazing into Our Greenhouse Future," *Audubon,* March 1991, 52–59, 124–129.

56. See S. Fred Singer, "Global Climate Change: Fact and Fiction," *You and I,* July 1991, 284–291.

57. S. Fred Singer, Roger Revelle, and Chauncey Starr, "What to Do about Global Warm-ing: Look Before You Leap," *Cosmos, 1,* no. 1 (1991): 28–31.

58. Ibid., 286.

59. See Stephen H. Schneider, *Global Warming: Are We Entering the Greenhouse Cen-tury?* (San Francisco, CA: Sierra Club Books, 1989).

60. For an explanation of this concept as it is used in ten case studies, see Michael H. Glantz, ed., *Societal Responses to Regional Climatic Change* (Boulder, CO: Westview Press, 1988).

61. See, for example, Dixy Lee Ray, "The Greenhouse Blues: Keep Cool about Global Warming," *Policy Review, 49* (Summer 1989): 70–72.

62. For this view, see Thomas Levenson, *Ice Time: Climate, Science, and Life on Earth* (New York: Harper & Row, 1989).

63. See E. William Colglazier, "Scientific Uncertainties, Public Policy, and Global Warming: How Sure Is Sure Enough?" *Policy Studies Journal, 19,* no. 2 (Spring 1991): 61–72.

64. See David Feldman, "Tracking Global Climate Change Policy," *Policy Currents, 1,* no. 4 (November 1991): 1–5.

65. See Schneider, *Global Warming,* 238–285.

66. National Academy of Sciences, *Policy Implications of Greenhouse Warming* (Wash-ington, D.C.: National Academy Press, 1991), 72.

67. Mobil Oil advertisement, *The New York Times,* June 8, 1995.

68. "US Acts on Global Warming at Geneva," *EDF Letter* (September 1996): 3.

69. Christopher Flavin, "Climate of Hope," *World Watch* (November/December 1996): 2.

70. For a narrative description of the rise of the ozone depletion issue to the top of envi-ronmental protection agenda, see John J. Nance, *What Goes Up: The Global Assault on Our Atmosphere* (New York: Morrow, 1991).

71. For an account of the early scientific evidence and the political debates that followed, see Paul Brodeur, "Annals of Chemistry: In the Face of Doubt," *The New Yorker,* June 9, 1986, 70.

72. Steven J. Shimberg, "Stratospheric Ozone and Climate Protection: Domestic Legis-lation and the International Process," *Environmental Law, 21,* no. 2175 (1991): 2184.

73. See Susan Solomon et al., "On Depletion of Antarctic Ozone," *Nature, 321* (June 19, 1986): 755–758.

74. Martha M. Hamilton, "The Challenge to Make Industry Ozone-Friendly," *Washing-ton Post National Weekly Edition,* October 7–13, 1991, 21.

75. For an analysis of the Title VI amendments, see Shimberg, "Stratospheric Ozone and Climate Protection," 2193–2214.

76. Debora MacKenzie, "Agreement Reduces Damage to Ozone Layer," *New Scientist,* December 5, 1992, 10.

77. Hilary F. French, "Learning from the Ozone Experience," in Lester R. Brown et al., *State of the World, 1997* (New York: W.W. Norton, 1997): 151–172, at 156.

78. Associated Press, "Data Point to Ultimate Closing of Ozone Hole," *The New York Times,* May 31, 1996, A11; Amal Kumar Naj, "Chemicals Bad for the Ozone Are Declining," *The Wall Street Journal,* May 31, 1996, B8A.

79. Paul Lewis, "U.S. and Other Donor Nations Plan $2 Billion for Environment," *The New York Times* (March 16, 1994).

80. For a summary of the U.S. position, as well as that of other countries, see Peter M. Morrisette and Andrew J. Plantinga, "Global Warming: A Policy Review," *Policy Studies Journal, 19,* no. 2 (Spring 1991): 163–172.

81. Shimberg, "Stratospheric Ozone and Climate Protection," 2188.

82. Peter M. Morrisette, "The Montreal Protocol: Lessons for Formulating Policies for Global Warming," *Policy Studies Journal, 19,* no. 2 (Spring 1991): 152–161.

83. Levenson, *Ice Time,* 204.

84. Morrisette, "Montreal Protocol," 158.

85. For an explanation of the difficulties of reaching an agreement on greenhouse warming, see James K. Sebenius, "Designing Negotiations towards a New Regime: The Case of Global Warming," *International Security, 15,* no. 4 (Spring 1991): 110–148.

FOR FURTHER READING

Timothy Beatley, David J. Brower, and Anna K. Schwab. *An Introduction to Coastal Zone Management.* Washington, D.C.: Island Press, 1994.

Allessandro Bonnano and Douglas Constance. *Caught in the Net: The Global Tuna Industry, Environmentalists, and the State.* Louisville, KY: University of Kentucky Press, 1996.

James M. Broadus and Ralphael V. Vartanov, eds. *The Oceans and Environmental Security.* Washington, D.C.: Island Press, 1994.

Elizabeth Cook. *Milestones in Ozone Protection.* Washington, D.C.: World Resources Institute, 1996.

Michael Grubb and Dean Anderson, eds. *The Emerging International Regime for Climate Change.* Washington, D.C.: Brookings Institution, 1995.

Pierre Marc Johnson and Andre Beaulieu. *The Environment and NAFTA: Understanding and Implementing the New Continental Law.* Washington, D.C.: Island Press, 1996.

Henry Lee, ed. *Shaping National Responses to Climate Change: A Post-Rio Guide.* Washington, D.C.: Island Press, 1995.

Arjun Makhijani and Kevin Gurney. *Mending the Ozone Hole: Science, Technology, and Policy.* Cambridge, MA: MIT Press, 1995.

Ronald B. Mitchell. *Intentional Oil Pollution at Sea.* Cambridge, MA: MIT Press, 1994.

Matthew Paterson. *Global Warming and Global Politics.* New York: Routledge, 1996.

Ian H. Rowlands. *The Politics of Global Atmospheric Change.* New York: St. Martin's Press, 1995.

Boyce Thorne-Miller and John G. Catena. *The Living Ocean: Understanding and Protecting Marine Biodiversity.* Washington, D.C.: Island Press, 1990.

Mark J. Valencia. *A Maritime Regime for North-East Asia.* New York: Oxford University Press, 1996.

Jon M. Van Dyke, Durwood Zalke, and Grant Harrison. *Freedom for the Seas in the Twenty-First Century.* Washington, D.C.: Island Press, 1994.

CHAPTER 10

Endangered Species, Forests, and Biodiversity

Nobody's told me the difference between a red squirrel, a black one or a brown one. Do we have to save every subspecies?
— Manuel Lujan, Secretary of the Interior under President Bush[1]

In 1996, southern California's largest developer made an agreement with the federal government that may be indicative of the types of changes that are occurring within the environmental policy process. The Irvine Company agreed to set aside 21,000 acres of prime land for a nature reserve, which will eventually become 39,000 acres when local governments in the region add another 18,000 acres to the Natural Community Conservation Plan. In exchange, the company was given a "no surprises" guarantee that it can build housing tracts, shopping malls and industrial parks elsewhere without having to face endless legal skirmishes with the Endangered Species Act (ESA). What makes the plan especially meaningful is that it was supported by several environmental organizations such as The Nature Conservancy and engineered by Secretary of the Interior Bruce Babbitt. In making the land swamp, the agreement assures protection of rapidly vanishing coastal sage scrubland and forty-two species of plants and animals believed to be the same level of danger as the California gnatcatcher, a tiny songbird that was designated a threatened species in 1993.[2] The plan also signaled a breakthrough in attempts to establish a regionwide network of natural habitat preserves from the Mexican border to the edge of Los Angeles. "This is a classic proving ground" of whether the Endangered Species Act can be made to work outside remote forests, Babbitt said in announcing the agreement. It is also exemplary of how the environmental community can work with real estate development interests to forge proposals that guarantee the survival of species without the kind of conflict that characterized the implementation of the ESA since its early inception.[3]

We have only the beginning of an understanding of the diversity and numbers of forms of life that currently exist on this planet. There may be as many as thirty million species currently in existence, primarily insects and marine invertebrates, with only about 5 percent of them named and identified. That number is though to be only a tiny percentage of the species that have inhabited earth during its millions of years of history—perhaps less than 1 percent of as many as four billion. Some species have disappeared as a result of cataclysmic change, such as changes in the level of the seas or massive ice movements, while others disappearing can be attributed to the appearance (and often, the intervention) of humans.[4]

Estimates of the current rate of species extinction vary considerably from one source to another and are largely dependent upon the period of time covered. From 1600 to 1980, for example, nearly two hundred vertebrate extinctions were documented, over half of them birds. But since 1980, habitat destruction, hunting, pesticide use, pollution, and other human-made causes have led to the extinction of as many as one thousand species per year, primarily in tropical regions. The *Global 2000 Report to the President* projected that between a half million and two million species extinctions would occur by the turn of the century. Most of those losses were attributed to the clearing or degradation of tropical forests, although marine species are threatened by damming, siltation, and pollution.[5]

This chapter focuses on the history of legislation, both in the United States and internationally, to protect wildlife, plants, and their habitats, the wildlife bureaucracy, and the role of nongovernmental organization (NGOs) in species protection. It reviews as a case study one of the most controversial issues related to the implementation of the Endangered Species Act: the wolf reintroduction program, which shows how policies change in response to various political forces. The last section of the chapter provides an overview of the forest debate by examining U.S. timber management and the ways in which other nations are attempting to preserve boreal and tropical forest diversity.

PROTECTIVE LEGISLATION

The development of laws protecting wildlife can be traced back to earliest legal history, but those laws have often differed in terms of what has been protected and why. Under Roman law, wild animals, or *ferae naturae,* were given the same status as the oceans and air—they belonged to no one. As Anglo-Saxon law developed, however, an exception was made: private landowners had the right to wildlife on their property. As land was parceled out to the nobility as "royal forests" around 450 C.E., hunting restrictions began to be imposed, and only the King was given sole right to pursue fish or game anywhere he claimed as his realm. As the English political system developed, there were very few changes in this theory except to perpetuate a system by which only the wealthy or nobles were qualified to take game. Those same restrictions found their way to American shores and flourished until the mid-nineteenth century, when a major policy shift occurred as the U.S. Supreme Court established the basis for a doctrine of state ownership of wildlife. The federal government's role in defining the legal status of wildlife was limited to an 1868 statute prohibiting the hunting of furbearing animals in Alaska and in 1894 a prohibition on hunting in Yellowstone National Park. The states began to regulate fishing within their waters just after the Civil War, a policy that was upheld by the Court using the commerce clause of Article 1, Section 8 of the Constitution. What is important about the decisions of this period, however, is that the states' regulatory authority was based on a fundamental nineteenth century conception of the purpose of wildlife law—the preservation of a food supply.[6]

Contemporary U.S. legislation protecting plants and animals can be divided into four categories: migratory and game birds, wild horses and burros, marine mammals, and endangered species. What is unique about these legislative provisions is that, in addition to offering protection for reasons of aesthetics or biological diversity, Congress has also sought to regulate the commerce and trade in these species. Generally, it is illegal to possess, offer for sale, sell, offer for barter, offer to purchase, purchase, deliver for shipment, ship, export, import, cause to be shipped, exported, or imported, deliver for transportation, transport or cause to be transported, carry or cause to be carried, or receive for shipment, transport, carriage, or export any of the protected plants and animals.

Three separate legislative efforts have been enacted—all within the last thirty years—which indicates how recently American concern for endangered species has reached the political agenda. The first, the Endangered Species Preservation Act of 1966, mandated the secretary of the interior to develop a program to conserve, protect, restore, and propagate selected species of native fish and wildlife. Its provisions were primarily designed, however, to protect habitats through land acquisition, and little else. The species protected under the law were those "threatened with extinction" based on a finding by the secretary in consultation with interested persons, but the procedures for doing that went no further. It did not limit the taking of these species, or commerce in them, but it was an important first step in the development of the law.

The Endangered Species Conservation Act of 1969 attempted to remedy those limitations by further defining the types of protected wildlife, and more importantly, by including wildlife threatened with worldwide extinction and prohibiting their importation into the United States—an international aspect not included in the earlier legislation. Instead of using the broad term *fish and wildlife* (which was interpreted as only vertebrates) the 1969 law included any wild mammal, fish, wild bird, amphibian, reptile, mollusk, or crustacean. The list of species was to be developed using the best scientific and commercial data available, with procedures for designation pursuant to the rule making in the Administrative Procedure Act. This formalized a process that had been haphazard and highly discretionary under the 1966 act.

President Richard Nixon warned that the two laws did not provide sufficient management tools need to act early enough to save a vanishing species and urged Congress to enact a more comprehensive law, which became the Endangered Species Act (ESA) of 1973. There are several notable features in the law that distinguish it from previous efforts. One, it required all federal agencies, not just the two departments identified in the 1966 and 1969 acts, to seek to conserve endan-

gered species, broadening the base of protective efforts. Two, it expanded conservation measures that could be undertaken under the act to include all methods
and procedures necessary to protect the species rather then emphasizing habitat
protection only. Three, it broadened the definition of wildlife to include any member of the animal kingdom. Four, it created two classes of species: those "endangered" (in danger of extinction throughout all or a significant portion of its range)
and those "threatened" (any species likely to become an endangered species
within the foreseeable future).

From an administrative standpoint, the 1973 law was considerably more
complex than were previous legislative efforts. It included a circuitous route by
which a species was to be listed by the secretary of the interior, delisted when the
species' population stabilized, and changed from threatened to endangered and
vice versa. The secretaries of commerce and the interior have virtually unlimited
discretion in deciding when to consider the status of a species, since the law did
not establish any priorities or time limitations.

Generally, a species is considered for listing upon petition of an interested
group that has developed scientific evidence regarding the specie's population. In
1992, for example, a single biologist working in Oregon's Willamette Valley discovered specimens of Fenders' blue butterfly, a one-inch-long species thought to
be extinct. Researchers found ten sites where the butterfly was found and estimated
that there were only 2,000–2,500 of the insects in existence. The biologist prepared
a report on the butterfly's status for the Fish and Wildlife Service as the first step
toward its possible designation as threatened. Reports are then considered by the
secretary of the interior, although the time frame for consideration is totally discretionary. Some species have become extinct while waiting to be listed.

Listing, however, is but the first phase in a very lengthy process. Once a
species is added to the list (which is made official by publishing a notice in the
Federal Register), the federal government must decide how much of its habitat
needs to be protected. The 1973 law is somewhat vague in indicating how "critical" habitat is to be determined and when that determination must be made. The
law then requires the government to develop a recovery plan for the species. Recovery is defined by the law as the process by which the decline of an endangered
or threatened species is arrested or reversed and threats to its survival are neu-
tralized to ensure its long-term survival in the wild. The plan delineates, justifies,
and schedules the research and management actions necessary to support the recovery of a species, including those that, if successful, will permit reclassifica-
tion or delisting. Typical recovery plans involve extensive public participation
and include the cost of each strategy.

One of the most controversial aspects of the planning process is the assign-
ment of individual species recovery priorities, which signifies the imminence of
extinction and the designation of those species to which a known threat or conflict exists (usually from development projects). About one-quarter of the listed
species are in conflict with other activities and receive the designation. The law
was amended in 1988 to make more specific the requirement that the secretaries

SEVEN MEN AND AN OWL

On May 14, 1992, a panel of seven men met in Washington and made a decision on the fate of a two pound bird which, if only symbolically, changed American environmental policy for decades to come. The Endangered Species Committee met for only the second time in history to exempt Endangered Species Act protection for the Northern spotted owl on thirteen timber tracts in southwest Oregon. The controversy over the spotted owl marked a dramatic departure from political decisions of the previous twenty years. Although the immediate impact of the committee's vote was negligible, affecting only 1,742 acres of timber land and a thousand jobs, it was the first such exemption ever granted in the history of the legislation. More importantly, to much of the public, the decision represented the choice that must be made between forest products jobs and preservation of the owl's habitat, a choice that has been made in countless other communities across the country.

The Northern spotted owl's habitat ranges along the Pacific Coast from Canada to the San Francisco Bay area. Fewer than three thousand breeding pairs are estimated to exist, preferring to nest in tree holes or snags and preying on flying squirrels and rodents. One of the keys to the owls' survival is its young; 70 to 90 percent of the young die, mostly from starvation and predation. Research shows that the surviving young owls must be dispersed in a range of about three thousand acres each to replace dead owls and mix the genetic pool. Concerns about the future of the bird convinced the U.S. Fish and Wildlife Service (FWS) to declare the owl "threatened" in 1990 and to begin development of a recovery plan and designation of critical habitat for its protection.

At issue in the 1992 hearing was a request by the Bureau of Land Management for forty-four timber sales in western Oregon to be exempted from the act. In an internal battle between competing federal agencies, the FWS had issued an opinion that the proposed sales would jeopardize the long-term survival of the owl by fragmenting forests that provide important dispersal routes for young owls. In the interim, a federal court granted environmental groups' requests for an injunction to block timber sales on all forty-four parcels. After a month-long series of hearings that produced fifty-thousand pages of exhibits and a four-thousand-page transcript at a cost of $1.5 million, the committee met to weight the alternatives.

To grant an exemption, the Endangered Species Committee must make tree findings:

- That there is no "reasonable and prudent" alternative to the proposed action,
- That the benefits of the action "clearly outweigh" any other alternatives, and
- That the action is in the public interest and of regional or national significance.

(continued)

The seven-member committee deciding the fate of the owl was comprised of the secretaries of agriculture, army, and interior, the administrators of the Environmental Protection Agency and the National Oceanic and Atmospheric Administration, the chair of the Council of Economic Advisers, and a representative of the state of Oregon, designated by the governor. Meeting far from the site of the controversy, the committee deliberated at the same time that the Department of Interior was releasing two other owl plans—a long-awaited Fish and Wildlife Service recovery plan and a proposed alternative plan prepared by Secretary of the Interior Manuel Lujan.

In a 5–2 vote, with EPA Administrator William Reilly and Oregon's representative Tom Walsh dissenting, the committee denied thirty-one of the forty-four timber sales for which the BLM had sought exemption. Reilly admitted in later interviews that the amount of timber involved would not seriously hurt Oregon jobs or the spotted owl, but the exemptions would set an unwise precedent. In May, 1992, the issue was complicated further when a federal judge ruled in response to lawsuits by several environmental organizations that the Fish and Wildlife Service protection plan for the owl was insufficient because it failed to take into consideration new scientific evidence about the owls' declining population.

The battle continues to be unresolved. President Clinton's forest policies came under criticism of environmental groups, which sought a total ban on logging of old-growth forests that might be owl habitat, and the timber industry, which successfully took advantage of a loophole in forest legislation that allowed for salvage logging to proceed. The issue is much more complicated than simply jobs versus owls, or any other species. But the rhetoric surrounding the controversy is exemplary of how a difficult decision, which ideally should be made using sound scientific principles, can be turned into a political battleground where only seven individuals decide who wins and who loses.

For Further Reading

"Critical Habitat Designation Proposed for the Northern Spotted Owl," *Endangered Species Technical Bulletin, 16,* no. 6 (1991), 3–4.

Kathie Durbin, " 'God Squad' Hearing to Make Conservative History," *The Oregonian,* February 2, 1992, C1.

Jonathan Lange. "The Logic of Competing Information Campaigns: Conflict over Old Growth and the Spotted Owl," *Communication Monographs 60,* September 91993, 239–257.

Steven L. Yaffee. "The Northern Spotted Owl: An Indicator of the Importance of Sociopolitical Context," in *Endangered Species Recovery: Finding the Lessons, Improving the Process.* eds. Tim W. Clark, Richard P. Reading, and Alice L. Clarke. Washington, D.C.: Island Press, 1994, 47–71.

Steven L. Yaffee. *The Wisdom of the Spotted Owl: Policy Lessons for a New Century.* Washington, D.C.: Island Press, 1994.

of the interior and commerce develop and implement recovery plans and to require a status report every two years on the efforts to develop recovery plans for all listed species and on the status of all species for which recovery plans have been developed.

Plants are also protected under the ESA, with the first four plants (all found on San Clemente Island off the California coast) listed in 1977. Before the 1988 amendments, it was illegal only to "remove and reduce to possession" listed plants, and then, only those on lands under federal jurisdiction. Under the amended provisions, there is a prohibition against maliciously damaging or destroying plants on federal lands, making it illegal to remove, destroy, or damage any listed plant on state or private land in knowing violation of state law.

INTERNATIONAL PROTECTION AGREEMENTS

The development of an international regime to protect endangered species has come largely from the leadership of the United States. The 1969 Endangered Species Conservation Act included a provision directing the secretaries of the interior and commerce to convene an international meeting before June 30, 1971, to develop an international agreement on the conservation of endangered species. Although it was a year and a half late, that meeting produced the Convention on Trade in Endangered Species of Wild Fauna and Flora, or CITES as it is better known. The United States was the first nation to ratify the convention in January 1974, and it became effective July 1, 1975.

It is important to note, however, that CITES is not strictly a conservation agreement; it focuses on matters of international trade rather than on preservation per se. One of the key aspects of the CITES treaty is that it creates three levels of species vulnerability: Appendix I (all species threatened with extinction that are or may be affected by trade), Appendix II (all species that are not now threatened with extinction but that may become so unless trade in specimens is strictly regulated), and Appendix III (species subject to regulation for the purpose of preventing exploitation). Within ninety days of the date when a species is added to an appendix, and upon a showing of an overriding economic interest, party nations may make a "reservation" to the convention. The reservation means that they do not accept the listing of a species in a particular appendix and, therefore, are not subject to the trade prohibitions.

CITES establishes an elaborate series of trade permits within each category and between importing and exporting authorities. Exempt from the trade restrictions are specimens acquired before the Convention applied to that species, specimens that are personal or household effects, and specimens used in scientific research. The CITES agreement is supported by a secretariat, provided through the United Nations Environment Fund, and a Conference of the Parties, which meets every two years for the purpose of regulating trade in each species.

When the CITES agreement was first ratified, it received the support of the majority of nations that are active in wildlife trading because it helps them to protect their resources from illegal traders and poachers. Several countries that are deeply involved in wildlife trading as importers and exporters of products chose not to sign on to CITES. The result is an active animal smuggling industry, much of it centered in Southeast Asia.[7] Japan, the world's biggest importer of illegally traded goods, initially made twelve reservations to the convention, including two species of endangered sea turtles, although it agreed to phase out its trade in those species.[8] The sea turtle shells, primarily those of the hawksbill and olive ridley species, are made into eyeglass frames, cigarette lighters, combs, handbags, belts, and shoes.

Perhaps the most publicized and controversial listing under CITES is the African elephant. The elephant had already been listed by the United States as a threatened species in 1978, but in 1988 the World Wildlife Fund and Conservation International sponsored a scientific study of the African elephant population and recommended that it be listed under CITES Appendix I—threatened with extinction. The listing was supported by the United States and several other nations (including Kenya and Tanzania) at the October 1989 Conference of the Parties, along with a proposed ban on trade in ivory products, a position opposed by Botswana, Malawi, Mozambique, South Africa, Zambia, and Zimbabwe. Their opposition was a result of several of the nations managing to increase their elephant herds through nationally supported economic incentives. They felt that there was no need for their countries to suffer the loss of the lucrative ivory trade because herds in other African states were being diminished through poor wildlife management practices.

In the end, the United States-led position won, and the elephant achieved Appendix I status. Prices in African raw ivory dropped by as much as 90 percent, reducing any real incentives for poaching and smuggling, and it appeared that the problem was resolved.[9] But the issue continued to be raised at the 1992 and 1994 Conventions of the Parties, as African representatives sought relief from CITES to sell ivory from culled elephants, arguing that they had managed their herds effectively to stabilize the population. They felt as if they were being penalized for their efforts, and denounced attempts by countries without elephants to dominate the discussion. Environmental organizations, who were actively monitoring the CITES meetings, pointed out that the elephant population still had declined, convincing members to keep the ivory trade ban in effect.[10]

In 1997, however, there was an abrupt shift of policy when environmental ministers representing 138 nations met in Zimbabwe. After years of rancorous debate, Botswana, Namibia, and Zimbabwe were given permission to sell previously stockpiled ivory tusks to Japan under an experimental program that included an international monitoring system and increased enforcement of anti-poaching laws. The three countries agreed that no elephants would be legally killed and that revenues from the ivory sales will go toward conservation and community programs for wildlife.

One of the flaws in the CITES provisions is that CITES has little real power over the actions of individual nations and whether or not they choose to comply with the treaty. For example, the parties established a panel comprised of affected states and nongovernmental organization representatives to monitor elephant populations and whether or not the species should be downlisted on a case-by-case basis. But the panel's recommendations are only advisory, and no mechanism exists within the secretariat to prosecute noncompliance with the convention. Thus, any real efforts at species protection are voluntary and reliant upon the parties' recognition of the value of preserving biodiversity.[11]

A second major international species protection agreement is the Convention on Biological Diversity, which was negotiated both before and during the Earth Summit in Rio de Janeiro in June 1992. Unlike the dissension that marked the initial reservations to CITES, the biodiversity convention gained the support of virtually every member of the United Nations except the United States. President George Bush, who had threatened to boycott the conference, refused to sign the biodiversity treaty in an action that embarrassed the U.S. delegation in a highly publicized dispute. Under the terms of the agreement, the parties agree that a state has sovereignty over the genetic resources within its borders, including any valuable drugs and medicines that may be developed from endangered animals and plants. The convention is an important extension of CITES because it commits countries to draw up national strategies to converse not only the plants and animals within their borders but also the habitats in which they live. Other provisions require countries to pass laws to protect endangered species and expand protected areas and restore damaged ones and to promote public awareness of the need for conservation and sustainable use of biological resources. When President Clinton assumed office, he signed the treaty, but because the Republican-controlled Congress refused to ratify it with a two-thirds vote, the United States was allows only an observer role when the first conference of the parties was held in 1994.[12]

Before the Earth Summit, habitat protection found international support largely through organization such as the International Union for Conservation of Nature and Natural Resources (IUCN) and by regime such as the International Convention concerning the Protection of World Cultural and Natural Heritage, which entered into force in 1972. More than 1,200 national parks have been established worldwide, covering nearly 2.7 million square kilometers—an areas larger than Alaska, Texas, and California combined. One of the challenges facing global efforts to preserve wildlife habitats is basically one of economics: in times of declining budgets, many governments are finding it difficult to support parks and reserves over human needs. Countries such as New Zealand, for example, are reorganizing their parks to earn more revenue from them, and several African nations are using tourism as a way of financing wildlife refuges. But there are less obvious problems as well. Most national parks are outlined by some type of physical barrier, such as a fence or moat, but animals within do not always respect those limitations. Large mammals and birds of prey, for example, demand a large ecosystem for their habitat, which may cross national borders. This makes it unlikely that, even when strictly protected, national parks by themselves will be able to conserve all, or even most, species.[13]

THE MAKING OF WILDLIFE POLICY

Federal authority for the regulation protection of wildlife is a case study in the growth of bureaucracy, characterized by name changes and power struggles within the agencies. Power is shared by a number of agencies, most of which have their counterparts at the state level. Until 1939, the Bureau of Biological Survey in the Department of Agriculture held regulatory authority for all wildlife, with the exception of marine fisheries, which were under the jurisdiction of the Bureau of Fisheries in the Department of Commerce. Both agencies were absorbed by the Department of the Interior and then consolidated into the U.S. Fish and Wildlife Service in 1940, but in 1956, the Fish and Wildlife Act divided authority into a Bureau of Sports Fisheries and Wildlife and a Bureau of Commercial Fisheries, much as had been the case prior to 1939. President Richard Nixon's federal reorganization of 1970 transferred the Bureau of Commercial Fisheries to the National Oceanic and Atmospheric Administration and the agency became the National Marine Fisheries Service, once again under the Department Commerce. The Bureau of Sports Fisheries and Wildlife went back to its previous designation as the Fish and Wildlife Service in 1974, remaining in the Department of the Interior.

The structure of congressional committees also contributes to the fragmentation of policymaking, since various committees and subcommittees have jurisdiction over different types of animals and their habitats. Political change can add to the confusion over which committee handles which species, as was the case in 1995 when the members of the 104th Congress eliminated entirely the Merchant Marine and Fisheries Committee, which had been in existence for 107 years. Its duties and staff were then parceled out to other committees, making the protection of the oceans and sealife more complex.

Congress, in the 1988 amendments to the ESA, directed federal agencies to more closely monitor those species facing substantial declines of their populations and to carry out emergency listing when necessary. Generally speaking, the longer a species has been listed, the better its chances for its population stabilizing or improving. For the most part, those species listed less than three years do not yet have final approved recovery plans, although they may have plans in some stage of development. Recovery outlines are developed within sixty days of publication of the final rule listing a species and are submitted to the director of the Fish and Wildlife Service to be used as a guide for activities until recovery plans are developed and approved.

In response to criticism from various interests about the way in which the ESA was being implemented, President Clinton established the National Biological Service within the Department of the Interior as a way of improving the existing bank of information on species and their habitat. The agency was given responsibility for developing an inventory of plant and animal populations, but some members of Congress viewed it as a base for advocates seeking to expand the scope of the ESA. Clinton's advisors believed that the new bureau was absolutely essential if the federal government hoped to speed up the process of listing and recovery, which had fallen far behind in the review process. By mid-decade, nearly 3,500 species were candidates for inclusion under the ESA, but with existing resources, it would take decades to even begin to make a determination of whether or not a species ought to be listed.[14]

But the 1995 change from a Democrat controlled Congress, which generally supported the ESA in principle, to a Republican one, which sought major reforms, marked a major turnaround for the nation's wildlife policies. The Endangered Species Act officially expired on October 1, 1992, but Congress had still appropriated funds and could continue do so unless the act is totally repealed. As one of its initial actions, the Republican leadership declared a moratorium on the listing of any new species under the ESA, using the argument that there was uncertainty about how best to implement its provisions. The moratorium lasted until May 1996, creating an additional backlog of casework for agencies already besieged by budget cuts and an overall lack of resources. Republicans also targeted the National Biological Service, whose budget was included under the Department of the Interior. In a conference agreement, legislators agreed to eliminate the agency and shift most of its functions to the U.S. Geological Survey, whose budget was slashed along with its ability to implement much of its chartered responsibilities. President Clinton vetoed the interior appropriations bill, objecting to provisions that included a 10 percent spending reduction for the department, along with a laundry list of issues relating to grazing on federal lands, offshore oil drilling, and mining patents.[15]

Amending the Endangered Species Act was one of the top priorities of congressional Republicans in the 104th Congress. House leaders established an Endangered Species Task Force. Representatives Don Young (R-Alaska and chair of the Resources Committee) and Richard Pombo (R-California) introduced a major ESA reform proposal. The bill sought to eliminate species recovery as the primary goal of the act, provided more opportunities for states and landowners to be more involved in decisions related to endangered species, created biodiversity reserves, gave more leeway to landowners, and would reimburse private property owners for loss in land value resulting from endangered species regulation.[16] The House Resources Committee approved the bill in October; the House leadership, however, refused to bring the bill to the floor for a vote in light of public outcry over the Republicans' environmental bills. But conservatives and property rights activists kept the pressure on the leadership to pass the bill.

Washington Senator Slade Gorton introduced his ESA reform bill in May 1995.[17] It was soon discredited by revelations that it had been largely written by timber and other industry representatives. Senator Dirk Kempthorne's (R-Idaho) reform bill was used by Democrats and Republicans on the Environment and Public Works Committee as the beginning point for compromise legislation.[18] Negotiators had produced substantial agreement on three issues by July 1996. First, state and local governments and private landowners would develop multiple species conservation plans that would protect listed as well as other "rare or declining" species in an area. The plans would permit "low-effect" conservation plans that allow for incidental takings of protected species as long as mitigation of the impact occurs and the taking does not decrease the likelihood of survival of the species and does not result in the "destruction or adverse modification of designated critical habitat." Second, listing decisions were to be based on the "best scientific and commercial data available." The Department of the Interior would be given 90 days from the time a petition is filed to list, delist, or downlist species from endangered to threatened or from threatened to recovered. Agencies would be required to release all information used in making decisions unless there was a "good cause" reason to keep it confidential. Agencies would subject all listing decisions to peer review from a panel of three independent referees from a list compiled by the National Academy of Sciences. Third, agencies would be required to publish draft recovery plans within 18 months and final plans within 30 months of listing. For species listed before January 1, 1996, plans were to be developed within 36 months of enactment of the law. Recovery plans would be formulated by representatives from the state, federal agencies, tribal governments, local governments, academic institutions, private individuals, and commercial enterprises. However, the bill died at the end of the 104th Congress, as Republicans were unable to generate any kind of bipartisan support for their proposal.

Both the Clinton administration and Congress agreed that the ESA was flawed, but one of the primary disagreements between the two branches was whether the law ought to be repealed so that policymakers could begin with a clean slate, or whether or not piecemeal, incremental changes could be made that would prove satisfactory to all the parties involved. Some reforms were made through the regulatory process, circumventing the legislature and therefore not require actual amendments to the law.

THE ROLE OF ORGANIZED INTERESTS

While government agencies are responsible for implementing the legislative aspects of wildlife protection, environmental organizations, industry trade associations, and grass-roots opposition groups have clashed over how the laws ought to be interpreted. Wildlife protection groups began to flourish in the late nineteenth century, and many of them survived to become the mainstays of the contemporary environmental movement, such as the National Aubudon Society, founded in 1905. Others, such as the Wilderness Society (1935) and the National Wildlife Federation (1936) were products of the surge of interest instigated by President Theodore Roosevelt. The vast majority of wildlife organizations, however, have a more recent origin, partly as a result of a spate of legislation activity just after Earth Day 1970. The National Wildlife Federation, which monitors environmental organizations, reported that, of the 108 national wildlife and humane organizations identified in its study, 14 percent had been founded before 1940, and 68 percent since 1966. The decade surrounding Earth Day (1965–1975) accounted for the founding of 38 percent of all groups with a species orientation.[19]

The tactics used by groups to influence the implementation of wildlife policy range from the traditional to the radical. Some organizations see their role within the context of legislation, such as the Wilderness Society's efforts at lobbying Congress to increase appropriations for habitat protection. Other groups focus on advocating for species by lobbying the implementing agency directly. In the mid-1990s, for example, the San Diego Biodiversity Project sought the listing of ten endangered plants and animals in southern California, while the Hawaii Aubudon Society wanted the government to designated critical habitat for seventeen species of Hawaiian forest birds.

Other groups have taken independent steps to preserve species, bypassing the federal bureaucracy. The Nature Conservancy, for instance, founded in 1951, buys up endangered habitats to save the species living on them from extinction. The organization has purchased or negotiated donations of more than five million acres worldwide, making the group the custodian of the largest private nature sanctuary in the world. Another notable accomplishment of the group is their Biological and Conservation Data System, a biogeographic database of more than four hundred thousand entries that can be used to assess species diversity on a region-by-region basis. It allows the group to establish protection priorities and is also used by public agencies and resource planners in preparing environmental impact studies.[20]

Somewhat ironically, sport hunting organizations, such as Ducks Unlimited and the Boone and Crockett Club, organized by Teddy Roosevelt in 1887, have also been active in species preservation. Many of the national hunting organizations have dedicated their efforts to preserving wildlife habitat and the enforcement of game laws. They have been instrumental in advocating management policies for species such as the North American deer, wild turkey, pronghorn antelope, and migratory waterfowl. Equally active have been recreational fishing enthusiasts, who have joined environmental organizations in seeking a ban on gill and entangled nets. The American Sportsfishing Association and fishing equipment manufacturers contributed funds toward a successful ban on netting in Florida waters, with most of the donations coming from rank-and-file anglers.[21]

Environmental organizations have been joined in their efforts by a number of corporate interests seeking to capitalize on Americans' love of wildlife. Firms such as the DuPont Chemical Company and General Wine and Spirits, Inc. (bald eagle), Manhattan Life Insurance Company (peregrine falcon), Sony Corporation (California condor), and Martin-Marietta (bighorn sheep) have made significant financial contributions to species restoration. As one publicist suggested, "People simply love animals. If your company is associated with kindness to animals, some of that love will rub off on you."[22]

The ESA has also been the focus of one of the environmental opposition groups discussed earlier in Chapter 2. Typical is the organization, Grassroots ESA Coalition, an umbrella group headquartered in Battle Ground, Washington. It claims to represent more than 350 other organizations seeking to "reform the ESA in a way that benefits both wildlife and people, something the old law has failed to do."[23] Unlike industry groups with the financial resources to make campaign contributions, the Grassroots ESA Coalition has urged its members to contact members of Congress through telephone calls and letter-writing campaigns in support of reform legislation. Other organizations have called for an outright repeal of the ESA rather than for incremental reforms.

THE PITFALLS OF POLICY IMPLEMENTATION

There is considerable disagreement over whether or not the federal government has been successful in its attempts to implement national policy for the protection of species. There is little disagreement that the numbers of species awaiting protection is growing, especially as a result of the 1995–1996 moratorium on listings and cuts in agency budgets which occurred during the first term of the Clinton administration. Despite the attention being paid to the loss of plant biodiversity within the tropical forests, resources have limited the government to researching and protecting only those species habitants within the borders of the United States and its geographic neighbors.

The United States can, with some justification, point to some successes in its efforts. The Aleutian Canada goose, for example, was once widespread throughout Alaska, but began to decline when commercial fox farmers introduced nonnative foxes from about 1836–1930. The geese made easy prey for the foxes, which decimated their numbers. When the species was listed as endangered in 1967, only about two hundred to three hundred birds were estimated to remain, restricted to a single island in the Bering Sea. But by relocating wild family groups on additional islands and protecting the wintering flock from hunting in Oregon and California, the population increased substantially. Other success stories include the peregrine falcon, the Gila trout, the piping plover, and the American alligator, which was reclassified from endangered to threatened.

Some efforts to preserve a species have created considerable controversy because of their cost or methodology. In 1987, for example, the San Diego Wild Animal Park captured the last of the known wild California condors. The 1985 decision by the U.S. Fish and Wildlife Service to remove the last six condors from the wild prompted an injunction by the National Aubudon Society and years of legal wrangling. The government eventually allowed several nonprofit groups to begin captive breeding programs, and they gradually began to release young condors back to their natural habitat in southern California and northern Arizona. Much of the tracking of the released birds has been done by organizations such as the Ventana Wilderness Sanctuary, and release efforts have not always been successful, leading critics to complain that human intervention may sometimes be counterproductive.[24] Another controversial project involved the translocation of the California sea otter. The Fish and Wildlife Service began capturing the animals in 1987 to move them to a protected habitat area on San Nicholas Island, off the coast of southern California, but the effort was largely ineffective because the otters returned to their old hunting grounds and others died.

In contrast, protection of some species may have come too late. The carcasses of the last two female Florida panthers known to exist in the wild were found in 1991 in the Florida Everglades, and preliminary analyses of the cause of death appeared to be mercury poisoning. Only two panthers, both of them male, are thought to remain in the southeast Everglades. Other species, such as Bachman's warbler and the Scioto madtom (a rare fish found in Ohio waters), are believed to be extinct, and unless representatives of these species are found in the wild, recovery plan preparation is curtailed. Outside the United States, extinction has already claimed hundreds of species, best exemplified perhaps by the dodo. The most famous of all animals on the island of Mauritius, the dodo was a dovelike flightless bird about the size of a turkey. Since it had no natural predators, it was naturally curious of the Dutch colonists who came to settle the island. The colonists did not kill the dodo for its meat (which is tough and bitter), but for sport, clubbing the last one to death around 1680.[25]

The bottom line on effectiveness, however, is a criticism shared by everyone who comes into contact with the Endangered Species Act. Only a handful of species have been recovered since the legislation was enacted. These "successes" have come at a cost of millions of dollars in recovery programs, staff time, and private and public studies. The ESA was scheduled for reauthorization in 1992, but a campaign-conscious Congress chose to defer action on new amendments, fearing both voter revolt and a Bush veto. Environmentalists were elated when President Clinton promised to make the legislation a priority of his new administration, but he was blocked by Republicans who had little intention of expanding the ESA and who, in fact, introduced dozens of amendments to revise or eliminate the legislation entirely. Although national organizations such as the National Wildlife Federation and Sierra Club put pressure on legislators to increase funding for the various agencies involved, they were met head-on by the Grassroots ESA Coalition. The coalition's members sought a revised ESA that would, among other provisions, give authority, for species preservation to the states rather than to the federal government and require conservation decisions to be made at the lowest possible cost to citizens. The group argued that priority should be given "to more taxonomically unique, genetically complex and more economically and ecologically valuable animals and plants."[26]

THE CONTINUING SAGA OF SPECIES PROTECTION

Much of the opposition to the ESA is focused on not whether the ESA has been effective in restoring or preserving species, but on its impact on development and jobs. The celebrated case of the snail darter is an example of how protection of a single species can affect a major federal project. In the late 1960s, the Tennessee Valley Authority (TVA) initiated its Tellico Development Project in the eastern part of the state, with plans to flood a valley behind a $120 million dam to make it a booming recreational area. The dam would also be part of a massive hydroelectric project, which would bring power to the region.[27] In 1971, opponents to the project, led by the Environmental Defense Fund (EDF), successfully sued to stop the project on the grounds that the TVA had failed to file an environmental impact statement. The TVA complied and filed a report that mentioned that a rare species of fish, the snail darter, was found in the river just above the dam site. In the interim, the Endangered Species Act was enacted in 1973, and biologists argued that the completion of the project would destroy the snail darter's habitat. The TVA attempted to transfer the fish to other streams nearby, but was unsuccessfully, yet at the same time refused to consider any alternative to completing the dam. The EDF and various citizens' groups sued again, and after working its way through the legal system, the case was heard by the U.S. Supreme Court, which ruled in favor of the environmental groups in June 1978.[28]

At the same time, Congress amended the 1973 legislation to create a special committee to review disputed projects such as Tellico, nicknamed the "God Squad" because its members could grant an exemption from the protection provisions of the ESA. The committee ruled in favor of the snail darter, but a separate piece of legislation, signed by President Jimmy Carter in September 1979, exempted the Tellico project from not only the act, but form all other laws which blocked its completion. The project continued, with some transplanted snail darters surviving in nearby waters.

Critics of the ESA often point to projects discontinued or stalled because of habitat protection requirements. When the golden-cheeked warbler was listed under the act, its listing brought a halt to residential and commercial development on some of the choicest real estate in Texas and led to an announcement by the 3M Company that it was delaying a multimillion-dollar expansion of its research and development center until the habitat issue was settled. Similarly, a spate of petitions to list species that are found only in the Pacific Northwest has caused a virtual crisis among the federal and state agencies that use the region's waters for hydroelectric power and agriculture.[29] California is believed to have more endangered species within its borders than does any other state, with species affecting housing developments (the gnatcatcher and the Stephens kangaroo rate) and agriculture (the Delta smelt).[30] In one of the more dramatic examples of dissatisfaction with the law, a disgruntled Florida land developer shot at several endangered red-cockaded woodpeckers and destroyed nesting sites because he believed concern for the birds was unduly delaying his application for a building permit on his property.

Despite examples like these, however, the actual number of projects blocked because of provisions in the ESA is very small. A study by the World Wildlife Fund found that only nineteen federal activities and projects of a potential pool of almost seventy-five thousand were blocked or terminated in one five-year period because of irreconcilable conflicts over species protection. The study tracked the results of more than two thousand formal consultations between other federal agencies and the Fish and Wildlife Service or the National Marine Fisheries Service required under Section 7 of the law, which calls for a determination as to whether a proposed activity would jeopardize a species. Only 353 "jeopardy opinions" were issued, and of those, the overwhelming majority did not result in a cancellation of the project or activity. In most of the cases, the government was able to find alternatives that allowed the actions to go forward without threatening protected species.[31]

The Wolf Reintroduction Controversy

Public policy is not static; it is responsive to factors such as changes in public opinion, electoral change, and in the availability of resources. One of the most dramatic examples of the dynamics of wildlife policy is the changing attitudes toward predator species such as the wolf. As early as 1630, the Massachusetts Bay Company paid trappers a one-cent bounty for killing wolves, a practice that continued with western expansion. In 1705, the government took an even more active role when the Pennsylvania colony hired the first predator control agent, who was paid to kill wolves using public funds. Throughout the 1800s, the public was uniformly supportive of policies such as strychinine poisoning and, eventually, the use of steel-jawed traps and rifles to kill unwanted predators. The United States Forest Service, responding to complaints by ranchers who were losing livestock to predators, began paying trappers to kill wolves on national forest grazing lands, and by 1915, a full-fledged wolf eradication program was under way. Eventually, local governments, livestock associations, and ranchers paid a tax to fund trapping operations. As a result, the wolf was virtually eradicated from the eastern United States by the 1880s,and by 1914, most had been killed in the western plains states, with only a few pockets persisting in the Southwest in the early 1920s. In 1931, pressure by the National Wool Growers Association and other groups led to the passage of the Animal Damage Control Act (ADCA), which gave the Department of Agriculture virtually unlimited power to eliminate animals that farmers and ranchers did not want or those considered "injuries." This included animals such as wolves and mountain lions in the national parks until the mid-1920s, when the National Park Service changed its policy and adopted one of wildlife protection and study. But the policy applied only to wolves inside park boundaries, and the eradication and control programs continued unabated nearly everywhere else. When environmental organizations became more active in the 1960s, they used audits prepared by biologists to show the significant effects of wolf poisons on the food chain and the inhumanity of using traps. The livestock industry regrouped in the 1970s and 1980s and lobbied Congress to continue the use of poison and to keep the ADCA program alive.[32]

Although the 1973 Endangered Species Act nominally provided protection for wolves because their numbers and habitat had been diminished, there was a conflicting Fish and Wildlife Service policy that permitted the killing of wolves that could be identified as predators. In 1978, a group of environmental organizations challenged the policy, and eventually, a U.S. Federal District Court judge ruled that wolves could be trapped only after a significant predation had occurred and that efforts must be directed at capture rather than killing.[33]

The court case did not resolve the wolf issue, however. State fish and game agencies had considerable discretion in determining how to implement the ESA and the court's ruling, with environmental organizations clamoring for a strict interpretation of the law's intention to conserve a threatened or endangered species. The Fish and Wildlife Service responded with a new policy of attempting to reintroduce wolves to the same areas of Wyoming and central Idaho where they had previously had a policy of killing them. In 1995, twenty-nine wolves from Canada were brought to Yellowstone National Park in an effort to build up the population, along with sixty wolves that had migrated on their own from Canada into Montana. The recovery program's goal is to remove the wolf from the endangered species list altogether by establishing ten breeding pairs for three consecutive years in each of the three recovery areas of Yellowstone, central Idaho, and northwestern Montana by the year 2002. The reintroduction program is expected to cost $6.7 million, a figure that some observers believe is excessive and unnecessary. One member of Congress even suggested that, if there was a need to cull the existing population of elk and deer in Yellowstone, a more cost-effective solution would be to open the park to hunters rather than reintroducing wolves. The wolf issue has been among the most controversial of the ESA recovery programs, generating a record-setting 160,000 letters of commit from fifty states and forty countries.[34]

The dispute over the program pits a number of interests against one another. While environmental organizations applauded the policy, groups such as the Montana Stockgrowers Association opposed it because of fears that the wolves would leave the park's boundaries to attack their livestock. In 1995, one Montana rancher was found guilty of shooting one of the Yellowstone wolves to death when a court rejected his contention that he thought he was shooting at a wild dog. He was sentenced to six months in prison and fined $10,000.[35] One organization, Defenders of Wildlife, set up a $100,000 fund to pay ranchers fair market value for any livestock kills attributable to wolves. Their efforts were countered by those of the Wyoming-based Abundant Wildlife Society of North America, which used dramatic photos of animals killed or mauled by wolves as evidence that the government's reintroduction program is misguided. And in 1995, the Montana legislature voiced its anger over the policy by passing a resolution that stated that, since Congress had sanctioned the reintroduction of wolves into the Yellowstone Park ecosystem, it should also do so in every other ecosystem and region in the United States including Central Park in New York City, the Presidio in San Francisco, and in Washington, D.C.[36]

The wolf policy is a mixture of politics and symbolism, with one observer characterizing the program as "the line in the sand that divides the old West from the new. Both sides want us to see this as a distillation of all endangered species conflicts, as a simple question of either/or."[37] Meanwhile, the wolves have begun to breed, are restoring the balance of predator to prey in the park, and have become a tourist attraction. The Republican-controlled 104th Congress, however, was successful in reducing the reintroduction program's budget, only to be countered by private contributions to help purchase radio collars to track the animals.

The wolf controversy is far from over and is notable because it so clearly indicates how policy is responsive to the political environment. Poisoning wolves was relaxed under one president's administration and totally lifted when another president took office. The public accepted predator control laws for centuries and then changed its mind as science began to play a more important role in the policy process. But the making of wildlife policy is still extremely politicized, and lobbying by interest groups or a change in party of the occupant of the White House could easily foster still another change in how wolves are protected.

The ESA in the Judicial Arena

One of the most successful strategies used by interest groups is the citizen suit, common to most environmental legislation. A provision in the 1973 Endangered Species Act allows individuals to enjoin the government for violating the provisions of the law. For example, the Sierra Club sued the government in 1976 when the group claimed that a proposed Army Corps of Engineers dam near St. Louis would flood caves inhabited by the endangered Indiana bat.[38] A similar suit was brought that same year by the National Wildlife Federation, which opposed construction of an interstate highway in Mississippi because it would affect the endangered Mississippi sandhill crane.[39] Often, the legal arms of the mainstream organizations will assist smaller organizations that could not, on their own, engage in litigation to protect a species. The Sierra Club Legal Defense Fund, for example, assisted the Bay Institute of San Francisco in its efforts to obtain ESA protection for the delta smelt and helped the Pilchuch Audubon Society in its suit to have the marbled murrelet, a threatened shorebird that nests in old-growth forests, listed under the ESA.

In the last decade, a somewhat different form of litigation has become more common, as property owners caught in the complex implementation of the ESA have sued for compensation for economic losses for which they believe they are entitled under the Constitution. Much of the litigation involves individuals or companies who own land that has been declared critical habitat for species listed under the ESA. The 1973 ESA prohibited the "taking" of a listed species, which meant killing, harming, capturing, or harassing. In 1975, the U.S. Fish and Wildlife Service expanded that prohibition to include the destruction of critical habitat as part of its definition of "harm." Various plaintiffs, including landowners, companies, and property owners affected by broadening of the definition, took the issue to court.[40]

In a 6-3 decision in 1995, the U.S. Supreme Court upheld the agency definition, resolving different interpretations of the law between two panels of circuit court judges. At issue was a policy enacted under President George Bush that allowed logging in areas that had been declared critical habitat for the Northern spotted owl, a threatened species. In *Babbitt v. Sweet Home Chapter of Communities for a Greater Oregon*[43], the latter a timber-industry-sponsored group, the court ruled that the common meaning of the term "harm" is broad and in the context of the ESA would encompass habitat modification that injures or kills members of an endangered species. The majority of the court also noted that the statute had been reasonably interpreted, while the dissenters on the court argued that the definition was so broad that it had the effect of penalizing actions regardless of whether they were intended or foreseeable.[42]

Environmental organizations hailed the *Sweet Home* decision as precedent for protecting entire ecosystems rather than individual species and believe that it gives government agencies such as the Fish and Wildlife Service more discretion in implementing the law. But groups within the environmental opposition called upon Congress to take action to alter the ESA, with one critic calling the court ruling "one more step down the road to agency control" and giving administrative agencies much more power than the Constitution intended.[43]

A second type of ESA litigation involves property owners who feel that the government is going too far in implementing the law. In 1992, two Klamath River Basin residents in Oregon filed suit against the Fish and Wildlife Service because the agency had curtailed their irrigation water to preserve two endangered fish, the Lost River sucker and the short-nosed sucker. The region includes about 275,000 acres of farmland, and the area had experienced a severe drought. Agency biologists monitoring the two fish set minimum water levels in two nearby lakes so that the fish could migrate to their natural habitat to spawn, but doing so meant that some users—farmers, city parks, and cemeteries— would get little or no water at all. Government officials admitted that they were unsure that the water diversion would be successful, but for many property owners, the efforts to save the fish came at a tremendous financial cost. Some were forced to try to drill wells to irrigate crops, while others found that they were expected to pay irrigation bills even though they received no water.[44]

In their suit, the ranchers argued that the protection measures were unnecessary and contrary to a provision of the law which requires regulators to consider the economic impact on a region when it declares an area a critical habitat. They alleged that the Fish and Wildlife Service irrigation cutoff had resulted in an estimated $75 million loss. In a unanimous 1997 decision, the United States Supreme Court agreed with the ranchers, ruling that individuals who feel harmed by what they see as overprotection of species may go to court to fight for less protection. Justice Antonin Scalia, writing for the Court, noted that the ESA allows "any person" to sue the government over an alleged violation, even when the plaintiffs seek to prevent application of environmental restrictions rather than to implement them. While the ruling was limited to only these two species, it did set a precedent that may someday be applied to persons adversely affected by other species' protection plans.

The Lingering Debate

There is a growing wave of opinion that the debate over the future of endangered species (and biodiversity in general) is becoming more political and less scientific in nature. Some observers of the process believed that many of the most important decisions about species survival are being made by political appointees who make policy only in response to the groups that provide financial support for their benefactors. This produces, they argue, a system in which there is a natural tension between politicians and scientists, and as the issue of conserving biodiversity becomes more important, it inevitably becomes more political.[45]

Critics of the ESA point to the numbers of species that have been delisted—an average of one species per year—as evidence that the law is not working effectively. They note that some species have been reclassified because their numbers improved, but that the improvement was the resulted factors other than the implementation of the law. The peregrine falcon, for example, was delisted in October 1995, but some have argued that the bird flourished not because of the ESA but because of a ban on pesticides that had previously been responsible for the death of many of the birds.[46]

Others note that many species that have been declining in population are making a comeback without the benefit of ESA protection. In 1930, for example, only thirty known trumpeter swans could be found along the Rocky Mountain flyway, a number that grew to an estimated three thousand by 1996. The Pacific Coast population of the bird grew fivefold from the 1970s to about fifteen thousand. The birds' comeback was a result of a management plan developed in the early 1980s by Ducks Unlimited and other private organizations such as the Wyoming Wetlands Society that helped create wildlife refuges. Opponents of the ESA believe that such private conservation efforts are both more cost-effective and efficient than the spending of millions of dollars by the federal government on recovery plans and surveys.

Environmental group leaders note that there are three factors that make it difficult to keep biodiversity on the public agenda: a lack of an easily identifiable opponent, a lack of any immediate impact on human life-styles, and a lack of cohesiveness by large groups around the widespread preservation of species. It is difficult, they say, to generate support or to motivate groups to mobilize to action even though species are becoming extinct because people's daily lives do not appear to be affected. The most difficult task seems to be convincing people, despite their concerns for endangered species, that there is a relationship between their own activities and the causes of endangerment. As a result, public attention begins to dissipate as policymakers realize the full costs of implementing protection measures.

One of the paradoxes of both the ESA and the CITES agreements is that a species is not protected until its population becomes so low that it is likely to become extinct. When that happens, recovery becomes both inefficient and costly. Recovery then begins to compromise the activities of other agencies (international, federal, state, and local), which must change their policies to accommodate the situation, increasing the probability of conflict. What this tells us about the future of endangered species and their habitats is that their protection requires the building of a much broader political constituency than currently exists. The actions of isolated organizations dedicated to the preservation of an individual species are unlikely to convince policymakers that there is a need for change. Instead, public policy is more likely to be politicized by groups whose economic prospects are influenced by what happens to their future.

THE FOREST DEBATE

While the protection of endangered species has been the center of the biodiversity controversy during the last three decades, an even longer running debate has continued over the world's forests, which cover almost one-third of the Earth's surface land. The issue is complicated by the fact that the planet is home to a variety of forest ecosystems, from the ancient forests of the United States, to the boreal forests of northern Canada and Russia, to the tropical forests circling the equator between the Tropic of Cancer and the Tropic of Capricorn. The management of forest resources has become an interest of global concern because in many instances, the conflicts that have erupted represent a duel between the "haves" and the "have nots." The issue has pitted environmental activists form urban areas against rural landowners, and representatives of industrialized nations against Third and Fourth World nations who have accused developed countries of "economic imperialism" in their attempts to control the fate of other countries' natural resources. The physical and biological diversity of forests, the large number of forest owners with often conflicting objectives, and increasing demands for wood for fuel, paper, shelter and artistic uses have made forest management especially challenging for policymakers.[47]

The rest of this chapter examines the forest debate from two perspectives. First, it provides an overview of the United States' timber management policy and the agencies charged with protecting forest resources. Second, it examines the ways in which other nations have attempted to preserve boreal and tropical forest diversity.

THE U.S. TIMBER MANAGEMENT POLICY

About one-third, or approximately 730 million acres, of the U.S. land area is forested, two-thirds of which (about 480 million acres) is considered timberland, capable of growing commercial crops of trees. The federal government owns about 20 percent of those lands, with 7 percent owned by state and local governments, 1 percent by Native American nations, 58 percent by private nonindustrial owners, and 14 percent by the forest industry. American timber management is complex, and involves concerns about jobs, economic diversity, endangered species and their habitats, and global warming. At opposite ends in the policy debate are timber companies and environmental groups, with federal agencies caught squarely in the middle.

Federal stewardship of the nation's forest resources can be traced back to 1873, when the American Association for the Advancement of Science petitioned

Congress to enact legislation to protect and properly manage U.S. forests. Despite the creation of a special bureau, the Division of Forestry, timber management practices were rife with scandal and exploitation. Forest policy was truncated by a division of responsibility between the Division of Forestry (in the Department of Agriculture) and the General Land Office (in the Department of the Interior). In 1901, the Division of Forestry changed its name, becoming the Bureau of Forestry, and four years later, became the Forest Service. From 1910 to 1928, the agency concerned itself primarily with fire prevention and control, and Congress had little power over forests on private lands.[48]

It was not until the Forest Service gradually began increasing the harvest of national forest land after World War II that the agency became the target of environmental interests. The need for timber that resulted from postwar economic growth was in conflict with public demand for recreational use of the nation's forests. Congress perceived that Forest Service as a commodity and income-producing agency, and timber harvests increased from 3.5 to 8.3 billion board feet during the decade of the 1950s.[49] In addition to competing public pressures, the development of a comprehensive federal forest policy was thwarted by the lack of congressional direction other than broad mandates.[50] As a result, the Forest Service operated under the dual traditions of planning—utilitarian and protective—that were the legacy of its first chief, Gifford Pinchot, who believed that wise use and preservation of forest resources were compatible goals. The resulting policy—multiple use—meant that the national forests were to serve competing interests: ranchers seeking land for grazing their livestock, recreational visitors seeking to spend their leisure time outdoors, and miners hoping to make their fortunes on as yet undiscovered lodes.

As a response to the fledgling environmental movement that advocated the setting aside of more wilderness areas, Congress enacted the Multiple-Use Sustained-Yield Act (MUSYA) of 1960, followed by the Forest and Rangeland Renewable Resources Planning Act (RPA) of 1974, and the National Forest management Act of 1976 (NFMA). The MUSYA gave equal footing to the use of forests for recreation, grazing, and wildlife as well as timber and watershed uses, although there was little direction as to how the law was to be administered. Critics argued that the Forest Service was out of step with the emerging ethic of environmentalism, and the agency became perceived as an enemy of the people. Congressional leaders began to recognize the growing criticism over the federal government's lead of long-term planning, and the increasing polarization of forestry issues between the timber industry and environmental groups. Both the RPA and its amendments (the NFMA) provided the Forest Service with some direction, requiring inventories of forest resources and an assessment of the costs and benefits of meeting the nation's forest resource needs.[51]

Although the legislation satisfied some critics, forest policy was far from complete, and the agency came under fire from its own employees, who alleged the Forest Service had been captured by timber interests and was inconsistent in its implementation of the law. In 1988, former staffer, Jeff DeBonis, founded a group called the Association of Forest Service Employees for Environmental Ethics as a way of encouraging its members to speak out against agency policies and abuses.[52] The organization began as an in-house protest against the Forest Service policy of clear-cutting—the logging of all trees within a given stand. The practice, in addition to being aesthetically unpleasing, often leads to erosion and has been widely criticized by environmental groups. DeBonis' organization marked one of the first time government employees had rallied against a particular cause, although some observers felt his actions were not constructive, given the Forest Service's history of institutional loyalty.[53] But DeBonis and his group believed the agency had forgotten its mission of serving the public and had become totally politicized.[54]

There is little doubt that American forest policy has focused on economic and political considerations, with the Forest Service at the center of the controversy. One group, Resources for the Future, found that Forest Service timber management expenditures are only minimally related to timber production potential, as measured by actual receipts from timber sales.[55] Another report by a congressional committee found that 110 of the nation's 120 national forests were losing money, since trees were being sold to timber companies at a price lower than what it costs to prepare a site for logging and managing the sales. The loss to taxpayers over ten years was estimated at $5.6 billion.[56] And a 1992 study by the congressional Office of Technology Assessment criticized the agency for favoring timber interests over protecting and preserving undeveloped land. The study said that the agency's budgets, planning process, and historical perspective favored physical production over the forests' other values. Industry sources agree that costs exceed revenues in some cases, but point out that the Forest Service has a mandate to improve the forest and manage revenues for the greatest net benefit, not the greatest dollar return. They agree that sales that fail to provide benefits to the public, multiple-use values, or the health of the forest should be eliminated.[57] Sweeping reforms, including a total restructuring of the agency, new budgetary incentives, and the introduction of ecosystem management practices, have been proposed as the criticism continues.[58]

The timber management debate has picked up steam over the past decade as environmental groups turned to the courts to protect forests through endangered species provisions and the timber industry sought relief at the ballot box, giving their support to public officials who side with loggers over preservationists. An initiative to protect old-growth forests in California was turned down by voters in 1990, and former Oregon governor Barbara Roberts became the target of three statewide recall efforts after comments that she made were interpreted as being anti-timber. In Maine, voters rejected a 1996 referendum that proposed a ban on clear-cutting on 10 million acres of northern forests. Governor Angus King said that the plan would have cost the state thousands of jobs. The paper industry spent mote than $5 million fighting the proposal, the most expensive referendum ever in Maine.[59]

Perhaps the most indicative measure of the continuing volatility of U.S. timber policy was the salvage logging rider attached to the 1995 Rescissions Act, an effort to cut spending that had already been appropriated by the 103rd Congress. The rider suspended the coverage of environmental laws in order to facilitate the logging of dead and dying trees. The language of the bill was expansive, allowing logging companies to remove healthy trees if they were associated with trees susceptible to fire or disease. As a result, the Forest Service expedited logging contracts and permitted some areas to be logged that likely would never have been approved if environmental reviews had been required. Industry groups defended the rider as an essential step to ensure supplies of timber and promote forest health. However, there was little commercial interest in much of the salvage timber that was put on the market. By April 1996 there were more than 100 sales announced that had not received any bids. The bids that were awarded included the price of some trees at less than a dollar each. Some areas that had been off-limits to loggers were suddenly made available and environmental groups claimed that the rider seemed aimed at opening old-growth forests to timber cuts, including areas that had previously been protected as habitat for bears and other species. But environmental organizations were unsuccessful in trying to get the Clinton administration to veto the Recessions Act and just as fruitless in getting Congress to pass new legislation to curb what they termed "logging without laws." The salvage timber rider expired on December 31, 1996, prompting a flurry of cuts before the end of the year.[60]

PROTECTING BOREAL AND TROPICAL FOREST DIVERSITY

Deforestation is an equally volatile issue outside the United States. The boreal forests of the far North comprise nearly one-third of the world's timberland, serving as a major carbon sink as well as home to plants and animals and to a million indigenous people who have lived in the forests for centuries. Massive logging in Canada has disrupted ecosystems, displaced native peoples, polluting rivers with toxic chemicals used in the bleaching of pulp, and subsidizing major multi-national corporations. An estimated 90 percent of boreal logging is clear-cutting, and 25 percent of these areas do not regenerate as topsoil erodes away during and after logging, which also destroys permafrost, the layer below the topsoil that acts as a heat reservoir in the winter. As the permafrost retreats, risks to the forests from fires, pests, and species composition grows; the downward spiral contributes to the threat of global climate change as the carbon sink is lost and carbon from dead trees is increasingly released into the atmosphere.[61]

Logging of similar forests in Russia is occurring even faster in an effort to generate much-needed foreign currency. Clear-cutting, combined with emissions from smelters and radioactive pollution, poses a serious threat to forests throughout the former Soviet Union. Scandinavian forests, largely in private hands, are facing similar problems. Private landowners log old-growth forests next to lands where trees are protected. While reforestation is standard practice and a few companies have switched to chlorine-free production of pepper, biodiversity has suffered. There are major challenges to boreal forests throughout the world: below-cost timber subsidies that waste resources, minimal environmental review of proposed logging efforts, disposal of timberlands that are home to indigenous peoples, and large-scale clearcutting that threatens the sustainability of forest production.[62]

Since almost all boreal forest policy is governed by sovereign nations rather than by international accord, individual countries have approached timber management in their own way. British Columbia, for example, has developed an ambitious program to replant forest lands that were heavily harvested in the nineteenth and early twentieth centuries. Little value had been assigned to forests, which were continuously cut so the land could be used for agriculture. By the 1940s, officials realized that the provincial forests were not limitless, and timber companies began replanting areas that had been clear-cut. The Forest Act of 1947 recognized the forests as economic resources and established the goal of ensuring a perpetual supply of timber under the principle of sustained yield forestry. By the early 1970s, provincial officials began to realize that logging rates were not sustainable, as timber cuts continued to climb as the promise of immediate jobs and profits overwhelmed a projected loss of sustainability. Modernization of logging technology resulted in job losses as timber harvests leveled off and increasing international competition impinged on profits. Preservationists lobbied successfully for the creation of parks that also reduced the potential supply of timber.[63] In 1993, the government, prompted by projections that forest harvests were likely to decline by 15–30 percent over the next fifty years, established a Forest Sector Strategy Committee to find ways to balance the competing values of forests and review policies that protect watersheds, wildlife, and the rights and concerns of indigenous peoples.[64]

Similar problems plague the world's tropical rainforests, four-fifths of which are concentrated in nine countries: Bolivia, Brazil (with one-third of the worldwide total), Columbia, Gabon, Indonesia (with another one-third), Malaysia, Peru, Venezuela, and Zaire. There are two major issues currently being addressed by global policymakers. One, although there is a lack of precise information about the rate of loss, there is consensus among scientists that tropical forests are disappearing at an alarming and ever-increasing rate. Two, there is also agreement that failure to effectively manage tropical forests can result in a number of negative impacts, including the loss of wood products for fuel and other uses, soil erosion, global warming, shrinking populations of plants in the wild, destruction of fish breeding areas, and loss of biological diversity and wildlife habitat.

Estimates as to how much tropical forest remains are notoriously unreliable and depend in large part on what definition of forest is used. One researcher believes that only 57 percent of Earth's original 8.65 million square miles of moist tropical forest remains, meaning that an area the size of the former Soviet Union has disappeared, much of it since 1945. The rate of worldwide tropical deforestation was about 120,000 square miles per year in 1979, between 175,000 and 220,000 square miles per year just ten years later, and may be as high as from 1.18 percent per year now.[65] While most of the loss results from burning for agricultural purposes, with another 20–25 percent of the deforestation attributable to commercial logging, some losses are not the result of human actions. In 1983, for example, a forest fire in northeastern Borneo during a period of severe drought resulted in the loss of an area of tropical forest the size of Belgium.

Deforestation in tropical areas occurs primarily on lands not held by private citizens, especially in developing areas, where over four-fifths of closed forest areas is public land. In some countries, nearly 100 percent of all natural forest is government owned, giving officials total authority over the use and preservation of the land. Thus, the rates of deforestation vary considerably from one region of the world to another. In Southeast Asia, rates range from less than 1 percent in Kampuchea to 8 percent in Thailand. China is estimated to have lost nearly 40 percent of its rainforest to rubber plantations, logging, and the pressures of feeding a rapidly increasing population. In the Philippines, natural forest cover has shrunk from two-thirds of total land areas to only 22 percent since 1945, while in Central America, forest areas declined by 38 percent between 1950 and 1983. Western Equador is estimated to have less than 10 percent of its original forests, and Madagascar, about 7 percent.[66]

The logging of tropical forests and their products has been occurring for nearly five hundred years, beginning with the collection of rare and valuable spices such as pepper and cinnamon by Southeast Asian traders. However, early merchants tended to collect only what they wanted and did not destroy the forests in their search for spices. During most of the nineteenth century, Europeans sought African hardwood for furniture but left the rest of the forest intact. Latin American forests, in contrast, were often burned to the ground as Spanish settlers established colonial outposts and set up plantation agriculture, with the export of agricultural commodities quickly proving to be a lucrative enterprise for several nations. The United States entered the picture in the 1880s when U.S. investors edged out their Spanish competitors and built huge sugar processing facilities dependent upon crops in Cuba and in the Pacific islands of Hawaii and the Philippines. The sugar barons' quest for increased profits meant that increasingly more forest acreage was cleared and sugar cane became the primary vegetation in many areas, pushing out tropical woods. The logging of native forests for sugar cane was followed by devoting massive acreage to growing tropical fruits, such as bananas in Costa Rica and Nicaragua.[67]

In the 1920s and 1930s, international journals of forestry documented the rapid destruction of tropical forests, but there was little political attention to the problem at that time, as was the case between World War II and the advent of the international environmental movement in the early 1970s. The more highly publicized issues of pollution crowded the top of the environmental protection agenda, especially in industrialized nations. It was not until the early 1980s that international organizations, such as the UN's Food and Agriculture Organization

(FAO), the UN Development Programme, and the World Bank began to systematically review scientific literature on deforestation.

Some of the forest protection issues are of relatively recent origin. In southern Chile, for example, widespread logging did not begin until the 1980s, when native trees were cut and ground into small chips that are shipped to Japan to be processed into paper. Although thirty million acres of Chilean forest are protected in reserves, the nineteen million acres estimated to be in private hands are often destructively cut by landowners seeking quick profits. The forestry industry has grown into one of Chile's main export earners. Attempts by groups such as the California-based Ancient Forests International and Chile's National Committee for the Defense of the Flora and Fauna have been largely unsuccessful in convincing the Chilean government to enforce existing regulations that limit cutting and provide for restoration. Few violators are prosecuted and even fewer are convicted by Chilean courts.

Now, as some countries' tropical forest resources are being depleted, international attention is being focused on regions where commercial logging was previously limited or inaccessible. Since the demand for tropical woods has not slowed, logging cartels are looking at areas of New Guinea, China, and New Caledonia, considered "hot-spot" regions of destruction.[68] This means that more nations, by necessity, will become stakeholders and involved in the debate over forest diversity.

Efforts to protect tropical forests are much better funded and organized than attempts to preserve the Earth's ancient and boreal forest regions. Environmental organizations throughout the world have rallied against tropical deforestation, agreeing, for the most part, on the urgency of the problem. But there is also a gulf that separates the groups in their approaches to what should be done.

Globally, there is a division between the more radical groups seeking to ban trade in timber from virgin rainforests (such as the World Rainforest Movement), and more traditional groups, primarily in the United States, that believe the solution is to "green" the development process. Mainstream organizations such as the World Resources Institute and Friends of the Earth have supported the World Bank's efforts to improve economic conditions in developing countries. Other groups, such as Greenpeace, have established tropical forest units within their organization, and have attempted to lobby government officials to add more land to existing forest reserves, such as Costa Rica's Monteverde Cloud Forest. Indigenous peoples's groups, such as India's chipko movement, have attempted to resist state encroachment upon their homelands. The groups are seeking to control not only forest practices, but also mining, the siting of dams, and other projects that affect natural resources and land management.[69]

To slow the world demand for exotic woods, the more radical groups have proposed a ban on the sale of tropical timber. They want the International Tropical Timber Organization (ITTO) to severely restrict timber harvests and trade. The organization administers the 1984 International Tropical Timber Agreement, but critics argue that the group has the somewhat contradictory role of both protecting forests and regulating the timber trade upon which many of its member nations depend.[70] Some attempts have been made to reduce trade in tropical wood under CITES, which covers both fauna and flora. In 1997, the U.S. worked out a compromise with Brazil to allow the United Nations to monitor trade in mahogany, although environmental groups had sought to have mahogany products included on a list that would have allowed only controlled trade. Developing nations have been critical of the U.S. and environmental groups for failing to recognize the desire of their people to overcome widespread poverty in areas dependent upon forest products and their allied jobs, including shipping and processing industries.

Other than an outright ban on timber, other solutions to tropical deforestation vary in their practicality and level of international support. The World Wildlife Fund and Friends of the Earth, for example, believe that the equipment and the types of forest management being used in these regions needs to be modernized. Current harvesting practices, they argue, are inefficient and waste much of the forest's resources. They have called for an end to existing logging practices and feel that technological advances could bring about extraction that is more compatible with sustainable management.[71] Other observers believe that a complete restructuring of timber taxing and sales practices is needed, since governments in these areas receive only a fraction of the rents from logging. Virtually all tropical countries also provide generous tax incentives for timber processing and logging, with the benefits accruing to the wealthiest strata of the population. The most commonly voiced solution is the creation of forest reserves, which many researchers argue is the only way to save tropical forests at this point. They believe that destruction is proceeding too fast for restoration to be effective because a damaged tropical forest does not regenerate quickly. The idea is costly, even when coupled with the concept of debt-for-nature swaps that allow developing countries to repay outstanding loans to industrialized nations and lending institutions by establishing forest reserves as a way of paying off their foreign debt. But even the most optimistic estimates show that tropical deforestation is outpacing any current attempts to slow the rate of loss.

SUMMARY

The protection of species dates back to the earliest legal history when, under Roman law, wild animals were given the same status as the ocean and air, belonging to no one. Gradually, laws began to be enacted that protected wildlife for commercial value, and later, for reasons of aesthetics and biodiversity. In the United States, the first laws to protect endangered species were passed in the 1960s, followed by a more comprehensive law in 1973. The process by which species are listed for protection has become extremely controversial, and environmental groups have criticized the federal government for the way it prioritizes recovery efforts and the development of critical habitat for each specie. Other critics of the legislation believe Congress has gone too far in its regulatory efforts, spending scarce resources on plants and animal protection without considering the economic impact on property owners or communities affected by a listing. Internationally, the development of a regime to protect endangered species paralleled U.S. laws, with passage of the Convention on Trade in Endangered Species of Wild Fauna and Flora in 1975. Unlike the U.S., the international community has limited its role to regulating trade rather than preservation of species. A second focus on diversity comes from efforts to protect the world's ancient, boreal, and tropical forests. In the United States, forest protection began in 1873, with the emphasis of timber management shifting from commercial logging on public lands to multiple use and sustainability. The issue has been extremely volatile, with environmental groups criticizing the U.S. Forest Service for policies perceived as favoring the timber industry, and logging interests angered by what they believe are unrealistic limits on how much timber can be cut and where. From a global perspective, there is little doubt that both boreal and tropical deforestation is a problem warranting international intervention. But there is a gulf between those who seek to ban timber from virgin rainforests and developing countries who feel environmental groups have failed to recognize the desire of their people to overcome widespread poverty in areas dependent upon forest products and their allied jobs.

NOTES

1. The comments were made in an interview with the *Denver Post* and quoted in Joe Hallinan, "Manuel Lujan: Genial Tender of the Interior," *The Oregonian,* December 5, 1991, A–3.

2. In 1994, a federal district court vacated the Department of the Interior's listing of the California gnatcatcher as a threatened species. The ruling came about as a result of a 1992 lawsuit filed by the Southern California Building Industry Association and other local agencies who argued that there were significant questions about the scientific merits of the study upon which the listing was based.

3. William Claiborne, "In California Compromise, Developers and Environmentalists Benefit," *The Washington Post,* August 18, 1996. A3.

4. See Paul Ehrlich and Anne Ehrlich, *Extinction: The Causes and Consequences of the Disappearance of Species* (New York: Random House, 1981).

5. U.S. Executive Office of the President, Council on Environmental Quality. *The Global 2000 Report to the President,* vol. 1 (Washington, D.C.: U.S. Government Printing Office, 1980), 37.

6. U.S. Executive Office of the President, U.S. Council on Environmental Quality. *The Evolution of National Wildlife Law* (Washington, D.C.: U.S. Government Printing Office,1977), 17. One of the critical decisions of this period, *Geer v. Connecticut,* 161 U.S. 519 (1896) upheld a state law regulating the transportation of game birds outside Connecticut. Despite the narrow legal issue raised in the case, it is considered to be the bulwark of the state ownership doctrine even today.

7. See John Nichol, *The Animal Smuggler* (New York: Facts on File, 1987).

8. Susan Lieberman, "Japan Agrees to Phase Out Trade in Endangered Sea Turtles," *Endangered Species Technical Bulletin, 16,* nos. 7–8 (1991): 4–6.

9. See Gareth Porter and Janet Welsh Brown, *Global Environmental Politics,* 2d ed. (Boulder, CO: Westview Press, 1996), 82–85; Nick Cater, "Preserving the Pachyderm," *Africa Report, 34,* no. 6 (November–December 1989): 45–58; Sue Armstrong and Fred Bridgland, "Elephants and the Ivory Tower," *New Scientist,* August 26, 1989, 37–41.

10. See "Elephant Skin and Bones," *The Economist,* February 29, 1992, 48; Peter Aldhous, "Critics Urge Reform of CITES Endangered List," *Nature, 355,* (February 27, 1992): 758–759: Peter Aldhous, "African Rift in Kyoto," *Nature, 354* (November 21, 1991): 175; and Steven R. Weisman, "Bluefin Tuna and African Elephants Win Some Help at a Global Meeting," *The New York Times,* March 11, 1992, A–8.

11. Lawrence E. Susskind, *Environmental Diplomacy: Negotiating More Effective Global Agreements* (New York: Oxford University Press, 1994), 102–103.

12. David E. Pitt, "A Biological Treaty to Save Species Becomes Law," *The New York Times,* January 2, 1994, Sec. 1, 4.

13. Jeffrey A. McNeely, "The Future of Natural Parks," *Environment, 32,* no. 1 (January–February 1990): 17–20, 36–42.

14. See Steven Lewis Yaffee, *The Wisdom of the Spotted Owl: U.S. Politics and the Protection of Biological Diversity* (Washington, D.C.: Island Press, 1994).

15. Bob Benenson, "Conferees' Interior Initiatives May Get Clinton's Veot," *Congressional Quarterly Weekly Report,* September 23, 1995, 2883–2884.

16. 104th Congress, H.R. 2275.

17. 104th Congress, S. 768.

18. 104th Congress, S. 1364.

19. James A. Tober, *Wildlife and the Public Interest: Nonprofit Organizations and Federal Wildlife Policy* (New York: Praeger, 1989), 24.

20. See John Cordell, "the Nature Conservancy: Databanking on Diversity," *Computerland Magazine,* November–December 1990, 19–20.

21. For a perspective on the role of hunters in wildlife conservation, see Roger L. Disilvestro, *The Endangered Kingdom: The Struggle to Save America's Wildlife* (New York: Wiley, 1989). For specific specie protection issues, see, for example, Oliver H. Hewitt, ed., *The Wild Turkey and Its Management* (Washington, D.C.: Wildlife Society, 1967); Douglas L. Gilbert, *White-tailed Deer: Ecology and Management* (Harrisburg, PA: Stackpole Books, 1984); William J. Chandler, *Audubon Wildlife Report* (San Diego, CA: Academic Press, 1988); and Jim Robbins, "When Species Collide," *National Wildlife, 26* (February–March 1988): 20–27. On the role of the recreational fishing industry, see George Reiger, "Good Vibes," *Field and Stream,* April 1995, 16–17, 22.

22. Tober, *Wildlife and the Public Interest,* 48.

23. *Mission Statement,* Grassroots ESA Coalition (Battle Ground, WA, 1995).

24. See Tober, *Wildlife and the Public Interest,* 59–83; Mark Crawford, "The Last Days of the Wild Condor? *Science, 229* (August 30, 1985): 845; David Phillips and Hugh Nash. *The Condor Question: Captive or Forever Free?* (San Francisco, CA: Friends of the Earth, 1981); and William W. Johnson, "California Condor: Embroiled in a Flap Not of Its Own Making," *Smithsonian,* December 1985, 73–80.

25. For a journalist's account of the plight of endangered species such as the dodo, see Douglas Adams and Mark Carwardine, *Last Chance to See* (New York: Harmony Books, 1990).

26. *Statement of Principles for Reform of the Endangered Species Act* (Battle Ground, WA: Grassroots ESA Coalition, July 10, 1995).

27. See William B. Wheeler, *TVA and the Tellico Dam* (Knoxville, TN: University of Tennessee Press, 1986), and William Chandler, *Myth of the Tennessee Valley Authority* (Cambridge, MA: Ballinger, 1984).

28. Ehrlich and Ehrlich, *Extinction,* 182–186.

29. See John M. Volkman, "Making Room in the Ark: The Endangered Species Act and the Columbia River Basin," *Environment, 34,* no. 4 (May 1992): 18.

30. See Tom Horton, "The Endangered Species Act: Too Tough, Too Weak, or Too Late?" *Audubon, 94* (March–April 1992): 68–74.

31. Donald J. Barry, *For Conserving Listed Species, Talk is Cheaper Than We Think* (Washington, D.C.: World Wildlife Fund, 1992).

32. See generally, George Cameron Coggins and Parthenia Blessing Evans, "Predators' Rights and American Wildlife Law," *Arizona Law Review, 24,* no. 4 (Fall 1982): 822–823;

Thomas R. Dunlap, "Values for Varmints: Predator Control and Environmental Ideas," *Pacific Historical Review, 53,* no. 2 (1984); David Todd, "Wolves–Predator Control and Endangered Species Protection: Thoughts on Politics and Law," *South Texas Law Review, 33,* no. 3 (July 1992), 461; and Donald G. Scheuler, *Incident at Eagle Ranch* (San Francisco, CA: Sierra Club Books, 1980).

33. See *Fund for Animals v. Andrus,* 11 E.R.C. 2189 (D. Minn. 1978).

34. Christopher Smith, "Wolf-Restoration Program Picks Up Private Support," *The Oregonian,* December 17, 1995, A27.

35. Gwen Florio, "Montana Ranchers Blame Wolf Issue on Washington," *The Oregonian,* March 17, 1996, A15.

36. Renee Askins, "Releasing Wolves from Symbolism," *Harpers, 290* (April 1995), 16.

37. Askins, "Releasing Wolves from Symbolism," 15–17. See also Rick McIntyre, *A Society of Wolves* (Stillwater, MN: Voyageur Press, 1993), and Rocky Barker, *Saving All the Parts: Reconciling Economics and the Endangered Species Act* (Washington, D.C.: Island Press, 1993), 175–198.

38. *Sierra Club v. Froehlke,* 534 F.2d 1289 (8th Cir. 1976).

39. *National Wildlife Federation v. Coleman,* 529 F.2d 359 (5th Cir. 1976).

40. See Lettie McSpadden, "Environmental Policy in the Courts," in *Environmental Policy in the 1990s,* 3d ed., eds. Norman J. Vig and Michael E. Kraft (Washington, D.C.: Congressional Quarterly Press, 1997, 168–186.

41. 115 S. Ct. 2407 (1995).

42. See John H. Cushman Jr., "Environmentalists Win Victory, but Action by Congress May Interrupt the Celebration," *The New York Times,* June 30, 1995; and "Regulating Habitat Modification," *Congressional Digest,* March 1996, 72.

43. "Sweet Home v. Babbitt," *Update* (Boise, ID: Stewards of the Range, August 1995), 3.

44. Mark Freeman, "The Year of the Sucker," *Medford (OR) Mail Tribune,* May 3, 1992, 1A.

45. Jeffrey A. McNeely, "Report on Reports," *Environment, 34,* no. 2 (March 1992): 25. See also Richard Tobin, *The Expendable Future: U.S. Politics and the Protection of Biological Diversity* (Durham, NC: Duke University Press, 1991).

46. Mark L. Plummer, "Is the Endangered Species Act Fundamentally Sound?" *Congressional Digest,* March 1996, 81–83.

47. For an overview of forestry policy, see Frederick W. Cubbage, Jay O'Laughlin, and Charles S. Bullock III, *Forest Resource Policy* (New York: John Wiley and Sons, 1993).

48. See Christopher McGrory Klyza, *Who Controls Public Lands? Mining, Forestry, and Grazing Policies, 1970–1990* (Chapel Hill, NC: University of North Carolina Press, 1996), 67–107.

49. See Paul Culhane, *Public Lands Policies* (Baltimore, MD: Johns Hopkins University Press, 1981).

50. See Charles F. Wilkinson and H. Michael Anderson, *Land and Resource Planning in the National Forests* (Covelo, CA: Island Press, 1987).

51. Cubbage, O'Laughlin, and Bullock, *Forest Resource Policy,* 327–336.

52. See, for example, Paul Schneider, "When a Whistle Blows in the Forest," *Audubon,* 7 (July 1990): 42–49; and Jim Stiak, "Memos to the Chief," *Sierra,* 75, no. 4 (July–August 1990): 26–29.

53. For perspectives on the U.S. Forest Service and its employees, see Herbert Kaufman, *The Forest Ranger: A Study in Administrative Behavior* (Baltimore, MD: Johns Hopkins University Press, 1960); and Harold K. Steen, *The U.S. Forest Service: A History* (Seattle, WA: University of Washington Press, 1976).

54. See William Dietrich, *The Final Forest: The Battle for the Last Great Trees of the Pacific Northwest* (New York: Penguin Books, 1992), 161–168.

55. Marion Clawson, "The National Forests," *Science,* 191, February 20, 1976: 762–767.

56. Schneider, "When a Whistle Blows in the Forest," 46.

57. The industry view is found in publications of groups like the American Forest Coun-

cil, American Forest Resource Alliance, the California Redwood Association, and the Timber Association of California. See, for example, *Forest Resource Fact Book* 2nd ed. (Memphis, TN: National Hardwood Lumber Association, 1991).

58. See, for example, Kathryn A. Kohm and Jerry F. Franklin, eds., *Creating A Forestry for the Twenty-First Century: The Science of Ecosystem Management* (Washington, D.C.: Island Press, 1997); Randal O'Toole, *Reforming the Forest Service* (Washington, D.C.: Island Press, 1988); and David A. Clary, *Timber and the Forest Service* (Lawrence, KS: University Press of Kansas, 1986).

59. Robert Pear, "The 1996 Elections: The States—The Initiatives," *New York Times,* November 7, 1996, B7.

60. Patti Goldman, "1995 Logging without Laws: Legislating By Budget Rider," *Environment,* 38, no. 3 (April 1996): 41–43.

61. Anjali Acharya, "Plundering the Boreal Forests," *WorldWatch* (May–June 1995): 21–29.

62. Acharya, "Plundering the Boreal Forests."

63. Western Canada Wilderness Committee, "How to Save Jobs in the B. C. Woods," Educational Report, 12, no. 8 (Winter 1993–94).

64. Government of British Columbia, "British Columbia's Forest Renewal Plan" (Victoria, BC: Queen's Printer, 1994): 1–5.

65. Malcolm Gillis, "Tropical Deforestation: Economic, Ecological, and Ethical Dimensions," *The South Atlantic Quarterly,* 90, no. 1 (Winter 1991): 7–38. See also C. J. Jepma, *Tropical Deforestation: A Socio-Economic Approach* (London: Earthscan, 1995).

66. See "Half of World's Deforestation Occurs outside the Amazon," *National Wildlife,* 27 (August–September 1989): 25.

67. See Richard P. Tucker, "Five Hundred Years of Tropical Forest Exploitation," in *Lessons of the Rainforest,* eds. Suzanne Head and Robert Heinzmann (San Francisco, CA: Sierra club Books, 1990), 39–52.

68. "Lost in the Forest," *The Economist,* August 31, 1991, 30.

69. An extensive survey of the chipko movement and its predecessor rebellions is chronicled by Ramachandra Guha, *The Unquiet Woods: Ecological Change and Peasant Resistance in the Himalaya* (Berkeley, CA: University of California Press, 1990). See also Vandan Shiva, *Ecology and the Politics of Survival: Conflicts Over Natural Resources in India* (New Delhi: Sage Publications of India, 1991); and Renu Khator, *Environment, Development, and Politics in India* (Lanham, MD: University Press of America, 1991).

70. See Nigel Dudley, Jean-Paul Jeanrenaud, and Francis Sullivan, *Bad Harvest: The Timber Trade and the Degradation of the World's Forests* (London: Earthscan, 1995); and Edward Barbier and Joanne Burgess, *Economics of the Tropical Timber Trade* (Delray Beach, FL: St. Lucie Press, 1995).

71. See Francois Nectouxa nd Nigel Dudley, *A Hard Wood Story: Europe's Involvement in the Tropical Timber Trade* (London: Friends of the Earth, 1987).

FOR FURTHER READING

William S. Alverson, Donald M. Waller, and Walter Kuhlman. *World Forests: Conservation Biology and Public Policy*. Washington, D.C.: Island Press, 1994.

Terry L. Anderson and Peter J. Hill, eds. *Wildlife in the Marketplace*. Lanham, MD: Rowman and Littlefield, 1995.

Solon L. Barraclough and Krishna B. Ghimire. *Forests and Livelihoods: The Social Dynamics of Deforestation in Developing Countries*. New York: St. Martin's, 1995.

Tim W. Clark, Richard P. Reading, and Alice L. Clarke, eds. *Endangered Species Recovery: Finding the Lessons, Improving the Process*. Washington, D.C.: Island Press, 1994.

Mary Byrd Davis, ed. *Eastern Old Growth Forests*. Washington, D.C.: Island Press, 1996.

R. Edward Grumbine, ed., *Environmental Policy and Diversity*. Washington, D.C.: Island Press, 1994.

Ginette Hemley. *International Wildlife Trade: A CITES Sourcebook*. Washington, D.C.: Island Press, 1994.

Chris Maser. *Sustainable Forestry: Philosophy, Science, and Economics*. Delray Beach, FL: St. Lucie Press, 1994.

Kenton R. Miller, *Balancing the Scales: Managing Biodiversity at the Bioregional Level*. Washington, D.C.: World Resources Institute, 1996.

Bryan A. Norton, Michael Hutchins, Elizabeth F. Stevens, and Terry L. Maple, eds. *Ethics on the Ark: Zoos, Animal Welfare, and Wildlife Conservation*. Washington, D.C.: Smithsonian Institution Press, 1995.

Reed Noss and Allen Cooperrider. *Saving Nature's Legacy*. Washington, D.C.: Island Press, 1994.

Susan E. Place, ed. *Tropical Rainforests*. Wilmington, DE: Scholarly Resources, 1993.

Simon Rietbargen, ed. *Tropical Forestry*. Delray Beach, FL: St. Lucid Press, 1994.

Kathryn A. Kohm and Jerry F. Franklin, eds. *Creating a Forestry for the Twenty-First Century*. Washington, D.C.: Island Press, 1996.

CHAPTER 11

The Human Explosion: Managing Population Growth

While you are reading these words four people will have died from starvation. Most of them children.
    —Dr. Paul R. Ehrlich, *The Population Bomb* (1968)[1]

In the six seconds it takes you to read this sentence, eighteen more people will be added [to the population.]
    —Dr. Paul R. Ehrlich, *The Population Explosion* (1990)[2]

In 1968, when Paul Ehrlich's book, *The Population Bomb,* first appeared, most Americans were shocked. Ehrlich predicted a population explosion accompanied by massive famine and starvation—a prophecy that nevertheless did not come to pass. The reason? In the mid-1970s there was a slight decline in the global population growth rate, and it looked as though the population might stabilize at about 10.2 billion toward the end of the next century. Many demographers called Ehrlich an alarmist, while others argued that population growth was actually a positive force because it accelerated progress and development, forcing humanity to use more ingenuity and resourcefulness. Regardless of the timeliness of the prediction, Ehrlich was correct in point out that the Earth is a closed system, with limited resources. At the same time, the world's population is increasing at a current rate of three people every second—a quarter of a million new mouths to feed every day. Ehrlich's comments in his 1990 book brought into focus an issue that has profound economic, ethical, religious, and political implications. What will happen to the environment if steps are not taken to *manage* population growth?

One of the key phrases often used to answer that question, and one that has appeared often in this book, is *sustainable development*. The term is used to describe policies that balance the needs of people today against the resources that will be needed in the future. It takes into consideration policies related to agriculture production, energy efficiency, health, reduction of poverty, and reduction in consumption. Individuals practice this concept when they recycle cans, bottles, newspapers, and plastics, carpool to work or bicycle instead of commuting alone in automobiles; or turn their thermostats down to use less electricity or install solar heating systems in their home. Each of these actions is taken in recognition that the Earth's resources are not unlimited and that we must restrict our consumption of those resources.

The possibility of sustainable development is built on the idea of carrying capacity. The carrying capacity of an ecosystem is the limit of resource consumption and pollution production that it can maintain without undergoing a significant transformation. If the carrying capacity is exceeded, then life cannot continue unless it adapts to a new level of consumption or receives external resources. Carrying capacity is affected by three main factors: the size of the human population, the per capita consumption of resources, and the pollution and environmental degradation resulting from consumption of each unit of resources. The task of residents of any ecosystem is to find what level of resource consumption and pollution production is sustainable. That may not be obvious until it is too late, but there are some intermediate indicators, such as the buildup of pollution and an increase in the resultant harms or a decline in a resource as it is depleted faster than it is replenished.

Population growth and consumption in the wealthy countries is the primary source of global environmental threats. While population growth rates have stabilized in these nations, consumption of resources and generation of pollution and wastes continue to grow. But population growth in the developing world increases the pressure on the biosphere. The problems of environmental degradation and poverty are intricately intertwined. Many of the most pressing environmental problems are the by-products of modern, industrialized life. As one writer put it, "poverty can drive ecological deterioration when desperate people over exploit their resource base, sacrificing the future to salvage the present." Environmental decline "perpetuates poverty, as degraded ecosystems offer diminishing yields to their poor inhabitants. A self-feeding downward spiral of economic deprivation and ecological degradation takes hold."[3] People in the developing world depend immediately and directly on natural resources for their survival. In their struggle for survival, the poor of the world are likely to harm their environment and make their survival even more tenuous. Further, as resources are stretched for survival, poorer countries will have even less ability to mediate the effects of climate change and other problems, unlike residents of the developed world who will have the resources to protect themselves against at least some environmental threats.

The idea of sustainable development as used by the World Bank, United Nations, industry groups, and others is a very optimistic concept that assumes that economic growth will produce the wealth to pay for technological innovations that reduce environmental impacts. Free trade, neoliberal restructuring of national economies and policies, and economic growth and consumption are all compatible with environmental sustainability. But this view of sustainability clashes with the idea of carrying capacity and scarcity.[4] Studies by ecologists point to an inevitable crisis as exponential growth clashes with the finite resources of Earth. Developed by the Club of Rome, the limits to Growth computer model, one of the earliest projections of the future of natural resources, technology, and pollution, concluded that by the year 2100 most nonrenewable resources would be exhausted, food supplies would dwindle, and massive famine and pollution would cause widespread deaths.[5] While there have been many critics of that study, few challenge the idea of limits; disagreements focus on when they will occur and how the variables interact.

Some optimists believe that pollution in the Western world "will end within our lifetime." They argue that the "most feared environmental catastrophes, such as runaway global warming," are unlikely. Environmentalism, "which binds nations to a common concern, will be the best thing that's ever happened to international relations." Nearly all technical trends are toward new devices and modes of production that are more efficient, use fewer resources, produce less waste, and cause less ecological disruption than technology of the past."[6] Others find that "just about every important measure of human welfare shows improvement over the decades and centuries"—life expectancy, price of raw materials, price of food, cleanliness of the environment, population growth, extinction of species, and the quality of farmland.[7] Some economists argue that we will never deplete resources—Earth's air, water, and crust will serve Earth dwellers for millions of years to come. The problem is not the existence of these resources, "but whether we are willing to pay the price to extract and use those resources."[8]

The optimists may be right in claiming that human ingenuity can respond to these problems and reverse these troubling trends. But the inexorable pressure from exponential growth threatens to overwhelm even the most optimistic projections. "We may be smart enough to devise environmentally friendly solutions to scarcity," one scholar has written, but we must emphasize "early detection and prevention of scarcity, not adaptation to it." But if we are not as smart and as proactive as optimists claim we are, "we will have burned our bridges: the soils, waters, and forests will be irreversibly damaged, and our societies, especially the poorest ones, will be so riven with discord that even heroic efforts at social renovation will fail."[9]

Population growth and the increased consumption and pollution accompanying it pose a profound challenge to the idea of ecological sustainability. This chapter explores the challenge of managing human population growth. It begins by presenting an overview of the scale of the global population boom and the factors that have caused the problems to be more acute in some areas than in others, placing U.S. population trends in perspective. It reviews the evidence for the assumption that there are not enough natural resources available, even with enhanced technology, to provide for the growing number of individuals born each year if present demographic trends continue into the next millennium. The chapter then outlines the political aspects of overpopulation and assesses the efforts by nongovernmental organizations and the United Nations to reduce birth rates and fertility through family planning programs. The chapter concludes with a brief summary of some of the challenges that population growth poses for policymakers.

TRENDS IN POPULATION AND PROJECTIONS

In 1798, Thomas Robert Malthus published "An Essay on the Principle of Population" in which he first argued that the "power of population" is indefinitely greater than the power of Earth to produce subsistence for humanity.[10] One of the ideas that has subsequently dominated the study of demography—the science of population—is demographic transition theory, a term used to describe a three-phase ecologic transition that leads to global overpopulation. In the first phase, human demands remain within limits that can be sustained by the environment, so there is enough food, water, and other resources for the needs of the population. In the second phase, human demands begin to exceed a sustainable limit and continue to grow. In the third phase, the ecosystem is unable to sustain the population, as there is little control over birth and death rates, and the system collapses.[11]

Although there has been criticism of the demographic transition theory,[12] there are many demographers who believe that Earth has already reached that third stage. The numbers of people already on the planet are staggering, and the projections for the future are considered even more alarming by some observers. The magnitude of growth in world population is disturbing, especially if we look closely at the last 150 years. Figure 11.1 provides a look at the milestone dates in world population growth from the year 1 C.E. through 1996.

As the growth curve indicates, while it took two hundred years (from 1650

Figure 11.1   World Population Growth

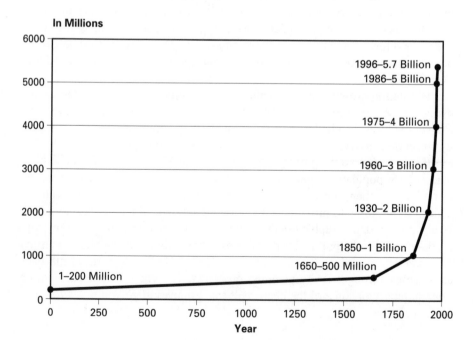

to 1850) for the global population to double from five hundred million to one billion, it took only forty-five years (from 1930 to 1975) for it to double from two billion to four billion, and the trend continues. The United Nations Population Division projections through the year 2025 show an even greater increase, as seen in Figure 11.2. The world's total population is expected to grow from a projected 5.6793 billion in 1995 to 6.1271 billion in 2000, and 8.1771 billion by 2025.

One of the primary difficulties in making decisions about population policy is that, in the past, demographic data were often insufficient or contradictory, especially in developing nations. Since the 1970s, however, nearly every nation in the world has conducted some type of census or national population register. Studies of world population by various agencies and organizations have identified several critical trends in the growth figures.

First, there are differences in the ages of populations in the industrialized and developing worlds. As we approach the turn of the century, about one of every three persons will be a child; one of five, a person in the late teens or early twenties, with the median global age being twenty-four. The most significant increase will be in the aged population; one of sixteen persons will be age sixty-five or older, with half of the world's elderly living in developing countries. The increasing number of older persons, when coupled with reductions in old-age mortality over the next four decades, will mean that there will be considerably greater demands upon the political system for social services and long-term care. Meet-

Figure 11.2   World Population growth, 1995–2025

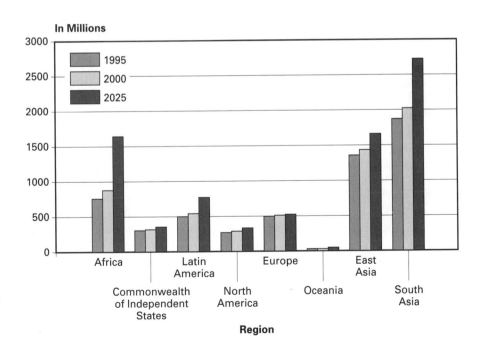

ing the demands for the global aged will necessitate shifting resources from the young to the old.[13] At the same time, the majority of the population will be of childbearing age; although women are having fewer children today, there are more women giving birth. This is a critical demographic fact. Even if fertility rates decline, population growth will continue if the number of women of child-bearing age increases. More than a third of the world's population lives in countries where the mortality for young children is greater than one in ten, posing problems for health care, mobility, and productivity.

Second, the population is becoming more urbanized, with 45 percent of the world's peoples living in urban areas by mid-1990, 51 percent by the year 2000, and 65 percent by 2025.[14] Urban populations are growing at a much more rapid rate in the less developed regions of the world than they ever did in the industrialized nations, but that growth is less the result of people migrating from rural to urban areas than of high birth rates and low death rates in the cities.[15]

Third, the distribution of population varies considerably from continent to continent, which affects the population's economic well-being and impact on the environment. The four largest countries in the world account for virtually half the world's population but only 30 percent of the world's land surface. For example, the richest 15 percent of the world's population consumes more than one-third of Earth's fertilizer and more than half of its energy, while at the other extreme, perhaps one-quarter of the world's population go hungry during at least some seasons of the year. The vast majority of the world's peoples exist on per capita incomes below the official poverty level in the United States.[16]

Similar findings were reported in *The Global 2000 Report to the President,* a U.S. study of global population trends. The study reported that populations in sub-Sharan Africa and in the Himalayan hills of Asian have already exceeded their maximum carrying capacity—the number of people who can be sustained by the land—and the entire planet is approaching that level as well. The study goes on to document shortages in water supplies and food, as well as a loss of arable land, insufficient sources of energy, and massive extinctions of plant and animal species.[17]

Another important aspect of population growth is *where* it takes place. Population growth in the industrialized countries of the world has been relatively modest, rising about 15 percent between 1970 and 1990. In contrast, the population of developing countries grew by almost 55 percent during the same period, and the disparity is expected to grow even larger in the future. The executive director of the UN Population Fund notes that most of the increase in population growth will occur in Southern Asia, which now accounts for about a quarter of the world's population but will have nearly a third of the increase by the end of the century, and Africa, which has 12 percent of the population now but will account for nearly a quarter by 2000. These changes represent a radical shift in population, with areas such as Europe and North America growing very slowly and areas such as India, which will overtake China as the world's most populous country by 2030, experiencing rapid growth.[18]

Demographers have identified a number of factors to which population increases in some regions can be attributed. Some of those changes began to occur long ago, while others are more recent in origin. First, there have been dramatic changes in our way of life and ability to survive. Humans' transition from hunting and gathering to the agricultural revolution about eight thousand years ago removed much of the risk of dying from starvation, raising the world's overall standard of living, and high death rates kept the number of people in the world from growing rapidly until the mid-eighteenth century. Second, in the category of more contemporary change, the rapid acceleration in growth after 1750 was almost entirely the result of the declines in death rates, which occurred with the Industrial Revolution. Rapid advances in science lowered the death rate by finding cures for common diseases that had previously wiped out large segments of the population. The introduction of the pesticide DDT, for example, dramatically reduced deaths from malaria, which is transmitted by mosquitos, and similar victories reduced deaths resulting from yellow fever, smallpox, cholera, and other infectious disease. Similarly, the acknowledgment of the theory that germs were responsible for disease caused a gradual acceptance of basic sanitary practices such as washing hands and bathing, which further reduced the spread of disease. The impact of DDT and other health and technological advances can be seen clearly in Figure 11.1 where the growth curve begins its steep incline. Advances in medicine have also reduced infant mortality rates to the point where the birth rate continues to exceed the death rate—the bottom line in population growth. The result is that many fewer people die than are born each year.

Third, food production has increased, keeping up with population growth until the mid-1950s, when food became more scarce and prices began to rise in developing nations. By the mid-1960s, only ten nations grew more food than they consumed: Argentina, Australia, Burma, Canada, France, New Zealand, Romania, South Africa, Thailand, and the United States.[19] Now, demand for food outstrips availability in most of the undeveloped world. Food output per person declined 11 percent between 1984 and 1993. The fish catch per person has fallen by 7 percent. There are some indicators that human demands are approaching limits of natural resources to produce food because soil erosion, air pollution, aquifer depletion, and land degradation decrease agricultural productivity.[20]

Part of the problem are the barriers to food production resulting from public policies. As economic reforms have opened up the economies of some nations, food production has increased. But much of the arable land in the less developed countries is dedicated to the production of cash crops that are used to generate foreign capital to service debt or finance economic development. Consequently, food production for domestic use suffers. Commodity prices are unstable; when they are high, exporting nations benefit, as revenues exceed those that would result from growing food. However, as world commodity prices have fallen, less revenue is available for debt service and development, and countries have to import food to make up for the shortfall in food grown for local people. Trade agreements prohibit exporting countries from processing food, thereby increasing their profits; shippers, brokers, processors, and wholesalers all live in the most developed countries (MDCs) and capture the bulk of the profits from food sales. Foreign debt, assistance programs that promote cash crop production, pressures to generate foreign capital to pay for industrialization, inexorable pressure from population growth, and the increasing use of marginal lands for food production have combined to produce the food crisis in Africa and parts of Asia and Latin America.[21] The problem is not one of scarcity as much as it is of the economic system by which food is distributed. Foreign aid is also a problem: sending large shipments of food for distribution to poor nations sometimes disrupts domestic food production, drives down prices, and harms local farmers.

Fourth, climatic changes may affect the population problem even more. The effects of population growth may be exacerbated by global warming, according to a three-year report published by the Environmental Protection Agency. The study, which was conducted by fifty scientists in eighteen countries, used three computer models, which predicted a doubling, by the year 2060, of the greenhouse gases that may be responsible for a rise in Earth's temperature. If those increases continue, the result may be a decline in crop yields, especially in grain production in developing countries, and an increase in prices from 25 to 150 percent. The reduced supply, together with increased prices, is estimated to increase the numbers of those at risk from hunger in developing countries by between 60 million and 360 million and to increase the total of the world's hungry to 1 billion by 2060. Still unknown is the impact of the acquired immunodeficiency syndrome (AIDS) epidemic, which may have an even longer effect on population trends, especially in developing countries. Until millions of people are thought to be infected with the human immunodeficiency virus (HIV), the majority of them in sub-Saharan Africa.

The pictures of starved and dehydrated children in Africa disguise a political reality, however. Although some of the problems associated with famine can be attributed to traditional food scarcity resulting from population increases and drought, some observers believe that the real issue is the radicalism of many African governments. One study of Ethiopia, for example, found that a long line of Marxist regimes and massive amounts of aid from the former Soviet Union exacerbated the traditional problems and resulted in persistent famine from 1983–1986. Despite $2 billion in worldwide aid, the Ethiopian government used its power to control food and water resources for purely political reasons.[22] In several African nations, millions of people have died because endless civil wars have made it impossible for other nations to safely bring in food and medical supplies. Even with a massive influx of aid in 1992, thousands of Somalis died each day because the country was in a state of virtual anarchy. Relief efforts were thwarted by roving bands of thugs who stole food and supplies as soon as they were brought in to refugee camps. Although the United States intervened alongside UN troops in 1992, many observers believe that Somalia's problems are exemplary of what is happening on much of the continent.

Not all of the forecasters have seen a vision of population doomsday, however. Others have a much more positive view of our ability to limit the desire to procreate or they point to errors in the population models that have been used to predict growth rates. One observer has termed the UN's projections as "so much statistical garbage," noting that the body has failed to accurately predict what is happening in major urban centers. In 1984, for example, the UN's World Population Conference demographers predicted that Mexico City's population would surge past seventeen million people, eventually overtaking Tokyo to become the world's biggest city, housing twenty-six million people by the year 2000. But in a 1996 study, the UN reported that Mexico City's population never did reach the seventeen million mark and was not likely to do so for another ten years. Most cities appear to reach a size beyond which urban problems such as pollution and congestion drive the population away in search of more liveable areas, as has been the case of cities such as London, New York, Sã̃o Paulo, Rio de Janeiro, Cairo, and Calcutta.[23]

Critics have argued that the UN's population projections are "utterly unrealistic"; no allowance has been made for death rates rising as a result of problems connected with rapid population growth, including the need for an expanded food supply. New viruses and resistant strains of old viruses, along with general environmental deterioration, will likely bring about a population limitation resulting from a combination of plague, famine, or war.[24]

Lastly, there is more evidence that family planning efforts, discussed in more detail below, are beginning to pay off, especially in industrialized nations. If so, policy direction is likely to change somewhat to stabilize the world's population while focusing on women's rights, education, and children's health.

U.S. POPULATION TRENDS AND POLICIES

Although population growth management is a global issue, few Americans have much of an understanding of where the United States stands in relation to other countries. This is partly because historically population has been a nonissue and there have been few policies established to deal with either the composition or distribution of the nation's citizens. Most public officials have been reluctant to tackle the problem, mainly because of the sensitivity of the issues of birth control and abortion. Not until the 1960s did Congress begin to develop specific proposals to define the nature of the population problem, and it was not until the mid-1970s and the U.S. Supreme Court decision regarding abortion in *Roe v. Wade* that the government was forced to address the issue directly.[25] Much of the U.S. population policy has subsequently focused on immigration and refugees and whether or not the government should lend support to international family planning efforts.

Several nongovernmental organizations (NGOs) have been formed in the United States to try to bring attention to the problems of overpopulation. One of the first was the Washington, D.C.–based Zero Population Growth (ZPG), established in 1968 in response, at least in part, to Paul Ehrlich's book. ZPG advocates a sustainable balance of people that basically stays the same from year to year. In contrast, another organization, Negative Population Growth (NPG) which formed in 1972, seeks to slow, halt, and eventually reverse population growth through several extremely controversial measures, including a reduction in legal immigration to the United States to stabilize the population between 100 and 150 million rather than the current 250 million. NPF members seek to limit immigration to 100,000 persons annually, which they believe will encourage developing nations to solve their own environmental and population problems. They also advocate a massive increase in U.S. funding for population assistance programs for Third World countries and the use of noncoercive economic and social incentives for family planning. Their goals are similar to another U.S. organization, Population-Environment Balance, which was founded in 1973 and has lobbied extensively on the immigration issue. Other groups have focused on the direct provision of services rather than on policymaking. In 1957, for example, the Pathfinder Fund began providing family planning services that include distribution of contraceptives, educational materials, medical kits, and training in developing countries.

The abortion issue has been raised for groups not directly associated with the UN programs or with population management. Prolife groups have also targeted environmental organizations such as the National Audubon Society, National Wildlife Federation, and Trout Unlimited, which had supported a moderate policy of voluntary family planning.[26] Threatened with boycotts of their advertisers and massive letter writing campaigns, the groups have personally witnessed the power and tenacity of the prolife movement.

Today, the United States has one of the higher population growth rates among developed nations in the world. Demographers predict that significant population growth is predicted to occur over the next fifty years, with the Census Bureau expecting a total U.S. population of 392 million by 2050, an increase of about 50 percent over the current population. About one-third of the growth will be attributable to immigration, specifically directed toward six states: California, New York, Texas, Florida, New Jersey, and Illinois. Immigration and births of those already living in this country will bring about dramatic changes in the ethnic population of the United States. In 1995, about one-fourth of the population was composed of racial minorities, which is defined as anyone who is not white and non-Hispanic. But demographers also predict that in the next fifty years that fraction will double, with nearly half the country composed of racial minorities. The Hispanic population, for example, is expected to rise from 22.5 million in 1990 to just less than ninety million by 2050, if immigration and high fertility rates continue. As a result, their share of the total population would increase from about 9 percent in 1990 to 22 percent in 2050.[27]

It is likely that the increase in the ethnic population will eventually be mirrored by changes in the political landscape, whether through an increase in the number of elected minority officials or by political backlash against immigrants.

During the mid-1990s, several states, led by California, considered citizen initiatives or legislation to limit immigration, to reduce social services available to nonresidents, or to declare English the nation's "official" language.[28]

GLOBAL FAMILY PLANNING EFFORTS

While most nations have not adopted explicit policies to manage their population, there is implicit agreement that the key to balancing resources to people is by reducing fertility, especially in those countries where resources are scarce. Family planning efforts vary considerably in various parts of the world, and thus some countries have made more progress in reducing birth rates than have others. Information about birth control and access to contraception are known to be major causes of declining fertility, according to a World Bank study that reported that family planning program account for 39 percent of the decline in population in developing countries.[29]

A historical review of the family planning policies shows that such programs have evolved relatively recently, considering that artificial birth control was illegal in most countries one hundred years ago. In the United States, birth control advocates first spread their doctrine of voluntary fertility in the late nineteenth century, based on the dual concerns of women's health and a rapidly growing poor population. Leaders such as Margaret Sanger, Marie Stopes, and Paul Robin were criticized for destroying the family structure, and opponents were successful in lobbying Congress to pass the Comstock Law in 1873, which outlawed advertisements or prescriptions of contraceptives. The federal statute was repealed in 1916, but similar state laws stayed on the books for another fifty years.[30]

Globally, the picture is different. Most of the countries that initially adopted family planning programs were Asian and included both large and small nations. India became the first country to adopt an official policy in 1951 to slow population growth, but no other nations followed suit until nearly a decade later, when Pakistan, the Republic of Korea, China, and Fiji adopted similar policies. In the early 1960s, when oral contraceptives and intrauterine devices were first becoming available, about sixty million women, or 18 percent of the women of childbearing age in the developing world, were practicing family planning. By the mid-1990s, about 55 percent of couples in developing countries were using contraception to control their fertility, with about 75 percent in the industrialized nations of the world.[31] Two factors have been identified as the causes behind this growth of an international family planning movement. First, there have been various cultural shifts, such as a growing sense of individualism and a corresponding decline in the perceived need to follow traditional ways. Second, people began to develop an awareness that rapid population growth represented a threat to their economic well-being.[32]

But there are a number of economic, social, and religious reasons why countries have shunned family planning as a way of bringing the birth rate down, especially in centrally planned countries such as China and Cuba. In many of these cultures, families simply *want* more children, even though more babies means more mouths to feed. It may also mean more hands at work in the field or more help in caring for aging parents. Population limitation is in direct opposition to the teachings of the Catholic Church, which has encouraged procreation and discouraged birth control and abortion, as is the case in most Islamic nations. When Pope John Paul II assumed office in 1978, the Vatican took a more active role than previously in opposing abortion and contraception. In 1984, the Pope sent a statement to the head of the UN Population Fund in which he noted that contraception "increased sexual permissiveness and promoted irresponsible conduct," a view that continues to represent the Vatican's perspective.[33] Many couples refuse to use birth control devices because of rumors and myths about their effectiveness. In India, women refused to use a loop-shaped intrauterine device when word spread that it would swim through the blood stream and reach the brain or give the man a shock during intercourse. Vasectomy has been only marginally successful because of fears by men that it reduced their virility. As a result, the use of contraception varies considerably from one nation to another.

Contraception use is generally highest in the nations of Europe and lowest in Africa—a trend mirrored in population growth rates. Some countries that have recognized the problem have taken steps to make contraception more available and acceptable, while others have made only nominal efforts. Government-sponsored family planning programs have been the primary mechanism for population control in most developing countries. About a dozen nations have established a cabinet-level ministry for population, generally in developing countries where the issue is considered serious enough to require an official program. The commitment is often not very firm, however, in countries with an Islamic or Roman Catholic religious tradition. The more successful efforts have been in countries where indigenous NGOs have been the most active. Working at the grass-roots level, NGOs appear to develop a greater sense of trust with people than programs offered by the government or foreign donors. They are also more adaptable to local circumstance and have more flexibility in their operations than do more structured programs.[34]

Generally speaking, economic inequality is the best predictor of fertility rates. Residents of poorer nations want more babies because they are a source of labor, while those in midrange economies choose goods over babies. Citizens of rich nations (such as the United States) can afford to have both—babies and goods. For them, family planning is less of a priority and there is little incentive to limit family size.

THE ROLE OF THE UNITED STATES

The United Nations has now become the primary agent of worldwide family planning programs and has made a number of efforts to address the overpopula-

CHINA'S CHOICE

As the world's most populous country, China long ago realized that it must take steps to bring about a decline in birth rates. From a strictly numbers standpoint, its population was growing much faster than its limited base of natural resources. Although China is about the same size geographically as the United States, it has four and a half times as many people. By the turn of the century, its population is expected to reach 1.3 billion, nearly one-fifth of the world's total, but it has only 7 percent of Earth's fresh water supply and 2 percent of its oil. Beijing and other urban centers in the dry northern part of the country have faced insufficient water supplies for decades—a condition exacerbated by attempts to increase economic development and, correspondingly, water consumption.

Between 1950 and 1994, China's population more than doubled, mainly as a result of the early efforts of the Communist Party, which exhorted women to have large families. Reductions in infant mortality during the 1960s was followed by a complete change in population policy. In the early 1970s, the government adapted an aggressive family planning program which became increasingly more stringent until 1979, when it adopted a one-child policy. Under the new law, the government made it illegal in most provinces to have more than a single child, although in rural areas, a second child might be permitted if the first was a girl. In the wealthier southern provinces, rural couples were allowed two children regardless of the gender of the first, and ethnic minorities were normally permitted one more child than the norm in their district. As a result, fertility rates dropped from 5.8 births per woman in 1970 to 2 births in the mid-1990s; the population growth rate declined from 2.7 percent per year to 1.1 percent.

The controversy over the country's population policy is based on how it has affected the status of women. Under Communism, numerous reforms were enacted that empowered women, including the banning of prostitution, female infanticide, child marriages, and the sale of brides. By the mid-1970s, women were encouraged to enter the labor force in numbers that were higher than those in most industrialized countries. But the one-child policy has been characterized as a major abuse of human rights because it is viewed as coercive. Various organizations have documented cases in which women have been forced to have abortions or have endured premature delivery because of quotas for births in a specific period. Other critics believe that women are still encouraged to over boys over girls. A 1994 survey conducted by the All China Women's Association noted that more than 40 percent of all women respondents said that they would prefer to be male.

To implement its policy, the government maintains an extensive record-keeping system that details the life of each village's women of childbearing

(continued)

age. Couples are issued permits to have babies, and statistics are carefully compiled on the number of women who have been sterilized, or what form of contraception a couple is using. Surveys in 1990 indicated that nearly half the women in Shanghai had aborted a child at least once, with more than a third having had two abortions or more.

Although from one perspective, China's population management policy is being successfully implemented, to those outside the country, there is criticism that the programs micromanage women's lives. Less attention is paid, for example, to the health care of unmarried women, those who have been sterilized, and those who are postmenopausal. International human rights organizations that have sometimes fought for the right for a woman to have an abortion believe that China has gone too far, with Chinese feminists warning of the complications associated with abortion. That view is not shared, however, by many in China's medical community, who believe that such stringent family planning measures serve the betterment of the society as a whole. Without the limitations, China's growth would have even further outstripped its natural resources. Some efforts are being made to enhance the "value" of girls through preferential programs that offer incentives such as pension plans and access to jobs for the parents of female children. But such perks do not satisfy those who believed that the policy has actually hurt the country more than it has helped women achieve any measure of equality, and may in fact, have set women's rights back to where they were before the Communist regime took over control.

China's policies received even closer world scrutiny in 1995 when it hosted the Fourth World Conference on Women. Although the meeting's general focus was women's equality, the Beijing Declaration and Platform for Action included strategic objectives related to women's health, human rights, and the girl child. Although it is difficult to assess whether the media attention and publicity surrounding the conference will have any impact on the nation's overall family planning strategies, the Chinese were forced to accept considerable criticism by delegates who considered the site of the conference somewhat hypocritical, given the country's past record on human rights.

For Further Reading

Judith Banister. *China's Changing Population.* Palo Alto, CA: Stanford University Press, 1987.
Elizabeth Croll, ed. *China's One Child Policy.* New York: St. Martin's Press, 1985.
Sheila Hillier and Xiang Zheng, "Rural Health Care in China: Past, Present, and Future," in *China: The Next Decades,* ed. Denis Dwyer. New York: Wiley, 1994.
Nicholas D. Kristof and Sheryl WuDunn. *China Wakes: The Struggle for the Soul of a Rising Power.* New York: Times Books, 1994.
Susan Lawrence, "Family Planning, At a Price," *U.S. News & World Report,* September 19, 1994, 56–57.
Megan Ryan and Christopher Flavin, "Facing China's Limits," in *State of the World 1995,* ed. Linda Starke, New York, W. W. Norton, 1995, 113–131.
H. Yuan Tien. *China's Population Struggle.* Columbus, OH: Ohio State University Press, 1973.

tion issue. The United Nations Fund for Population Activities was established as a trust fund in 1967, financed by voluntary contributions from members. During its first fifteen years, it allocated over $1 billion in family planning assistance to member states. Following the 1968 United Nations Conference on Human

Rights, the "Tehran Proclamation" identified the ability to control one's fertility and therefore access to birth control as a basic human right. The UN organization, renamed the United Nations Population Fund, has held five world conferences: in Rome (1954), Belgrade (1965), Bucharest (1974), Mexico City (1984), and Cairo (1994). At the Bucharest conference, the UN's World Population Plan of Action was established, led by the United States and other industrialized nations that urged developing countries to set targets for lowering their fertility rates. Many Third World nations and Eastern bloc nations rebelled, accusing the UN of supporting efforts by former colonial masters to suppress emerging nations and limit the strength of their armies.[35] Ten years later, at the Mexico City conference, those misconceptions vanished as leaders from 149 nations committed themselves to a voluntary reduction in population growth and a strong national family planning program. Although there was continuing concern about the continuation of high population growth rates in developing nations, fertility rates had declined modestly since the Bucharest meeting.[36]

In the intervening years between the population conferences, the UN's Conference on Environment and Development, held in 1992 in Rio de Janeiro, indicated how hesitant delegates were to tackle the population issue head on. For example, the term "appropriate demographic policies" was substituted in conference documents for the more traditional phrase "family planning," and many of the representatives of NGOs were critical of industrialized countries, which they perceived as failing to take responsibility for their own overconsumption of resources. But the meeting did produce, as part of its Agenda 21, a chapter on demographic dynamics and sustainability. Delegates agreed that the role of women should be strengthened and their rights fully recognized and noted that governments should ensure that women and men have the same right to decide freely and responsibly on the number and spacing of the children. But representatives of the Vatican and the Philippines were successful in weakening the exact language on family planning and in removing any remarks on contraceptives.[37]

At the 1994 Cairo conference, the issue of abortion overshadowed nearly every other agenda item. Delegates reached an uneasy compromise after what one observer termed "a Vatican-led handful of countries held the meeting hostage."[38] The final document provided that abortions "should be safe" where they are legal and that they should "in no case . . . be promoted as a method of family planning."[39] Vatican officials argued that economic reform should be the major focus of global leaders: "Demographic growth is the child of poverty. . . . Rather than reduce the numbers at the world's table, you need to increase the courses and distribute them better."[40] Other religious groups and foundations launched campaigns aimed at drawing attention to overconsumption in the United States and other wealthy nations, paralleling arguments of economists that the United States needs to save and invest more and consume less.[41]

The "Program of Action," a 113-page document approved in April 1994 by the UN committee responsible for the Cairo meeting, provides the basic outline for a twenty-year plan to promote women's rights and reduce population growth to 7.27 billion by 2015. A central theme embraced by nearly every one of the 150 delegates was the empowerment of women.[42] While few participants were completely happy with the results of the report, as one observer put it, "conferences and documents like these never get out ahead of where the people who agree to them are comfortable. What these conferences do is take an aerial snapshot of where we're at."[43]

One of the most promising products of the conference was the creation of "Partners in Population and Development: A South-South Initiative," announced by ten developing countries that came together to share their successes in reducing population growth. These successful strategies include offering a wide range of choices for family planning and careful integration with local cultural and political conditions.[44] The Women's Environment and Development Organization, formed in 1989, played a major role in shaping the agenda of the Cairo meeting and promised to maintain the pressure on governments and international bodies to include gender equality and empowerment of women in family planning and reproductive health efforts.[45]

Many challenges remain, however, in determining how to finance and deliver family planning and related services in ways that are consistent with local religious, cultural, social, and economic conditions. In many less developed countries, family planning services are still widely seen as a First World idea. Much of the focus will have to be on those countries that have the greatest population growth rates and the fewest resources to help empower women.[46] Some of the success stories touted at the Cairo meeting have been questioned by other experts. Bangledesh is often cited as an example of a model program, having reduced the average number of children from more than seven to fewer than four per women between 1975 and 1994, with contraception use increasing from 19 percent to 45 percent in a decade. The achievements came during a time when the country faced severe socioeconomic problems, floods, and storms, which placed extraordinary pressure on the country's political and economic resources. But one of the critics of the program believes that the decrease in Bangladesh's fertility rate has come at the expense of women who were pressured to undergo sterilization and through the diversion of funds needed to support the country's primary health care system.[47]

The United States's role in global population management has been somewhat contradictory. The U.S. Agency for International Development (AID) began promoting large-scale national family programs funded through international aid in the early 1960s, providing health care workers in many developing countries. Congress first earmarked foreign assistance appropriations in 1968, with nearly $4 billion in assistance allocated through AID over the next two decades. Initially, the United States also supported UN programs for education and family planning. But during the administration of president Ronald Reagan, the United States adopted what came to be known as the Mexico City Policy—an abrupt change in policy direction. The United States cut off its support (as the major donor) of the UN Fund for Population Activities and the International Planned

Parenthood Federation, the largest multilateral agency and the largest private voluntary organization providing family planning services in developing countries.

The sudden policy about-face became tied to the issue of abortion, even through U.S. law (the 1973 Helms Amendment of the foreign assistance act) explicitly prohibits government funding for abortion programs overseas and even though legal abortions are permitted in only a few countries. In 1985, the Kemp-Kasten Amendment to the foreign assistance act banned any U.S. contribution to "any organization or program that supports or participates in the management or a program of coercive abortion or involuntary sterilization." The passage of the legislation effectively cut off U.S. support to China's family planning program, which was alleged to have forced women to have abortions, despite denials by the Chinese government. Congressional attempts to restore the UN funding by stipulating that the money not be spent in China were vetoed by President George Bush in November 1989.[48] The Bush administration's position puzzled those who pointed out that, by cutting back its aid to the UN program, the United States was actually encouraging the demand for abortion in those nations where there are no other alternatives.

The United States stood virtually alone in its refusal to contribute to the United Nations programs, having previously been the primary donor, contributing $38 million of the $122 million program budget in 1984. But after the U.S. policy change, Germany, Canada, the United Kingdom, Japan, and the Scandinavian countries increased their donations, with Japan becoming the major donor and exceeding what the United States previously contributed.[49] After years of congressional debate, the result was that from 1986 to 1992 the United States eliminated all contributions to the UN program, with only a few bilateral assistance programs remaining intact.

In 1993, the Clinton administration reversed prior policies and began restoring U.S. aid to the UN programs, with $430 million earmarked for international population assistance—the most ever contributed in the history of the program. In 1996, Congress agreed to appropriate $385 million for international family planning assistance and defeated a proposal by House Republicans to limit assistance to any international program that spent its own funds on any kind of abortion-related services (everyone agreed that U.S. funds could not be used to provide these services). The law required another vote by Congress before the funds could be released, and one of the few pieces of legislation enacted during the first few months of the new Congress in 1997 released the funds.[50]

IMPLICATIONS FOR POLICYMAKERS

Because population growth management is inextricably linked to other types of public policy, social, cultural, and religious beliefs, economics, and political forces that are constantly changing, it has become one of the most critical, yet unresolved, issues facing policymakers today. The consequences of population growth, regardless of the exact magnitude and timing, have considerable repercussions for the resources of both developed and developing nations. The problem is exacerbated by the substantial disagreement among scientists as to the seriousness of the problem, making it difficult for policymakers to decide what kind of action, if any, to take. There are also opposing views on whether the population issue ought to be addressed by individual nations, allowing them to develop policies to control their own fertility rates and resource use or whether the problem should be dealt with on a global scale by organizations such as the United Nations.

There are a number of reasons why population management has slipped from the top of the political agenda, both in the United States and globally. Biologist and "population buff" Garrett Hardin, who was at the forefront of the ethical debate over population management, argued that a change in public attitude is to blame, among other factors. He noted that population is a chronic problem rather than a critical one, with the media preferring the latter to the former. As a result, there is much more media interest in covering "crises" such as the continuing conflict in the Middle East than the fact that a quarter of a million people were born on the day that Iraq invaded Kuwait. He also pointed out that many people fail to make the connection between population size and problems like air pollution from too many automobiles. Finally, Hardin believed that population questions raise issues that might be perceived as being selfish, bigoted, provincial, or even racist—criticisms that he himself had to bear.[51]

In the United States, members of Congress have not made population a high priority because there is little political incentive to do so. There are few interest groups to support a particular policy and a lack of a strong constituency for policy change in a system where institutional fragmentation is the norm.[52] Most environmental organizations have only tangentially addressed population growth management, preferring instead to focus on more specific resource issues.

But the most important policy implication relates to whether or not there will be sufficient natural resources to sustain the growth in population, wherever it may occur. One of the key indicators is the adequacy of the food supply, which has thus far kept pace with population growth in all regions of the world except Africa. But most studies of world population projections note that world food production potential is dependent upon increasing the amount of land under cultivation and increasing inputs of capital and fertilizers. Developing countries seeking to modernize their agricultural practices risk causing additional harm to the environment, whether it be by cutting timber in order to grow crops or adding more chemicals to the soil and water supply. Another important consideration is whether there will be sufficient energy resources for the growing population. Developing countries seeking to modernize and grow will place additional demands on natural resources to produce the power needed for everything from household appliances to factories.

Lastly, there is still suspicion among developing nations that countries such as the United States are more interested in curbing population growth in poorer countries as a way of protecting the environment rather than concentrating on reducing excess consumption in wealthier nations. This view has been expressed at numerous international conferences and exemplifies the continuing divisiveness between the industrialized nations of the world that already have the benefits of development and those countries that are still seeking to attain them. Some in the South also contend that the real population growth problem is in the North, since the environmental and natural resource impact of each person in the wealthy world is many times that of residents of the developing world. If population growth is to be curtailed in the South to reduce pollution and resource use, it should be combined with restraint on the consumptive patterns of the North.

SUMMARY

One of the most controversial environmental issues—population growth management—deals with whether Earth's limited resources can sustain the growing number of human beings born each year. The world's population has skyrocketed since the Industrial Revolution as a result of improved living conditions and scientific advancement, which reduced the number of deaths. Although those declines initially occurred in the more developed countries of Europe and the United States, technological advances are now available worldwide. In addition, the age structure of the population is changing, with the largest segment of the population now of childbearing age. Although the risk of death has been lowered dramatically in developing nations, birthrates have decreased slowly, with a resulting boom in population growth in those regions. With varying degrees of success, efforts to reduce fertility have focused on two strategies: providing information about birth control and providing access to contraception. Although adopted initially by several Asian nations, family planning programs have been stymied for various economic, social, and religious reasons. While the United Nations remains the primary focus of global family planning efforts, nongovernmental organizations have become more active in working directly with indigenous people in developing countries. The ongoing abortion controversy led to an end to U.S. support of UN family planning programs during the Reagan and Bush administrations and became a continuing source of conflict under President Clinton and at the 1994 Cairo conference on population, although Congress has appropriated money to fund international family planning programs.

NOTES

1. Paul R. Ehrlich, *The Population Bomb* (New York: Ballantine Books, 1968). The statement is conspicuously placed on the cover of Ehrlich's book.

2. Paul R. Ehrlich and Anne H. Ehrlich. *The Population Explosion* (New York: Simon & Schuster, 1990), 9.

3. Alan B. Durning, *Poverty and the Environment: Reversing the Downward Spiral,* Worldwatch Paper 92 (Washington, D.C.: Worldwatch Institute, 1989): 40–41.

4. For further discussion of these issues, see World Commission on Environment and Development, *Our Common Future* (New York: Oxford University Press, 1987), and Robert

Repetto, ed., "Agenda for Action," *The Global Possible: Resources, Development, and the New Century* (New Haven, CT: Yale University Press, 1985): 496–519.

5. Donella H. Meadows et al., *The Limits to Growth* (New York: Universe Books, 1927).

6. Gregg Easterbrook, *A Moment on the Earth: The Coming Age of Environmental Optimism* (New York: Viking Penguin, 1995), xvi.

7. Julian Simon, "Pre-Debate Statement," in *Scarcity or Abundance? A Debate on the Environment*, eds. Norman Myes and Julian L. Simon (New York: W. W. Norton, 1994), 5–22.

8. Tom Tietenberg, *Environmental and Natural Resource Economics*, 3d ed. (New York: Harpercollins, 1992), 356–357.

9. Thomas F. Homer-Dixon, quoted in William K. Stevens, "Feeding a Booming Population without Destroying the Planet," *The New York Times*, April 5, 1994.

10. See Philip Appleman, ed. *Thomas Robert Malthus: An Essay on the Principle of Population* (New York: W. W. Norton, 1976). For biographical material on Malthus and his theories, see Jane S. Nickerson, *Homage to Malthus* (Port Washington, NY: Kennikat Press, 1975); David V. Glass, *Introduction to Malthus* (New York: Wiley, 1953); William Petersen, *Malthus* (Cambridge, MA: Harvard University Press, 1979); and Donald Winch, *Malthus* (New York: Oxford University Press, 1987).

11. See Maurice King, "Health Is a Sustainable State," *The Lancet, 336,* no. 8716 (September 15, 1990): 664–667. For a historical perspective on demographic transition theory, see the work of Kingsley Davis, "The World Demographic Transition," *The Annals of the American Academy of Political and Social Science, 237* (January 1945): 1–11, and George Stolntiz, "The Demographic Transition: From High to Low Birth Rates and Death Rates," in *Population: The Vital Revolution*, ed. Ronald Freedman (Garden City, NY: Anchor Books, 1964).

12. See, for example, Ansley Coale, "The History of the Human Population," *Scientific American, 231* (1974): 40–51; and Kingsley Davis, "The Theory of Change and Response in Modern Demographic History," *Population Index, 29,* no. 4 (1963): 345–366.

13. William H. Frey, "Global Aging," 1 *HD Focus,* no. 1 (Winter 1994), 13.

14. "Population Conference Set for 1994," *UN Chronicle, 28,* no. 2 (June 1991): 74.

15. See, for example, Richard E. Stren and Rodney R. White, eds., *African Cities in Crisis: Managing Rapid Urban Growth* (Boulder, CO: Westview Press, 1989).

16. William C. Clark, "Managing Planet Earth," *Scientific American, 261* (September 1989): 48.

17. U.S. Executive Office of the President, Council on Environmental Quality, *The Global 2000 Report tot he President* (Washington, D.C.: U.S. Government Printing Office, 1980). For a different view of the need for a new strategy for sustainable agriculture, see David Norse, "A New Strategy for Feeding a Crowded Planet," *Environment, 34,* no. 5 (June 1992): 6.

18. Nafis Sadik, "World Population Continues to Rise," *The Futurist,* March–April 1991, 9–14. See also *World Resources 1994–95* (New York: World Resources Institute, 1994), 27–42.

19. Ehrlich, *Population Bomb*, 38.

20. Lester R. Brown, et al., *State of the World 1994* (Washington, D.C.: World Watch Institute, 1994), 4–5, 177.

21. Norman Myers, *Gaia* (New York: Oxford University Press, 1988), 46–48.

22. See Steven L. Varnis, *Reluctant Aid or Aiding the Reluctant* (New Brunswick, NJ: Transaction, 1990), 3.

23. See, for example, Fred Pearce, "Where Have All the People Gone?" *New Scientist, 149* (March 9, 1996), 48.

24. Paul R. Ehrlich, Anne H. Ehrlich, and Gretchen C. Daily, "What It Will Take," *Mother Jones, 20* (September–October 1995), 52–56.

25. See P. T. Piotrow, *World Population Crisis: The United States Response* (New York: Praeger, 1973).

26. Frank Graham Jr., "Thoughts," *Audubon, 92* (January 1990): 8.

27. Carl Haub, "Global and U.S. National Population Trends," *Consequences,* Summer

1995, 10. See also Sam Roberts, "Hispanic Population Outnumbers Blacks in Four Major Cities as Demographics Shift," *The New York Times,* October 9, 1994, A34.

28. On the bilingualism debate, see Gilbert Narro Garcia, *Bilingual Education: A Look to the Year 2000* (Washington, D.C.: National Clearinghouse for Bilingual Education, 1994); James Crawford, *Hold Your Gongue: Bilingualism and the Politics of English Only* (Reading, MA: Addiston-Wesley, 1992); and Kenji Hakuta, *Mirror of Language: The Debate Over Bilingualism* (new York: Basic Books, 1986).

29. Nathan Keyfitz, "The Growing Human Population," *Scientific American, 261* (September 1989): 123.

30. See Peter Fryer, *The Birth Controllers* (New York: Stein and Day, 1965); and James Reed, *From Private Vice to Public Virtue: The Birth Control Movement and American Society Since 1930* (New York: Basic Books, 1978).

31. Frances Fitzgerald, " A Manageable Crowd," *The New Yorker* (September 12, 1994), 7–8.

32. See Ronald Freedman, "Family Planning Programs in the Third World," *Annals of the American Academy of Political and Social Science, 510* (July 1990): 33–43.

33. Barbara B. Crane, "International Population Institutions: Adaptation to a Changing World Order," in *Institutions for the Earth: Sources of Effective International Environmental Protection,* eds. Peter M. Haas, Robert O. Keohane, and Marc A. Levy (Cambridge, MA: MIT Press, 1993), 365–366.

34. See Julie Fisher, "Third World NGOs:A Missing Piece to the Population Puzzle," *Environment, 36,* no. 7 (September 1994), 6–11.

35. See Jason L. Finkle and Barbara B. Crane, "The Politics of Bucharest: Population, Development, and the New International Economic Order," *Population and Development Review, 2* (September–December 1976): 87–114.

36. Werner Fornos, "Population Politics," *Technology Review* (February–March 1991), 43–51. See also Jason L. Finkle and Barbara B. Crane, "ideology and Politics at Mexico City: The United States at the 1984 International Conference on Population," *Population and Development Review, 11,* no. 1 (March 1985): 1–28; and Michael E. Kraft, "Population Policy," in *Encyclopedia of Policy Studies,* 2d ed., ed. Stuart A. Nagel (New York: Marcel Dekker, 1994), 631–633.

37. See Michael Grubb, et al., *The Earth Summit Agreements: A Guide and Assessment* (London: Earthscan Publications, 1993), 106–108.

38. Emily MacFarquhar, "Unfinished Business," *U.S. News & World Report* (September 19, 1994): 57.

39. United Nations Conference on Population, "Plan of Action," Paragraph 8.25.

40. Alan Cowell, "Is This Abortion? *The New York Times,* August 11, 1994.

41. Wade Greene, "Overconspicuous Overconsumption," *The New York Times,* August 28, 1994.

42. Barbara Crossette, "Population Meeting Opens with Challenge to the Right," *The New York Times,* September 6, 1994.

43. Barbara Crossette, "U.N. Meeting Facing Angry Debate on Population," *The New York Times,* September 4, 1994.

44. Barbara Crossette, "A Third-World Effort on Family Planning," *The New York Times,* September 7, 1994.

45. "Keeping Alive Cairo Goals for Women," *The New York Times,* September 25, 1994.

46. Tim Carrigan, "Viewing Population as a Global Crisis, Cairo Conferees Have Missed the Point," *The Wall Street Journal,* September 12, 1994.

47. For the conflicting observations, see B. Sison, "Bangladesh Succeeds with Family Planning," *The New York Times,* October 6, 1994, A28, and Betsy Hartmann, "What Success Story?" *The New York Times,* September 29, 1994, A25.

48. See Phillip Davis, "The Big O: Zero Population Growth," *Buzzworm,* November–December 1992, 54.

49. Peter J. Donaldson and Amy Ong Tsui, "International Family Planning Movement," *Population Bulletin, 45,* no. 3 (November 1990): 14.

50. P.L. 104–208.

51. Garrett Hardin, "Sheer Numbers," *E Magazine, 1,* no. 6 (November–December 1990): 40–47.

52. Kraft, "Population Policy," 635.

FOR FURTHER READING

Douglas L. Anderson, Richard E. Barrett, and Donald J. Bogue, eds., *The Population of the United States.* New York: The Free Press, 1996.

Lourdes Arizpe, M. Priscilla Stone, and David C. Major, eds., *Population and the Environment: Rethinking the Debate.* Boulder, CO: Westview, 1994.

Bryan Cartledge, ed., *Population and the Environment.* New York: Oxford University Press, 1995.

Janice Jiggins. *Changing the Boundaries: Women-Centered Perspectives on Population and the Environment.* Washington, D.C.: Island Press, 1994.

Laurie Ann Mazur. *Beyond the Numbers: A Reader on Population, Consumption, and the Environment.* Washington, D.C.: Island Press, 1994.

Donella H. Meadows, Dennis L. Meadows, and Joergen Randers. *Beyond the Limits.* Post Mills, VT: Chelsea Green, 1992.

Rick Searle. *Population Growth, Resource Consumption, and the Environment: Seeking a Common Vision for a Troubled World.* Waterloo, Ontario, Canada: Wilfrid Laurier University Press, 1995.

CHAPTER 12

Reflections on Problems and Solutions

If we do not change the direction we are going, we will end up where we are headed.
—Old Chinese proverb

Thus far, this book has focused on environmental issues and problems that have developed over the past 150 years, the majority of which have made their way to the domestic and international political agenda since 1960. The early legislative efforts dealing with environmental questions have been called the "react and cure" phase of environmental politics. Some global environmental problems, such as air and water pollution, are likely to be around well into the next century in the "anticipate and prevent" stage of policymaking.[1] Many observers believe that the framework for environmental legislation has been in place in the United States for over 30 years, and subsequent changes to domestic policy amount to only a fine-tuning of those efforts. The decade of the 1990s has seen an emphasis on the globalization of environmental issues, with new regimes being formed to deal with biodiversity, transboundary pollution, and oceanic resources. This last chapter reflects on the environmental issues that are likely to become the focus on the twenty-first century and the potential solutions that are being considered to deal with them.

FROM GEOPOLITICS TO ECOPOLITICS

The term *geopolitics* was first used in the late nineteenth century to describe the science that conceives the state not as an inanimate body, but as a geographical organism or as a phenomena in space. The living state is characterized by its territory and people; its form of government and the economy; its space, size, and shape; and its relationship to the sea. Early authors described geopolitics in terms of Charles Darwin's evolutionary theories; states compete with one another for scarce space, and the laws of natural selection, which favor the most biologically fit, apply equally to nations as to species.[2] More recently, geopolitics has given way to concerns about the connection between national security and environmental degradation.[3] Why is there a connection between these two disparate issues, and what are the implications for the political agenda in the twenty-first century?

The connection exists because of both ecological and economic linkages. For many countries, national security is threatened by the failure of governments to adequately address issues of overpopulation and resource depletion. It has been argued that the next century will see a redefinition of what constitutes national security, as the previously sharp dividing line between foreign and domestic policy becomes blurred, forcing governments to deal with environmental problems on an international scale, rather than just internally.[4] In addition, the development of an increasing number of trade linkages, such as the General Agreement on Tariffs and Trade (GATT) and the North American Free Trade Agreement (NAFTA), and the globalization of the world economy make the fate of any one nation, developed or developing, dependent upon others as well. Even the national security of the United States is affected by environmental issues in other parts of the world. For example, the Third World now accounts for about 40 percent of U.S. exports and supplies about 40 percent of U.S. imports. American private investment in developing countries has also increased significantly. This gives the United States an important stake in the stable development of the global economy, which is dependent, in large part, on the equally stable development of environmental resources.[5]

There are a number of reasons why these phenomena are occurring. The burgeoning human population has placed enormous stress on the environment, which as in turn led to an economic decline in many countries worldwide. That economic decline is at the root of the kind of frustration that leads to domestic and civil unrest and makes countries ripe for political upheaval, which threatens not only internal order, but the stability of the international political system.

The most acute examples involve refugees. When economic and political problems force citizens to leave their national borders, frustration is spread to surrounding regions. In Haiti, for example, the government has failed to deal with the problem of an expanding population that has systematically destroyed the country's once heavily forested landscape. The resulting soil erosion has limited any attempts at productive agriculture and left the country with only a minimal economic base. In their frustration, thousands of Haitians have attempted to flee their island home for the United States, many of them on board boats with little chance of safely completing the rough sea journey to the mainland. Rescuing the refugees is a thorny political issue for the United States and results in the importation of a Haitian environmental problem to the United States. Although thousands of the refugees have sought political asylum in the United States, a more plausible explanation for their flight is that they sought economic sanctuary when their own economy failed.

Similarly, desertification, believed to affect as much as one-third of the planet's surface, has resulted in a lack of arable land in several countries on the African continent and has led to massive human migrations. Food outputs have fallen behind economic growth, leading to famine and starvation and fueling civil unrest. The Sudan, for example, is home to nearly three-quarters of a million refugees from Chad, Ethiopia, and Uganda; the tiny nation of Malawi holds over a million, and Zaire holds much of Rwanda's population, nearly 400 thousand of whom fled to Zaire in the mid-1990s.[6] Fleeing to other countries, whose resources are already tapped out, forces the receiving nations to rely on imported food sources further compromising their sovereignty and destroying their own trade balance. More people means further demands on the economy and further stress on the environment's ability to provide enough food and water for residents.[7]

Water scarcity is another issue assured of affecting national security in the coming decades. This is true particularly in the Middle East, where fifteen nations depend upon three primary river systems: the Nile, the Jordan, and the Tigris-Euphrates. With high birthrates throughout the region, researchers believe that all renewable water sources will soon be depleted unless more sustainable development plans are launched. Conflicts over water supplies could lead to increased instability in many areas, especially when water sources are shared among countries. International water law is poorly developed, with the most common conflict being disputes over competing claims. Although there are an estimated 2,000 regimes relating to common basins, efforts to insure an equitable sharing of scarce water resources remains illusive despite attempts to include such provisions in the ongoing process of peace settlement.[8]

In urban areas of the developing world, at least 170 million people lack access to clean water for drinking, cooking, and washing; in rural areas, more than 855 million lack clean water. According to one study, water pollution is the most serious environmental problem facing developing countries because of its direct effect on human welfare and economic growth.[9] Water quality issues are becoming so acute in some regions of the world that the magnitude of the deaths they cause can no longer be ignored by industrialized countries. In Africa, for example, the magnitude of waterborne diseases is almost impossible for Westerners to comprehend. Six tropical diseases—malaria, schistosomiasis (caused by a flatworm and carried by snails), sleeping sickness (trypanosomiasis), leishmaniasis (an infection carried by flies that is usually fatal within two years), filariasis (which leads to elephantiasis or river blindness), and leprosy—are rampant. In addition, diarrheal illnesses— caused by a variety of intestinal germs and parasities—kill hundreds of thousands of people each year and are the leading cause of death in some countries. These illnesses know no national boundaries, and as more and more tourists visit these areas, there is concern the diseases will be transmitted to developed countries as well.[10]

The current strategy of the United Nations's World Health Organization is to concentrate on those diseases responsible for the greatest mortality and morbidity and for which effective treatment is known. This means control of diarrheal diseases first, followed by respiratory infections and malnutrition second, and with lowest priority given to diseases of lengthy/costly care, such as sleeping sickness and leprosy. These are not choices made easily, but they are choices made on the basis of limited resources and incalculable human costs.

Other geopolitical changes are having environmental repercussions as well. The Iraqi invasion of Kuwait in August 1990 further emphasized national security issues in the form of environmental terrorism. The Gulf region experienced several impacts from the war: destruction of fragile desert ecosystems as a result of the activity of more than a million troops, their equipment, and supplies; localized by severe fouling of Kuwait's harbor and the Saudi coastline from the deliberate sabotage of oil tanks and U.S. bombing of Iraqi oil tankers anchored nearby; unknown health effects from the smoke and toxic gas produced by 732 burning oil wells; and unquantified loss of marine life, vegetation, wildlife, and birds, as well as unknown impacts on crops and farm animals.[11]

Even more important than what appears to be these somewhat localized impacts is the realization that existing international law and regimes have little effect on ecoterrorism. Conventions on the conduct of war proved ineffective, and UN sanctions against Iraq have had questionable utility. Even the UN resolution making Iraq financially responsible for the environmental damage it caused Kuwait is not likely to be complied with.[12]

THE BAG BETWEEN THE NORTH AND THE SOUTH

The 1992 Earth Summit underscored the widening division between the industrialized nations of the North and the developing countries of the South, especially in the area of resource consumption. It is somewhat ironic that the developing countries are now facing environmental protection issues that are the result of, in some cases at least, growing consumer demands in the North. The problem of global climate change (see Chapter 10) is mainly a result of the consumption of fossil fuels and the use of chemicals by industrialized nations. Even more ironic is that the consumers in the South *want* those same goods for themselves. In recent decades, the nations of the South have been responsible for the consumption of most natural resources at a faster pace than developed countries, although per capita levels are still far below those of the North.[13] The old battles between the "haves" and the "have-nots" have an added dimension where the environment is concerned. Developing nations with extractive resources (minerals, oil, and timber) are loath to relinquish total control of those resources simply to satisfy the concerns of environmental groups. Developing nations' gross national product is highly reliant upon natural resources, generating almost two-thirds of their employment and half of their exports. These nations have no choice but to continue development of those resources as a way to help pay for their mounting foreign debt.[14]

Environmental organizations in developed regions still have difficulty understanding why Third- and Fourth-World governments are less eager to absorb the costs of pollution control and limitations on development that are now commonplace in the United Stats. Why, they ask, can't countries such as China, India, and Brazil, which are home to almost half of the world's population, agree to sign accords that would limit the production of greenhouse gases? Such questions are more than just philosophical—they are at the heart of the debates over who should pay for cleaning up the environment. Developing countries with limited capital and limited technology look to the leaders of the industrialized world and note that foreign aid has decreased over the past two decades.

Leaders in industrialized countries, saddled with political and economic problems of their own, dislike the "deep pockets" attitude of countries who are unwilling or unable to enact strict environmental protection laws and enforce them. The cost of transferring the technology for chlorofluorocarbon substitutes to developing countries is estimated at between $2 billion and $7 billion over the next several years. Who should pick up the tab? Even though developing countries are responsible for less than 10 percent of the total industrial carbon dioxide emissions that contribute to global warming, any attempt at reducing emissions by the countries of the North will be negated unless they are also willing to pay for the cost of reducing greenhouse gases in the South as well.

The environmental degradation in Eastern Europe presents a somewhat unique challenge for the leaders of developed countries. The three most pressing problems are the threat of another "Chernobyl catastrophe" from aging nuclear facilities, the threat posed to the Arctic Ocean and the Baltic and Japan Seas from nuclear and toxic waste dumping, and the wanton destruction of forests. Although the problems are easily identifiable, Western environmental groups and researchers are experiencing considerable difficulty assessing the magnitude of the problems caused by the legacy of policy avoidance.[15] Environmental and health data from the region tend to be fragmented, incomplete, and generally unreliable, according to one observer. As a result, it is difficult to assess exactly how much damage has been done in such areas as nuclear, industrial, medical, and household waste. The lack of reporting by military facilities, nuclear weapons complexes, and industrial and agricultural production units conceals both the extent and the potential cost of cleanup, making it difficult for researchers to convince policymakers that international assistance is crucial. The problems caused by decades of environmental indifference are, however, extremely clear. Mortality rates are increasing dramatically, especially among infants, while birth rates decrease. Medical care is often unavailable, and reported cases of infectious diseases such as polio and diphtheria (considered conquered in other industrialized regions) are on the rise. Solving such problems will require, as one author notes, patience and local partnerships focused on strengthening local institutions and building political support at the grass roots, with cooperative action and burden sharing at the centerpiece of every project.[16]

The factors leading to the current rift are contrary to the notion of interdependence, which should be at the center of the political debate over the environment. As an economic and political superpower, the United States is in a unique position to help bridge the gap by initiating global environmental agreements. The United States cannot insulate itself from the environmental degradation that is creeping over its borders or that its companies are causing in other countries.

But the United States has lost its position of environmental leadership to Japan and Germany, as evidenced by the negotiations at the Earth Summit over biodiversity and carbon dioxide emission limits and by the U.S. reluctance to fund UN family planning programs. Perhaps the United States' decision in 1996 to support binding greenhouse gas emission limits will help renew American leadership. However, unless there is a reversal of U.S. policy on these issues, other nations will, by default, take over the policy agenda and mold it to fit their own national security needs and environmental priorities.

THE NEW DIPLOMACY: REGIMES FOR THE TWENTY-FIRST CENTURY

To deal with the rift between the North and South, some observers are calling for the development of what has been called "a new diplomacy"—including new institutions and regulatory regimes. With the increased awareness of the transboundary nature of many environmental problems comes an acceptance that existing strategies for developing international agreements are no longer viable. Some environmental problems cannot withstand the ten- to fifteen-year delays common in building new regimes. Some nations, for example, still have not signed the 1987 Montreal Protocol, despite almost unanimous scientific consensus that chlorofluorocarbons (CFCs) are depleting Earth's protective ozone layer. Other attempts at regime formation, such as a new Antarctic agreement, will require negotiations among nations such as the republics of the former Soviet Union, which themselves are still undergoing economic and political upheaval. Nations reluctant to surrender their sovereignty have in the past been reluctant to join regimes, fearful that they are "giving up" their power. For example, although the Convention on Biological Diversity signed at the 1992 Earth Summit addressed to some degree the issue of "bioprospecting" for plants cultivated and sanctified by indigenous peoples, there is still enormous pressure for developing countries to sign trade accords to grant broad access to their genetic resources. But there is a fine line between exploration and exploitation, and little agreement on appropriate compensation or regulations on access to biochemicals found in tropical forests and other ecosystems.[17]

The new diplomacy may wear a different face entirely. Rather than seeking multilateral acceptance of new regimes (an extremely time-consuming and often unsuccessful process), some nations are simply proceeding on their own and working toward agreements among like-minded countries. Such "environmental alliances" are already beginning to appear and are likely to grow in the next millennium. The so-called 30-percent Club (originally Canada and nine other European countries) was formed in 1984 to reduce sulfur dioxide emissions, which result in the formation of acid rain; more countries have since joined. In Central America, "peace parks" straddling the borders of Costa Rica, El Salvador, Guatemala, Honduras, Nicaragua, and Panama have been developed to preserve rainforests and to help promote sustainable development. The parks serve not only as nature preserves but also as demilitarized buffer zones.

The globilization of environmental issues has also led to a call for a world government approach—creation of an institution whose powers far exceed those of the existing structure of the United Nations. Other observers have urged a rethinking of conventional economic theory so that the emphasis is on balancing the debt between civilization and the biosphere rather than balancing the federal deficit.[18] The fiftieth anniversary of the United Nations in 1995 prompted several calls for strengthening the institution and making it more efficient. A similar anniversary of the World Bank generated proposals to abolish it and replace the bank with an organization more committed to environmental preservation.

One reason why world leaders are looking toward a new form of environmental diplomacy is the need for, yet avoidance of, some form of mutually acceptable sanctions for nations that violate environmental regimes. Considerable controversy has erupted over the use of trade sanctions in the enforcement of the Montreal Protocol and the Convention on the International Trade in Endangered Species of Wild Fauna and Flora. Using punitive measures is not always appropriate, especially in the case of developing countries, where violation of international agreements may be a consequence of a lack of resources and technical capability to enforce the law, rather than deliberate noncompliance. As a result, many accords include a provision that a fund be created and made available to nations needing financial assistance to meet the terms of the treaty—an action that has not only led to more participation by signatory countries, but one that has also led to voluntary compliance, as in the case of the ozone treaty.[19]

ENVIRONMENTAL JUSTICE AND INDIGENOUS PEOPLES

During much of the twentieth century, environmental problems were often addressed with little consideration about the impact of the policy on those directly affected by the decision. Members of the public were rarely consulted about whether or not they approved or disapproved of a project, and not until relatively recently has legislation given affected parties a formal decision-making role. Since the late 1980s, however, nongovernmental organizations (NGOs) are playing an increasingly important role in the global policy process in their attempts to influence environmental politics at both the local and international levels. NGOs have become the voice for those who previously had neither the resources, skills, or legal standing to have their concerns heard. One of the reasons why NGOs have become more successful in their efforts is the development of the concept that all people have a communal right to a healthy and healthful environment. This often creates a linkage with human rights organizations around the world who are working toward full acceptance of the 1948 Universal Declaration of Human Rights and the 1994 Draft Declaration of Principles on Human Rights and the Environment. Activists are seeking to have governments agree to the rights all citizens should expect from society, such as clean air and water and the universal right to a "secure, healthy, ecologically sound environment" while also protecting the rights of indigenous peoples.

In the United States, concerns over perceived inequalities of environmental risk spawned the environmental justice movement (see Chapter 5). In the early 1970s, grass-roots groups, churches, and civil rights leaders made public their claims that toxic waste dumps, landfills, and other locally unwanted land uses (or LULUs, as they are often called) were being disproportionately sited in minority or poor neighborhoods. In areas such as South Chicago, Kettleman City, California, and the St. Regis Reservation in New York, local residents have battled with federal regulators, arguing that they have become the victims of environmental racism.[20]

The issue of environmental justice has become one of global concern as well. Frequent clashes between native peoples and industrial world environmental organizations, who have been accused of caring more about the South's wildlife than its people, demonstrate that the goals of the two groups are not always parallel. In Kenya, for example, environmental organizations convinced the government to set aside wilderness preserves such as Amboseli National Park, forcing the Masai people from their traditional homelands. Similarly, in India, fifty-two tribal villages were displaced through the creation of tiger and buffalo preserves, an action that also led to an insurgent movement that occasionally harasses game wardens and conducts poaching raids.[21]

Similarly, efforts to establish an exclusively rights-based approach to protecting local peoples has occasionally had the unintended consequence of further degrading the environment. The sea cucumber harvesters of the Galapagos Islands, known as the *pepineros,* have decimated the population of the marine animals by selling them to China and Japan, where they are considered a gourmet delicacy. Although a 1994 plan establishing the Galapagos National Park protected subsistence fishing for the islands' indigenous population, many of the *pepineros* are new residents who have come to the islands specifically for the commercial harvest. As a result, there is no way for the government to either monitor or limit the harvest to subsistence levels—a situation that is likely to destroy the species in that area.[22]

In many countries, corporate interests have been targeted for ignoring the needs of the local population, leading observers to conclude that many projects are unduly disruptive, with most of the benefits accruing to the wealthy and most of the costs borne by marginalized communities. In southern Nigeria, for example, nine leaders of the Movement for the Survival of Ogoni People who protested a Shell Petroleum Development Company oil drilling project were executed by the country's repressive military in response to their activism. The organization had been founded in 1992 to combat alleged "environmental terrorism" by the company, with the organization's leaders demanding that Shell conduct economic impact and social impact studies and provide compensation for damage caused by the project. The Worldwatch Institute has compiled numerous examples of community-level environmental injustices, which appear to be growing in number and visibility as more NGOs are formed in developing countries.[23]

One of the more publicized cases in which indigenous people have fought back against environmental "progress" involves the Cree and Inuit communities of northern Quebec, Canada. The target of their resistance was a hydroelectric project under the control of the James Bay Development Corporation, established by the Quebec government in 1971.[24] Termed "the project of the century" when it was first announced, the James Bay complex involved nineteen waterways and twenty-seven reservoirs that were expected to provide power to not only Canadian utilities but to the United States as well.

The 17,500 people who live within the complex boundaries argued that their hunting life-style had been altered as a result of the building of project roads linking them with cities in the south and that social problems such as prostitution and alcoholism were increasing. In 1975, they settled with Hydro Quebec for $136 million in compensation, plus exclusive hunting, fishing, and trapping rights, and a guaranteed income for Cree hunters living in the bush.[25]

Subsequently, researchers found evidence that the soil in the lands being flooded by the James Bay dams was heavily contaminated with mercury, and accumulations along the food chain finally made their way to human beings. Tests on Cree who ate fish caught in the region revealed that 47 percent had levels of mercury in their bodies above World Health Organization standards, and nearly 10 percent had levels high enough to risk developing mercury poisoning—effects that may linger for decades, and possibly as long as one hundred years.[26]

The Cree experience and others involving indigenous peoples in other parts of the world have resulted in the creation of hundreds of NGOs specifically related to the environment and its impact on native groups. In 1977, the Inuit formed their own NGO—the Inuit Circumpolar Conference—to serve as a forum for issues of mutual interest. Representatives from Alaska, Canada, and Denmark joined together to urge their governments to establish an international Arctic policy, demilitarize the region, and establish Inuit health care, education, and cultural exchange programs. The organization was granted consultative status by the United Nations in 1982 and is the primary continuing forum for indigenous peoples of the region.

It is clear that the active participation of local individuals and groups with a vested interest in program outcomes is a prerequisite to making environmental policy acceptable to the greatest majority. If policies are designed with the premise that involvement by indigenous peoples is a necessary component of the process, such "stakeholder" participation can enhance the effectiveness of environmental protection programs in both the industrialized and developing world.[27]

THE INTEGRATION OF SCIENCE AND POLITICS

One of the more intriguing issues in environmental politics is the question of how important a role science should play in the policy process. Most analysts agree that the appropriate application of science to political decision making will, as Kai N. Lee states, provide humanity with the guides it needs to direct itself away from its current course of destruction.[28] The issue, however, is how science can adapt its methodology to the adversarial arenas that are common to politics. Researcher Lawrence Susskind answers that question by identifying five roles that scientific advisers can play in the policy process: trend spotters, theory builders, theory testers, science communicators, and applied-policy analysts. The key to effective policymaking, he argues, is to bring together not only each of the five types of scientists at each step in the process, but to also force them to confront the sources of their disagreement.[29] Another observer, political scientist Lynton Caldwell, has noted, however, that scientific information is far from being fully utilized and that science may be limited to slowing the pace at which environmental degradation is occurring.[30]

When there is scientific uncertainty or differences over the reliability of data, policy is more likely to be challenged. In the case of the Endangered Species Act, for instance, biologists are often at the forefront of the problem identification phase of policymaking (see the Preface). In making estimates of a species' population and habitat, biologists make a reasoned decision as to whether or not they should petition the federal government for protected status for a species. Since the ESA was first enacted, several species have been delisted because original estimates of their population were incorrect. In the case of the Northern spotted owl, uncertainty over the methodology used to calculate the extent of the bird's habitat led to controversy when timber companies argued that the number of remaining birds was actually greater than had been originally estimated. Several firms engaged their own experts to challenge the U.S. Forest Service's findings, thus extending the listing process and eventually bringing the issue to federal court.

Internationally, studies have shown that science has been of minimal importance in global environmental negotiations. While reports by researchers have helped to call attention to issues such as acid rain, biodiversity, and ozone depletion, science has had little impact in the development of treaties dealing with whaling, migratory species protection, trade in hazardous waste, tropical deforestation, Antarctic mineral exploration, trade in African elephant ivory, ocean dumping, and wetlands and world heritage site designations.[31]

A number of reasons have been identified as to why science often is ignored or given little credibility during the policymaking process. First, stakeholders in the policy process often make decisions based on their own self-interest and reject any scientific findings that are contrary to those interests. Despite international pressure to enact a multilateral agreement on acid rain, for instance, the United States resisted attempts at a substantive treaty because to do so would have placed a severe financial cost on the American utility industry. Sometimes, the difficulty lies in that the professional goals of scientists and policymakers appear to be extremely different. In considering ways to dealing with the issue of climate change, scientists developed and tested plausible explanations and subjected their findings to peer review, publication, and replication. Policymakers, in contrast, are more likely to interpret scientific findings in terms of their own political ambitions or agendas, and they may value public opinion, budget priorities, or the costs and risks of taking action.[32]

Second, science is often complex and inexact, so policymakers disregard what they do not understand. Long-term models that predict trends in population growth have often been inaccurate because of the methodology used to predict birth and mortality rates. The apocalyptic warnings of some researchers have later been found to be unfounded, leading political leaders to disregard any perceived threat as unlikely. Third, there are many areas of scientific inquiry where the findings of researchers have been inconsistent or contradictory, making it difficult for decision makers to choose which course of action is most desirable. In the case of climate change, for example, scientists at first warned of a coming ice age, then later theorized that global warming was imminent. As a result, some policymakers were hesitant to make abrupt (and costly) changes in resource use for fear that the science community might change its mind again.

Controversy may also arise over the issue of which scientists should be invited to participate in the policymaking process and at which phase their input should be solicited. The drafting of the London Dumping Convention, which included the issue of ocean dumping of low-level radioactive waste, is exemplary of these problems. Several nations that had been signatories to the original 1972 treaty proposed that the International Atomic Energy Association and the International Council of Scientific Unions be included in the review of the original provisions of the ban, while other countries sought the creation of a panel comprised of represented nations and international organizations. After considerable deliberation, a two-part review was agreed upon, but the experts were unable to come to a consensus to submit to the political leadership, and thus decisions about the future of the convention were made in what was essentially a scientific vacuum.[33]

Nowhere is the conflict between science and politics more apparent than in the issue of environmental risk assessment. The issue first emerged in the United States in 1969 with the passage of the National Environmental Policy Act. The legislation required that major projects undergo an analysis of their environmental impacts, a strategy increasingly used by policymakers to justify controls on various toxic substances in the air, in water, and on land. In 1983, the National Research Council defined risk assessment as a technique used to estimate the effects on the health of individuals or populations exposed to certain materials or situations that are regarded as hazardous.[34] Risk assessment consists of four basic steps:

- Hazard identification: determining whether a particular agent is causally linked to certain negative health effects
- Dose-response assessment: determining the relationship between the amount of exposure to the agent and the probability of occurrence of any health effects.
- Exposure assessment: determining the extent to which humans are exposed to the agent
- Characterization of risk: describing the nature and the magnitude of risk to humans

Risk assessment has been applied to a wide range of situation, including exposure to various pollutants, occupational exposures to chemicals or radiation, the discovery of chemicals in the environment or in products, and in the disposal of wastes. Naturally, risk from exposure to environmental pollutants must also be put into perspective with the risks that are a part of everyday living, such as riding in a car or airplane, or walking across the street. Some risks such as making the decision to smoke a cigarette, are voluntary, while others, such as passive exposure to environmental tobacco smoke, or not. For environmental risks such as those posed by indoor air pollution, researchers use medical data concerning the effects of the pollutant: time patterns of occurrence of the effects; the distribution of the effects within the population, including age, sex, and racial groups; cofactors, such as diet or occupation, that influence the effects; and demographics for exposed and control populations.

Risk assessment performs a valuable function by assisting policymakers and individuals in setting priorities and in comparing new and existing technologies to reduce or mitigate risks. It is expected that risk assessment will play an even more important role in political decision making as the costs of cleaning up prior environmental damage and hazards are calculated and science tells us more about the nature of risk.

Members of Congress have given significant attention in recent years to risk assessment. In 1993, the Democratic-led Senate overwhelmingly passed a bill that would require the EPA to assess the costs and benefits of regulations and to do comparative risk assessments to ensure that the problems addressed were sufficiently serious, in comparison with other problems, to merit regulation.[35] The bill died in 1994, only to be resurrected by the Republicans in 1995. The House passed a bill that would have required the EPA and eleven other agencies, when proposing major regulations, to 1) assess the nature of the risk being regulated, including the range of risk; 2) compare the risk at issue with similar risks, including everyday risks such as automobile accidents; 3) assess how effectively the rules would reduce risks to the public, based on detailed scientific analysis; 4) assess risks that might occur if alternatives are substituted for the substance or practice to be regulated; and 5) demonstrates that the costs of compliance are justified by the expected benefits and that the proposal is the most cost-effective option. The Senate came close to passing its own version of the bill, but was blocked by a filibuster. Although there is strong support for changing the rules about how risks are assessed, there is little agreement over exactly how to do that.

The primary dilemma faced by those who seek to integrate science even more into politics is that individuals make decisions from different viewpoints, with some seeing risk only in terms of a purely economic or personal perspective. How much will it cost me to remove the old asbestos pipe form my building versus the chance of my employees dying from asbestosis? We each make choices whether to eat foods (such as peanut butter) that are known to contain trace amounts of toxic substances. We measure the likelihood of suffering adverse health effects against our desire to eat. We also know that it is impossible to remove all potential risks from our lives, so we identify those risks that we are willing to take and those that we are not.

Unfortunately, science does not give us an answer to the question of what constitutes "acceptable risk," so a consensus is difficult to achieve. While one individual might consider the risk of exposure to a toxic waste incinerator to be minimal in light of the costs of other types of disposal, his or her neighbor might not—hence, a political dispute develops. Government agencies have often attempted to establish what is known as *de minimis* risk—a specific level at which the risks are so small that they are usually ignored. Proponents of this concept believe the regulatory agencies should establish *de minimis* levels and regulate only those hazards that pose a risk greater than those levels. Others prefer to rely on cost:benefit analysis to analyze alternative courses of action. This has the advantage of being a quantifiable method of improving economic efficiency, but critics point out the difficulties of putting a price tag on aesthetics such as clear vistas in the Grand Canyon. The problem remains, for the most part, unresolved, with many of these political disputes expected to enter the judicial arena as courts determine that constitutes "reasonable" risk.[36]

Why is risk assessment likely to be an important issue in the next century? Political decision makers are responding to a public that no longer is willing to "pay" for environmental protection unless there is a perceived "benefit." As the costs of other government programs and services (such as health care and interest on the federal deficit) skyrocket, decision makers must choose among competing priorities for limited tax dollars. Unless society perceives that the risks are serious, taxpayers are likely to want to prioritize other needs ahead of environmental problems. Those who are truly concerned about risk must make their case to the people in such a way as to enhance that perception. Similarly, efforts toward voluntary pollution reduction are more likely to gain acceptance than are costly disincentives and increased governmental regulation.[37]

COOPERATIVE ENVIRONMENTALISM

While much of this book has been devoted to a discussion of the environmental problems that will continue into the twenty-first century, there is reason for cautious optimism about the future. Reporter Gregg Easterbrook, for example, has argued that there needs to be a separation of major environmental issues to determine those alarms that have been genuine and those that have been exaggerated. His "ecorealism": views the future in terms of a world where humans coexist with nature rather than attempting to conquer it, protected by technology against natural ecological devastation and by conservation strategies that stop extinctions.[38]

Easterbrook need not be viewed as Pollyanna, nor should the environmental doomsayers continue to employ end-of-the-world rhetoric to exhort their followers to make draconian efforts to preserve the planet's resources regardless of the human or economic cost. There is already convincing evidence that some progress has been made in developing viable solutions to deal with environmental degradation if there is sufficient political will to implement new policies and to approach problem solving in new ways. Author Wallace Kaufman has echoed Easterbook's perspective when he writes. "The good news is that we have indeed entered a critical period in human and natural history, and we are superbly equipped to have a great time. . . . There is a vast cornucopia of hope, a shining mother lode, not of metals or oil or timber, but of human knowledge and imagination."[39]

One of the most promising strategies is cooperative environmentalism—a broad term that refers to attempts to change the decision-making process from an adversarial one, pitting environmental organizations against a perceived "enemy" (whether corporate or government), to one where the parties agree to discuss their differences in hopes of reaching consensus. Cooperative environmentalism does not necessarily mean that both sides will be in agreement or that they will accept the other side's point of view. But it does imply a willingness to try to find solutions and to enter into a dialog rather than litigating, protesting, or using violence to express grievances.

One strategy of cooperative environmentalism takes its cue from criminal justice policy. In several developing nations, government leaders have attempted to institute community-based forest management, returning control of a region's natural resources to the people who live there. This concept has been applied in Indonesia, the Philippines, Thailand, India, Nepal, Sri Lanka, and Papua New Guinea with varying degrees of success. As yet there is no "boilerplate" model that can be used by countries seeking to allow for these initiatives to be introduced, and there are significant roadblocks because of differences in culture and legal and political systems. But by allowing indigenous populations to have a voice in the use of forest resources, policymakers often circumvent the types of civil unrest and revolt usually associated with the timber industry.[40] Other applications have been made to protecting species diversity, especially in rural areas,[41] and in promoting sustainable coral reef management.[42]

Local management of property does not necessarily mean a complete turnover of lands or resources, as has been advocated by members of the environmental opposition's county supremacy groups. Rather, it can mean that lands are viewed from a multiple-use perspective in which all stakeholders are invited to decide how lands should be managed. Success stories abound, both domestically and globally. For example, since 1898, efforts to preserve the natural resources of the Black Hills National Forest in South Dakota have been mired in controversy between local residents and the U.S. Forest Service. But when government officials agreed to allow local stakeholders to participate in the process of deciding *what* uses were compatible with the area's overall management plans, resources were enhanced rather than degraded.[43]

One other strategy, and perhaps and the one most likely to be used in the United States, is termed "civic environmentalism." The concept was initially proposed by two researchers, Stan Johnson and DeWitt John, who sought to develop a new style of environmental politics that would replace the traditional command-and-control, top-down style of environmental regulation with "decentralized, bottom-up initiatives using new tools to address newly recognized environmental problems."[44] In this paradigm, state and local officials and citizens, rather than the federal government, take primary responsibility for pollution prevention and ecosystem management.

Civic environmentalism is an outgrowth of the frustration that both government regulators and environmental activists felt during the administrations of presidents Ronald Reagan and George Bush, when environmental policymaking was hampered by congressional gridlock and massive budget cuts to key regulatory agencies. It is viewed as a complement to, rather than a substitute for, federal regulation. The idea of crafting a new approach to environmental policy has won the support of mainstream environmental groups such as the World Resources Institute as well as the bipartisan National Commission on the Environment, which includes agency representatives appointed under both Republican and Democratic administrations.

Because civic environmentalism involves a style of decision making that is collaborative, it reduces the potential for conflict. Examples of successful implementation of the model already abound in the United States. Iowa, for example, has relied almost exclusively on voluntary, nonregulatory tools to deal with the issues of nonpoint source pollution by farm chemicals, winning praise for its 1987 Groundwater Act and a 1992 EPA award for pollution prevention.[45] Other attempts at finding common ground include the efforts made to restore the Florida Everglades[46] and Oregon's Applegate partnership.[47]

Each of these strategies is aimed at finding a way to reduce the adversarial nature of environmental policymaking, but they are likely to be implemented on an incremental basis, rather than adopted in totality as a reform package. And they provide hope for the next millennium as science uncovers new problems and stakeholders strive for new solutions. The stakes are high, the commitment deep, and the application broad-based, limited only, as Kaufman says, by human knowledge and imagination.

NOTES

1. See Michel Potier, "Towards a Better Integration of Environmental, Economic, and Other Governmental Policies," in *Maintaining a Satisfactory Environment: An Agenda for International Environmental Policy,* ed. Nordal Akerman (Boulder, CO: Westview Press, 1990), 69–81.

2. For a history of these early writers, see Jeremy Rifkin, *Biosphere Politics* (New York: Crown, 1991), 119–123. Among the key works cited are those of Frederick Ratzeland Ellen Churchill Semple.

3. Some observers believe that the concept of security should be expanded from the narrow interpretation as security of territory from external aggression to a broader definition of "human" security, encompassing seven categories: economic security, food security, health security, environmental security, personal security, community security, and political security. See "Redefining Security: The Human Dimension," *Current History* (May 1995): 229–236.

4. Jessica Tuchman Mathews, "Redefining Security," *Foreign Affairs, 68,* no. 2 (Spring 1989): 162–177.

5. Norman Myers, *Not Far Afield: U.S. Interests and the Global Environment* (Washington, D.C.: World Resources Institute, June 1987), 9.

6. See Kathleen Newland, "Refugees: The Rising Flood," *World Watch, 7,* no. 3 (May–June 1994): 10–20.

7. See, for example, William H. Bender, "How Much Food Will We Need in the 21st Century?" *Environment, 39,* no. 2 (1997): 6.

8. See Gareth Porter and Janet Welsh Brown, *Global Environmental Politics,* 2nd ed. (Boulder, CO: Westview Press, 1996), 156–159; and World Resources Institute, *World Resources 1994–1995* (New York: Oxford University Press, 182–183.

9. *World Resources 1994–95,* 6.

10. For more on the likelihood of global disease epidemics, see Anne Platt, "The Resurgence of Infectious Diseases," *World Watch* (July–August 1995): 26–32.

11. See Carl Pope, "War on Earth," *Sierra* (May–June 1991): 56; Roy Popkin, "Responding to Eco-Terrorism," *EPA Journal* (July–August 1991): 24; and Sir Frederic Warner, "The Environmental Consequences of the Gulf War," *Environment* (June 1991): 9.

12. See U.S. Congress, Senate, Committee on Environment and Public Works, Gulf Pollution Task Force, *The Environmental Aftermath of the Gulf War* (Washington, D.C.: U.S. Government Printing Office, 1992).

13. *World Resources 1994–95,* 4.

14. See Mustafa Tolba and Rudolf Bahro, "The Ecological Balance of Power," *New Perspectives Quarterly, 7,* no. 2 (Spring 1990): 60–62.

15. Murray Feshbach. *Ecological Disaster: Cleaning Up the Hidden Legacy of the Soviet Regime* (New York: Twentieth Century Fund Press, 1995). See also Murray Feshbach and Alfred Friendly, Jr. *Ecocide in the USSR: Health and Nature under Siege* (New York: Basic Books, 1992).

16. See Philip R. Pryde, *Environmental Resources and Constraints in the Former Soviet Republics* (Boulder, CO: Westview Press, 1995).

17. John Tuxill, "Biopirates on the Loose," *World Watch, 9,* no. 6 (November–December 1996): 9.

18. Michael Renner, *National Security: The Economic and Environmental Dimensions* (Washington, D.C.: Worldwatch Institute, 1989), 282–285.

19. Hilary F. French, *Partnership for the Planet: An Environmental Agenda for the United Nations* (Washington, D.C.: Worldwatch Institute, July 1995), 22–25.

20. There is considerable debate among researchers as to the validity of the citizens' claims that they are deliberately and inequitably being subjected to environmental health risks. See, for example, Even J. Ringquist, "Environmental Justice: Normative Concerns and Empirical Evidence," in *Environmental Policy in the 1990s,* 3rd ed. Normal J. Vig and Michael E. Kraft (Washington, D.C.: Congressional Quarterly Press, 1997, 231–254; Robert D. Bullard, ed., *Unequal Protection: Environmental Justice and Communities of Color* (San Francisco, CA: Sierra Club Books, 1994); Andrew Szasz, *Ecopopulism: Toxic Waste and the Movement for Environmental Justice* (Minneapolis, MN: University of Minnesota Press, 1994); and Robert Bullard, ed., *Confronting Environmental Racism: Views from the Grassroots* (Boston, MA: South End Press, 1993).

21. Aaron Sachs, *Eco-Justice: Linking Human Rights and the Environment* (Washington, D.C.: Worldwatch Institute, December 1995), 13–14.

22. Ibid., 15. See also, Laura Westra and Peter S. Wenz, Faces of Environmental Racism: Confronting Issues of Global Justice (Lanham, MD: Rowman and Littlefield, 1995).

23. Ibid., 25–26.

24. Boyce Richardson, *Strangers Devour the Land* (Post Mills, VT: Chelsea Green Publishing, 1991).

25. See D'Arcy Jenish, "Creating a New Way of Life: Changes Threaten Cree Tradition," *Maclean's,* May 21, 1990, 55; and William Hamely, "Hydroelectrick Developments in the James Bay Region, Quebec," *The Geographical Review, 73* (January 1983): 110–112.

26. Rae Corelli, "Fateful Consequences: Development Could Take a Heavy Toll," *Maclean's,* May 21, 1990, 56.

27. See Kent H. Redford and Jane A. Mansour, *Traditional Peoples and Biodiversity Conservation in Large Tropical Landscapes* (Washington, D.C.: Island Press, 1996), Aaron E. Zazueta, *Policy Hits the Ground: Participation and Equity in Environmental Policymaking* (Washington, D.C.: World Resources Institute, 1995), and Peter G. Veit, Adolfo Mascarenhas, and Okyeame Ampadu-Agyei, *Lessons from the Ground Up: African Development That Works* (Washington, D.C.: World Resources Institute, 1995).

28. Kai N. Lee, *Compass and Gyroscope: Integrating Science and Politics for the Environment* (Washington, D.C.: Island Press, 1993).

29. Lawrence Susskind, *Environmental Diplomacy: Negotiating More Effective Global Agreements* (New York: Oxford University Press, 1994), 76–78.

30. Lynton Keith Caldwell, *Between Two Worlds: Science, the Environmental Movement, and Policy Choice* (New York: Cambridge University Press, 1992), 20.

31. Susskind, *Environmental Diplomacy,* 62–63.

32. Lamont C. Hempel, *Environmental Governance: The Global Challenge* (Washington, D.C.: Island Press, 1996), 103.

33. Susskind, *Environmental Diplomacy,* 68–69.

34. National Research Council, *Risk Assessment in the Federal Government: Managing the Process* (Washington, D.C.: National Academy Press, 1983).

35. Congress, Senate, *Report on S. 171,* 103rd Cong. 1993, 103–38, 39.

36. See John J. Cohrssen and Vincent T. Covello, *Risk Analysis: A Guide to Principles and Methods for Analyzing Health and Environmental Risk* (Washington, D.C.: U.S. Government Printing Office, 1989).

37. See William Reilly, "Taking Aim Toward 2000: Rethinking the Nation's Environmental Agenda," *Environmental Law, 21,* no. 4 (1991): 1359–1374. See also Robert F. Blomquist, "The EPA's Science Advisory Board's Report on 'Reducing Risk': Some Overarching Observations Regarding the Public Interest," *Environmental Law, 22,* no. 1 (1992): 149–188.

38. Gregg Easterbrook, *A Moment on the Earth: The Coming Age of Environmental Optimism* (New York: Penguin Books, 1995).

39. Wallace Kaufman, *No Turning Back: Dismantling the Fantasies of Environmental Thinking* (New York: Basic Books, 1994), 158.

40. See Owen J. Lynch and Kirk Talbott, with Marshall S. Berdan, *Balancing Acts; Community-Based Forest Management and National Law in Asia and the Pacific* (Washington, D.C.: World Resources Institute, 1995).

41. See Jeffrey A. McNeely, ed., *Expanding Partnership in Conservation* (Cambridge, England: World Conservation Union, 1995); and David Western and R. Michael Wright, *Natural Connections: Perspectives on Community-Based Conservation* (Washington, D.C.: Island Press, 1994).

42. Alan T. White, et al., eds. *Collaborative and Community-Based Management of Coral Reefs* (West Hartford, CT: Kumarian Press, 1994).

43. Martha E. Geores, *Common Ground: The Struggle for Ownership of the Black Hills National Forest* (Lanham, MD: Roman and Littlefield, 1996).

44. De Witt John, *Civic Environmentalism: Alternatives to Regulation in States and Communities* (Washington, D.C.: Congressional Quarterly Press, 1994), xiv.

45. John, *Civic Environmentalism,* 85–86.

46. See David Gluckman, "The Margery Stoneman Douglas Everglades Protection Act," *Environmental and Urban Issues* (Fall 1991): 17–27; James Webb, "Managing Nature in the Evergaldes," *EPA Journal* (November–December 1990): 50; and Majory Douglas *The Everglades: River of Grass* (Sarasota, FL: Pineapple Press, 1988).

47. For a discussion of the Applegate Partnership's attempt to reach consensus over the issues of logging in sensitive species' habitat, see Brett Ken Cairn, "Peril on Common Ground: The Applegate Experiment," in *A Wolf in the Garden: The Land Rights Movement and the New Environmental Debate,* eds. Philip D. Brick and R. McGreggor Cawley (Lanham, MD: Rowman and Littlefield, 1996), 261–277.

FOR FURTHER READING

Ken Conca, Michael Alberty, and Geoffrey D. Dabelko, eds., *Green Planet Blues*. Boulder, CO: Westview Press, 1995.

Gregg Easterbrook. *A Moment on the Earth: The Coming Age of Environmental Optimism.* New York: Penguin Books, 1995.

Paul R. Ehrlich and Anne H. Ehrlich. *Betrayal of Science and Reason: How Anti-Environmental Rhetoric Threatens Our Future*. Washington, D.C.: Island Press, 1996.

Robert R. Gottfried. *Economics, Ecology, and the Roots of Western Faith*. Lanham, MD: Rowman and Littlefield, 1995.

Lamont C. Hempel. *Environmental Governance*. Washington, D.C.: Island Press, 1996.

Roger E. Miners and Bruce Yandle, Eds., *Taking the Environment Seriously*. Lanham, MD: Rowman and Littlefield, 1995.

Norman Myers. *Ultimate Security: The Environmental Basis of Political Stability*. Washington, D.C.: Island Press, 1996.

APPENDIX

Major United States Environmental Legislation, 1947–1997

Year	Air Quality	Water Quality	Pesticides— Toxics	Solid Waste	Land	Other
1947 Truman			Federal Insecticide, Fungicide, and Rodenticide Act			
1956 Eisenhower		Water Pollution Control Act				
1963 Kennedy	Clean Air Act					
1964 Johnson					Land and Water Conservation Fund Act	
1965 Johnson		Water Quality Act				Highway Beautification Act
1966 Johnson						Endangered Species Preservation Act
1967 Johnson	Air Quality Act					
1968 Johnson					National Wild and Scenic Rivers Act/National Trails System Act	

Year	Air Quality	Water Quality	Pesticides— Toxics	Solid Waste	Land	Other
1969 Nixon						National Environmental Policy Act/Endangered Species Act Amendments
1970 Nixon	Clean Air Act Amendments	Water Quality Improvement Act		Resources Recovery Act Act		Environment Education Act
1971 Nixon					Alaska Native Claims Settlement Act	
1972 Nixon		Federal Water Pollution Control Act	Federal Environmental Pesticides Control Act	Coastal Zone Management , Act		Marine Protection Research and Sanctuaries Act/Noise Control Act
1973 Nixon						Endangered Species Act
1974 Nixon		Safe Drinking Water Act				
1976 Ford			Toxic Substances Control Act	Resource Conservation and Recovery Act	Federal Land Policy and Management Act/National Forest Management Act	
1977 Carter	Clean Air Act Amendments	Clean Water Act Amendments			Surface Mining Control and Reclamation Act/Soil and Water Conservation Act	

Year	Air Quality	Water Quality	Pesticides—Toxics	Solid Waste	Land	Other
1978 Carter						Public Utility Regulatory Policies Act/ National Energy Act
1980 Carter			Comprehensive Environmental Response, Compensation, and Liability Act (Superfund)		Alaska National Interest Lands Conservation Act	Fish and Wildlife Conservation Act
1982 Reagan						Nuclear Waste Policy Act
1984 Reagan				Resource Conservation and Recovery Act Amendments		
1985 Reagan						Food Security Act
1986 Reagan		Safe Drinking Water Act	Superfund Amendments			
1987 Reagan		Clean Water Act Amendments				Nuclear Waste Policy Act Amendments/ Global Climate Protection Act
1988 Reagan				Federal Insecticide, Fungicide, and Rodenticide Act Amendments		Ocean Dumping Act

Year	Air Quality	Water Quality	Pesticides—Toxics	Solid Waste	Land	Other
1990 Bush	Clean Air Act Amendments					
1992 Bush						Energy Policy Act
1994 Clinton					California Desert Protection Act	
1996 Clinton	Safe Drinking Water Act Amendments					Food Quality Protec-tion Act

Index